A Journey to the East:
Asia in Focus

A Journey to the East: Asia in Focus

Michael H. Prosser, Ph.D.

Professor Emeritus, University of Virginia

Dignity Press
World Dignity University Press

Copyright © Michael H. Prosser 2015
This work is published under the Creative Commons Attribution-Non-Commercial-ShareAlike 4.0 International (CC BY-NC-SA 4.0) license. Details can be found at: http://creativecommons.org/licenses/by-nc-sa/4.0/

Published by Dignity Press
16 Northview Court
Lake Oswego, OR 97035, USA
http://www.dignitypress.org

More about this book at www.dignitypress.org/journeytotheeast

ISBN 978-1-937570-69-9

Dedication

To all of my coauthors, coeditors, translators, and editorial assistants with whom I have collaborated on my published books from 1969 to the present:

Thomas W. Benson, Cui Litang, He Daokuan, Ray T. Donahue, Nemi C. Jain, Steve J. Kulich, Li Mengyu, Lu Jun, Joseph M. Miller, Melvin H. Miller, Adil Nurmakov, Roichi Okabe, Ehsan Shahghasemi, Mansoureh Sharifzadeh, Lawrence H. Sherliick, K.S. Sitaram, William J. Starosta, Weng Liping, Muneo Yoshikawa, Zhang Shengyong, And and S. L. Zhou.

Contents

Preface 13

Acknowledgements 15

Introduction 17

Part One
Thinking Globally – Acting Locally

1. Being There: Monocultural/Eurocentric/Afrocentric/Asiacentric/Multicultural/World Citizen? The Intercultural Communication Field: a Founder, North America, 1970–2014; a Participant: China, 2001–2014 35
2. Forewording the SISU Intercultural Research Series: 2010–2014 48
3. Applying Discourse Analysis to Cultural Dialogue 53

Part Two
Opening Up to the Broader World

4. Eurocentrism: 1958–2006 63
5. Russia: 1959, 1989, 2005, 2006, 2008 68
6. Latin and Central America, 1960–2011 77
7. USIA/VOA: 1977–1980 81
8. The Middle East: 1980–81 82
9. Swaziland: Black/"Bloody Wednesday:" November 14, 1990 87

Part Three
My Journey to the East and West: Asia in Focus

10. Globalization, Asian/Chinese Modernity, and Values 97
11. Social Media and Cybernetics in Asia: Implications for Regional Security 121
12. Bicultural Japanese-American Research Conference, Nihonmatsu, Japan: 1974 135
13. India, 2003, 2005, 2011 141
14. Vietnam: 2004, 2011 149
15. Cambodia: 2005, 2010 153
16. South Korea: 1980, 2004 157
17. The Semester at Sea: 2011 161

Part Four
My Journey to the East: China in Focus

18. Contemporary Chinese Youth: Language and Culture 163
19. Chinese Education 190
20. Chinese Media 204
21. Meeting the Chinese for the First Time: 2001–02 213
22. Some Thoughts on the Beijing Language and Culture University: 2002–05 221
23. Two Chinese Weddings: 2005 235
24. Michael, Are You a Chiamerican? A Photo Essay 241
25. The Culture of Guanglinyilu Road: Shanghai International Studies University 250
26. Shangdong Province, Qingdao and Jinan: 2011 258
27. Yangzhou University Once More: 2013 263

28. Cultural Health Detour, Food Poisoning: 2013 265
29. Three Conferences in China, 2013/2014 270

Part Five
Voices of the Youth

30. Winter and Summer Camps: 2003, 2013 277
31. Russian and Chinese Sophomore Cultural Stories: 2013 288
32. Beijing Language and Culture Students' Comments,
    Arguments, Debate, Essays, and Poetry 317
33. The Sars Panic: 2003 348

Part Six
Public Conversations

34. Bingjuan Xion, Applied Linguistics and Intercultural
    Communication 359
35. Man Cheong Tsoi: Hong Kong and Mainland China 369
36. Chew Fong Peng: the Chinese Disapora 377
37. Laura Gostin (2007: 12–06) the Journey of an Intercultural/
    International Scholar: Dr. Michael Prosser 393
38. Intercultural Dialogue: an Interview with Professor Michael
    H. Prosser, Ph.D. by Li. Mengyu, Ph.D., Ocean University
    of China 414

Biography 423

Books by Michael Prosser 426

References 428

Favorite Expressions

"[Confucius] The Master says: At fifteen, I set my heart on learning. At thirty I know where I stand (my character has been formed). At fourty, I have no more doubts, at fifty, I know the will of Heaven, at sixty, my ears are attuned (i.e. my moral sense is well-developed), at seventy, I follow my heart's desire without crossing the line (without breaking moral principles)."

Confucius: "It does not matter how slowly you go as long as you do not stop."

Socrates: "I am neither a citizen of Athens, nor of Greece, but of the world."

St. Matthew [Jesus]: "How blessed are the poor in spirit: the kingdom of Heaven is theirs./Blessed are the gentle: they shall have the earth as inheritance./ Blessed are those that mourn: they shall be comforted./ Blessed are those who hunger and thirst for uprightness: they shall have their fill./Blessed are the merciful: they shall have mercy shown them./Blessed are the pure of heart: they shall see God./Blessed are the peacemakers: they shall be recognized as children of God./Blessed are those who are persecuted in the cause of uprightness: the kingdom of God is theirs."

St. Matthew [Jesus]: "You must love the Lord your God with all your heart, with all your soul, and with all your mind. This is the greatest and the first commandment. The second resembles it. You must love your neighbor as yourself."

Thomas Jefferson: "I was bold in the pursuit of knowledge, never fearing to follow truth and reason to whatever results they led."

Paulo Freire: "For apart from inquiry, apart from the praxis, individuals cannot be truly human. Knowledge emerges only through invention and re-invention, through the restless, impatient, continuing, hopeful inquiry human beings pursue in the world, with the world, and with each other."

Pope Francis: "This is important: to get to know people, listen, expand the circle of ideas. The world is crisscrossed by roads that come closer together and move apart, but the important thing is that they lead towards the Good."

Pope Francis: ""Life is a journey. When we stop, things don't go right."

Preface

My early and adult life has always inclined toward intercultural and international adventures. At 17, my parents took me to Ontario, Quebec, New Brunswick, and Prince Edward Island, Canada. When I was 22 I took a ship from Montreal to Liverpool and traveled for two months in 12 European countries, participating in an international youth conference, and returning to the US by plane. The next year, my wife and I traveled to Germany, Scandinavia, and the Soviet Union. With several international graduate students, we spent a month in Mexico in 1960. We took our three children: Michelle Ann, Leo Michael, and Louis Mark to England, the Netherlands, and Germany in 1968. Michelle celebrated her sixth birthday in Heidelberg. In 1970, Churchill, Manitoba beckoned us.

My first trip to Asia was for the bicultural Japanese-American bicultural research conference in Nihonmatsu, Japan, during 1974. We spent a month each in London and Ottawa as a family in 1975. My wife and I explored Berlin and four central European countries in 1977; Poland, Hungary, Czechoslovakia, and East Germany. In 1979 I was in Mexico and in 1980, I gave lectures in Singapore and South Korea. Part of a Middle East faculty study tour in 1981, I was in Lebanon, Jordan, and Israel. I was in Europe twice in 1983, visiting Italy, Sweden and the Netherlands. I was back in Europe in 1986, including Portugal, Spain, France, Germany, Denmark, Sweden, and Finland. During 1989, my second wife and I participated in an international peace and communication conference in Moscow and in a "solidarity retreat with the poor" in Haiti. During 1990-91, I was a Fulbright Professor at the University of Swaziland, which also included our visits to South Africa, Botswana, Zimbabwe, Kenya, and Burkina Faso.

From 2001 to 2014, I taught at four universities in China and I traveled also to Argentina, Australia, Cambodia, Chile, El Salvador, Europe, India, Indonesia, Japan, Malaysia, New Zealand, Peru, Russia, Singapore, South Korea, Thailand, and Vietnam. As a faculty advisor for life-long learners on the 2011 Semester at Sea around the world study tour, I visited Ghana, Mauritius, Morocco, and South Africa in Africa; in Asia, China, India, Japan, Malaysia, and Vietnam, and in Central America: Costa Rica,

Honduras, and Panama. I have returned to China in November 2014 and Indonesia in 2015.

As a part of my own intercultural learning experience, I hosted international high school students from Sweden, Belgium, Brazil, El Salvador, France, South Africa, Spain, and Swaziland during the 1980s and early 1990s. In the later part of the 1990s, several young adult refugees from Sudan lived with me.

I have combined living an intercultural and international life with my edited and authored books, all of which have similar interests.

Development of *A Journey to the East*

A Journey to the East is partially academic and semi-scholarly, but it is also mixed with many short and more popular essays about my experiences teaching and lecturing in Chinese universities, or as Deng Xiaoping said, "developing theory from practical facts." It is both autobiographical/autoenographic in terms of my own writing, and even also by twenty-two cultural story student voices from Russia and China for themselves, and then biographical about me with comments by my own earlier Chinese students and in part Six in two of the public conversations and dialogues with Laura Gostin and Li Mengyu who are the questioners and I am the respondent.

Many of the earlier and later essays on the same topic have been combined for greater clarity and longitudinal developments over the 2001–14 period of teaching in Chinese universities. There are six parts to the book: 1. Thinking Globally: Acting Locally; 2. Opening Up to The Broader World; 3. My Journey to the East and West: Asia in Focus; 4. My Journey to the East: China in Focus; 5. Voices of The Youth; and 6. Public Conversations.

Michael H. Prosser, Ph.D.
Charlottesville, Virginia
March 1, 2015
International blog: *www.michaelprosser.com*
Email: *mlchaelhprosser@hotmail.com*

Acknowledgements

Dr. Uli Spalthoff, director of operations at Dignity Press, Dr. Linda Hartling, its director, and Dr. Evelin Lindner, founder of the Human Dignity and Humiliation Studies Network and a self-proclaimed global citizen, have all been most helpful and encouraging my publishing efforts for Dignity Press, including *Finding Cross-cultural Common Ground* with Mansoureh Sharifzadeh and Zhang Shengyong (2013); *Social Media in Asia* with Cui Litang (2014); and Chinese Communicating Interculturally with Li Mengyu (2014). Presently, I and Ehsan Shahghasemi are coediting *Social Media in the Middle East* also for Dignity Press. I owe all of them great thanks for their support and digital friendship.

I have included many essays originally posted on the Communication Research and Theory Network, and often simultaneously from my own international blog, *www.michaelprosser.com* often as composites written from 2003 to 2014.

My opening essay, "Being There," has evolved from earlier ver-sions which I presented at the German-Chinese symposium on intercultural communication at the Shanghai International Studies University in June, 2010, and at the International Academy for Intercultural Research in Reno, Nevada in June of 2013. The IAIR essay has a link on my Wikipedia page.

My essay, "Contemporary Chinese Youth: Chinese Language and Culture" was originally published in Olga Leontovich (Ed.) (2010). *Chinese Linguoculture in the Modern Global World*. Volgograd: Russia, Peremena Press. It is included here with kind permission.

An earlier version of "Globalization, Asian Modernity and Values" was published in *Finding Cross-Cultural Ground* (2013), pp. 166–174) as "Asian Modernity and Intercultural Communication."

My series preface for the Intercultural Research series at the Intercultural Institute of Shanghai International Studies University, Shanghai, China, 2010–2014 was published in Intercultural Re-search in volumes 2–7 by Shanghai Foreign Language Education Press. Names cited in the preface have been deleted.

Laura Gostin: "The Journey of an Intercultural/International Scholar: Dr. Michael Prosser" was originally published in *China Media Reports*, 2007, and is republished here with kind permission.

Li Mengyu's public conversation with me in Part Six, "Intercultural Dialogue: An Interview with Professor Michael H. Prosser" was later published in the *Shangdong Foreign Language Teaching Journal* and is published here with kind permission.

My essay, "Social Media and Cybernetics in Asia: Implications for Regional Security" was my keynote address at the Cultural Security Conference at the National University of Defense Technology in Changsha in November 2014 and it is expanded as my keynote address for my Lifetime Achievement Award at the 2015 Biennial Conference for the International Academy for Intercultural Research in Bergen, Norway.

Introduction

Wu Cheng'en [?], *Journey to the West*

Liam Matthew Brockley, in his *Journey to the East: The Jesuit Mission to China: 1579–1724* (2009) writes:

> One of the greatest works of Chinese literature … being produced, *Journey to the West,* or *Xiyou Ji,* a prose masterpiece derived from centennial folk traditions, was first printed in 1592. It is a book of disputed authorship, most frequently attributed to Wu Cheng'en (ca. 1500 – 1582), a minor scholar-official with a taste for the supernatural. The plot reworks the historical journey made by Xuanzang, a seventh century monk, to India in order to acquire the Buddhist scripture, elaborating on the trials undergone by a group of adventurers to bring a foreign religion to China. What rendered this tale so compelling to the generations of storytellers who had passed it on, embellished it, and made it an appropriate subject for a former mandarin to write down was that it combined adventure and religion set in epic fashion set against the boundless landscapes of inner Asia.
>
> In *Journey to the West,* Xuanzang must travel across deserts and mountain ranges, confront the perils of the fabulous and the unknown, and defeat monstrous foes on his way to far-distant India. The perilous road trodden by the seeker allegorically represents the Buddhist path to enlightenment. Fortunately for Xuangzang, he is escorted and protected from harm by three companions with supernatural powers, of whom the best known is the monkey Sun Wukung [Zhu Bajie, and Sha Wujing, together with a dragon prince who acted as Xuangzang's steed, a white horse]. While the religious quest of the wandering monk provides the central motif of the fabled journey, the tale of the monkey with his extraordinary ingenuity and wit has made this one of the canonical works of Chinese fiction (Brockley, 2009, pp. 2 – 3).

Although I did not read any of this classic novel, I did see over several years in China many of the very popular English-language television episodes of Xuanzang, the monkey, the white horse, and the pig, in their humorous journey to the West, and like the book, including overcoming many trials and scoring many victories over various monsters.

With ten years of experience as a foreign teacher/"expert" of English and communication in China from 2001–2014, and as a traveler in many other Asian countries beginning in 1974, it seemed time to write an autobiographical book about my forty year experience, broadly in Asia, and more specifically about my adventures living and teaching in China as an ongoing sojourner there from 2001–2014. Lu Jun, my former postgraduate student at Yangzhou University in 2001–02, and now with his doctorate in applied linguistics was one of my major hosts in my last semester of teaching there in 2013–14. He gave me wise advice to call my book: *A Journey to the East*, as a continuing emphasis on my own Asian adventures and counterbalance to Wu Cheng'en's *Journey to the West*. Religiously, I have long been intrigued about St. Augustine's fourth century book, *City of God* and Harvey Cox's counterpoint book, *Secular City* (1966), making, then my own book *Journey to the East* as a counterpoint to Wu Cheng'en's *Journey to the West* became an appealing concept.

Since I participated in a 1974 bicultural research conference in Japan, and I have traveled to a total of eleven Asian countries from 1974 to 2014, I decided to become more inclusive of my Asian experience, rather than only focusing on my time in China. I also gave lectures in South Korea and Singapore in 1980; in India in 2003 and 2005, in Cambodia in 2004, and in Japan after giving a keynote at a conference there in 2009. In 2010, I participated in an international conference in Singapore. I traveled also to Vietnam, the Philippines, Thailand, Malaysia, and Indonesia during my time in China, and in 2011 on the Semester at Sea, we spent time in Vietnam, Malaysia, India, China, and Japan.

Thus, for my own book, I have added a subtitle: *Focus on Asia*. Additionally, since I have traveled to a total of 69 countries, including teaching in Swaziland and traveling to Europe, Russia, the Middle East, and Latin and Central America, I have incorporated some of these experiences in *A Journey to the East*, as prologue material and thereby rounding out some of my international experiences autobiographically and autoethnographically.

While considering my title development, I was surprised to learn of Hermann Hesse's book, published originally in German in 1932, and translated into English in 1956 as *A Journey to the East*. The promotional information about the book makes the following statement:

> In simple, mesmerizing prose, Hermann Hesse tells of a journey both geographic and spiritual. H.H., a German choirmaster is invited on an expedition with the League, a secret society in whose members include Paul Klee, Mozart, and Albertus Magnus [as well as Plato, Pythagoras, Don Quixote, Puss in Boots, Tristam Shandy, Baudelaire, the ferryman Vasudeva, and Siddhartha]. The participants traverse both space and time, encountering Noah's Ark In Zurich and Don Quixote at Bremgarten. The pilgrims' ultimate destination is the East, the "Home of the Light" where they expect to find spiritual renewal. Yet the harmony that ruled at the outset of the trip soon degenerated into open conflict. Each traveler finds the rest of the group intolerable and heads off in his own direction with H.H. bitterly blaming the others, for the failure of the journey. It is only long after the trip, while pouring over records in the League archives that H.H. discovers his own role in the dissolution of the group (back cover).

There appear to be linkages, at least marginally between Wu Cheng'en's version and that of Hesse, and possibly with Chaucer's *Canterbury Tales* where there is also a spiritual pilgrimage involved which also degenerates into quarrels among the pilgrims. Whether my version, *A Journey to the East,* has any realistic counterpart to Cheng'en's book remains to be seen. At a conference in 2000, Chinese colleagues suggested that after I retired from teaching in 2001 from the University of Virginia and Rochester Institute of Technology, I should consider teaching in China, and I responded: "Why not?" I thought that a year teaching in China might be an interesting adventure, followed perhaps by a year in India, or South Korea, or Vietnam. As it turned out, however, a year teaching in Yangzhou (2001–02) was followed by three years in Beijing (2002–05), then four years in Shanghai (2005–09), still later by a single semester in Qingdao (2011) and again for my final semester in Yangzhou (2013–14). Earlier, in 2003–05, 2005–06, 2009, 2010, and 2014, I gave several weeklong lecture series at Chinese universities. I gave keynote addresses in China, India, Japan, Russia, and the United States. I was featured in *China Semi-monthly Talents Magazine* in 2005 (in Chinese.

Fortunately, my life in China over fourteen years was indeed an adventure, without any terrible monsters to overcome, and at a point in teaching in Shanghai, some of my students started teasing me that, in fact, I was becoming a ChiAmerican. My adventures in China expanded more broadly in Asia, and even earlier to Africa in 1990–91 and later in 2011, and also to Europe in 2006 and Russia again in 2004, 2006, and 2008. My life was very blessed by having both American faculty in China and younger Chinese as friends. Only a few Chinese faculty over my fourteen years in China became friends, though most were marginally friendly. I can say, without reservation, that my experiences in Asia, and more especially in China, framed a significant period in my life-world and greatly deepened my interest in intercultural communication and competence. I was very happy that my daughter, Michelle Ann, visited me in Beijing in 2005, and with her three children, Darya, Sanders, and Sophia in 2009 in Shanghai. Among the 2,550+ students that I have taught in China, I hope that I have had an important contribution to their educational and cultural development, with the goal of encouraging them to become creative and critical thinkers and moving toward global citizenship.

Reading Chinese Literature

During my teaching in China (2001–2014), I had the opportunity to read in English translation parts of three of the four literary Chinese classics: Cao Xuegin's and Gao E's *Dream of Red Mansions/Dream of the Red Chamber* (Sixteenth century), *The Water Margin/ Outlaws of the Marsh* (Song dynasty), and the Romance of the *Three Kingdoms* (Three Kingdoms period). *I* read Confucius' *The Analects* (Ancient) several times, Lao Tzu's *The Art of War* (Ancient), Pearl Buck's *The Good Earth* (1932), Lin Yu Tan's *My Country and My People* (1935), *The Importance of Living* (1937), and *Moment In Peking* (1939), Edgar Snow's *Red Star over China* (1937), Lao She's *The Camel Driver/The Rickshaw Boy/ Camel Xiangzi* (1945), Ch'ien Ching –shu's *Fortress Besieged* (1947), and Lu Xun's *Selected Works* (1956). Lu Xun died three months after I was born, causing some students to whom I had mentioned both dates to quip that he died in shock when

I was born. While teaching at Shanghai International Studies University, students and I paid frequent visits together to the Lu Xun Museum near the main campus. Going with a first year group of young women from Shanghai International University to the museum, and meeting a group of first year Tongjin University men, it was interesting to see that the freshmen/women student leaders from each university had organized a match making event for future dating opportunities. I was sorry not to visit Qufu, the home of Confucius since the *Analects* appears often in my writing.

Although many of my Chinese students knew a lot about these works, only a small number could concede that they had actually read most of them, except in short versions, almost like the American versions of Cliff Notes. The library lobby at Shanghai International Studies University Songjiang campus has a giant statue of Lu Xun, while the English College lobby has a small bust of Shakespeare. Each sophomore English major class there annually presents a well done Shakespeare play, compacted to thirty minutes each. Annual favorites are *A Midsummer Night's Dream, the Merchant of Venice, Romeo and Juliet,* and *Hamlet*. However, I never heard of any class readings or student enacting in plays of the works of Lu Xun.

More recently, I have read, with enthusiasm, eight of the 2011 Nobel Laureate in Literature, Mo Yan's highly satirical books (in English) in which he is often himself a very naughty character, all translated by Howard Goldblatt: *Garlic Ballads* (1988), *Republic of Wine* (1992), *Red Sorghum* (1993), *Big Breasts and Wide Hips (1996), Shifu, You'll Do Anything for A Laugh* (2001), *Sandlewood Death (2001/2013), Life and Death are Wearing Me Out* (2006), and *Pow!* (2012). I had read many of Han Han's individual blogs translated into English, which often attracted an immediate audience of 300 million readers in Chinese, and I had the opportunity to read his first blog collection in English, *This Generation* (2013). Another recent novel about China which I have read was Ian Buruma's *The China Lover: A Novel* (2008). I have read three of Amy Tan's Chinese-oriented novels: *The Kitchen God's Wife* (1991); *The Bonesetter's Daughter* (2001); and *The Joy Luck Club* (2006).

Over time, I have also almost obsessively read books, many of which would have been banned, perhaps 40–50%, about China as: Robert T. Oliver, *Communication and Culture: Ancient India and China* (1971); Michael Albert and Robin Hahnel, *Unorthodox Marxism; An Essay on*

Capitalism, Socialism and Revolution (1978); Godwin Chu, *Popular Media in China: Shaping New Cultural Patterns* (1978); Nien Cheng, *Life and Death in Shanghai* (1986); David Turnley, Peter Turnley, and Melinda Liu, *Beijing Spring* (1989); Jan Walls and Yvonne Walls, *Classical Chinese Myths* (1989); Jung Chang, *Wild Swans: Three Daughters of China* (1991); Godwin Chu and Yanan Ju, *The Great Wall in Ruins; Communication and Culture in China* (1993); Richard Evans, *Deng Xiaoping and the Making of Modern China* (1993, 1994); Anne F. Thurston with Karin Turner and Linda A. Reed, *China Bound, Revised* (1994); *Ten Chinese Myths of the Creation* (1998); Iris Chang, *The Rape of Nangking: The Forgotten Holocaust of World War II* (1999); Jonathan D. Spence, *The Chan's Great Continent; China in Western Minds* (1999).

Among books beginning in 2000 TO 2010, I read Jasper Becker, *The Chinese* (2000); D. Ray Heisey, *Chinese Perspectives in Rhetoric and Communication* (2000); Orville Snell, *Virtual Tibet: Searching for Shangri-La from the Himalys to Hollywood* (2000); Joseph M. Chan and Bryce T. McIntyre, *In Search of Boundaries: Communication, Nation States, and Cultural Identities* (2001); Guo-ming Chen and Ringo MA, *Chinese Conflict Management and Resolution* (2001); Karin Evans, *The Lost Daughters of China: Abandoned Girls, Their Journey to America, and Their Search for a Missing Past* (2001); Deng Rong, Deng Xiaoping and the Cultural Revolution (2002); James Farrer, *Opening Up: Youth, Sex, Culture and Market Reform in Shanghai* (2002); Jia Wengshang, Lu Xing, and D. Ray Heisey, *Chinese Communication and Research: Reflections, New Frontiers and New Directions* (2002); Lu Xing, Jia Wenshan, and D. Ray Heisey, *Chinese Communication Studies: Contexts and Comparisons* (2002); Zhang Liang, *The Tinanamen Papers: The Chinese Leadership's Decision to Use Force against Their Own People — in Their Own Words* (2001, 2002); David Aiken, *Jesus in Beijing: How Christianity Is Transforming China and Changing the World* (2003); Iris Chang, *The Chinese in America: A Narrative History* (2004); Maria Hsia Chang, *Falun Gong: The End of Days* (2004); Ji Fengyuan, *Linguistic Engineering: Language and Politics in Mao's China* (2004); Peter Hays Gries, *China's New Nationalism: Pride, Politics, and Diplomacy* (2004); Robert Lawrence Kuhn, *The Man Who Changed China: The Life and Legacy of Jiang Zemin* (2004); Gregory Wang and Betty Barr, *Between Two Worlds: Lessons in Shanghai* (2004); Jung Chang and Jon Halliday, *Mao: the Unknown Story* (2005); Stephanie Hemelryk, Donald Benewick, and Robert Benewick, *The State of China Atlas: Mapping the World's Fastest*

Growing Economy (2005); Sun Shuyun, *The Long March: The True Story of Communist China's Founding Myth* (2005); Chen Guidi and Wu Chuntao, *Will the Boat Sink the Water? The Life of China's Peasants* (2006); John Gittling, *The Changing Face of China from Mao to Market* (2006); Sang Ye, *China Candid: The People on the People's Republic* (2006); Zhou Ji, *Higher Education in China* (2006); Margaret Macmillan, *Nixon and Mao: The Week That Changed the World* (2007); Hu Yang, *Shanghai Living* (2006); Oliver August, *Inside the Red Mansion: On the Trail of China's Most Wanted Man* (2007); Gao Wenqian, *Zhou Enlai: The Last Perfect Revolutionary* (2007); An Ran, *Learning in Two Languages and Cultures: The Experience of Mainland Chinese Families in Britain* (2008); Rob Gifford, *China Road: A Journey into the Future of a Rising Power* (2008); Abram Lustgarten, *China's Great Train: Beijing's Drive West and the Campaign to Remake Tibet* (2008); John Mann, *The Great Wall: The Extraordinary Story of China's Wonder of the World* (2008); George T. Haley, Usha C.V. Haley, and Chen Tiong Tan, *New Asian Emperors: The Business Strategies of Overseas Chinese* (2009); Martin Jacques, *When China Rules the World: The End of the Western World and the Birth of a New Global Order* (2009); Guo-ming Chen, *Study on Chinese Communication Behaviors* (2010); R. Edward Grumbine, *Where the Dragon Meets the Angry River* (2010); Robert Lawrence Kuhn, *How China's Leaders Think: The Inside Story of China's Reform and What It Means for the Future* (2010); and Hui ching Chang, *Clever, Creative, Modest: The Chinese Language Practice* (2010).

In the second decade of the twenty first century, I read Frank T. Gallo, *Business Leadership in China: How to Blend Best Western Practices with Chinese Wisdom* (2011); Yinglan Tan, *Chinnovation: How Chinese Innovations Are Changing the World* (2011); Henry Kissinger, *On China* (2011, 2012); Edward N. Luttwak, *The Rise of China vs. The Logic of Strategy* (2012); Dambisa Moyo, Winner Take All: China's Race for Resources and What It Means for the World (2012); David Shambaugh, *China Goes Global, The Partial Power* (2013); Howard W. French, *China's Second Continent: How a Million Migrants Are Building a New Empire in Africa* (2014); Evan Osnos, *Age of Ambition: Chasing Fortune, Truth, and Faith in the New China* (2014).

My Books Published Relating to China and Asia

With S. L. Zhou and Lu Jun, I published a cross-cultural manual for Chinese students preparing to take the CET 4 AND CET 6 (Chinese English Test): *Sino-American Compositions of Shared Topics* (2003); with Steve J. Kulich I coedited *Intercultural Perspectives on Chinese Communication* (2007); with Kulich and Weng Liping: *Value Frameworks at the Theoretical Crossroads of Culture* (2012), and *Value Dimensions and Their Contextual Dynamics across Cultures* (2014); and with Li Mengyu, a coauthored textbook for Chinese students: *Communicating Interculturally* (2012) and its North American edition: *Chinese Communicating Interculturally* (2014). One third of my, Mansoureh Sharifzadeh's, and Zhang Shengyong's book, *Finding Cross-cultural Common Ground* (2013) emphasizes Asia and especially China. Addressing Asia more broadly, Cui Litang and I have *coedited Social Media in Asia (*2014). My book, The Cultural Dialogue (1978, 1985, 1989) touches only marginally on China but includes one fourth of the book related to a 1974 Japanese-American dialogue. It was the beginning of western intercultural comparisons and contrasts with the East, as China had not yet begun its "Opening up" (1978–1980). The book was translated into Japanese by Roiche Okabe (1982), and into Chinese by He Daokuan (2013).

My Journey to the East and West: Asia in Focus: 1974 – 2014

In learning about China from 2001–14, I had personally made my own journeys to the west from China — India, three times while teaching in China, as well as southeastern countries such as Cambodia, Indonesia, Malaysia, Singapore Vietnam, and Thailand, all of which made my interest in Lu Jun's title recommendation even more interesting to me. I also decided to broaden the subtitle to "Asia in Focus." This book also serves as my autobiographical remembrance of my earlier international travel as a prelude to my contemporary forty-year plus Asian experiences.

Coming to China in 2001 very shortly before the 9/11 event, with a far too simplistic knowledge of Chinese education, and especially Chinese higher education, qualitatively, I have learned a lot about contemporary China, although not yet enough. I have now taught in four Chinese universities, on and off from 2001–14, and junior middle school environments and youth camps. A major fault lies in my total lack of written or spoken Chinese. I have always taught in English. Often asked if I speak Mandarin well, I typically respond: "yes, very well, but only a few words." I have attended sixteen Chinese communication conferences, giving keynote addresses at many of them, and also because of my books published in China, I can honestly claim to be well known and respected in Chinese communication circles, especially in intercultural communication organizations. Because of my dozen appearances on China Central TV'S "Dialogue" program and as an interviewee on five Shanghai International Channel programs, several million people have seen me on Chinese television. I have moved from knowing rather little about China to having a reasonable grasp of much of contemporary China, youth, media, education, and culture.

Autoethnography

Sarah Wall in her 2008 article, "Easier Said than Done; Writing Autoethnography," indicates that the key words for her essay required the terms: "autoethnography, reflection, representation, objectivity, data, ethics, and legitimacy." She notes that this qualitative method comes from postmodern critiques, which give a voice to personal experiences and thereby enhances sociological studies about individuals and cultural groups. Wall stresses that this method offers an intimate and personal narrative, but which clearly may not be representative of others in the group. It presents considerable challenges to the observational and informal lived experience of the participant-observer, providing an intersection between the personal and societal situation. She claims that "personal narratives can address several key theoretical debates in contemporary sociology: macro and micro linkages; structure; agency and their intersection; reproduction and social change" (p. 392). Naturally, all humans are inherently story tellers with ongoing narratives. Wall argues that autoethnography begins with the personal story where there remains considerable latitude, perhaps in contrast to other qualitative, quantitative and mixed method research.

Wall recommends that this type of study should be linked to an appropriate literature review and theory, and she proposes that it can provide new avenues for conceptual, theoretical, and research development. To become more than merely a story teller, Wall calls upon such researchers to have criteria to judge their self-narratives, and also their self-examinations, while exploring the available collected data, its validity, motivation, and self-reflection. Personally, in constructing a very broad and eclectic literature review as noted above, I have read every book related to contemporary China available to me, and I have reviewed several dozen books about China (Prosser, 2007, Zhang and Prosser, 2011, Prosser, Sharifzadeh, & Zhang, 2013).

Autoethnography offers, Wall claims, more interpretative, experimental, critical, creative, and imaginative new approaches of space and time, while understanding that claiming representativeness cannot be a fully accurate reflection of lived lives. At the same time, measuring one's objectivity and methods of progressing with the narrative are tied to the subjective values, attitudes, and beliefs of the narrative writer. Still, these narratives may be sometimes more reliable than field notes or empirical quantitative studies, as field notes may mediate and alter the accuracy of one's memory as it continually progresses within the narrative over time while empirical studies often evaluate a small group of samples, not necessarily linked to the individual participant narrator. Wall concludes that autoethnography can engage one as well in ongoing self-reflection of the narrative experience.

In my paraphrase of the Japanese-American dialogues in *The Cultural Dialogue* (1978, 1985, 1989, pp. 216–286) and in the eleven imaginary dialogues between imaginary students, an imaginary Professor Zhang, and my "real" self which I created for Li Mengu's and my intercultural textbook, I have purposefully used cultural dialogue as a teaching tool. Both D. Ray Heisey and I have considered this trend in the study and practice of intercultural communication as a major aspect of our lived, teaching, writing, and intercultural experiences. He argued, too, that joint intercultural collaboration is an essential ingredient for the intercultural researcher. In this way, I have been the host parent on an extended basis for several young people from European, Latin American, and African countries. Also, as noted in my dedication for this book, I acknowledge my interculturally shared cooperation with several scholars, including Chinese, Indian, Iranian, and Japanese. In several of my books, many of the authors in my books come from a variety of different countries and cultures as I have sought to give voice to some whose voices might otherwise be silent or underrepresented.

Developing My Personal Narratives and Longitudinal Experiences in Teaching in China, 2001–14

Since coming to China in 2001, besides reading widely in the available literature about contemporary China, its educational systems, most often at the higher education level, and Chinese youth, I have briefly discussed some of this literature review at different places in the text of the book itself. A special type of reading that I have done is to review forty-five articles for the Journal of *Middle Eastern and Islamic Studies (in Asia)*, several doctoral dissertations, and more than 140 MA theses in intercultural communication at the Shanghai International Studies University. I have read electronically considerable information available more broadly about Asia, but as noted above almost all of my print reading has been about China.

Thus, I often knew much more about contemporary China than most of my Chinese students, while still not knowing many other aspects of which they were far more informed as Chinese, where I neither understood the spoken nor the Chinese written language. Additionally, they have lived lives, or micro worlds as Chinese that I never could have had as an American, even spending more than ten years in China. Also, I have lived a much longer life, and one that they cannot explicitly experience, though I have never led their lives as Asian nor Chinese youth. I can claim to have certain expertise, especially on Chinese education, contemporary China and youth longitudinally over the fourteen year experience, but much less so because of my less lived experiences about Asian society in general. Generally speaking, I have grounded my observations through my own interest in the study of intercultural communication, and particularly on the concept of cultural dialogue for which I give many examples in my research and narrative story, and a theme that informs much of my professional editing and authoring.

I have made many attempts to be as objective as possible in my knowledge of China and Asia; more broadly, I have conducted some qualitative research on areas that interest me; and I have continued a process of self-reflection and many stereotypical/cultural bias corrections over these years. I have made every possible effort to observe the Asian and Chinese society in an ethically acceptable way, without over representing my own societal background and American societal impact on my own beliefs, attitudes, values, motivations, and world view as indicative of the broader American academic society, or typical Americans. I have high hopes that my comments provide rich data and legitimacy for future studying or teaching about China. In Li Mengyu's and my intercultural textbook for Chinese university students, we guide the students to think creatively and critically about their own assumptions and stereotypes and to reflect on the philosophical statement of Rene Descartes, "Dubito, ergo Cogito, ergo Sum" — I doubt, therefore I think, therefore I am."

While I am a considerable friend of Asian and Chinese culture, education, and contemporary youth, there are statements that I make in *A Journey to the East* which might not please all readers from the region or China, which might be strongly critiqued by many Chinese faculty and students, and certainly might make me unwelcome by the authorities. These critiques are as objective as possible from my own experience as an American sojourner, especially in China. With reasonable freedom in most of my classes, I did sometimes criticize Asian or Chinese government leaders, institutions, media, or social media censorship, and opening up the students' knowledge base, which would have much been less likely in public lectures, conferences, or the Chinese media. It is a necessary condition in writing such an autoethnographic/autobiographical book as a foreigner and American, reasonably unfettered in my external application of the freedom of expression, but with sensitivity and an effort to provide a balanced cultural viewpoint and friendship for the thousands of young students whom I met there.

In my final class with my Yangzhou University sophomore students in the autumn semester of 2013–14, I urged them to seriously "consider my following proposals: get a passport for future possibilities of overseas travel, study, or work; doubt all messages that come from the Chinese media without checking other possible sources; think more creatively and critically; ask "why?" and "why not?" regularly; prepare yourselves for positive future doors or opportunities to open; and work toward becoming more multicultural, and eventually world citizens, remembering the clarion call of Socrates, "I am neither a citizen of Athens, nor of Greece, but of the world."

A Journey to the East 29

Subjectivity in Evaluating Cultural Stories for Russian and Chinese Sophomore Students; 2013–14

In the autumn semester of 2013–14 at Yangzhou University, I assigned the creation of their personal cultural stories for all of my students; fifteen first year English education postgraduate women; fifty-five senior Japanese and French majors; and 270 sophomore Arabic, French, Japanese, Korean, business English, English translation, and English education majors. Illustratively, they were expected to include creatively critical thinking about such aspects as their family, community, and educational backgrounds; their interests, beliefs, attitudes, values, and world views; and their goals for five years from the present; with good English composition (a potential problem for the Arabic, French, Japanese, and Korean majors). For the semester-long post graduates and seniors, this was only one of several assignments, but for the sophomore nine-week course on western culture, because their cultural stories took me forty-five hours to grade, correct minor mistakes, and post about 160 of them onto my international blog, (2013), writing their cultural stories turned out to be their only assignment. Objectively, there should have been two assignments for a nine-week class. In fact, for one of the two classes, because of the Christmas [for the foreign teachers only] and calendar New Year holidays, there were only seven weeks available.

As I was working with their cultural stories over several weeks, some of the grading was simply subjectively intuitive, or varied on how well the students met the rather vague criteria for the assignment, or even varying on when or how I personally felt at the time that I read their essays. What if students developed one part well, but others less well? What if they paid no attention to one of the criteria, for example, their goals for the next five years, as many of them failed to do, but did well on other aspects? What if the business English, English translation, and English education majors typically could meet the various English language criteria better than the Arabic, French, Japanese, and Korean language majors, but these language students had other positive aspects in their cultural stories? What if students turned in assignments on time, but never or only rarely attended the classes? Did they deserve equal consideration with all of those who attended every class? What if some students wrote the cultural stories for others? Earlier at Ocean

University of China, one young woman turned in a cultural story which I accidentally found on Google by someone else.

Total objectivity was nearly impossible in assessing these sophomore cultural stories, particularly for those students in an English language class, but who were other foreign language majors. Also, with 120 students in one sophomore class, and 150 in the other one, and fifty-five senior Japanese and French majors, I learned only a few names in each class, those who were more responsive to questions or statements that I offered. Even as university French and Japanese seniors, many students followed the Chinese tendency never to speak in class unless directly called upon, and this was even truer among the sophomores.

Nonetheless, when a young man from another institution helped me enter the final grades both in paper copies and online for the College of Foreign Language records, he remarked: "What high grades! Why are all of your grades so high?" I discussed with him the fact that one student had an internship in Shanghai, and notifying me of that situation, turned in very well done papers on time. "Fail him!" my young friend exclaimed. However there may have been others who did not attend class but did turn in assignments on time. This was a difficult situation to solve since class roll calls were too cumbersome with so many students in the two sophomore classes. Even passing around attendance sheets each week could easily have found friends signing in absent classmates.

Since this was my last semester teaching in a Chinese university, and there was less possibility of cheating by the autobiographical and qualitative nature of the assignments, I had decided at the beginning of the semester senior and post graduate courses and nine week course for the sophomores, to grade everyone relatively generously, another subjective decision on my part. Typically, in the Chinese universities where I taught, American teachers already had the reputation of grading closer to the top of the grading scale than otherwise. No doubt all of the students were pleased with their grades, despite my own inherent positive subjectivity in grading their cultural stories. Over ten years of teaching in China, almost none of the students whom I taught ever had any objections about their grades that I was aware of, neither by their own complaints, nor from their class monitors who served as spokespersons for their classes, nor from the faculty supervisors of the foreign teachers. Of course, there is an important cultural element here as well, as I have found that very few of my Chinese students over ten years have ever objected about my grading patterns as their American professor, unless to challenge my often well-founded assertions of cheating or plagiarism on their part on research papers.

To be sure, in teaching more than 2,550 Chinese students from 2001–14, I estimated that about 25% of my previous undergraduate students in the four universities had seriously cheated or plagiarized on term papers or essays that required supportive and accurate citations and evidence. Before this last semester, I typically gave a final grade of 60, a barely passing, but not failing grade, for those whom I caught plagiarizing rather stridently, but I also probably missed 10 or 20% or more such instances. At the same time, most of my Chinese students would rank honesty among their top five values. Rampant cheating was less likely in oral assignments and those which I developed over time that tended to be designed as relatively cheat-or plagiarism-proof, and not at all likely in assessing MA theses, where the Shanghai International Studies University Graduate School used such software as "Turn me in," causing the documents to turn red whenever plagiarism or even near plagiarism was evident. In group oral assignments, it was often apparent that some members of the group worked much harder on the assignment than others — another subjective problem in grading.

What about students who became close friends, or traveled internally or internationally with me, if they cheated, was I able to overcome any positive feelings that I had about our friendship? Michael, a student friend in three of my classes, cheated on the research paper in each class. He didn't mind the low grade as long as he could pass the course and his argument was that he had not cheated on any of the other course assignments. Later, when he was teaching English in a college, he wrote me and said that because of many of his students were cheating, he now really understood why I was so angry at him because of his regular cheating and plagiarism. What about the frequent implicit administrator's view that publically endorsed strict standards, but who also did not wish to have their departments or colleges embarrassed by a large number of failing or very low grades by foreign teachers? All of these factors are important despite being as objective and with the highest ethical standards as possible in each of these situations. Are honesty and high ethical behavior relative by Chinese students, especially when they see regular signs of dishonesty by their faculty and administrators? Is this a problem only of the Chinese students? Certainly not, as it is prevalent in western culture as well. Even in the 1980s when I was heavily involved with high school international students, I would receive such responses from some of them as "Of course we cheat, but do not want to get caught. All of the institutions are corrupt." "Why?" "Because all of the institutions are corrupt."

I used one class period for the nine week class as a Christmas sing-along — as an example of the significance of Christmas and its religious and secular music for western culture. One student monitor read expressively "Twas the night before Christmas" and other class monitors of Arabic, French, Japanese, and Korean majors each sang a Christmas song in their major languages. I considered this to be an important aspect of western culture and made a self-reflection that all of the seniors and sophomores had the text book from which they could learn much more, if they were really motivated to do so, rather than one more day of my lectures and class dialogues.

Communicating Interculturally includes eleven dialogues between imaginary students, an imaginary Professor Zhang, and myself; ten substantive chapters, thirty short essays; case studies; and discussion questions for each chapter. At the end of the semester, I urged all of these students to retain the book as it would provide them considerable knowledge on a number of topics. For the fifteen first year postgraduate women in English education, we used Steve J. Kulich's and my coedited book, *Intercultural Perspectives on Chinese Communication* (2007) for which teams of two were assigned to discuss the intercultural implications of two chapters (eleven of which were written in English and three in Chinese) each week. During the semester, I frequently recommended their purchase of *Communicating Interculturally* as I made numerous references to the book. This led some of the women students to suggest that both books should be required, despite the extra cost. In that class, I led them to have a self-reflection weekly on whether they had met the expectations of leading the class discussions in terms of the summary and analysis. This group was small enough that we were able to have a very pleasant dinner party at my apartment (on a different campus) on Christmas day with games developed by the young women.

Apparently being well-liked by students at these institutions, I wondered if my efforts to increase their creativity and critical thinking had been unsuccessful because these mostly undergraduate students were not interested or were too shy to continue a long distance relationship with me. In contrast, perhaps thirty-forty of my students at Yangzhou University in 2001–02, Beijing Language and Culture University in 2002–05, and mostly MA students at Shanghai International Studies University in 2005–09 have continued to keep in touch with me by email. A likely reason for this contrast might be that we had many activities outside of class such as open houses and parties at my apartment and several of them traveled with me, as well as greater maturity for my postgraduate students. Many of these students remember with fondness my annual Halloween, Christmas, and my birthday parties, as well as my annual Christmas concerts. Very recently, I received the following message from one of my MA students at Shanghai International Studies University:

"The time we spent together are now treasures in my memory. I have various photos about us in my home PC. I will never forget t your help when I was just a poor student. Your generosity and help meant a lot to me at that time, as I was just a poor student from a rural area. Life is never an easy thing in Shanghai for a young man from a poor family. I'm forever grateful to your noble deeds. I wish one day I could do the same thing as you do. I cherish our friendship. (Mike)"

PART ONE
THINKING GLOBALLY – ACTING LOCALLY

1. Being There: Monocultural/Eurocentric/Afrocentric/Asiacentric/Multicultural/World Citizen? The Intercultural Communication Field: a Founder, North America, 1970–2014; a Participant: China, 2001–2014

My father jumped out of his southern Indiana classroom window in the seventh grade and never returned. I think that he never read a book. My mother was unable to teach in the 1920s through the Ku Klux Klan's interference because she was Catholic. When I was a child, there were still signs at the roads leading into the southern Indiana town warning blacks not to let the sun set on them there.

I grew up monoculturally in Muncie, Indiana (often called little Kentucky, because of the surge of uneducated Kentuckian workers moving there after World War II), an industrial lower and middle class city of about 70,000. Ball State Teacher's College then enrolled about 6,000 students, who were expected to be friendly. There were only thirteen academic departments. Walnut Street divided where African Americans and the lower middle class whites generally would unofficially live only on one side. Ball state teacher's college was located mostly in an area of the city inhabited by the better educated, richer, and higher middle class white population.

I was perhaps destined to remain monocultural, as many of my thirty St. Lawrence grade school classmates remained in Muncie for most of their lives, except for two who became Catholic nuns and later served as missionaries in Latin America. When I graduated from high school, my parents took me to Montreal and Quebec City where I practiced a little of my limited high school French.

With an early interest in becoming a Catholic priest, the Church's near universal appeal (the oldest NGO in the world), my study of Greek, Latin, and French, and the inspiring statement in St. Matthew's gospel, "go and teach all nations," all provided a positive Eurocentric counter balance to the more likely potential monoculturalism on my part. In the seminary, a number of young men went to study in Rome or Innsbrook, Austria, which encouraged me early to dream to go to Europe. Later I lived at home and walked to classes at Ball State Teachers College, majoring in English, with minors in Latin and communication, later earning my master's degree in English, with a minor in Latin — thus having a double major. In 1956 as a member of the college debate team, my partner and I won many debates at various intercollegiate tournaments on both sides of the national debate resolution: "Resolved that the United States should recognize Red China." The US military academies were not allowed to compete that year because of the government's insistence that it was impossible for these elite future officers to debate the affirmative side of the question. I cannot remember if I recognized the proposition's slur against China that was imbedded in the national debate resolution, then, but later I more clearly understood its derogatory nature. However, is it possible that the year's intensive debates as a college sophomore about China sowed the seeds for my later interest in China?

Joining the international club and attending some local National Association for the Advancement of Colored People meetings, as far as I can remember, I never had any racist tendencies, despite mild religious prejudices. Graduating from college in 1958, and traveling on a 1,000 passenger student ship from Montreal to Liverpool, I spent two months traveling alone in twelve western European countries which created considerable early intercultural dialogue for me. I attended an international Pax Romana (international Catholic Youth) conference in southern Germany.

The next year, my wife and I participated in an International Youth Hostel Festival in Munich, with travel to Copenhagen, Stockholm, Oslo, and Helsinki. Then we joined a group of twenty-four young people for a two week tour to Leningrad and Moscow, my first of five visits to the Soviet Union and Russia. A late 1959 *Newsweek* cover announced that for the first time, 15,000 Americans had traveled to the Soviet Union that year. One young Jewish member of our group gave each of us a Torah so that he could distribute them to Russian Jews. If he had carried them all, Soviet customs officials would have confiscated them. In Leningrad we visited the former orthodox cathedral which had been converted into a museum of religion and atheism. In Kremlin Square, we followed tearful citizens past the mummified bodies of Lenin and Stalin in their joint mausoleum.

We were at the American exhibit in Moscow before vice president Nixon and Soviet chairman Nikita Khruschev had their aggressive "kitchen debate" at the model American home. I also saw the "soft power" of the US as the exhibit started with 15,000 books by American authors, very lightly monitored, and by the time that we were at the exhibit, 7,500 books had fortuitously disappeared into Russian visitors' possession. At the American Embassy, we were given many copies of the United States Information Service Russian language magazine "Amerika" to leave randomly on the metro or in the department store Gum, or to give to individual Russians, as the police constantly and immediately rounded up the copies for sale at magazine kiosks with the explanation to the embassy staff that no one was buying them. Several Russian students invited us to visit their homes, but when the meeting times arrived, none of them came to meet us. Even though we were closely monitored by our Intourist guide, many members of our group managed to sell western records, jeans, and cigarettes to eager young Russians.

At the Ph.D. level in the University of Illinois, majoring in communication with a strong emphasis in classical rhetoric, I wanted to write my dissertation on Khruschev's translated speeches in his 1959 US visit. My advisor wisely vetoed this proposal as I knew no Russian. Next, I suggested writing my dissertation on UN Secretary General Dag Hammarskjold's speeches in English, but my adviser also vetoed it as his view was that Hammarskjold's initial thinking was in Swedish, despite the speeches being written in English. He was probably incorrect in rejecting the second proposal as Hammarskjold was a fluent speaker of English from his youth. We settled on a classical rhetorical analysis of Ambassador Adlai Stevenson's UN statements in the fifteenth and sixteenth general assemblies (1964). My adviser found me a $1,000 University of Illinois grant to spend six weeks at the UN and US mission to the UN in the summer of 1962. I recorded and copied all of Stevenson's UN statements, and I also copied all of his speeches from 1936 through 1962. This led to the publication of a well- regarded collection of his international speeches (1969). My two volume set. *Sow the Wind, Reap the Whirlwind: Heads of State Address the United Nations*, (1970) was published as a twenty-fifth anniversary deluxe and numbered commemorative edition. The first numbered set was given to the United Nations Library, where it remains today.

My dissertation led also to my joint authorship with Ray T. Donahue of *Diplomatic Discourse: International Conflict at the United Nations* (1997). Later, I planned to edit a collection of United Nations documents, and still later to edit a several volume collection of the addresses of heads of state and government at the United Nations from 1970 to 1995, but both anticipated publishing projects never materialized, the second as I could find no American university presses willing to commit to such a large project.

Robert T. Oliver gave a one week course on international communication in Denver in 1963 which I attended, using his book, *Culture and Communication* (1962) as the text. No doubt, this brief experience also influenced my later interest in intercultural and international communication. In 1963, he offered me a faculty position at Pennsylvania State University, but I also had an invitation to join the faculty at the University of Buffalo instead. How might my professional academic career have differed if I had joined the faculty with Professor Oliver? He was always a distant mentor for me.

In the 1967 final meeting of the Committee for Cooperation with Foreign Universities meeting in Memphis and inspired by Edward T. Hall's books, we began to discuss informally the creation of an academic field of intercultural/cross-cultural and international] communication. Under the leadership of Fred L. Casmir, we agreed to have a 1968 bicultural German-American oral communication conference in Heidelberg which I attended with my family where my daughter turned six years old. Earlier that summer, I represented the Catholic Diocese of Buffalo at a three week international ecumenical conference at Oxford University and with my family we traveled in England, Scotland, Wales, the Netherlands, and Germany.

Under the leadership of Mitsuko Saito and John C. Condon, our committee promoted a Japanese-American conference at International Christian University in Tokyo in 1972. This conference and a second one in January, 1976, resulted in their two publications in Japan: *Intercultural Encounters with Japan: Communication-Context* and Conflict, (1974) and *Communicating across Cultures: For What?* (1976).

Meanwhile, intercultural/cross-cultural communication courses began to be offered in several American universities in the late 1960s and early 1970s, I offered my first cross-cultural communication course at Indiana University in 1970. David Hoopes had also created the Regional Council for International Understanding at the University of Pittsburgh and produced a number of issues of his work-book-sized annual s from 1972 through 1975: *Readings in Intercultural Communication, Vols. 1–5.*

William C. Howell, second vice president of the Speech Communication Association, unsuccessfully advocated that the Association hold its 1969 convention in Hong Kong as an Association commitment to its commitment to interculturalism and internationalism. Failing the acceptance of that proposal, he and we members of the committee argued, also unsuccessfully, that Miss Angie Brooks of Liberia, the president of the United Nations General Assembly in 1969 be invited to deliver the keynote address for the convention in New Orleans of that year. In that case, subtle racism or fear of a backlash may have prevailed among the organization's leaders

From 1968 through 1970, I served as editor of ten issues of *Today's Speech, the journal of the Eastern Communication Association,* with special issue topics and essay reviews such as "communication, human rights and social protest"; "communication in nonwestern cultures"; "selected sources on modern international communication"; "communication and development: a review essay"; and "cross-cultural communication: a review essay." These were some of the early communication academic journal emphases on intercultural and international communication from our discipline.

On May 6, 1970, K. S. Sitaram and five others, proposed to the board of the International Communication Association meeting in Minneapolis the creation of Division 5: Intercultural and Development Communication. The proposal was adopted, and the Division began to operate on May 7, 1970, with Sitaram as the first chair, effectively giving the field's development its first formal endorsement by an important professional international communication association. I served as the Division's third chair from 1975–77, culminating in the association' second conference outside of North America in Berlin where I was responsible for thirteen panel sessions. That summer, my wife and I also traveled to Poland, Hungary, Czechoslovakia, and East Germany in our own European journey to Eastern Europe. This experience was complicated by several negative developments with the customs agents from each of these countries.

In 1971, under the auspices of the [US] Speech Communication Association and the Canadian Oral Communication Association, I chaired the Indiana University (Brown County State Park) consultation to begin to formulate the academic field of intercultural communication. Twelve faculty leaders, including the president of SCA, William Howell, and Grace Layman, president of the Canadian Oral Communication Association, and twelve of my Indiana university graduate students were present. We considered both the process of establishing intercultural communication as an academic study and the content that such a field should emphasize, borrowing heavily from anthropology, sociology, and psychology. Casmir became the first editor of the SCA *International and Intercultural Communication Annual* in 1974. Simultaneously, I was the chair of the International Communication and Development Commission of the Midwestern University Consortium for International Development.

I was a visiting professor at Memorial University of Newfoundland in the summer of 1972, teaching what we believe was the first intercultural communication course in Canada. At the University of Virginia, we established several undergraduate and graduate courses related to intercultural and international communication. The US Office of Education awarded me a $55,830 grant to internationalize our undergraduate program, which brought to the University John C. Merrill and Edward C. Stewart as visiting professors each for a semester. In 1974, I chaired the summer Chicago conference on establishing intercultural communication as an academic field of study and I was a participant in the Nihonmatsu, Japan Bicultural Japanese/American Research Conference. During the summer of 1975, I participated in a three week course on British media in London taught by Hamid Mowlani, and I taught jointly at St. Paul's University and at the University of Ottawa at the invitation of Professor Andrew Ruscowski. In 1980, I returned to St. Paul's University to present a paper on intercultural communication and religion at an international ecumenical conference.

My coedited books, *Readings in Classical Rhetoric* (1969, 1972, 1985, 1989), *Readings in Medieval Rhetoric* (1973) and my edited books, *Intercommunication among Nations and Peoples* (1973) and *Sow the Wind: Reap the Whirlwind: Heads of State Address the United Nations* (1970, two volumes) illustrated my two different early emerging academic interests: rhetoric and public discourse and intercultural and international communication, both of which I have developed over my professional career.

In May, 1973, a number of us met at the University of Pittsburgh to establish the International Society for Intercultural Education, Training and Research (SIETAR International) which held the first of twenty-five international congresses in 1975 in Gaithersburg, Maryland, and electing Molefi K. Asante as the first president. I was a member of the first two Governing Councils; I was an active participant at the Congress in Mexico City, and later I chaired the 1980 international congress at which twelve Latin American diplomats were present. I was vice president in 1982–84, leading toward international congresses in Italy in 1983, and the Netherlands in 1986, plus regional 1983 and 1986 conferences in Sweden. I was president in 1984–86, and past president and chair of the Society' International Advisory Board in 1986–88. In 1986, the Society awarded me its first and only "Citizen of the World" award. The statement by Socrates, "I am neither a citizen of Athens, nor of Greece, but of the world" inscribed on the award plaque has become an ongoing guide in my interest in eventually becoming a global citizen myself. In 1990, I received the Society's "Senior Interculturalist" award. Earlier in 1978, I had been honored with a Distinguished Alumnus Award at Ball State University and also by the International Communication Association.

In the summer of 1974, SCA, ICA and SIETAR International jointly cosponsored the Chicago founding conference for intercultural communication which I chaired, attracting 200 persons and using Edward C. Stewart's "Outline of Intercultural Communication" as the guideline for about ten small group discussions. Nemi C. Jain, I, and Melvin Miller coedited *Intercultural Communication: Proceedings of the Speech Communication Association Summer Conference, X.* (1974).

In the same summer, the Japanese-American bicultural research conference was held in Nihonmatsu, Japan, cosponsored in part by the Japan Expo Foundation and the Eli Lily Foundations. I devoted the last quarter of my book, *The Cultural Dialogue,* (1978, 1985.1989. pp. 216–286) to a paraphrase of the dialogue of our group of eight Japanese and American participants at the conference. Muneo Yoshikawa provided an introduction to the dialogue detailing his experiences as a Japanese professor teaching in Hawaii. My first Asian conference and my inclusion of the paraphrased Japanese-American dialogue in *The Cultural Dialogue* were early steps in my later movement toward an Asiacentric orientation, reinforced by my 1980 United States Information Agency sponsored lectures in South Korea and Singapore and by my visits that year to the homes in Japan of six of my former MA advisees at Indiana University and the University of Virginia.

In the summer of 1975, I participated in a course on British media in London taught by Hamid Mowlana of American University. Later that summer, I taught intercultural communication jointly at St. Paul's University and the University of Ottawa). In 1977, I was the professor of the intercultural communication course for midlevel executives at the United States Information Agency, resulting in the publication of my edited *USIA Intercultural Communication Course: Proceedings* (1978). I was also the co-chair for a series of scholar-diplomat seminars sponsored by the Agency. During that period (1979–1980), I organized a twenty-four part series on intercultural communication for the Voice of America's world-wide broadcast in English and I was an interviewee in four of them.

During the winter and spring quarters of 1978, I was a distinguished visiting professor at Kent State University while D. Ray Heisey was serving as president in his last semester at Damavand College in Tehran. I was heavily involved in the SIETAR congresses until 1989, including the 1983 conference in San Giminano, Italy, and the 1986 conference in Amsterdam, plus regional conferences in 1983 and 1986 in Sweden. After my 1990–91 Fulbright year in Swaziland, I also attended the 1992 and 1993 SIETAR congresses. Besides being deeply involved professionally in the development of the academic field of intercultural communication, I was making a consistent effort to live the most positive intercultural life possible, partly at the microworld level, especially with international high school students, serving in the 1980s as host father for students from Sweden, Belgium, France, Spain, Brazil, El Salvador, and South Africa and as president of the local chapter of the American Field Service (AFS).

As a member in a faculty study tour of Lebanon, Jordan, and the occupied territories of Israel in 1980/81, we had meetings with the Jordanian Council of Foreign Relations, the out-going US ambassador to Lebanon, the UN High Command, and Chairman Yasser Arafat, as well as women's groups, orphanages, and refugee camps. In Israel's occupied territories, we met the mayors of Ramallah and Nabulus, who had recently suffered car bomb attacks, and leaders of various groups.

As the Fulbright communication professor in 1990–91 at the University of Swaziland, I initiated the fifteen junior communication major students as communication majors. We had several field trips to various embassies and their development programs. I represented the University for a meeting with UN officials in Nairobi, and then at the African Communication Association conference in Burkina Faso. We had planned a two week media class field trip to Zimbabwe, but because of a dangerous military intervention on the University of Swaziland campus on November 14, 1990, the trip had to be canceled for the students. The intended launching of a biweekly newspaper by the communication students was prevented by the two month closing of the university, while the establishment of a daily thee hour radio broadcast was delayed until the following year because the radio training station had not yet been completed. Following my Fulbright year, my wife and I brought back to the US two teenage Swazi students for future high school education. Still later in 1995–2001, three young Sudanese refugees lived with me in Rochester, New York. I was a strong supporter for the "lost boys of Sudan" often being called "American father of the Sudanese." These years, 1990–2001, became the most important Afrocentric phase of my personal cultural advancement.

While retaining tenure at the University of Virginia, I accepted the William A. Kern and Distinguished Visiting Professorship of communication at the Rochester Institute of Technology (1994–2001). Unfortunately this meant my loss of a selected Fulbright professorship in Bulgaria. Teaching one course each quarter (intercultural communication, a model United Nations Security Council simulation, and communication and social change), I received generous funding for special projects including organizing thirty-three lectures on intercultural, international, and global topics, and delivering eleven of these lectures. I took students to four model international United Nations conferences in Toronto and Montreal, where I gave a lecture at each conference. I attended four annual NGO conferences at the United Nations, plus Fulbright, communication, and third world development conferences. I founded and served as the first president for the Rochester Area Fulbright Association (1995–98) and I was the president of the United Nations Association of

Rochester (1997–98). More recently, I have been a member of the Blue Ridge United Nations Association.

K. S, Sitaram and I initiated the first of six Rochester Intercultural Conferences (1995–2001), first celebrating the 25th anniversary of his May 1970 founding of the ICA Division for Intercultural Communication and Development. Sitaram was the keynoter at the first conference, and later I served as well as a conference keynote speaker. Later, Sitaram's and my other co-chaired Rochester Intercultural Conferences included such topics as communication, technology, and values; social justice and peace; intercultural and international media; human rights; and social media (1996–2001). Sitaram and I published *Civic Discourse: Multiculturalism, Cultural Diversity and Global Communication* (1998) and *Civic Discourse: Intercultural, International, and Global Media* (1999).

After Ray T. Donahue and I *published Diplomatic Discourse: International Conflict at the United Nations* (1997), I was appointed the series editor for my own series, "Civic Discourse for the Third Millennium" for Ablex Publishing Company and later also for Praeger and Greenwood Publishing Group (1998–2004) with the publication of seventeen books on intercultural, international, and global topics, including, for example, two books related to China; one related to south East Asia; two related to Africa; two related to North America; two related to the Middle East; one related to Central and Eastern Europe; and three books related to human rights, peace, and social justice. Three more books were completed in 2000 relating to communication, technology, and values; human rights; and African communication and were submitted to Ablex, but because of a change of ownership and complicated negotiations with Greenwood Publishing Group, they did not get published. This remains one of my professional regrets as a large number of chapter authors were unable to get their research published in our books. This was a case of my applying short term orientation in moving the books forward, rather than a long term orientation, as seen in the concept of Confucian Dynamism.

Becoming an emeritus professor at the University of Virginia and retiring from the Rochester Institute of Technology both in 2001, I became a professor in the Foreign Language College at Yangzhou University for the academic year of 2001–02. My postgraduate course there in intercultural communication may have been among the earlier courses in Chinese universities on this topic, just as my course at Memorial University in Newfoundland had been in 1972 for Canada.

In October of 2001, I gave a keynote address at the fourth biennial China Association for Intercultural Communication conference in Xi'an, meeting Professor Jia Yuxin of Harbin Institute of Technology for the first time, a founder of the study of intercultural communication in China. He later wrote the foreword for Li Mengyu's and my text book, *Communicating Interculturally* (2012). I gave keynote addresses at CAFIC conferences in 2003, 05, 07, and 2011 while also attending the 2009 and 2013 conferences. In 2009 and 2011, the Association gave me special recognition awards for promoting teaching and research in intercultural communication in China.

In November 2001, I lectured at the Beijing Language and Culture University, plus being interviewed by Yang Rui for the China Central International Television program "Dialogue" which was placed on the Yangzhou University website. Subsequently, I was interviewed eleven more times for the "Dialogue" programs (2002–04) Professor L. S Zhou, my post graduate student Lu Jun, and I coedited *Sino-American Compositions of Shared Topics* (2002) for Chinese students preparing for the CET exams (College Test of English) 4 and 6.

From 2002–05, I was a distinguished professor in the College of Foreign Languages of Beijing Language and Culture University, popularly known as the little United Nations as nearly 1500 international students were studying Chinese there from more than 140 countries.

I attended two Fullbright conferences in Athens in 2004. I had lecture series at Luchnow University in India in 2003 and 2005 and at Kursk State University in Russia in 2005 and later in 2008 at Volgograd State Pedagogical University. I took a different Chinese student each to Vietnam, Cambodia, South Korea, and India while a faculty member in Beijing, giving them "Opening UP" experiences.

At Shanghai International Studies University (2005–09), I was a distinguished professor first in the English College from 2005–07 and then in the College of Communication and Journalism from 2007–09. Steve J. Kulich and I were delegates to the Asian Foundation for Education conference in Beijing in 2005. I participated in Kulich's subconference related to intercultural communication in the Second World Forum on China Studies in 2006, organized by the Shanghai Municipal Government and the Shanghai Academy of Social Sciences. The forum had the theme of "China and the World: Harmony and Peace." Our subconference theme was "China Communicating Interculturally and Internationally." On the same weekend, the Intercultural Institute was founded under Kulich's leadership as executive director, where I became the chair of the International Advisory Board and with him, senior co-editor of the intercultural research series. Kulich and I coedited *Intercultural Perspectives on Chinese Communication* (2007) for which I wrote a ninety page history of the field of intercultural communication in North America and China; "One World, One Dream: Harmonizing Society through Intercultural Communication: A Prelude to China Intercultural Communication Studies" (pp. 22–91).

Kulich's, my, and Weng Liping's coedited book, *Value Frameworks at the Theoretical Crossroads of Culture* was published (2012), in which my essay, "Universal Human Rights as Universal Values: A Historical Perspective" appeared (pp. 383–434) and Kulich's, Weng Liping's and my *coedited Value Dimensions and their Contextual Dynamics across Cultures both* applied the theoretical and practical aspects of cross-cultural values (2014). I wrote the foreword for Volumes 2 to 7 of the *Intercultural Research* series.

Laura Gostin's "The Journey of an Intercultural/International scholar: Dr. Michael Prosser," appeared in *China Media Reports,* 2007:12, 06. It is republished in this book in Section Six. Peter Zhang Long's 2009 MA thesis: "Investigating into the influence of an intercultural communication founder — Michael H. Prosser and his contemporaries" was completed in 2009 and is available in my international blog, www. Michaelprosser. com as well as in various US and Chinese search engines.

From 2007 through 2011, I served as the English editor for forty-five articles in *The Journal of Middle Eastern and Islamic Studies (in Asia)*. My article, "Reading Discourse on the Middle East for Intercultural Understanding," was published in the *Journal* in 2010. I was also a keynoter at the German/Chinese Intercultural Communication Discipline Development Symposium at SISU (2010), and at the International Association for Intercultural Communication Studies conference at Kumamoto Gakuin University, Kumamoto, Japan (2010).

For the spring semester of 2011, I was a distinguished professor in communication and journalism at Ocean University of China in Qingdao; then during the autumn semester of 2011, I was the faculty advisor for sixty lifelong learners and the Asia/China expert on the University of Virginia/Institute for Shipboard Learning around the world study voyage Semester at Sea.

Higher Education Press published Li Mengyu's and my coauthored book, *Communicating* Interculturally (2012), later published by Dignity Press for a North American version, *Chinese Communicating Interculturally* (2014). Under my and Kulich's coeditorship, we published "Special issue: Early American pioneers of intercultural communication" in *the International Journal of Intercultural Relations* (2012: November). My, Mansoureh Sharifzadeh, and Zhang Shengong's book, *Finding Cross-cultural Common Ground,* was published by Dignity Press (2013). Dignity Press has published Cui Litang's and my coedited scholarly *Social Media in Asia* (2014) and now, I, Adil Nurmakov, and Ehsan Shahghasemi are coediting *Social Media in the Middle East* for publication in 2016 and to complete the trilogy, I and Debhasis (Deb) Aikat are planning to coedit *Social Media in Africa,* targeted for publication in early 2018.

As I have concluded my Chinese university teaching career in 2014, in September of 2014, I have had my doctorate from the University of Illinois for fifty years. I have taught full or part time almost fifty-five years, with 8800 students in Canada and the US, fifteen in Swaziland, and more than 2550 in China. I have given lectures to more than 8,500 secondary and tertiary students in Cambodia, China, India, Japan, and Russia; and teaching basically as a volunteer about 500 kindergarten, primary school, and junior middle school children in China. Among other former students, it has been a great pleasure that my former postgraduate student at Yangzhou University in 2001–02, now Associate Professor Lu Jun, and his wife, my former oral English student, Kathleen Jin, provided me immense friendship and assistance during my final 2013–14 semester in China, especially during and following my hospital stay because of food poisoning.

More or less, my sojourning, teaching, and travels in Africa, Asia, Europe, Latin America and the Middle East have greatly enhanced my life and intercultural communication competence. My forty years more broadly with short experiences in Asia and my ten years teaching in China were not only an adventure in my journey to the east (and west Asia) but also were challenging intellectually as a teacher and learner.

My ultimate personal and professional goal, emerging from a potentially monocultural individual, to an Eurocentric one, Afrocentric, and Asiacentric person, eventually to a multicultural one, is to move to *global citizenship* in the not too distant future. I very much appreciate Confucius's quote attributed to the *Analects:* "The Master says: At 15, I set my heart on learning. At 30 I know where I stand (my character has been formed). At 40, I have no more doubts, at 50, I know the will of Heaven, at 60 my ears are attuned (i.e. my moral sense is well-developed), at 70, I follow my heart's desire without crossing the line (without breaking moral principles)."

2. Forewording the SISU Intercultural Research Series: 2010–2014

Kulich's and my first coedited volume in the Shanghai International Studies University's Intercultural Iinstitute's intercultural research series, *Intercultural Perspectives on Chinese Communication* (2007) was nominated for the outstanding book award of the International and Intercultural Communication Division of the [US] National Communication Association in 2008. Subsequently, his, my, and Weng Liping's book, *Value Frameworks at the Theoretical Crossroads of Culture, Volume 4* (2012) was nominated for an outstanding book award in the International Academy for Intercultural Research at its biennial conference in 2013.

Professor Guan Shijie of Peking University wrote the foreword for volume 1. He noted that "IC studies [in China] have achieved encouraging progress in various aspects such as the expansion of research groups, the founding of more research institutes, extended exchanges with overseas scholars, more frequent symposia, the increase of the number of schools that have begun to offer ic courses, as well as the recruitment of more postgraduates" (2007, p. xi). These developments created, he argued: "(1) the study of interpersonal communication across different cultures has been integrated with the reality of China….(2) intercultural communication between different countries has become an important topic in communication study. (3) research on ic between China and foreign countries has gone beyond the range of intercultural communication between China and the united states,… (4) intercultural communication between Chinese ethnic groups has become a focus of research as well…. (5) interdisciplinary study combining ic [intercultural communication] theories with other disciplines has also become a research interest" (2007, pp. xi-xii).

Writing specifically about the intercultural research series, Guan praised the volume for the following reasons: "It serves as an interdisciplinary platform for China's ic research…. It emphasizes on the importance of scientific methodology in ic research…. it focuses on the localization of ic research' (xiv-xvi). He concludes; "the publication of this series is an occasion to celebrate for the entire Chinese ic [intercultural communication] community. It is my sincere wish that these volumes can continue and grow, and my hope is that it develops into a series that is interdisciplinary, methodology-promoting, indigenized into the Chinese setting and blends well theories and practice"(xvi.)

In 2009, the China Association for Intercultural Communication gave me their first special recognition award for my promotion of teaching and study of intercultural communication in China, and in 2011, the Association gave special recognition awards to Kulich, Guo-ming Chen of the University of Rhode Island, He Doakuan, emeritus professor of Shenzheng University (and later translator of my book, *The Cultural Dialogue* into Chinese), Ling Chen of Hong Hong Baptist University and me.

Steve J. Kulich has kindly invited me, as his senior coeditor, to write the series preface for volumes 2–7 in the intercultural research series. My series preface, slightly changed over time and to meet the topic for each book, follows for volumes 2–7.

Series Preface: Intercultural Research Series, Volumes 2 – 7, Intercultural Institute, Shanghai International Studies University

Ancient Athens served as an intercultural and intellectual crossroads for Asia and Europe. The Greek philosopher, Socrates' famous statement "I am neither a citizen of Athens, nor of Greece, but of the world" speaks eloquently of the impact of intercultural communication, comparative analysis, and the importance of identity clarification both in his and contemporary society. Greek philosophers, Socrates, Plato, and Aristotle all looked outward from their own culture, identifying or debating major world value orientations such as goodness, justice, truth, and happiness. For East Asia, multiple schools of thought developed were put forward during the spring and autumn period, shaping China's cross-state communication. Confucius' Analects articulated the role of *ren* (benevolence and kindness), *li* (propriety and right living through ritual), *de* (moral power), *dao* (internalized moral direction), and *mianzi* or *lian* (externalized social image and harmony). These Confucian orientations were integrated into what became the fabric of not only the Chinese state, but the educational and philosophical orientation of much of East and South Eastern Asia.

All of these early cultural conceptualizations of identities and values strongly support the potentially positive intercultural, multicultural, and global world orientations that have enhanced a dialogue of civilizations and cultures, and stress factors that are unifying rather than divisive. The challenge continues to be substantial since intercultural, multicultural, and global communication might just as easily be highly negative with increasing war, poverty, crime, and pandemics. The goal of all those interested in promoting a better local and global society vastly prefers the former.

The location from which this series is originated shows some of these dynamics and contradictions. Just as each nation and people must deal with highs and lows, China is grappling both with some of the positive dialogues of modernization and internationalization, and also as well as the challenges of divergent cultural or global discourses — each nation and people deal with highs and lows. from the depths of the Wenchuan earthquake in Sichuan [may 12, 2008] that rallied not only the nation's, but the world's sympathy, engagement and commitment to rebuild, to the heights of the spectacularly well-orchestrated and successful 2008 Beijing Olympics; from the ongoing challenges of natural disasters like floods or human tragedies like mining and accidents or the global financial crisis, to the futuristic development of Shanghai and its visionary and record-breaking participation and cooperation at the 2010 Shanghai Expo, we see these human and intercultural dynamics at work.

Later Chinese scholars…and their contemporaries each brought and Sinocized many of these western intercultural theories and practical implications for China…. Others have also sought to indigenize social and cultural psychology to strengthen into Chinese scholarship on intercultural communication. Currently many Chinese scholars, either in China itself, in North America, or other regions around the world, have developed robust theories and models or have postulated newer ones, as has been well articulated and documented ..., in the premier volume of this series, *Intercultural Perspectives on Chinese Communication* (2007).

The SUSU Intercultural Institute (SII) of Shanghai International Studies University's (SISU), under the executive leadership of Steve J. Kulich, D.Phil. has accepted a mandate to undertake an intercultural research series of volumes which seeks to publish "cutting edge and seminal articles on the state of the intercultural field" in a variety of areas. as formulated in the establishment of the series, Kulich emphasized that "each volume will focus on one primary domain and will include diverse theoretical and applied research from cultural, intercultural or cross-cultural approaches for that area, seeking to present and frame a 'state of the art' or an extended development summary on the topic."

The SII is committed to close cooperation with both Chinese and international scholars, and that was reflected both in the first volume entitled intercultural perspectives on Chinese communication, where both domestic scholars of the CAFIC were joined by international scholars from communication studies, indigenous and cross-cultural psychology to contribute seminal reviews of ic in their areas of focus. SII is also committed to highlight and bring some integration to the diverse disciplines that influence form, contribute to or are informed by intercultural scholarship. This is illustrated particularly by efforts in that first and subsequent volumes to invite contributions from communication studies at both the interpersonal (jiaoji) as well as mass communication (chuanbo) levels and also to include the perspectives of cultural psychology, cultural anthropology and other related fields. The interdisciplinary nature of ic motivates the SII team to identify and integrate those aspects that contribute to shared foundations for the field, especially as these reflect intercultural, multicultural human development, in keeping with our motto to "develop a discipline to develop people."

This focus on cooperation continues with the biennial thematic ic conferences held by Shanghai normal university, part of the dynamic cooperation among CAFIC Shanghai branch institutions (which also includes regular cross-city scholar forums and the annual ic outstanding MA thesis conference). The next two volumes highlight such interdisciplinary and multi-perspective scholarship on identity and intercultural communication: focusing on i: "Theoretical and contextual construction" (vol 2.) [co-edited by Xiaodong Dai and Steve J. Kuilich, Methodologies and other important topics for ic disciplinary development. The next volumes in the series take up the important topic of ic values -. "Values Frameworks at the Theoretical Crossroads of Culture" (Vol. 4) co-edited by Steve J. Kulich, Michael H. Prosser, and Weng Liping (2012), and "Value Dimensions and their Contextual Dynamics across Cultures" (Vol. 5) co-edited by Steve J. Kulich, Weng Liping and Michael H. Prosser (2014).

Naturally, since the series is being published by the Shanghai Foreign Language Education Press, Chinese academic contributions are especially encouraged, as well those as from the wider international academic community. Based on Professor Kulich's many years of scholarship on values, it is very meaningful that the SISU Intercultural Institute's fourth second and fifth volumes are centered on the continuing examination and invaluable aspects of value studies and their applications. Indeed, the first year postgraduate course that he has taught since 2002 for intercultural communication MA students focuses specifically on the theoretical and applied research on value studies, identities, and core-culture domains. It may be one of the few such courses internationally to stand alone on these topics within the broader academic study of intercultural communication. Related to other strands of research, since 2005, the course that he and I developed in 2005 on "intercultural research foundations: history and status" has become the springboard for the first doctoral program in intercultural communication (kuawenhua jiaoji) in China and coursework, conference papers and contributions for the "interdisciplinary survey of intercultural communication research" will surely provide an ongoing stimulus and ready application for future volumes.

In his foreword for the first volume, *Intercultural Perspectives on Chinese Communication* (2007), Shijie Guan noted that three features characterize the book: 1. it serves as an interdisciplinary platform for China's ic research. 2. it emphasizes the importance of scientific methodology in ic research. 3. it focuses on the localization of ic research. he concludes his remarks by saying that "the publication of this series is an occasion to celebrate for the entire Chinese community: my hope is that it develops into a series that is interdisciplinary, methodology-promoting, indigenized into the Chinese settings and blends well theories with practice (p. xvi)." As he also notes in his foreword for volume 1. For human beings, just as Lourdes Arizpe, chair of the Scientific Committee of the

World Culture Report, 2000, says, "Cultural exchanges are in fact the axis of the new phenomena' as global cultures develop and change (p. ix)."

Since the initial books by Edward T. Hall, *The Silent Language, The Hidden Dimension, Beyond Culture,* and *The Dance of Life,* began to shape the early study of intercultural communication theoretically and practically, so too, it is reasonable to assume that these volumes might provide new impetus for the academic study of values in various cultural contexts. The historical development, frameworks and research approaches presented both by well-established and emerging scholars in these volumes will surely move the academic understanding of key intercultural topic areas ahead. Each volume's contribution toward highlighting theoretical constructs, clarifying the "state of the art" and presenting cutting edge research and practical applications will hopefully contribute to a new apex in the field of intercultural communication. To the ongoing development of the intercultural communication discipline both in China and abroad this series is dedicated. [Listed names have been omitted.]

3. Applying Discourse Analysis to Cultural Dialogue

In *The Cultural Dialogue* (1978, 1985, 1989), the fourth section, "The Cultural Communicator in Dialogue: Observations on Japanese and American Cultures," includes in pages 216–286 a reconstructed cultural dialogue between Americans and Japanese at the bicultural research conference in 1974 at Nihonmatsu, Japan. Now, in Li Mengyu's and my 2012 intercultural communication text book for Chinese university students, Communicating Interculturally, we have ten dialogues preceding each of the ten chapters and one as the epilogue between imaginary Chinese university students in an intercultural communication course, an imaginary Professor Zhang, and myself, relating to each of the chapters and the ending of the course.

D. Ray Heisey wrote in "A Dialogue Proposal" in 2002, the following comments about the goal of cultural dialogue:

First, how can dialog be used in the substance of teaching intercultural communication?...In the process of teaching, as well as in the substance of teaching, we should engage in dialog....Still another approach to dialogic teaching is to engage the students in the process.... The argument [in a case study which he cites from Peking University] is an excellent example of a creative mind at work, which grew out of an intellectual dialog where there was a disagreement between her and the professor's position on a subject.... This case study serves as an example of a very useful tool for teaching intercultural communication to students who may not have much opportunity experiencing other cultures....[L]et me say a word about dialogue in research. Again, in terms of both the substance and the process of research, we should engage in more dialog.

Hilaire Roseman's book, *Generating Forgiveness and Constructing Peace through Truthful Dialogue; Abrahamic Perspective* (2014) stresses that "Communication and dialogue are essential for survival....Dialogue occurs through global and local forms of communication, enhanced over the past 50 years by new technologies. One of the major goals of dialogue in intergroup settings is peace. The modes of communication in the twenty-first century are therefore essential to the peace movement and to the creation of new memories of history to replace old destructive memories" (pp. 21–22). She believes that

Conflict and cooperation are fundamental to the human experience. Intercultural cooperation is harmonious communication among people from different backgrounds, people who are speaking different languages and carry different pictures in their heads that shape their constructions of reality. Under these conditions, people are more likely to disagree than to agree. Love is perhaps the perfect motivator for cooperation as hate is for war. It is a challenge for mankind to take the value of love, and put it into practice" (p. 30).

In Part Five of *A Journey to the East,* there are several examples of the importance of love in various cultural dialogues. Curiously enough, many Chinese students are unable, because of recent traditions, to tell their parents that they love them, but within the context of intercultural dialogue, they are able to say it to a foreign teacher such as myself. There are a half dozen young Chinese males, three of whom are married and have a child, and one young Chinese woman friend, also married and a mother, who regularly sign their email messages to me with "Love." In Part Five, a number of young Chinese men and women use such expressions to me as "I love you forever." In my view, love (*philos* from the ancient Greeks) among friends is one of the most universally important of human values.

In Ray T. Donahue's and my 1997 book, *Diplomatic Discourse*, within the discussion of discourse analysis, some major terms include: framing, contextualism (Context: The Matter of Definition); words: empty containers; scripted language; expectancy: a key to discourse; interactive processing; motivated discourse; critical communication (language and culture awareness); and application.

Musing Heisey's understanding of the importance of dialogue and several of the terms which Donahue and I introduce, providing examples from the Japanese and American dialogue in *The Cultural Dialogue* and from the simulated Chinese and American dialogues in *Communicating Interculturally*, discourse analysis will be employed to consider its application to cultural dialogues, both as a teaching and research contribution for an understanding of intercultural communication as an academic field of study.

In Jia Yuxin's Foreword to *Communicating Interculturally*, he remarked:

It is really gratifying to let the readers — teachers and students — know that scholarly and sophisticated soundness in the *Dialogue* will find a practical resonance with them. The *Dialogue* is truly what is called for by 21st century as a response to the challenge of intercultural communication predisposed by globalization....

I have been reading or to be exact, learning intercultural dialogues from this book It is really rewarding. It is not only original in content but also in form. I believe what Marshall McLuhan stated: "The medium is the message," and the form of the creation is itself really the message as the Platonic Dialogue is the source of ethical enquiries and philosophical explorations....

The Dialogue is at the same time serious and light hearted and the serious side of the Dialogue is imbued with authoritative knowledge while the light hearted side always shines with humor and induces students' interesting responses with a grain of humor too (Jia Yuxun, 2014, p. xix.)

The following introductory dialogue in *Communicating Interculturally* is illustrative:

Professor Zhang: Good morning boys and girls. This class is "Intercultural Communication," and the text for the class is *Communicating Interculturally.* Active class participation is important. I am Professor Zhang, and this is my visiting co-teacher, Professor Michael Prosser. I have studied in America, and have been a teacher at this university for several years. Before you were born, students, Professor Prosser wrote a book called *The Cultural Dialogue.* Professor Prosser, would you like to introduce yourself?

Professor Prosser: Ni hao, ladies and gentlemen! In China, I am regularly called Michael (Mikai). You can all call me Michael. I have taught at several universities in the United States, as well as in Canada and Swaziland and for several years in Chinese universities. Some of my Spanish friends call me Migueleito! "Little Michael!" It's just a pun. As you can see, I am quite tall and big.

Class laughter

Jason: Professor Zhang and we look small compared to you. Did you play basketball?

Michael: I played it very badly. In my first game in high school, I hit the basket at the wrong end of the court! Then the other boys called me "Wrong Way Michael!"

Class laughter

Michael: Class, I would like to ask you some questions. Don't be too shy to respond. Ok? What color are your eyes?

Silence

Ava: Black of course!

Michael: Really? I see some people in the class with brown eyes. You all learned as children that you had black eyes. This is a cultural stereotype. I have a mirror here. Pass it around and see if you have black or brown eyes.

Class laughter

Ivy: I have brown eyes. I never knew that.

Ruby: I have brown eyes too. Teacher, what color are your eyes?

Michael: I think that they are blue. One of my children has blue eyes, another has green eyes, and the third has brown eyes. I wonder how we can explain that genetically.

Cindy: Perhaps there are three different mothers?

Laughter

Michael: Here is a second question. What color is your skin?

Class members: Our Chinese skin is yellow. We come from the Yellow River, you know.

Gloria: We are children of the Dragon.

Michael: I don't see anyone here with yellow skin. Look at this student's shirt. It's yellow. Do you look like that?

Jason: No. Perhaps we are brown?

Class laughter

Michael: Here's another question. How many foreigners are in this room?

Sophia: Just one, you.

Michael: Oh my! I see many foreigners in the room, Professor Zhang and all of you! You see, it's a matter of cultural perspective as you are all foreigners to me. You can see that we have many stereotypes about ourselves and others. For example, in the US, many people have positive stereotypes about Chinese students being so bright in science and math. Are you so bright?

Class laughter

In this short example, when we emphasize contextualism and framing, we understand that this is the first day in an imaginary intercultural communication class for Chinese university students, with an imaginary Chinese Professor Zhang and an American teacher, Michael. The dialogue might be very different in a class in Japan or in a class in South Korea. Although Professor Zhang seems more formal than Michael (aninteresting concept in the naming), he or she (the gender is never identified in all of the dialogues), after a brief introduction of his/her own experience in the United States, Zhang provides a useful introduction of Michael. It appears that Professor Zhang, though potentially a more traditional Chinese professor, is very open to dialogue and encourages Michael to introduce himself. Because his initial self-introduction is humorous, the class immediately has an expectancy of the likelihood of humor as the class progresses. Some stereotypes are identified and challenged both by Michael and class members (Michael being tall and therefore playing basketball; class attention to the myth of Chinese creation from the Yellow River and as children of the Dragon; eye and skin color). It is evident that the initial language is contextually scripted ("Good morning, boys and girls" — a common expression by Chinese teachers), but that words as empty containers (outside of the context of the class) move toward interactive processing; motivated discourse; critical communication (language and culture awareness); and application, which then can be expected to develop more fully in future dialogues in the text book. It is important to note that in reality, I am writing the dialogue for all of the imaginary students, the imaginary Professor Zhang, and myself, thus controlling the narrative, here and in all of the book's dialogues. However, in the paraphrased dialogues of the Japanese and American participants at the Japanese-American bicultural conference are based on real and often conflicting, not imaginary, dialogues where humor is developed as a part of the imagined interaction.

In the Epilogue:" A Final Conversation: Think Globally and Act Locally," the context has changed as the semester is over, but the framing of a serious subject remains humorous. This dialogue recaps some of the earlier statements and brings the class to a conclusion with the imaginary students, imaginary Professor Zhang, whose gender has still never been indicated, and myself.

> *True Nation:* You all know that I am very nationalistic. But, you will be happy to know, Professor Zhang and Michael, that I have learned how to become more conscious of the beliefs, attitudes, and values of people from other cultures, and to be more tolerant of other points of view.
>
> *Catherine:* On the first day of the class, I told you, Professor Zhang and Michael, that so far we hadn't learned anything about intercultural communication.
>
> *Michael:* How do you feel now, Catherine?
>
> *Catherine:* I really appreciated that you both kept encouraging us to be creative and to become critical thinkers.
>
> *Forest:* I decided during the class that I really want to work for an international chocolate company.
>
> Laughter
>
> *Forest:* But seriously, the class did help me to decide that I would like to work in an international company…..
>
> As the dialogue comes to a close, Cindy says:

Cindy: My favorite parts of the class were the very interesting and often very humorous dialogues.... It made me feel that a class like this one is really a good way to learn both serious and humorous ideas about culture and intercultural communication.

Lucky: Michael, in this class, who was more humorous, you or I? Maybe should I be a comedian for my future career? ... A good comedian knows what jokes work best to make an audience laugh. Forest and his obsession on chocolate have taught us that. So perhaps I will become prosperous by making others laugh!

Laughter

Mike: Yes, Lucky. I feel lucky (a pun) to have been in this class with you, Perhaps because of this class I will become an AmeriChinese and then I can meet our Chi American friend Michael in his own country. I have a haiku for Michael: "Today, it's over./Come outdoors with us to play/So sunny and warm."

Laughter

Professor Zhang: Thank you for your comments, class. Don't forget the slogan: "Think globally and act locally."

Michael: And remember the goal so that you can say with Socrates, 'I am neither a citizen of Athens, nor of Greece, but of the world." Or, "I am neither a citizen of Beijing, Shanghai, Guangzhou, nor Xi"an, nor of China, but of the world."

Tony: Let's take a class photo, shall we?

(Class applause and dismissal)

Joy: Professor Zhang and Michael, is that a tear I see in your eyes?

Professor Zhang: Meo. Meo. I have had much joy having you all in class.

Michael: I hear Beethoven's "Ode to Joy" about to begin! And who are the most beautiful young women and most handsome young men here in China?

Class: It's us! Michael and you are our best grandpa!

In this way, we can see both Heisey's and my interest in the importance of dialogue as a key ingredient in the study, teaching, and research in intercultural communication. Because of the frequent humor in the dialogues, one might expect that the text itself will also be humorous, but this is not the case as the text is more traditional in the study of intercultural communication, but at the same time, leads the students toward creative and critical thinking. Other examples can be provided from the Japanese and American dialogue that will occur later in *A Journey to the East,* which can then develop into cross-cultural dialogical analysis between Chinese-American and Japanese-American cultural dialogues.

Because of the dialogical humor, I requested the Higher Education Press to include a picture of a laughing Buddha on the cover, but they did not do so, instead having the image of a mosque. This was curious, even though we had two imaginary Muslim students, and an imaginary Muslim visitor, in the class setting, in terms of discourse analysis, it was unexpected. Many of the imaginary students in the class actually represented students whom I had taught previously with characteristics that resembled the real students, such as True Nation, Catherine, Gloria, Forest, Lucky, and Mike. True Nation and Gloria were actually both very realistic impressions of some of my own students' nationalism; the real Forest did offer class humor about 'Forrest Gump' and took his English name after the character in the movie; Lucky was a humorous student in a sophomore class; and Mike did start the trend of some students calling me a "ChiAmerican." Jia Yuxun says in the Foreword: "I like these young people and their self-identify performance. I like the young Mike. Great! I feel young again. How good it is to be a young guy and to be an intercultural young guy like you (2014, p. xxvii).

Later, in *A Journey to the East,* there are several examples that relate back to these dialogues, for example, " Michael, are you a ChiAmerican? A Photo Essay," and questions by Li Mengyu's in her and my public conversation about statements that I have introduced in *Communicating Interculturally.* My created dialogues in the book reflect my own modeling of creative and critical thinking that is developed throughout the book. It is important to note however, that these dialogues were created by an American trying to think like a younger Chinese professor and like Chinese students. Further discourse analysis, after the book's publication, indicates that my contributions were generationally, geographically, and culturally no longer entirely accurate. When I taught intercultural communication to more than 300 students in the autumn of 2013–14 at Yangzhou University, many of the students had no connection to identified movies and television programs that had been quite familiar to students at the earlier Chinese universities where I taught. One amazing example, not identified in the dialogue illustrations above, was the tremendous earlier student enthusiasm in the television series, "Friends," which many of my students used both for the plots and as a way to learn informal and casual American English and humor, and on the other hand, virtually no connection to the series by the 2013–14 autumn semester students. Thus it is important to recognize that both discourse analysis and intercultural communication change dramatically and quickly over time, geography, and space.

Part Two
Opening Up to the Broader World

4. Eurocentrism: 1958–2006

At St. Meinrad High School, in St. Meinrad, Indiana, I was a student for the Catholic priesthood. Two of my classmates later became bishops and one became the archabbot at the Archabbey. At Ball State Teacher's College, with a major in English, and undergraduate minors in Latin and Communication and then as a Master's student in American literature, and a minor in Latin. At the University of Illinois doctoral program in speech communication emphasizing classical Greek and Roman rhetoric and English as my minor, I had a very classical European/American education. With my nine years of Latin providing me a double major, I taught, curiously, three years to 100 students each year of junior high school Latin while I was a doctoral student in communication. In high school, I took a year of Koinei Greek to study the New Testament. Over my educational period, I also had two years of French, a year of German, a semester of old English, and an undergraduate and Master's emphasis on American literature, writing my MA thesis on "Solitude in the Works of Nathaniel Hawthorne."

Later my Ph.D. dissertation was on the addresses of Ambassador Adlai Stevenson in the United Nations General Assembly (1964), using as my analytical basis classical rhetorical theory and criticism. I taught classical rhetoric at the University of Buffalo, Indiana University, and the University of Virginia. Still later, I coedited two books related to this classical background, *Readings in Classical Rhetoric* with Thomas W. Benson, for many years since a distinguished professor at Pennsylvania State University (1969) and *Readings in Medieval Rhetoric* (1973) with him and my own Ph.D. advisee, Father Joseph M. Miller (then teaching at St. Meinrad College). He and one of my former teachers there both translated medieval rhetoric treatises from Latin to English. With my nine years of Latin, it would still have been a considerable challenge for me to use these skills as a translator for these treatises.

Benson and I had planned a series of five sets of rhetorical readings: in the Renaissance, the Enlightenment, and contemporaneously for Indiana University Press, but by then we were then teaching in different universities, he at Pennsylvania State University, and I at Indiana University, and we each moved into different research areas, in his case, first in cinema criticism, and I as a founder during that period of the academic field of intercultural and international communication.

After my BA graduation from Ball State Teacher's College in 1958, I made a two month trip alone to twelve countries in Western Europe, going by a student ship from Montreal to Liverpool; attending an international youth congress, Pax Christi, in Eichstatt, Germany which was a very rich cultural experience; and flying to the US from Europe where I was immediately a candidate for the presidency of the national US Catholic student movement. None of my friends were able financially or wanted to travel with me to Europe. During my travel, after crossing the English Channel, I met many of the students from the ship, even biking with some of them through Paris. I hitchhiked from Switzerland to Florence, and stayed in many youth hostels in Europe. I had earlier requested a brief meeting with Chancellor Konrad Adenauer in Bonn, whom I admired, but it was declined. I was a part of the weekly general audience given by Pope Pius XII, the pope of my youth, at Castel Gandolfo in Italy. I had applied for a scholarship for a week-long class on ancient cultures on the Island of Parma, but I was unsuccessful. I wanted to go to Athens. However, my two month period was too limited, and instead I finally went to there in 2004 where I participated in two Fulbright conferences, as I continued to enhance my own background in classical western cultures. In 1959, after completing my MA degree, I returned to Europe for an international youth hostel festival in Munich, after which I traveled to Denmark, Sweden, Norway, and Finland. Then I spent two weeks as a member, with my wife, of twenty-four youth tour of Leningrad and Moscow. Newsweek noted that as many as 15,000 were among the early American tourists there in 1959, the largest annual number to that date.

At Oxford University, I was a delegate to a three week international ecumenical conference at Christ College, Ox representing the Catholic Diocese of Buffalo New York in 1968 with my family. I participated in the first small German-American oral communication conference in Hei1delberg the same summer. My daughter, Michelle, turned six years old at that conference and sons Leo and Louis were four and a half and two and a half. The communication conference became a biennial event, and expanded to include Austrians. For the 1976 conference celebrating the US bicentennial, we held it in Tampa, Florida. During 1977, I was in Berlin for the International Communication Association Conference as the third chair of the Intercultural and Development Division. There, I met Edward T. Hall, often called the father of the field of intercultural communication. My wife and I traveled to Hungary, Poland, Czechoslovakia, and East Germany, getting a brief first hand harassed understanding of life in Eastern Europe then under the control of the Soviet Union.

Serving as a host father of year-long international high school students during the 1980s in Charlottesville, Virginia, Bjorn-Olaf Stenmalm of Kalmar, Sweden was the first of my several such students. Sadly, in 1991 while I was in Swaziland, he and his wife were killed in an icy truck/car accident. He was followed by Jean-Louis Dislaire of Malmady, Belgium, now a grandfather; Nicolas Danigo from Lyon, France; Ze Fogaca from Porto Alegre, Brazil, for a half year; Pablo Alonso, from Salamanca, Spain; and Bernard Arthur with an Indian background from Durban, South Africa. While Bernard was with us, we also hosted Tulio, a refugee boy from El Salvador. Bernard returned to the US for an undergraduate degree and lives with his wife in Charlotte, North Carolina. Later, Paulos Dlamini and Amariah Mybusi from Swaziland lived with us in Charlottesville, Virginia. Amariah lived with us for three years, and now remains in Charlottesvile, the father of two daughters and divorced. Later, there were several adult Sudanese refugees living with us at our home in Rochester, New York, where I was also involved with "the lost boys of Sudan, and I was widely called the father of the Rochester South Sudan community. Reat Tuany, who received both his American citizenship and the first BA recipient among the South Sudanese in Rochester, has now returned to South Sudan to help establish that new country. Hosting all of these young men added significantly, earlier on a one at a time basis and later with several young refugees, to my increasing practical intercultural understanding and competence.

In January, 1983, I gave a lecture at the Royal Tropical Institute in Amsterdam, with travel to Denmark and Sweden. I was also in Rome and at San Gmiginano near Florence in 1983 for the International Society for Intercultural Education, Training, and Research Congress where

I became the vice president, and a year later its president from 1984 to 1986. I participated in the 1986 SIETAR Amsterdam congress, plus regional conferences in Sweden in 1983 and 1986. This was my last lone thirty-five day trip to Europe in 1986. In 1990, in route to Swaziland to serve as a Fulbright professor in Kwalasene, my wife and I briefly visited London, and in 1991, she and I and two young men from Swaziland, Paulos and Amariah, who were going to spend a year for high school with us in Charlottesville, Virginia, we again briefly spent time in London.

Europe: 2006

David Xu and I spent thirty-five days in ten European countries in 2006. It was David's first trip out of China. We flew on his twenty-eighth birthday from Shanghai to Beijing to Moscow to St. Petersburg for the Fourth Russian Communication Association Conference in which I provided, curiously enough, a paper about Chinese communication.

From St. Petersburg, we flew to Cologne, having our first experience with the world cup fever as Germany had beaten Ghana the evening that we were there. We took a night train to Dresden which I had earlier visited in 1977 while it was part of East Germany. About 1800 attended the International Communication Dresden conference, including many Europeans. In Berlin, with the world cup fever intensifying, we saw Ukraine beat Tunisia on a large screen at the Brandenburg Gate. We began to see extensive grafitti on walls and in the metro cars and considerable litter on the berlin streets. This continued throughout the large cites that we visited. After Berlin, we spent a rather miserable rainy day and night in Copenhagen, and then went to Kalmar, in southeast Sweden, for a very pleasant visit to the family of my first exchange son, Bjorn-Olof. He and his wife had been killed in 1991 in an icy car/truck accident three months after their marriage while I was a Fulbright professor in Swaziland. This visit to his family was very special and nostalgic for me and Bjorn-Olof's family.

We took a night train to the Hague to see the World Court. We visited my second exchange son, Jean-Louis and his two daughters in Malmedy, Belgium, a quiet interlude in our hectic schedule. In Paris, the French had beaten Germany in the world cup and we were once again caught up in the world cup fever, but in a different country. Going to

Italy, the only night train available south was to Nice along the Mediterranean Sea. In Monaco, we visited Cannes, and another night train took us to Naples where we visited Pompeii.

Ending our excursion in Rome, Italy had beaten France for the final victory in the world cup and the streets were again filled with jubilant, happy and rowdy young people. On this trip, David and I spent time in three of the world's greatest museums: the Hermitage, the Louve, and the Vatican museum. We flew overnight to Beijing, and then to Shanghai. We enjoyed many activities together and overcame some negative situations through our own cultural dialogues.

I have now traveled in Europe in 1958 (twelve countries); 1959 (seven countries including the Soviet Union); 1968 (four countries); 1977 (six countries, including East Germany, Hungary, Czechloslovakia, and Poland); 1983 (twice in six countries, attending conferences in Italy, the Netherlands, and Sweden); 1986 (four countries, including conferences in the Netherlands and Sweden); 1989 (the Soviet Union); 1990–91 a brief visit in London going and coming from Swaziland; 2004 (Greece), 2005 2006, and 2008 in Russia (and nine other countries in 2006). Each European experience increased my intercultural awareness, and traveling with David helped me to develop my Chinese awareness even more. In Rome, I froze as a car came directly at me. David reminded me to "think Chinese" as the auto there would swerve around me, as the Italian driver also did.

In June 2015, I will travel potentially with family members to Bergen, Norway to receive a life-time achievement award from the International Academy for Intercultural Research and to present a keynote address: "Social Media and Cybernetics in Asia: Implications for Regional Security," an expanded version of the keynote address which I gave at the November, 2014 Cultural Security conference at the National University of Defense Technology in Changsha, China.

The experiences in studying the past in Europe, and my travel there all enhanced my own Eurocentric life experiences, which remain a significant complement to my American life-world.

5. Russia: 1959, 1989, 2005, 2006, 2008

When I was twenty-three, traveling with the youth group to Leningrad and Moscow in 1959 as early American travelers to the Soviet Union, we were watched over carefully by our assigned guides in both cities. We were generally shocked at the poor conditions, the lack of products in the GUM showpiece store, and the small number of autos on the streets, but we were treated well, despite the near constant Russian supervision. We had several good conversations with young Russians, but when it was time to meet them to visit their family apartments, none of them appeared, perhaps under pressure from government officials or fear of their families to admit Americans into their homes. Visiting both the Russian exhibit in New York City where the theme was heavy machinery, and the American exhibit in Moscow showcasing a one floor ranch style house — whose kitchen was the site of the Khrushchev-Nixon debate, following Khrushchev's earlier 1959 three week travel to the US, it was a very exciting opportunity for us. I assumed, incorrectly that I would be back to Leningrad and Moscow in the near future.

Instead, it was thirty years later in 1989 when I returned to Moscow as an American delegate to an international conference on peace and communication in the satellite and computer age, hosted at the Russian Peace Center, but the conference, hospitality, and lodging were probably sponsored by the Soviet government. Five months after the Tiananmen Square event and three weeks before the fall of the Berlin Wall, the Russian media were filled with news in Russian about Gorbachev's calls for glastnoss and perestroika and the liberalizing incidents toward democracy and freedom in central and Eastern Europe. I visited five Russian apartments and gave a speech at Moscow State University. The GUM department store was relatively full of items to buy, unlike my previous experience, and the streets were reasonably full of cars. Stalin had been moved from his shared mausoleum with Lenin, and buried. I had a meeting at one of Russia's largest publishers about having my 1978 book *The Cultural Dialogue* translated into Russian and published by the Press. When the Soviet Union was in the near process of collapse, however, I was notified that the state subsidies for the publisher had ended, and therefore the book could not be translated nor published by the Press.

Kursk State University: 60th Anniversary School of Foreign Languages: Keynote and Lectures -May 2005

Through the kind assistance of Igor E. Klyukanov (Eastern Washington University) and Fulbright alumna Tatiana Sazogova (head, Department of English, Kursk State University, Kursk, Russia, 500 kilometers south of Moscow), I was invited to participate in the sixtieth anniversary conference of the university's foreign language school April 27–29, 2005. My keynote speech was on "global languages." During my visit, April 26-May 9, I had the opportunity to provide eleven additional power point lectures on intercultural and international communication. I also spoke informally in several classes and showed the last two videos on the end of the cold war from the CNN "cold war" series to classes which provided lively discussions. I met several hundred enthusiastic English majors at the University and enjoyed excursions to Russian orthodox churches, a former palace, and the Kursk area battlefield memorials. I had several pizzas with a number of women students, and visited a village for a weekend about 50 kilometers from Kursk. I was in Moscow May 9 for the annual national day, but I was not able to get close to Red Square where the celebration was being held by the leaders of several countries. We were able, however, to eat at the world's largest McDonald's in Moscow, an interesting experience.

Except for my keynote address, most of the conference was in Russian. English majors at Kursk State University had very good English, but outside of the English department, not so many students appeared to be speaking English fluently. Where many Chinese universities have several foreign native English teachers, Kursk State University had none. Also, in China, English seemed to be much more apparent on store fronts and road signs, but in Kursk Russian was largely dominant everywhere. As in foreign language colleges in China, most of the students in Kursk State University's foreign language school were women. Also similar to English majors in China, the English majors had to take a second foreign language, in their case, either French or German. They appeared to have a better grasp of their second foreign language than many of the English majors whom I had taught in China. The dean of the Foreign Language School spoke fluent French, but relatively little English. Many of the English majors had the opportunity in the summers to work in American camps or to have American work/travel experiences in the

US through the leadership of their director of international cooperation who had met me in Moscow before our train trip to Kursk. This was a difference between them and my Chinese students who never discussed having such opportunities. Curiously, I met two such students from Russian universities working summer jobs at upscale restaurants near the Great Smoky Mountains in 2014. Later, I attempted, unsuccessfully, to obtain a year-long assignment for my chief host in a Chinese university.

The Third Russian Communication Conference St. Petersburg: June 12–16, 2006

At the State Educational Center in St. Petersburg, the Russian Communication Association, the North American Russian Communication Association, St. Petersburg State University, Bruevich State University for Telecommunications, St. Petersburg Institute of Foreign Economic Relations, Economics and Law, and the Nevsky Institute of Language and Culture co-sponsored the Third Russian Communication Association Conference which my close Chinese young friend David Xu and I attended.

St. Petersburg was especially interesting because of its imperial past dating from the early 1700's and as I had visited there in 1959 when it was called Leningrad. We visited Peterkoff, the tsars' summer palace and the Hermitage, one of the world's greatest museums. There was naturally a large Russian delegation of about 200 at the conference, but also thirty-six Americans, and a few from other nearby countries. David and I were the only participants coming from China.

Local university leader, Olga Matyash, President of the Russian Communication Association Barbara Monfils, President of the World Communication Association (and my former Ph.D. student); and American leaders all gave welcomes to conference delegates. Perhaps there were about 200 Russians, thirty-six North Americans, and a few other international delegates from Turkey, Poland, the Netherlands, South Africa, Ukraine, Australia, and Belarus. Many Russian university students provided excellent hospitality and technical support.

The plenary session included addresses by American communication leader Steven Beebe "Communication and values: The search for unifying principles of human communication"; Dmitry Gavra (St. Petersburg State University), "Basic paradigms in defining the category 'communication'; Robert T. Craig (University of Colorado at Boulder), "Communication theory as a field"; Olga Matyash, "The challenges of developing communication education in Russia"; David Cratris Williams and Noemi Marin, "'Citizenship' in Russian presidential discourse: (Re)making publics in global times"; Alexander Yuriev (St. Petersburg State University), "Psychological characteristics of information in political communication"; Swetlana Shaihitdinova (Kazan State University), "Tolerance to 'otherness' in Russian mass-media: problems of measurement and evaluation"; and Grigory Tulchinsky (St. Petersburg University of Culture and Arts), "Social communication in business: Pr as public relations and public responsibility." My power point conference presentation was on Chinese media. It would have been a good idea for David Xu, as the only Chinese present, to give a presentation on his life as an undergraduate in China, but I did not think about suggesting it. Later, he wrote an essay for *Communicating Interculturally* (2012) on his life as an average Chinese youth. He now has an MBA from Tongji University and an executive position with a major western country in China.

There was considerable diversity of topics presented by the various delegates. specific sections included : philosophy and theory of communication; mass and media communication; modern theories of mass communication: analytical review of trends for the last twenty years; organizational, professional and business communication; from theory to practice: workshop, business communication and simulating realities in teaching business English; political communication and political rhetoric; student debates; interpersonal and small group communication; gender politics: communication problems and issues; the role of applied communication research in (re) making social worlds; communication education (1 and 2); from theory to practice workshop: computer-mediated communication and advanced information technologies; instructional practices in public speaking pedagogy (1 and 2); seminar defining the communication discipline in Russia; communication and culture; teaching business communication and virtual business, and workshop, techniques of speech communication process. My paper presentations also included mass media and the internet in China.

St. Petersburg is probably one of the most interesting and charming cities in Europe because of its imperial past dating to the early 1700s. Our Russian hosts provided outstanding hospitality and included for the international delegates attendance at "Swan Lake" ballet, and a

Russian folk show. A number of us visited Peterkoff and the Hermitage Museum. There was considerable multicultural dialogue, not only between Russians and North Americans, but also with participants from other nations. Some of the sessions were hampered because of interpretation problems from one language to another, the wide diversity of topics, and time constraints causing a number of younger Russian scholars not to be able to present their papers. There also appeared to be very different views about the nature of communication as expressed by older Soviet- period trained scholars and younger Russian scholars as well as between Russian and North American scholars which led to some confusion about our definitions, theories, and case studies. Some North American scholars failed to take into consideration adequate cultural sensitivity for the Russian hosts, leading some Russian scholars to note politely and informally that sometimes it seemed like an American conference transplanted onto Russian soil. This is a frequent problem for conferences internationally in which there is a strong American presence and leadership. A similar negative expression was made by European delegates to the SIETAR International congress in San Gimignano, Italy in 1983 and the Lima, Peru Congress of the Americas which my daughter, Michelle, and I attended in 2007. It appears to be a common problem in international conferences with a broad cross-cultural participation.

Overall, it was a well-developed international conference and we benefited not only interculturally with our Russian colleagues, but also multiculturally with those from other countries.

Russia 2008

On May 7th, Dmitry Medvedev was inaugurated as the new president of Russia, held in the grand hall of the Kremlin, only the second president to be sworn in at that hall, the first being Vladimr Putin eight years before. President Medevev pledged to preserve Russian human rights freedoms and civic freedoms for every Russian citizen. He indicated that he supported "the rule of law," promising to keep Russia stable and strong, becoming again a leader in innovations, and encouraging different religious groups and regions. In his short speech, he said: "My duty is to serve the people of Russia every day and every hour." Unfortunately, the present situation in Russia appears to moved away from his likely pivot toward Europe and the West, and under the current presidency of Vladimir Putin toward a dictatorship and a high level of corruption. He is identified as among the richest persons in the world. The average Russian annual income is about $850, lower than the annual wage in India which is about $1050 per annum.

I began reading Antony Beevor's 1998 book *Stalingrad* (now Volgograd), in order to have background about the city and region before Charles Cheng, my former MA student and I were to go there on June 8, 2008. Orlando Figes called the book, discussing the Nazi siege of Stalingrad in the autumn and winter of 1942 to February, 1943, a "tour de force." Later in Volgograd, I gave it to the university library, along with the entire set of intercultural communication books published by Shanghai Foreign Language Education Press, two books on intercultural communication, also published by the Press in Chinese, all as a gift from Steve J. Kulich, of the Shanghai International Studies University Intercultural Institute, as well as copies of my 1978 *The Cultural Dialogue*, Kulich's and my co-edited book, *Intercultural Perspectives on Chinese Communication* (2007), and my daughter Michelle Epiphany Prosser's new book, *Excuse Me, Your God Is Waiting* (2008).

After Charles and I were flying ten hours from Shanghai to Moscow, and then two and a half hours to Volgograd, Olga Leontovich, the chair of American Studies, Chinese Language and Studies, and Interpretation and Translation, met us at the Volgograd airport at about midnight. Olga had taught a year in a New Jersey university and had visited Beijing and Tiangin in 2007. We later had a tour of Mamayev Hill, with the monument "of Mother Russia," larger than the Statue of Liberty, of a Russian woman holding a giant sword to celebrate the victory in the battle of Stalingrad in 1943, and holding a dead Russian soldier. She represented all mothers in Russia who had lost fathers, husbands, sons, brothers, and sisters in WWII. Two young women with us had worked in the US during the summer of 2007 under the special work-travel program between the US and Russia. We visited the "encampment" along the Volga River, which had been the defensive line for the Russians protecting Stalingrad as the final line beyond which Josef Stalin declared no Nazis would pass.

We had a tour of Volgograd State Pedagogical University where we met a first and fifth year Chinese language class. I showed my Asian and western values power point presentation and we met the doctoral students and faculty. Professor Leontovich spoke about attending the International Communication Association conference in late May in Montreal. Charles presented his MA thesis, "On Becoming Interculturally Competent" which fascinated the postgraduate students who were not used to doing empirical research but only highly theoretical papers and theses. I talked about value studies to the faculty and doctoral students. Asked what my own hierarchy of values would be and what an anthropological hierarchy of values might be, I discussed the work of Kulich and the Israeli expert on cross-cultural values, Shalom Schwartz, noting that my own leading value was happiness. Later we were both interviewed by a local journalist and an article appeared about us in the local newspaper. Based on the more passive involvement of David Xu in our 2006 conference experience, with Leontovich's encouragement, we made more use of Charles, including his chance to talk to the Chinese majors, which the fifth year students could understand and respond to, but his Chinese was too difficult for the freshmen.

We both spoke at the Academy of Social Services to seventeen and eighteen year old students, where I showed the first half of the international media power point as I had done also for the Chinese majors. We talked to a freshman class in interpretation and translation, who had reasonably good English, as well as to the American studies majors. We had a two hour research consultation with four doctoral students and I presented a short power point on the internet.

We went to a dacha about thirty minutes from Volgograd for an afternoon with several faculty and students. One young woman played the guitar and the women sang in Russian, Charles sang in Chinese, and I sang in English, for example, "America the Beautiful." That evening we were met at the Moscow airport by eighteen year old Yarak and the driver, staying at the dormitory of the University of Cooperation, which really meant "small businesses," where the Fourth Russian Communication Conference was being held. We were the first foreigners, either American or Chinese, whom he had ever spoken to, as was true with some of the other eighteen year old students whom we met during the conference. When he received the information with my name, he later said that it had really confused him as the name didn't sound at all Chinese, despite the fact that we were coming from China to the conference. It was of course curious that at both the 2006 and 2008 conferences, my young Chinese friends were the only real representatives from China, though I was also coming from China and all of my presentations were about Chinese education or media.

The Fourth Russian Communication Conference began with the usual "high face" opening, and a keynote speech by Stephen Beebe who is now the past President of the [US] National Communication Association. He used the metaphor of a home, coming home, the crossroads of the communication discipline, and the centrality of the study of communication as a uniquely human endeavor. I gave my presentation on North American and Chinese developments in intercultural communication and a talk to Russian teachers of English on how I taught my courses in China without having any ability to speak, understand, or write in Chinese.

We toured the Monastery of St. Sergius, founded by the fourteenth century monk, Sergius, the seat of the Russian Orthodox Church and Patriarch Alexi. It was my second visit to the Monastery — either in my 1959 visit or in 1989. This time, we witnessed a procession of "black" monks who lived in monasteries and remained celibate, as well as "white monks" who worked in parishes and had families, several with three or four young children. This happened to be the graduation day for the young seminarians and thus it was a very festive occasion.

June 12 is the Russian Independence day, and our young interpreter, Yarak, asked "independence from what?" Except for our conference, the University was closed. Charles gave his presentation on his thesis to an interested audience of thirty or forty persons. We toured the Kremlin, my third time to do so. As it was a three day holiday, the area around the Kremlin was very crowded with families and tourists. Conference leaders decided to cancel the afternoon programs on this last day of the conference, meaning that several young Russian scholars were unable to present their papers, an incident which had also occurred in the 2006 conference. It appears that they were expected to do the research, and to have their names in the conference program, but not to actually present their papers. A similar situation occurred for young Chinese faculty at the National University of Defense Technology cultural security conference in 2014, when the expected two day conference suddenly became a one day event. I have also noted this situation at other Chinese conferences.

Charles and I took three eighteen year old students, Yarak, Dasha, and Stephen to the Moscow zoo. We went from the zoo to the world's largest

McDonalds, my second meal there. Coming out of McDonalds, there was a large Hare Khrisna band which we watched. Charles, Dasha, and Stephen went to the Kremlin, and Yarak and I chatted in the park across from McDonalds as he wanted to know more about China and the US. I asked him when he had first met and conversed with a foreigner, and looking at his cell phone calendar, he said it was at the airport when he met us. Yarak, Dasha, Charles and I went to the Moscow circus, my third one (1959, 1989, and 2008).

This trip to Volgograd, and then to the Fourth Russian Communication Association conference was my fifth and last trip to Russia. My Chinese friend Jacky Zhang and I had planned to go to the 2010 conference, and I was to give presentations in two Russian universities and one in Poland, but because of incorrect invitations, the Russian Consulate in Washington was unable to issue visas for us. These five experiences in Russia, 1959–2008, were all very important in my own understanding of different dimensions of intercultural and cross-cultural communication both with the Russian and other national delegates, and between Charles, a Chinese, and myself. Just as had happened in 2006 with David Xu when we were in St. Petersburg, and then nine other European countries. Charles and I had traveled to the Philippines together during the Spring Festival, providing us two very different cultural experiences. Olga Leontovich invited me to submit an essay on Chinese language, youth, and culture for her book, *Lingoculture in the Modern Global World* (2010), which introduces Part Four in this book. It was the only essay in her book not written in Russian and therefore a double honor, and curiously, an American professor discussing Chinese youth for a Russian language book. Additionally, eleven of her sophomores wrote their cultural studies, which with eleven sophomore Chinese students, are in Part Five of this book.

With agreements for lecture series from two Russian universities, one at which the 2010 Russian Communication Conference was to be held, where I was also scheduled to give a keynote address, and one Polish university, my friend Jacky Zhang and I received an invitation letter from the Russian host. Unfortunately, the invitation had several errors for both of us. When we went to the Russian Consulate in Washington, D.C. for the visas, because of the errors, we were unable to receive the visas. There was too little time to receive correct invitations and so I had no chance to take a third young Chinese friend with me to Russia.

In 2012, I was interested to travel to the Russian Communication Association conference in Siberia. I attempted to set up the missing lecture series in two Russian universities and one Polish university, but at this time their funding had become too difficult even for modest hospitality, and this experience in Russia, and potentially also in Poland, no longer materialized.

6. Latin and Central America, 1960–2011

My first substantial tourist visit to Mexico was in 1960 for a month with my wife and four others, driving from the University of Illinois together as far south as Puebla, where a civil uprising was occurring. All of us were graduate students with three from the US, including Soter Kokalis, my wife and me, plus Maarten Chrispeels from Belgium, Jaime Esaiguire from Chile, and Jose Nieto from Mexico, who was returning for his wedding with Laticia. We attended their civil wedding in Mexico City. His family was poor, but he was studying for a Ph.D. in science, while his wife's family were reasonably wealthy, sporting fur coats in the summer. Five of us later received Ph.D. degrees, four in the sciences and one in communication.

Having received a two year $58,300 grant from the United States Office of Education to internationalize our undergraduate communication program at the University of Virginia in 1973, with other colleagues from the University of Virginia and our visiting professor, John C. Merrill, famous in the field of journalism, my wife and I attended the 1974 Mexico City conference on international mass media sponsored by local universities and media there. It was my first international conference in Latin America, but I had attended international conferences previously in England, Germany, and Canada.

In 1979, I was present as a Governing Council member at the International Society for Intercultural Education, Training, and Research Congress in Mexico City, followed by another week of individual tourist travel as far south as Oaxaca near the Guatemalan border. At the Mexico City congress, I was appointed the chair of the Society's 1980 congress to be held in The Pocono Mountains, Pennsylvania, which included a dozen Latin and Central American diplomats attached to embassies and consulates in the United States. For some time, I hoped to teach for a year in a Latin American university, but then all visiting faculty members in Hispanic Latin America had to be fluent in Spanish, for which I had no background.

As a part of a two-week "Solidarity with the Poor" retreat with university students in Haiti in late 1988 and early 1989, we spent several days with the poor in the capital Port au Prince, where we visited maternity hospitals, schools, orphanages, clinics, the university, the Catholic radio station, relief agencies, the US embassy, and soup kitchens. Then the entire group stayed with the bishop in the Catholic Diocese of Hinch, the twin diocese of the Catholic Diocese of Richmond, Virginia. At St. Michel's Parish in Soltadare, the twin parish with our American university parish, near the border of the Dominican Republic, my second wife and I were hosted by a Belgian missionary who was the only one in the village who spoke English. He took us briefly to the Dominican Republic, a sobering experience, being in a fifth world setting in Haiti, and then contrasted with a short third world experience in the Dominican Republic. The Haitians were most generously hospitable although we had a lot to learn about intercultural communication competence with the poor, not as easy as with others who shared our elite professional background, and causing us to express assumptions that were unfounded in their own lives and to cause problems over our unwise use of scarce water.

Already enthusiastic about the study of liberation theology, this experience had a major effect in my later teaching, including a long segment on liberation theology in Latin America and South Africa in my communication and social change courses at the University of Virginia, Kent State University, University of Swaziland, as a visiting professor at the George Washington University, and the Rochester Institute of Technology. Sometimes, people have referred to me as a Catholic intellectual, and if it is true, this period in my life would have been my most obvious expression as a Catholic intellectual, and interpreter for my students of the role of liberation theology primarily in Latin and Central America, but also in terms of South Africa. This teaching was an important prelude to my autoethnographic experiences in Asia and China. However, I have more recently written and spoken publically about Asian religions such as Hinduism, Buddhism, and Islam, rather than about Catholic or Christian faith, partly due to my experiences in China, where writing and speaking about these religions is more acceptable than about Catholic or Christian faith.

In 1992, I attended the SIETAR International Congress in Jamaica, where I had the opportunity to meet Paulo Freire, the leading Brazilian indigenous teacher of the oppressed, a liberation theologian, and internationally known author of *Pedagogy of the Oppressed* (1970), which was one of my main text books in my communication and social change class. One of my most important secular quotes that I often cite was his statement: "The ontological role of being human is to be fully human, fully alive, fully creative and fully free" (paraphrased).

I also used as a text in the class segments on liberation theology, *The Power of the Poor in History* (1972), by the Peruvian founder of the study of liberation theology, Gustavo Gutierrez. I wanted to visit him in Peru in 2007 as an admirer of his when my daughter anere present in Lima for an international conference, The Congress of the Americas, but our time was too short and without Spanish, it was too difficult to locate him. The *Voice of the Voiceless* (1985) was another of my text books by Archbishop Oscar Romero of El Salvador, who had been assassinated while saying Mass in 1980 and is now promoted by Pope Francis for beatification and sainthood as a martyr for the faith. I have always been impressed with Romero's sermon on March 23, 1980, just before he was assassinated while saying Mass, only the second Catholic bishop killed while celebrating a religious service since the assassination of Archbishop Thomas A Becket in 1170. On March 23, Romero delivered a very significant homily at the cathedral in San Salvador: "I want to make a special appeal to soldiers, national guardsmen, and policemen: each of you is one of us. The peasants you kill are your own brothers and sisters. When you hear a man telling you to kill, remember God's words, 'Thou shalt not kill.' No soldier is obliged to obey a law contrary to the law of God. In the name of God, in the name of our tormented people, I beseech you, I implore you; in the name of God I command you to stop the repression."

Rigoberto Menchu, the 1992 Nobel Peace Prize Laureate's book: *I, Rigoberta Menchu: An Indian Woman of Guatemala* (1983) was also important in my classes on communication and social change in the 1980s and 1990s and was especially important to my women students at the University of Virginia and Rochester Institute of Technology. In fact, one year when I taught this class at the Rochester Institute of

Technology, there were twenty-one women and one man, an unusual feature for most classes there.

In my classes, a book which was also very touching for my university students was Mark Mathabane's *Kaffir Boy* (1986). At University of Virginia graduations, students often told me that this book had been one of the most important ones that they read as an undergraduate. Even some parents told me at the graduations that their sons and daughters in my class had urged them also to read the book and that reading it had brought tears to their eyes.

During the number of years that I had my university students reading and discussing these books, I made a sustained effort to increase their own understanding of social justice and the role of liberation theology in Latin and Central America and South Africa. Sometimes others have called me a Catholic intellectual. If this is reasonable, it was most appropriately identified during my years of teaching liberation theology as an important aspect of my teaching in a course entitled, Communication and Social Change. Such a course was impossible in Chinese universities.

Attending the 2000 International Communication Association conference in Acapulco, Mexico, my wife and I followed this professional conference with tourist travel in Guatemala and Honduras, and learning more about the atrocities against religious figures especially in Guatemala and El Salvador. Earlier I had been a member of a in 2011 Central American support group and I was an admirer of Chomsky's books and lectures on these subjects. Later with members of the Semester at Sea around the world study voyage, we spent time at the Honduran island of Ruritan, since the US Department of State had designated the Honduran mainland as unsafe because of extensive gangland violence there. On that voyage, we also visited Costa Rica and crossed the Panama Canal.

I had the opportunity to visit as a tourist Argentina, Uruguay, and Chile in 2009, spending time with one of our 1983–84 Charlottesville, Virginia American Field Service exchange students and his wife and four children in Santa Fe, Argentina, Magister Daniel Alonso, writer of a short essay about Latin America for *Communicating Interculturally* (2012) and now an Argentinian judge. In Santiago, Chile, I had dinner with two university students, with whom I have kept in touch, and one, Pablo, who appeared in the imaginary dialogues as a foreign student from Chile in *Communicating Interculturally*. I left Chile the day before the February 27, 2010 massive 8.8 earthquake and Tsunami that reached Japan, which temporarily closed the airport in Santiago.

7. USIA/VOA: 1977–1980

Having finished my five year term as chair of the University of Virginia Department of Speech Communication, in the autumn of 1977 I served as the professor in the tenth annual intercultural communication course sponsored by the Training and Development Division of the United States Information Agency in Washington, D.C. for the Agency's mid-level executives under the leadership of the Division Chief, L. Robert Kohls, later author of the very popular book *Survival Kit for Overseas Living* (2001). I was also the co-chair for a series of scholar-diplomat seminars at the Agency as well as the editor of *USIA Intercultural Communication Course: 1977 Proceedings* (1978). In the winter and spring quarters, I was a distinguished visiting professor at Kent State University replacing D. Ray Heisey who was completing his last year as President of Damavand College in Tehran.

The USIA course included presentations by Agency chief L. Robert Kohls and eight other Agency officials, as well as scholars: psychologist Edward C. Stewart, and his contrast American model Cajetan DiMello; anthropologist Roy Wagner; intercultural communication field founders K.S. Sitaram and Nobleza Asuncion-Lande; translator Edmond Glenn; intercultural and international communication scholar Marshall R. Singer; internationally recognized scholar, Walter J. Ong, S.J; my former Ph.D. student, William J. Starosta; Canadian sociologist Gertrude J. Robinson; international development experts, Nojoku Awa, originally from Nigeria; Daniel J. Kealey, one of my students in my 1975 summer course on intercultural communication at St. Paul University and the University of Ottawa; Robert C. Morris, leader of the Michigan State University departure seminars for official six month guests from emerging countries in the United States; and international communication scholar Hamid Mowlana. Pilot empirical studies and book reviews were provided for the book which I edited based on the course by several mid-level executives who were members of the course.

In 1979–80, I designed and served as the coordinator of twenty-four half hour interview programs on intercultural communication for presentation in English on the world-wide Voice of America radio network. I was interviewed in four of the programs. The presenters all prepared essays on their topics which were intended to be included in a book that I was editing for the Voice of America to be published in 1981. Unfortunately, with the change of the US administration from President Carter to President Reagan, this specific program was canceled shortly after Reagan's inauguration and the book was not published.

In 1980, I provided a four day training program for new officers of the USIA. Also, in 1980, under the auspices of the Agency, I gave lectures on intercultural communication and social change to several different audiences in South Korea and Singapore, which received very favorable local newspaper reports. These were my first visits to these countries and my second direct exposure to Asia.

These USIA/VOA experiences all moved me out of the traditional university classrooms for the first time to a more practical US-sponsored program understanding of the developments in the academic field of intercultural communication put into realistic practical as these diplomats had to transfer the theoretical implications into practice overseas in the diplomatic and cultural environments in which they led their professional lives.

8. The Middle East: 1980–81

In the end of 1980 and beginning of 1981, I was one of a faculty delegation on a study tour to Lebanon, Jordan, Israel and its occupied territories in the West Bank and Gaza, which included twenty-two faculty members from various universities and colleges in the US, two students, including my own University of Virginia student who was the president of the US Student Model United Nations Association, and two working journalists who planned to report on the Middle East when they returned to their media outlets in the US.

We were sponsored by the US Faculty Model United Nations Association, the Palestinian Liberation Organization in Beirut, which had a very strong influence in Lebanon, and the Jordan Council on Foreign

Relations. The PLO leader Chairman Yasser Arafat was then located in Beirut, identifying himself a "stateless" person, able to travel internationally only by a United Nations issued passport. We met him for two hours as the eighty-sixth unofficial American delegation to meet with him. We had a very vigorous dialogue between him, his officers, and us. My student asked him a rather mild question about one of his topics: "But wouldn't that betray your revolution?" Arafat was suddenly so angry that he "apparently" could no longer speak in English and he reverted to a diatribe in Arabic. He apologized with tears in his eyes to my student for suddenly becoming so upset, stating that he could not accept any allegation that his motives would be capable of betraying his revolution. Later, we learned that it was a typical theater stunt by him with almost every American delegation to stimulate sympathy for him and the Palestinian Liberation Organization cause.

Our delegation visited various groups and leaders in Beirut and other cities in Lebanon, including at refugee camps, orphanages, women's and youth groups, the leader of the Syrian military, the outgoing US ambassador, the United Nations High Command, and many other groups, and an academic group of professors at the American university in Beirut. Although the US had forbidden American officials from having direct contact with the PLO, following the election of President Reagan, President Carter's outgoing American ambassador made positive remarks that seemed to be directed toward the PLO, while there were PLO members present with us in the room. We assumed that this was an intentional indirect message to the PLO from the American government.

In the imaginary dialogue relating to the Chapter: "Cultural Patterns and Cross-cultural Value Orientation, in *Chinese Communicating Interculturally,* I made the following true statement:

I had an interesting experience in Beirut, Lebanon in 1981. While the PLO Controlled a large part of the city, there was a New Year's parade, and I saw what seemed like the same red haired boy pass by three or four times. In this case, the parade circled around several times or it would have been much smaller. But, a young soldier accidentally brushed the bayonet on his rifle again against me and pulled my shirt open. Later in the week, I foolishly went by myself to the bombed out Christian area. A uniformed soldier stopped me and spoke to me in French, so our conversation was very vague as he had very little English and I had very little French. I was a bit nervous both about the language barrier, but also because of the rifle with the bayonet that I thought he was carrying. To my surprise, I had not written about him having a rifle with a bayonet. Fortunately, I was writing a daily journal, and perhaps a year later, I was rereading my writing about the incident with the French-speaking soldier. Again, because of my earlier experience, I had had my own selective perception since the young soldier at the parade did indeed have a rifle with a bayonet, but while the soldier in the bombed out area may have had a gun, if so, it was a pistol instead of a rifle with a bayonet (Li & Prosser, 2014, p. 117).

In travel to Tyre in southern Lebanon, we were suddenly hustled into an air raid shelter as Israel was shelling the area, verified by the *International Herald Tribune* the next day, although the Israeli government was well aware that our delegation was traveling there at that time. There were also women, children, and some old men in the air raid shelter with us. We were reasonably safe in Lebanon under the protection of the PLO, but later, several Americans were taken hostage, including Terry Anderson for six years by Hezballah Shiite Muslims, and author of *Den of Lions: A Startling Memoir of Survival and Triumph (1995)*.

In Amman, we had meetings with the Jordanian Council of Foreign Relations and visited several refugee camps. Crossing into Israel from the Allenby Bridge, we spent two hours passing through customs as some of our members had carried PLO material with them from Lebanon. We spent several days particularly in the occupied territories, meeting various leaders, including representatives of the US diplomatic mission and the Palestinian mayors of Ramallah and Nabulus, both of whom had recently had their lower legs blown off when they turned their motors on. I served as the delegation spokesperson when we met the mayor of Nabulus, repeating the enduring statement by Thomas Jefferson in my opening remarks, "All the land belongs to the living."

Israeli leaders refused to meet us because they had been informed that we had met with Chairman Arafat. A few members of the delegation admitted that there were only one primary reason for joining the largely sponsored study group, being able to visit the holy places in Jerusalem, Bethlehem, and Nazareth. Some rumors circulated among the group that one Jewish couple in the delegation were actually Israeli spies, but there was no direct proof of this assumption, beyond their frequent pro-Israel and negative PLO statements throughout the trip.

When we returned to the US, I wrote a long feature essay on the visit which was published in the University of Virginia student weekly newspaper, *The Declaration* (an allusion to Thomas Jefferson's "Declaration of Independence)," but when the second essay on our experience in the occupied territories of Israel was scheduled for publication, suddenly the student editors indicated that they had decided that it should not be published, perhaps from pressure of local Jewish leaders.

Starting with this study tour, I have maintained a long term interest in the Israeli –Palestinian situation. Ray T. Donahue and I included in our coauthored book, *Diplomatic Discourse: International Conflict at the United Nations* (1997)Arafat's May 25, 1990 address to the UN Security Council, meeting in Geneva, and interpreted from Arabic, about "Black Sunday" when he claimed that a "heinous massacre was perpetrated against Palestinian workers who early that morning were in search of bread for their children....Further, the massacre is being continued by the Israeli forces in the West Bank, the Gaza Strip and Jerusalem, accompanied by an outburst of Israeli racism against the Palestinian masses in the Galilee, the Triangle, and the Negev" (p. 249). We also included a three page summary reaction by elite media (pp. 258–261) and we noted: "In the UN Security Council on May 31, 1991, the United States formally vetoed a Security Council resolution, supported by all 14 other Council members that would have dispatched an observer mission to the occupied territories" (p. 261).

Later, I was a member of the editorial board of SISU's *Journal of Middle Eastern and Islamic Studies (in Asia)* for which Journal, I reviewed its first forty-five articles published during 2007 through 2011. I also wrote several articles for the *Journal* during this period including (2008: April) "The Palestinian Issue in the Eyes of Jimmy Carter: A Book Review"; (2009: September) "Obama's Culturally Transformative Identities and Accommodations toward the Middle East and Islam"; and (2011: December) "Reflections on Readings on the Middle East for Intercultural Understanding." Zhang Shengyong and I also had an article for the *Journal:* (2011, September). "A Comparative Review: 2010: Middle East Books."

Presently, the second volume in my trilogy on social media is in progress with the following contents:

Social Media in the Middle East

Michael H. Prosser and Ehsan Shahghasemi [University of Tehran, Iran], Coeditors

Dignity Press (scheduled for publication, early 2016)
Contents:
Preface: Michael H. Prosser
Introduction: Michael H. Prosser and Ehsan Shahghasemi
Part 1: Cross-cultural Studies
Issam S. Mousa: Digitalism and Development of Arab Media in the 21st Century
Debashis (Deb) Aikat: Social Media in the Arab Spring and Its Broader Influence: The Role of Social Media in Promoting Social Change in the Middle East
Mohammed Al Emad and John L. Hocheimer: Social Media and the Arab Spring and the "Spiral of Voice": Toward a New Public Opinion Theory
Chengzhang Bao: Social Media of the Islamic State
Taher Khadiv and Ehsan Shahghasemi: Dumbing Down or Reaching Out? Facebook in Kurdistan and Nassir Rozazi
William J. Brown and Benson P. Fraser: A Cross-Cultural Study of Social Media Access and Online Communication in Egypt and the West Bank
Fatema Akbar, Ingmar Weber, and John Pavlik: Social Media and the Politicization of Migrant Communities in the Gulf Cooperation Council
Elaine Hatfield, Shari Paige, and Paul Thornton: The Business of Matchmaking in the Middle East
Part Two: Selected Individual Case Studies
John L. Couper and Mahmoud Khalili: Social Media Messages for Young Afghanis: Hopes, Uses, Impacts
Maha Bashri: Failure to Launch: Social Media and Revolution in Sudan
Amal Ibrahim: Social Media in Egypt during the 2014 Presidential Campaign
Philip J. Auter and Abdel Ei Reheem Ahmed Sulyman Darweesh: Facebook and Twitter Use among Female University Students in Egypt
Kathleen German: Social Media and Citizen Iranian 2009 Protests: The Case of Neda Agha-Soltan

Zahra Golestaneh: Facebook and Young Adults: The Issue of Online Privacy in Iran
Haneen Mohammad Shoaib and Samar M. Shoaib: Social Media in Saudia Arabia: A Dramaturgical Analysis of Identity
Hesham Mesbak and Nasser al-Myaibel: Do Independent Arab YouTube Broadcasters "Broadcast Themselves?": The Saudia Case Explored
David Delulius and Inci Ozun Sayrak: Chapulling for Freedom and Democracy in Gezi Park and Beyond: A Case for Communication Ethics, Conflict, and Social Media
Catlin Miles: Moving Beyond the Public Screen: Perspectives and Debates on Gendered Media during the Gezi Park Protests
Author biographies
Index

The third volume in the trilogy will be *Social Media in Africa*.

9. Swaziland: Black/"Bloody Wednesday:" November 14, 1990

November 14, 1990, "Bloody Wednesday" in Swaziland still lingers as one of the most important moments in my life and that of my wife. It was the only day that we thought that we surely might die. I was a Fulbright Professor initiating the communication and journalism major for fifteen juniors at the University of Swaziland that year and my wife was teaching two religion courses to seventy-five juniors and seniors. As we had returned from Kenya and Burkina Faso two days before November 12, university students began boycotting classes on November 12 in protest of a lack of faculty lecturers, poor food conditions, and the suspension of a popular young sociology lecturer for promoting democracy in the Kingdom.

    Early on November 12, many of the 1600 university students held a protest meeting and boycotted all classes, arriving at an authoritarian consensus, and led by the Student Council. At noon, they dumped their plastic wrapped lunches at the administration office door. The Swazi radio and TV stations and Swaziland's two newspapers gave extensive coverage to the dumping of the lunches. Many Swazis were subsistence farmers who often went to bed hungry; thus this student decision reflected very badly on them. All students received a university notice demanding the end of their class boycott on November 13. They decided again by authoritarian consensus to continue it. The University Council demanded their return to classes on November 14, or be considered in defiance, and thus at war, toward the twenty-three year old King Mswatti III.

Another authoritarian consensus student meeting on November 14 continued the boycott. About 500 students peacefully barricaded themselves in the two-story university library. Several hundred students left campus or stayed in their student hostel area. At about five pm, many faculty and students watched, including my wife and me, as armed Swazi (and as later confirmed drunken) soldiers entered the high fenced campus which only had two gates. A university official drove through the campus announcing on a loud speaker the immediate campus closure. Five young women rushed to my wife and me and asked for emergency protection in our home. We took them there immediately. Since we had just returned from Kenya and Burkina Faso, a neighbor discreetly brought us food to feed the five young women. When we asked Hariet what would she do if the King selected her as a bride at the annual Reed dance, where he could select a new bride, she surprised us despite the immediate threat to her life by the King's command for the soldiers to invade the campus, by commenting: "It would be God's will." A fifteen hour rain and thunderstorm had just begun and the young women were quite terrified. A Canadian couple with three children took six young men, one who had been beaten, into their home.

We did not witness as the young soldiers broke into the library and the student hostels, dragging them out, beating both men and women with their night sticks on their arms and legs, and forcing them to run a gauntlet toward the front gate while the soldiers gave them sharp blows. The uneducated soldiers taunted the students: "We'll beat the English out of you." They were especially vicious toward the women, simulating rape with their truncheons. The soldiers had been stationed that day at the high school next door to the campus and drank lots of beer before they attacked the campus, making them even more violent than otherwise so likely.

A neighbor warned us that at 10 pm, soldiers would search our houses and arrest any students found there or on campus. Two Canadian families, and my wife and I, in a caravan of three autos, took students to the front gate to take them to safety. With a gun pointed at the first Canadian driver's cheek, he got permission from the guard to leave the campus with the students. In the swirling rain, lightening, and thunder storm, and with some difficulty in the rural area near the campus, since we were unfamiliar with possible safe locations, we took the students to safe shelters. Foreign faculty members living in the nearby city, Manzini, shut off their lights when we came to their houses seeking a place for the students to stay.

When we returned to campus late in the evening, two soldiers were posted all night in the back and two more in the front of our houses. In the meantime, the Catholic bishop hid the Student Council members at the Catholic orphanage for several days. It was reported that at least two or three bodies were delivered to the national morgue. The next morning, with some students, we drove to the nearby hospital where more than 120 students had received emergency treatment, many not giving their correct names. Small clinics within the general range of the university also received injured students. We visited more than a dozen badly injured students and learned that soldiers possibly had injured as many as 300–400 of the 1600 students.

The two national newspapers, read only by elite members of the society, did give the event considerable coverage over several weeks, decrying the incident and calling for a national judicial enquiry. The radio and tv announcers gave no more information after reporting on the dumping of the lunches. Full statements by the Vice Chancellor and Assistant Vice-Chancellor of the University (the king was the Chancellor) were published in the newspapers as well as lengthy statements by members of the Student Council. Some of my own communication majors, wrote imaginary tongue-in-cheek positive letters to the newspaper editors, to counter the many negative letters. Reuters News Agency and the South African press gave it some coverage.

The university remained closed for two months, reopening on January 14. A national judicial enquiry, more heavily critical of the student boycott than the hostile military response, began on March 14, 1991, treating the students appearing before it very harshly and ended on May 14. The enquiry panel never released any details to the public.

Many students returned privately to the campus while it was closed and told us stories of their beatings and humiliation by the soldiers and then by the National Enquiry.

The print media called the incident "Black Wednesday" (Prosser, 1999) but my students and I attempted to have the newspapers rename it "Bloody Wednesday" since so much innocent student blood had been shed and all the students at the University were black. My wife and I always recalled that day as our worst and best day in Swaziland when much evil occurred but many good Africans, Canadians, and European faculty and staff risked imminent danger by helping the students. At the campus, the hospital, and nearby clinics, many Swazis generously helped the students. The only other American faculty member shut her drapes and refused to open her door, later becoming dean of the business school; a Canadian staff member in charge of building infrastructure for the University pointed a gun at students coming for refuge at his campus house. Some faculty members living in the nearby industrial city, Manzini, refused to answer our knocking to seek shelter for the students and turned off their lights. The two Canadian families with whom we cooperated in getting the eleven students to safety out of campus were in the first year of a two year contract and returned to teach in the 1991–92 academic year. Earlier my wife and I had been invited to return to teach for a second Fulbright year, but after the University reopened, the situation was made so ambiguous by the administration that we could not return.

We drove to Johannesburg, where we learned from the American cultural director in Swaziland that it might be dangerous for us to return as some administrators had claimed that we had driven two individuals, Ray Russon and Sabelo Dlamini, in the trunk of our car to the American embassy who were being sought by the police on charges of treason. In Johannesburg, my wife had a serious case of the nerves, and when we met a doctor, we provided him with a written report of what we had witnessed. He said that he would provide our hand-written report to South African newsletters. When we did return to Kwalaseni, we drove to a different border crossing, very nervous that we might be arrested or more likely refused reentry when we sought to enter the country. Our Canadian friends alerted us to the highly unlikely arrest of foreign families, since there were faculty members from Canada, the UK, and us because all three countries were investing heavily in Swaziland and the University, while Swazi students were very vulnerable in such a situation.

Amnesty International cited the military and police violence against the students in their 1991 annual review (1991):

Amnesty International

Document — Further information on UA 468/90 — (AFR 55/05/90, 16 November)
Swaziland: Legal Concern: Sabelo Dlamini, Boy Magagulu, Dominic Mngomezulu, Ray Russon, Mphandlane Shong Document — Further information on UA 468/90 — (AFR 55/05/90, 16 November) — Swaziland: Legal Concern: Sabelo Dlamini, Boy Magagulu, Dominic Mngomezulu, Ray Russon, Mphandlane Shongwe
EXTERNAL (for general distribution) AI Index: AFR 55/06/90
Distr: UA/SC
23 November 1990
PLEASE BRING THIS ACTION TO THE ATTENTION OF THE SECTION REFUGEE COORDINATOR
Further information on UA 468/90 (AFR 55/05/90, 16 November) — Legal concern
SWAZILAND Sabelo DLAMINI Dominic MNGOMEZULU
Boy MAGAGULU Ray RUSSON Mphandlane SHONGWE
Ray Russon and Sabelo Dlamini, who on 14 November had sought refuge in the embassy of the United States of America in Swaziland, are in the custody of the Swaziland police. At 5.45 am on 17 November 1990 the two men are reported to have been escorted out of the embassy. They had been placed under pressure to leave the embassy despite the fact that, by the time they left, the Prime Minister had confirmed publicly that he had authorized Ray Russon and Sabelo Dlamini to be arrested under 60-day detention orders. After leaving the embassy they went into hiding and apparently fled the country to neighbouring South Africa.

At 5.05 pm on 22 November 1990, armed officials of the South African Police at Oshoek border post between South Africa and Swaziland handed the two men over to four members of the Swaziland police, at least one of whom was armed, who were waiting on the other side of the border. They were put into a police van and driven off to Mbabane, and are reported to be in detention.

Amnesty International believes that, like Dominic Mngomezulu, Boy Magagulu and Mphandlane Shongwe (the three detained on 14 or 15 November 1990), Ray Russon and Sabelo Dlamini are now being held under 60-day administrative detention orders issued under the terms of the King's Decree No. 1 (1978). These detention orders enable the police to hold a person incommunicado, and the period of detention can be renewed indefinitely at the Prime Minister's discretion. Amnesty International believes that all five are prisoners of conscience and is calling for them to be released immediately and unconditionally. In addition, Amnesty International is particularly concerned that Sabelo Dlamini, who was assaulted by police on the university campus on 14 November before he fled to the United States embassy, may be at risk of further assaults or torture. One of the other defendants in the recent Swaziland treason trial was reportedly assaulted at the time of his arrest and for some time afterwards the police refused to allow him medical treatment. This serves to increase concern that all five now detained are at risk of ill-treatment or torture.

Background Information

Amnesty International has received eye-witness accounts of the police raid on the campus of the University of Swaziland on 14 November 1990, following student protests over the expulsion of Sabelo Dlamini from the University for his involvement in the treason trial. The accounts indicate that the police deliberately used excessive force against unarmed students and that at least 87 students were subsequently admitted to hospital for treatment of injuries inflicted by the police with clubs, sjamboks (whips), sticks, and branches torn from trees on the university campus.
FURTHER RECOMMENDED ACTION: Telegrams/telexes/faxes/express and airmail letters:
TO THE SWAZILAND AUTHORITIES:
- expressing concern at reports that Ray Russon and Sabelo Dlamini, as well as Dominic Mngomezulu, Boy Magagulu and Mphandlane Shongwe, are now detained incommunicado under renewable 60-day administrative detention orders;

- seeking assurances that they are not being subjected to torture, ill-treatment or other forms of duress;
- urging that they be granted immediate access to their lawyers, relatives, and independent medical advice;
- expressing concern that they are prisoners of conscience, imprisoned on account of their non-violent political activities and calling for their immediate and unconditional release.
TO THE SOUTH AFRICAN AUTHORITIES:
- expressing concern at reports that on 22 November 1990 Ray Russon and Sabelo Dlamini were forcibly returned from South Africa to Swaziland in spite of the fact that administrative detention orders permitting their indefinite incommunicado detention had been issued by the Swaziland authorities;
- urging the South African authorities to respect international standards relating to people who seek protection from human rights violations, most essentially the principle of non-refoulement which, as set out in Article 33 of the 1951 Convention relating to the Status of Refugees, states:

> "No contracting State shall expel or return ("refouler") a refugee in any manner whatsoever to the frontiers of territories where his life or freedom would be threatened on account of his race, religion, nationality, membership of a particular social group or political opinion".

This principle is recognized by the international community as a norm of general international law binding on all states, irrespective of whether they are party to the 1951 Convention itself.
- requesting assurances that in future no one in need of such protection will be expelled to any country where he or she risks being imprisoned as a prisoner of conscience, or being tortured or executed;
- urging that all who seek protection in South Africa be given a full opportunity to present their request for protection and have it examined by the appropriate authorities. Document — Further information on UA 468/90 — (AFR 55/05/90, 16 November) — Swaziland: Legal Concern: Sabelo Dlamini, Boy Magagulu, Dominic Mngomezulu, Ray Russon, Mphandlane Shongwe
EXTERNAL (for general distribution) AI Index: AFR 55/06/90

As an evaluation of the events, I wrote an essay: "Media Reactions to 'Bloody Wednesday' in Swaziland" which was published in my and K.S. Sitaram's coedited volume: *Civic Discourse; Intercultural, International, and Global Media* (1999: pp. 241–254).

During the year, we became close friends with our two day a week Swaziland housekeeper, Mrs. Masinni, her four children: Godfrey, Sweetness, Deborah, and Well Done, plus three high school students and weekend garden boys, Amariah Mybuisa, Paulos Dlamini, and Muzi Manango. We assisted Sweetness and Muzi to get hearing aids; we took the mother to the hospital once for dental work, and a second time when a sixteen year old boy raped her. On that occasion, she and her four children stayed with us for a week until she could find a cousin whose family allowed her to stay with them as she did not want to return to her home. Since she had been raped, her Christian minister husband divorced her. We were able to assist modestly the education of her four children for ten years after first meeting the family, as well as Muzi and some other poor young Swazis whom we supported in two year technical programs.

We brought Amariah and Paulos to the US for an extra year of high school education. Paulos graduated from the Charlottesville, Virginia High School and returned to Swaziland, where he became a computer science major at the University. Amariah also completed high school, attended a year of community college, and married a fellow student there. Now divorced, he is the father of two daughters, both in their twenties. From 1995 to 2001, three adult Sudanese refugees lived with me and my wife in Rochester, New York. One who graduated from college and became an American citizen, Reat Tuany, has now returned to South Sudan to assist its development as a new nation. He has two daughters in the US and two sons in Africa.

While living in Swaziland, my wife and I visited Botswana, Zimbabwe, South Africa, Kenya (where we met leaders of the United Nations), and Burkina Faso, where we attended the African communication conference. Still with an ongoing interest in Africa, I was glad to visit Morocco, Ghana, and Mauritius, and a revisit to South Africa during the 2011 University of Virginia/Institute for Shipboard Education Semester at Sea. I had a great desire to return to Swaziland during this voyage, but it was not possible. I wrote to my former Swazi students each year on November 14 for several years, but I gradually lost contact with them.

One died in an auto accident. The hospital's two most frequent admissions related to rape and auto accidents, many of which occurred on Saturday evenings because of drunk driving.

Do these former Swazi and other African students caught up in this Black/Bloody trauma, now in their mid-forties, still remember that terrible day of November 14, 1990? I assume so. I certainly always remember it as an anticultural event against our students. It was the most dramatic practical day of both very bad and very good communication in my wife's and my lives. It left a profound impression on me as a major phase of my Afrocentric era. More student boycotts have occurred often over the years at the University of Swaziland, but to the best of my knowledge King Mswati III has not sent any more soldiers to attack the students.

Forty-five year old King Mswati III of Swaziland chose his fifteenth wife in 2014: an eighteen-year-old beauty pageant contestant named Sindiswa Dlamini. Mswati III has thirteen lavish palaces and an estimated net worth of $200 million, but 69 percent of the nation, 1.2 million people, live below the poverty line, according to Forbes. Additionally, Swaziland has the highest national rate of HIV in the world, with 26.1 percent of adults between 15 and 49 diagnosed with the disease (Newsmax).

Part Three
My Journey to the East and West: Asia in Focus

10. Globalization, Asian/Chinese Modernity, and Values

We are well aware through the concept of globalism and the actual process of globalization that a new world order has begun to emerge in the recent past several decades, much different than international relations experts might have predicted even in the mid-1980s. The *Encarta World English Dictionary* (1999) defines globalism as "the belief that political policies should take world-wide issues into account before focusing on national or state concerns, or the advocacy of this concept," and globalization as "the process by which social institutions become adopted on a global scale" or "the process by which a business or company becomes international or starts operating at the international level."

From this merger, we have the concept of glocalization and the mantra: "Think globally; act locally." Evelin G. Lindner proposes: "A global culture and global institutions of social and societal cooperation can create meaningful life on planet earth....We need to seek optimization of balance within each individual's life, as one integrated life, embedded in one united global community.... Today, it takes a decent global society to give humankind a future" (2010: p. 141). As an optimist for a positively connected and interdependent global society, Lindner argues: "Global brotherhood and sisterhood, global connectedness, cohesion, mutuality, solidarity, and loving care for our human family and its habitat are desperately needed. In Europe, the term 'social cohesion' is preferred, while in Asia, the phrase 'the harmonious society' is more commonly used. Whatever the phrasing, the meaning behind the words is solidarity among all of humankind for the common good" (xvii). For her forthcoming book, *Humiliation and Terrorism,* Lindner is spending one month in Rwanda in 2015 interviewing leaders and survivors of the genocidal massacre there of 500,000–1,000,000 Rwandans.

William R. Slomanson, an international relations expert, says that none of the experts might have imagined in the mid1980s that by the end of the decade the Soviet Union would begin to collapse, the wall separating east and west Germany would fall, the two Germanys would reunite, apartheid would begin to end in South Africa, or that China would become a more and more important world power (2000). Samuel P. Huntington in his 1996 book, *The Clash of Civilizations: and the Remaking of World Order,* asks whether the Judao/Christian west and the Muslim middle east and North African nations and cultures and the Asian Confucian/ Buddhist/ Hindu cultures are fundamentally different and at odds with each other.

Can we engage in a "dialogue of civilizations" as suggested by Zhu Weilie instead (2007: September)? If China is a civilization state more than a nation state, as Martin Jacques postulates, it is an important intercultural/multicultural issue for Asia and China and for other states to pursue, as well as for individuals interacting with Asian and Chinese citizens and the reverse. Jacques proposes, "It is this civilizational dimension which gives China its special and unique character" (2009: 374). He argues that "previously, the US was regarded as the overwhelming agent and beneficiary of globalization. Now the main beneficiary is perceived to be East Asia and especially China" (352). We can also note the increasing international significance of India and Indonesia (See Cui and Prosser, 2014).

In this case, we may have to consider globalization, not as moving Asians towards westernization, but increasingly as the west moving more toward East Asia and China. Globalization always includes the geographical movement across cultures of goods, currency, people, and ideas. Migration is one the most important aspects of globalization from one country to another or in China's internal circular migration with more than 100 million migrating from the rural areas to and from the urban areas or more than 40% of the population. A significant problem for many of these migrant Chinese workers, besides a low economic and educational level, is the Houkou system which restricts such internal migration in terms of social welfare, education of their children in the cities and legal status, but some provinces and cities are starting to ease these restrictions on their permanent or semi-permanent residency situation, which affects not only the workers, but also their children's quality of education, and thus as future contributing citizens in a Chinese civil society. In 2013, China indicated that a couple with one member as a single child can now have a second child. However, in the expectation that one million couples would seek permission to have a second child, in the first year, only 700,000 couples made this request.

Does globalization bring us closer together as a "global village" as Marshall McLuhan, Canadian guru of communication, asked in the 1960s and early 1970s (1964 & 1970), or does it move us ever farther apart, as the Australian newspaper and magazine entrepreneur Rupert Murdoch envisions with a "global city?" A village brings people together where all of the villagers know each other, often very well, and may collectively be opposed to cultural change, but it is often intrusive on one's privacy. A city allows for greater anonymity, where people do not know each other, but where cultural change is constant, often non harmonious and unstable. In China, there are many streets that act as a type of close knit village, but when residents leave it to enter the city, their lives are constantly organized in the larger and broader society. Men and women wearing pajamas on the "village within the city" streets, as happens also in Japan and South Korea, must give way to regular street clothing when they go even blocks away in the city, blocks away. I saw this phenomenon on a daily basis when I lived for four years in China's largest city, Shanghai.

There are 336 cities in the world now with more than one million residents. More than 150 of these cities are in Asia. More broadly, the World Gazzetter claims that Asia's twenty largest cities are as follows: Tokyo, Jakarta, Seoul, Shanghai, Delhi, Mumbai, Manila, Beijing, Osaka, Kolkuta, Karachi, Guangzhou, Shenzhen, Bangladore, Hong Kong, Tehran, Bangkok, Chennai, and Nagoya. The China International Urbanization Development Strategy Research Committee selected the following Chinese cities as China's top developing cities for 2009: Shanghai, Beijing, Tianjin, Guangzhou, Hangzhou, Chengdu, Nangjing, Fuzhou, Changsha,and Ji'nan, all which have more than six million inhabitants except Fuzhou (*Globaltimes*, 2009:November 30). In contrast, the US with its 366 million population has only four cities with more than 2 million residents: New York City, Los Angeles, Chicago, and Houston (US Census Bureau, 2000). Which society is more likely to fit the pattern of global cities, Asia in general, and specifically China, or the United States?

The post WWII anthropologist George Murdoch stressed that certain cultural traits are common to all societies, such as the cycle of life: birth, adolescence, youth, courtship, mating, maturity, old age, and death as cultural universals. He and other similarly oriented anthropologists also noted other universals, such as bodily care, bodily ornaments (especially for women), male and female bodily differences, cleanliness, hygiene, modesty, sexual customs and restrictions, relations with others in the community, including local governance, kinship, cooperative labor, community organization, education, law, status differentiation, and customs relating to a belief in the supernatural or a higher power and religious power (Murdoch, 1945: pp. 123–145).

The theory of cultural universals offers important intercultural and cross-cultural communication insights. However, Clifford Geertz warns that having identified such concepts as cultural universals, we must test the most significant ones which are thoroughly grounded in particular biological, sociological, or psychological processes, empirically across cultures and cross-culturally. He believes that saying that all people have a religious impulse [and we are aware that while Asia basically does have such a religious background, most Chinese do not recognize such an impulse], or have reasonably similar views on mating or marriage, or the concept that all people have a common interest in private property, for example, then "the question still remains whether such universals should be taken as the central elements in the definition of man [and woman], whether a lowest common denominator of humanity is what we want anyway?.... in short, we need to look for systematic relationships among diverse phenomena, not for substantive identities among similar ones" (Geertz, 1973: pp. 39–44).

Without briefly considering the basis of Eastern and Western values broadly in their ancient and contemporary context, it is difficult to understand the pull between tradition and modernity in Confucian societies such as China, Japan, Korea, and Southeast Asia and western Graeco/Roman, Judao/Christian societies. Robert T. Oliver, in his book: *Communication and Culture in Ancient India and China* (1971), argues: "For centuries, the 'Confucian industry' of China has matched the 'Shakespearean industry" of Anglo-American scholarship in its production of books, lectures, and educational programs. Nowhere has any political apparatus been more influential than the dominance in Chinese life and politics by the prescription of Confucianism. No other culture has been so strongly marked by the characteristics of so unsystematic a philosophical system…. Confucius resolutely kept his attention devoted to the practical problems of the world as he observed it." Far from being modernist, yet, Oliver says: "The goal he [Confucius] deliberately set for himself was to change the nature of Chinese civilization with a bloodless revolution.... It is part of the quality of his genius that its influence extended backward in time as well as forward....He was the quintessence of a revolutionist....What Confucius sought above all was a society in which harmony would prevail, because propriety and loyalty would be practiced by the rulers and the people....this philosophy was cogent, clear, consistent, and practical" (1971, pp. 123–144). Oliver concluded his thoughts about Confucius on harmony and justice: "The focus of his inquiry was upon effective means of adjusting people to ideas, ideas to people, and people to people. This was the humanist way, as he conceived it" (p. 144). Are harmony and justice prevalent today in most Asian societies and particularly in China?

Basically, Confucius was concerned about the social order, based on love for one's kind and family, authority, social stability and harmony: "goodness: in private life, courteous; in public life, diligence; in relationships, loyal." *The Analects* are well known as the core of contemporary Chinese culture even today, with the brief exception of the anti-Confucian campaign initiated by Madame Mao and the rest of the Gang of Four during the latter period of the Great Proletarian Cultural Revolution, apparently a veiled attack against Deng Xiaoping.

Among the Greek philosophers, Socrates, Plato and Aristotle, there was an ongoing debate about the ultimate values as truth, wisdom, goodness, and justice, leading toward the good life from the perspective of Plato, or from the point of view of Aristotle, his student, whether these values must be complemented by happiness, then leading to the good life. Socrates, the main protagonist in Plato's dialogues, always modestly, but firmly, identified with the idea of what a philosopher should be, an individual with wisdom, truth, and a sense of justice. He argued that dialectical reasoning and logic were far superior to the monological persuasion of an individual speaker. In a more practical way, Aristotle called for the speaker to have qualities of ethos (credibility, knowledge, and good will for the audience), logos (reasoned logic) and pathos (appropriate emotional appeals for the audience).

Where Plato compared argument with dialectic having the favored place over rhetoric, Aristotle identified dialectic as the counterpoint of politics — thus promoting happiness and movement for the community toward the good life. the philosopher Greek teachers of rhetoric saw themselves as guiding young Greek male citizens to become active members of the civic society and able to argue directly, forcefully, and persuasively their well-considered points of view, in contrast to the Confucian hierarchical five levels, authoritarian based reasoning — modeling justice and goodness by the leaders, and thereby naturally but implicitly encouraging the populace to follow. While the Confucian "golden mean" was negative ("Do not do unto others what you would not have them do unto you,"), the western Greek and Christian prescription was positive ("Do unto others what you would have them do unto you." Later, in Jesus Christ's "Sermon on the mount," he offered both a set of positives, "blessed are the..." and a set of negatives, "woe unto them that...." Perhaps we can argue that the positives are values and the negatives are drives, noting that the renowned chronicler of cross-cultural values, would place both positive and negative attributes as values.

In terms of the comparison of eastern and western values, K.S. Sitaram (1995) identifies two primary values and value orientations: *Eastern responsibility vs. Western individuality.* He regards many easterners seeing themselves collectively, with modest respect for responsibility, authority, benevolence, and propriety for their groups and others as well as loving care for family members, while westerners see themselves first as individuals which leads to the importance of values such as competitiveness, aggressiveness, challenges to authority, public opinion polls, political differences, court-protected individual rights, success, high personal earnings, private property, personal identity, self-centeredness, and ethnocentrism. I would challenge that those which are negative aspects should not be called values; instead I call them drives (Prosser, 1978).

To be more specific, Sitaram lists the following contrasting values and goals in Asian and western cultures. In Asian culture, he believes that the key values are authoritarianism [authoritarian consensus], brotherhood, collective responsibilities, education, gratefulness, loyalty, respect for elders, and hospitality. While in western culture, the primary values are human dignity, individuality, firstness, frankness, directness, punctuality as well as respect for youth. According to his illustration, the following are key values stressed in the eastern cultures. Naturally, culture is not static, and so some of these characteristics also change as the cultures evolve. What Sitaram saw as clear when he was writing *Communication and Culture: A World View* in 1995 may already have changed currently. Certainly, it appears to me that in the 2000's China has fully adopted the concept of "firstness:" the world's largest political party, the largest Olympics, the largest world expo, the largest national museum, the largest new architecture, and the most students being educated at all levels.

According to Sitaram, Asia has the following dominant values [or drives]:

> *authoritarianism* [authoritarian consensus]: a primary value in Asian, African, and Middle Eastern cultures. Eastern societies in their respect for authority have established a set of hierarchical systems. For instance, birth may predict status in the Hindu caste system; and Confucianism underscores hierarchical order as well.
>
> *brotherhood:* a value cherished by Confucianism as well as Islam. Chinese culture speaks highly of brotherhood with many young Chinese calling their cousins brothers and sisters, and it is the same case in Islam. According to the Qu'ran in Islam, all Muslims are brothers but this often does not extend to outgroups or non-Muslims.
>
> *collective responsibility:* it is the Hindus' and Buddhists' highest value, which is also cherished broadly in Chinese culture.
>
> *cooperation:* Qu'ran-value of brotherhood results in cooperation (and sometimes Jihad) among all Muslims. It is also a primary value in Chinese culture, though this may be changing as the Chinese become more individualistic and competitive.
>
> *education:* Eastern cultures place high priority on education and show great respect for teachers. According to the Sanskrit saying: "The teacher is god." Chinese, Korean, and Japanese culture values education as well. Para-

mount Leader Deng Xiaoping re-established "teachers' day" annually on September 10, as during the Cultural Revolution, young Red Guards had the authority to denounce their teachers, make them wear dunce hats, and treat them harshly, or even kill them.

gratefulness and loyalty: it is an eastern and long-lasting value. Loyalty is especially expected for members of one's family or in-group.

hospitality: to some extent, the guest is god in Eastern sacred books. for instance, in Hindu, Buddhist, and modern Han weddings, the hosts serve the best food to guests.

respect for elders: both African and Asian cultures hold the values of ancestor worship; showing respect and caring for the elderly. In Korea and Japan, the eldest son has the responsibility to honor the ancestors. In China, "tomb sweeping day" has been made an annual holiday period to honor the ancestors.

sacredness of the land: in the Hindus' eyes, "the sacred cow is like the mother who nurses her children." Taoists [Daoists] also hold the view of earth as mother.

Sitaram contrasts the key values underscored in the western culture as human dignity, individuality, firstness, directness and respect for youth.

human dignity: a basic concept in the UN Charter, and equality among persons is highly valued in Western culture. Team-building now starts among kindergarten children and develops throughout their entire education.

individuality: a clear western value which stresses achievement, success, winning, and competition. Robert

D Putnam's book, *Bowling Alone: The Collapse and Revival of American Community* (2000) stresses this sometimes unhealthy sense of individuality and personal superiority.

"*firstness:*" westerners generally want to be first. For instance, the Soviet sputnik was a great shock to the US in 1957. (the US: first to land on the moon, to make an auto, to fly a plane.) (*Guinness Book of World Records*.) We can note, however, that in contemporary China, there is more and more emphasis on "firstness" as I noted above.

frankness and directness: most Western people prefer the direct way of speech. Particularly, Americans like frank and direct expressions instead of vagueness or ambiguity in communication. Many western leaders announce: "I mean what I say, and I say what I mean." When Americans become more Easternized, this trait diminishes.

respect for youth: Western cultures are youth-oriented. The value of youth is highly appreciated. In the Asian societies, classrooms are teacher-oriented, whereas in the American classrooms, they are much more likely to be student-oriented.

Tom Bruneau, speaking at the 2007 CAFIC conference in Harbin, reasoned that "Throughout the world in traditional societies, there is a yearning for a paradise, a place of peace, of rest, place where there is no conflict, only joy, bliss, and stillness without tension, a great harmony at last.... All religions harbor images of harmony, constructed in 'sacred places' as a characteristic of mind, or a transcendental consciousness"(2007). However, China is also well known for its four ancient, but even then modernizing, technological inventions: the compass, gunpowder, papermaking, and clay printing techniques. All of them, plus mechanics, hydraulics, and applied mathematics had a major impact on early Chinese traditional culture.

The traditional society, nonetheless, remains static in time and tends to most often culturally accept submission to authority, filial piety, conservatism, fatalism, pessimism, and a patriarchal society, with authoritarian consensus, or a potentially multicultural and harmonious integration, such as Asian societies like Singapore and Malaysia, while the still modernizing society moves, often only gradually, toward egalitarianism and open mindedness, gender equality, social isolation, individualism, self-reliance, optimism and new assertiveness.

Asia's future may include an integration of an individualistic and collectivistic society, with an increasingly modern scientific education which leads to western cognitive intelligence and rationality, identity as global citizens and international stakeholders, and more hybrid identities. The new cross-cultural prism may be Asians in Western dress and customs, and Westerners in traditional Asian dress and customs (Jacques, 2009).

What is the role of technology in shaping, changing, or modernizing our cultures? Is the technological global society helpful to the continuation of the best human cultural values, or a detriment? Will new technologies come out of East Asia or China? How will China's rapid modernization complement or conflict with its traditional values? Will it lead to cooperation or competition and conflict with the already technological societies in the west?

Jules Henry, in his *Culture against Man* (1963), Jacques Ellul in *The Technological Society* (1964), and B. F. Skinner, in *Beyond Freedom and Dignity* (1971) were all "cultural determinists." Even in the period of the American, Chinese and European 1960s and 1970s cultural revolutions; in every cultural generation and time, the irreversibility of technical progress and its geometric cultural diffusion and expansion across space, according to Henry, Ellul, and Skinner, offer the conclusion that technology in modern life is so pervasive that it has produced a global society in which human culture has become the subject rather than the master over technology. Henry argued that in contemporary society, the technological society is a driven one, seeking to become expansive, competitive, individualistic, consuming and achievement-oriented, all cultural factors that are usually subscribed to Westernization and even global Americanization (1963: pp. 23–25). Although some value theorists such as Shalom Schwartz include such drives among universal values, it would seem that they are the antithesis of universal values such as those espoused by the ancient Greeks of truth, wisdom, happiness and the good life or by Confucius of benevolence, ritual, right thinking, and harmony.

Hinduism and later Buddhism accepted the concept of a divine supernatural being, just as the Jews, Christians, and Muslims did, but added other divinities as also the Greeks and Romans accepted. The Hindus, without a definite founder or time for its initiation, accepted as universal principles four broad categories based on moksha — the search for liberation from unhappiness and a past chain of lives, and *samsura* — one's involvement in the universe. These four broad categories included *kharma* — the central role in life of having a sense of doing right, but which had both positive and negative aspects, *artha* — the pursuit of material wellbeing, kama — the pleasure of the senses, and dharma — leading a right and virtuous life. These combinations are accepted at least as near universals,

All have the power in Hinduism and Buddhism, to lead one ultimately to happiness or linkage with Brahman or unity with the divine spirit. Buddhism, coming first from India and traveling east to China, Japan, and Korea, enriched first by Sidhartha, and later living Buddhas, articulates for "all humans" "four noble truths:" life is suffering; all suffering is caused by ignorance of the nature of reality and craving for material well-being and attachment; suffering can be overcome by overcoming ignorance and attachment (which Schwartz might call hedonism). Buddhism adopted the Hindu notion of life as cyclical. The "four noble truths" can lead to the "eightfold way:" which consists of right views, right intention, right speech, right action, right livelihood, right effort, right-mindedness, and right contemplation. These eight are usually divided into three categories that form the cornerstone of Buddhist faith: morality, wisdom, and *samadhi,* or concentration. We can see certain parallels to Wu's novel, *Journey to the West.*

Confucianism, based in the *Analects,* provides a hierarchical system of five universal values: and proposes such concepts as *ren* — benevolence, kindness, filial piety, love of kind (a particularistic value), respect for authority and elders, social stability and harmony, goodness in life, courteousness in public life, diligence in relationships, and loyalty to family or superiors; jen or humaneness, *li* — moral propriety through established rituals which include several of the characteristics of *ren;* *di* — moral righteousness or moral power; *lian* — one's internalized dimension including face practices; and *mianzi* — one's externalized images, including also face practices, or more broadly harmony or creating a harmonious society (a major goal of the Chinese leadership of President Hu Jintao, for example). While we do not necessarily see happiness as a central factor such as Hinduism, Buddhism, and the Greeks provide in their belief systems, it certainly must be a result in Confucianism in the process of being benevolent or kind, in having moral righteousness or power, and in both the internalized and externalized images which the Confucian life-world illustrates. Despite setbacks, the Confucian world view remains a dominant philosophy in societies such as China, Japan, Korea, and others. Justice (and social justice) is certainly a major value in Hinduism, Buddhism, Confucianism, Christianity, and Islam and may indeed be a universal value.

The Chinese "four modernizations" were articulated first by Zhou Enlai in 1974 (Gao, 2007) and promoted by Deng Xiaoping in 1978 with a dedicated 36% of China's GDP (agriculture, industry, technology, and defense), "seeking truth from facts" and socialism "with Chinese characteristics." It is a key element in all current Chinese education. In 2002, President Jiang Zemin promoted his version of "the three represents" which was promulgated in the Chinese Communist Party Constitution at the March 2002 Sixteenth Party Congress: advanced social productive forces (representing economic production); advanced culture (representing cultural and scientific development); and interests of the overwhelming majority of the people (representing political consensus, and inviting intellectuals, business persons, and entrepreneurs into the CPC which now has eighty-eight million members).

President Hu Jintao called for a stable, harmonious, and an increasingly "all round moderately prosperous society" by the year 2020. Each year, 450,000 engineers in China graduate from university engineering programs, 50,000 with master's degrees, and 8,000 Ph.D. degrees. Most of the recent leaders of China have engineering degrees, including Jiang Zemin (electrical engineering, Shanghai Jiao Tong University), Zhu Rongji (electrical engineering, Tsinghua university), Hu Jintao (hyraulic engineering, Tsinghua university), Wen Jibao (geological structures, Beijing Institute of Technology), Xi Jinping (chemical engineering, Tsinghua University), and Li Xeqiang (law, LLB, and Ph.D. in economics, Peking

University) became very important Chinese leaders in 2013. In contrast, most political leaders in the United States have law degrees, promoting often divisive legislation rather than bold new or renewed architecture and infrastructure.

Here, we note that as recent current leaders in China typically have had engineering degrees, they have led massive engineering feats in China in the last two decades, including the creation of a multitude of express roads, fast bullet trains traveling 300 kilometers an hour, exceptional rail infrastructure, the Three Gorges project (the world's largest hydraulic project), as well as the extraordinarily bold architecture in the last twenty years in Pudong, Shanghai, along the Wampu River and other metropolitan cities, many of which are entirely new mega cities. The 2010 World Expo was a part of Shanghai's redevelopment from its "tired old lady" image in the early 1990s, as was also Beijing's 2008 Olympic Bird's Nest, the Aquatic Center and the new modernistic rather curious CCTV center in Beijing, which unfortunately had a major fire in 2009, destabilizing the structure. Now that all but five pavilions at the World Expo have been destroyed as required in the Expo regulations, Shanghai is poised to construct and develop the world's most eco-friendly modern urban/park/residential landscape in the entire world in the next ten years. The 2010 Expo theme, "Better city, better life" is very likely to occur in this reconstruction of most of the five kilometer square area near Shanghai's waterfront which is now in progress. Disney is also building a major entertainment center in this area of Shanghai.

Hu's and Wen's successors in 2012, especially President Xi Jinping, who has adopted the slogan of "China dream" and Premier Li Keqiang, considered as the fifth generation of PRC leaders, are expected to continue to lead expansively toward an "all round moderately well-off society by 2020" (Kuhn, 2010). A major concept of Xi is "the China dream" which he emphasized in his December, 2013 address marking the 120th anniversary of the birth of Mao Tsedong, in which he noted that over time this dream had developed and expanded considerably since the dream that Mao had for China during his leadership, but still based on the foundation which Mao had established. This linkage allowed him to distinguish himself from Mao, but at the same time to show that his China dream was also a continuation of Mao thought.

China has been moving toward a significant role as an international stake-holder since 2000. Both Presidents Obama "pivot to Asia" and his and Hu and Obama and Xi have sought a closer collaboration on many issues following Hu's 2011 state visit to the US and Xi's and Obama's private Sunnydale California meeting in 2013. Nonetheless, many tensions continue between the two countries, as are also developing between the US and Russia, causing China and Russia to move closer together. Conditions between China and Japan also are finding many points of tension, while Japanese and Indian relations are improving.

Chinese industry and commerce have moved beyond Germany and Japan as an exporter and now sell more autos than the US. China owns a large proportion of American debt, several trillion dollars. Among other factors, this debt ratio requires both China and the US to establish more of a partnering and ongoing cooperative relationship than one which sees the other side as a threat ("the China threat" for Americans, and "the America threat" for Chinese). China is moving closer to good economic and political relationships with the European Union, and now has major economic and political influence in many African, Asian, Latin American and Middle Western countries.

Martin Jacques' *When China Rules the World: The End of the Western World and the Birth of a New Global Order: Second Edition* (2012); Edward N. Luttwak's book: *The Rise of China vs. the Logic of Strategy* (2012); Dambisa Moyo's book: *Winner Takes All: China's Race for Resources and What It Means for the World* (2012); David Shambaugh's book: *China Goes Global: The Partial Power* (2013); Howard W. French's book: *China's Second Continent: How a Million Migrants Are Building a New Empire in Africa (2014)*; and Evan Osnos' book: *Age of Ambition: Chasing Fortune, Truth, and Faith in the New China* (2014) all provide considerable detail about China's increasing international development and strength.

In an American 2009 poll by the Pew Research Center, 44% of those polled said that China is now the top world economic power while only 27% felt that the US remains the top economic power; 49% wanted the American government to "mind its own business internationally," indicating that many in the us public were growing more isolationist; 53% identified China's emerging economic strength as posing rising competition for the US, and 63% still saw the US as the leading military power (*English People's Daily Online,* 2009: December 4). Arthur Kroeber, managing director of Gavekald, an economic research firm in Beijing, wrote in the April 11, 2010 *Washington Post* that Americans tend to hold five easily disproven myths about the Chinese economy:

(1) China will quickly overtake the United States as the world's most powerful economy. (2) China's vast holdings of us treasury bonds means it can hold Washington hostage in economic negotiations. (3) leting its currency grow in value is the most important thing China can do to reduce its trade surplus. (4) China's hunger for resources is sucking the world dry and making major contributions to global warming. (5) China's economy has grown mainly through the cruel exploitation of its cheap labor.

One of the most interesting earlier recent western books about Chinese culture is the first bestseller edition of Martin Jacques' *When China Rules the World* (2009) in which he argues that: understanding China will be one of the greatest challenges of the twenty-first century.... First, China is not really a nation-state in the traditional sense of the term but a civilization-state.... Second, China is increasingly likely to conceive of its relationship with East Asia in terms of a tributary-state, rather than nation-state system....Third, there is a distinctively Chinese attitude toward race and ethnicity. The Han Chinese see themselves as a single race....Fourth, China operates, and will continue to operate, on a quite different continental canvas than other states. There are four other states that might be described as continental in scale [the United States, Australia, Brazil and India].... Chinese modernity will come continental-sized, in terms of both population and physical size.... Fifth, the nature of the Chinese policy is highly specific....The dynastic state was replaced not by Western style popular sovereignty but by state sovereignty.... Sixth, Chinese modernity, like other East Asian modernities, is distinguished by the speed of the country's transformation.... Seventh, since 1949 China has been ruled by a Communist regime.... Eighth, China will, for several decades to come, combine the characteristics of both a developed and a developing country.... In the light of these ... characteristics, it is clear that Chinese modernity will be very different from Western modernity, and that China will transform the world far more fundamentally than any other global power in the last two centuries (417–429).

Jacques suggests that modernity in East Asia and the West can be measured by several different characteristics: language, the body, food, power, and politics. In Japan, despite years of learning English, the level of English is rather low; in India, English is one of fifteen official languages and a typical school language; in Singapore and Hong Kong, where Chinese ethnicity is prevalent, the official language for schools at a certain level is English; and although English has not replaced Mandarin on the Chinese mainland, English is now the elite second language.

Jacques proposes that the body, including especially skin color and style of dress, offers a very strong tilt toward a desire for Western white or light skin, and except in Japan to some extent among women and more directly in India, Pakistan, or Bangladesh, the style of dress is distinctly Westernized.

In terms of Westernized food in East Asia, the total of Western fast food chains is growing consistently, but still represents only a small percentage of fast food restaurants, with KFC having 2,200+ restaurants, McDonalds having 950 restaurants in China and 3, 500 in Japan in 2009. However, indigenous restaurants, including Asian fast food restaurants, such as the Yum franchises, still are the overwhelming food choice for most Asian residents. At the same time, Jacques notes that in China almost all those living in rural areas and migrants to the cities eat in Chinese restaurants. Jacques quotes K. C. Chang's book, *Food in Chinese Culture*, in which he says: "The importance of food in understanding human culture lies precisely in its infinite variability – variability that is not essential for species survival."

Jacques states that in terms of power in Western and East Asian societies, there is a profound difference; in the west, people are driven by a search for an individual autonomy, identity and utilitarian government, but in East Asia, whether Confucian-based North-East Asia or in South-East Asia, the key goal of individuals is to be a part of group identity from which they find security and meaning, with a separation of governmental power and group responsibilities. In Confucian societies like mainland China, Japan, Korea, Taiwan and Vietnam, Jacques maintains that generally the family is the basis of society, and by extension, the nation itself.

Thus both stability and harmony are of great importance to these Asian societies. These values, plus the scientific development of China, were major contributions made for China by Hu Jintao. Jacques draws two general conclusions about East Asian modernity: "first, if the impact of Westernization is limited, it follows that these societies – and their modernities – remain individual and distinctive, rooted in and shaped by their own histories and culture. It also follows that their modernization has depended not simply or even mainly upon borrowing from the west, but on their ability to transform and modernize themselves. "Second," he notes, "if the process of modernization is simply a transplant then it cannot succeed. a people must believe that modernity is theirs in order for it to take root and flourish" (113-138). In terms of China, we can then surmise from Jacques' arguments that Chinese modernization, while borrowing from the West is useful, it must be with "Chinese characteristics" as Deng Xiaoping articulated: "It doesn't matter if it is a black cat or a white cat, as long as it catches mice."

In contrast to the cross-cultural national characteristics or dimensions, as are suggested in the studies of Geert Hofstede, when we discuss international and global communication, Thomas L. McPhail, in his book: *Global Communication* (2010) defines it as referring "to the cultural, economic, political, social, and technical analysis of communication and media patterns and effects across and between nation-states. international communication focuses more on global aspects of media and communication systems and technologies and, as a result, less on local or even national aspects or issues" (2010, 2). McPhail believes that "what is significant, then, is that international communication is no longer solely focused on the role of the print press and the newsgathering habits of the international news agencies, such as AP or Reuters. It is growing to encompass a broad range of issues that arose from the emergence of global broadcasting, global advertising, and the global economy" (34).

Noting a number of critical issues relating to international communication, he argues that they can be explained through three major theories or movements: NWICO (New World Information and Communication Order), electronic colonialism, and world system theories: "international communication will have a greater impact on the future of the planet than exploration and transportation combined" (35). McPhail identifies the debate about the NWICO as dominating the international communication agenda for about two decades late in the twentieth century, with its final objective to restructure the system of media and telecommunication priorities so that lesser developed countries could "obtain greater influence over their media, information, economic, cultural, and political systems" and represents:

(1) "an evolutionary process seeking a more just and equitable balance in the free flow and content of information;

(2) a right to national self-determination of domestic communication policies; and

(3) at the international level, a two-way information flow reflecting more accurately the aspirations and activities of less developed countries (IDCS) (12–13)."McPhail identifies the electronic colonialism theory (ECT) as passing through four epochs of empire-building: the Greco-Roman period; the crusades of the Middle Ages, also called Christian colonialism; the mercantile colonialism in the seventeenth and eighteenth centuries of the British, French, Spanish, Belgians, Italians, Dutch, and Portuguese conquests of the Americas, Africa, Asia, and the Middle East; and finally, with the rise of nationalism and decolonization, the recent and current electronic colonialism represents the dependent relationship of poorer regions on the post-industrial nations, especially in the area of communication transfer. This has resulted in a new global culture created by "the large multimedia conglomerates.""ECT focuses on how global media, including advertising, influence how people look, think, and act…. just as the era of the industrial revolution focused on manual labor, raw materials, and then finished products, so also the information revolution now seeks to focus on the role and consequences concerning the mind and global consumer behavior" (16–24).

McPhail labels what he considers the third major aspect in considering both the international and global communication revolution as the world system theory (WST), which identifies the core, periphery, and semiperiphery zones in today's global setting. He defines the core zone as "capital intensive, high-wage, high-technology production, involving lower labor exploitation and coercion"; the semi-periphery zone as "core-like activities, peripheral-like activities"; and the periphery zone as "labor-intensive, low-wage, low-technology production involving high labor exploitation and coercion." He contends that the "world system theory states that global economic expansion takes place from a relatively small group of core-zone nation-states [the industrialized west] out to two other zones of nation-states, these being in the semi-peripheral and peripheral zones." He identifies China as among the semi-peripheral nations, along with Brazil and India, all of which can expect in the near future to become core nation-states, rivaling both the US and European Union's initial ten nation-states. McPhail sees both the recent electronic colonialism theory and the world system theory as being closely linked (24–30).

In this sense, we can also see the merger of both international and global communication through what McPhail calls "three new strong hegemonic communication forces stemming from: (1) expansion of cable and satellite broadcasting systems; (2) an avalanche of western, primarily American, television and movie programming, and (3) the collective rules of the World Trade Organization, the World Bank, and theI Monetary Fund." McPhail notes that issues facing both international and global communication are explained through the three major theories or movements which he has proposed: "collectively, they help organize or frame the trends, economics, technologies, and stakeholders involved in the dynamic, globally significant, and expanding role of international communication" (31–35).

Chinese Communication and the Civil Society

John H. Powers and Randy Kluver suggest that while China has one of the longest civilizations, it has only been building a truly civic society since 1976 with the death of Mao Zedong. Earlier periods were framed by "fragmentation, civil war, and Japanese occupation, wherein little progress was made toward the evolution of civil society in the modern sense. From the founding of the People's Republic to the death of Mao, the development of 'civil society with Chinese characteristics' floundered while the nation lurched from one top-driven political movement to another." They propose that "from a communication framework" civic society may develop on either a top down or bottom up basis, or within various groups in the society, and also between the central government and other international and global actors. Not only has there been the possibility of internal and external civic communication but also between the internal Chinese society and the world-wide Chinese diaspora" (1999: pp. 1–2).

Kluver writes that civil society allows citizens a voice in influencing social and political life outside the power of the state itself. He calls civic discourse the ability to define the nature of the society and its people, including economics, cultural and social issues, and popular culture, by which the national identity can be expressed.Civic discourse helps to create the society, and the civil society helps to promote civic discourse, much like Edward T. Hall's claim that culture is communication and communication is culture. Civic discourse is seen not only in political matters in China, where those in power in the party and government provide the substantial part of the discourse, but also in popular culture including the arts, music, books, tv, advertisements, the internet both as a form of exercising communicative interactions and in a major way in China as entertainment. Given the ever increasing importance of education at all levels in China, not only do the political leaders exercise power in the civic society, but also intellectuals (zhishifenzi) from the major universities (1999: 12–13), [and also so do younger popular cult figures like Han Han and Guo Jingmeng]. In the tradition of the dyanastic periods, the Confucian scholar-officials tended also to serve as "the conscience of the emperor." The cultural assumption that the scholars have a moral duty not only to innovate, but also to concern themselves about the progress of the society, remains true today, Kluver believes "that intellectuals have been and will continue to be a vital element of Chinese civic discourse."

Additionally, Kluver claims that the guiding principles of Marxism-Leninism/Mao Zedong thought also contribute to the role that intellectual elites play in China's civic discourse, which Deng Xiaoping reinforced through the centrality of the party to the development of social order, with a strong and well educated set of leaders leading and guiding the general population (1999: 12–20). Just as Martin Jacques (2009) has argued, Kluver also believes that the new Chinese society may develop some democratic tendencies quite unlike the western model of democracy: "the future is likely to bring an even more diverse set of ideas into a culture and a society that is rapidly constructing a new identity, and a new Chinese world" (20–22).

In my 2007 essay, "One World, One Dream" (2007, pp. 22–91), I concluded by saying that: "Some scholars claim that the twenty-first century will be the China/India century, since the two countries are expanding quickly economically, and more and more providing significant contributions internationally. We may also speculate that indeed China itself will be a major harmonizer interculturally for the twenty-first century, and, that in fact, the twenty-first century can be the China century" (2007, 77). Nevertheless, Shambaugh sees China as only a partial power (2013). If in Jacques' 2009 first edition, *When China Rules the World,* his view that the strong economy, more responsibilities of an international stake-holder leadership emerging, continuing infrastructure and environmentally friendly developments, the rise of the middle class through more and more well educated citizens, and potential successes of the coming fifth generation of leaders are all accurate, then we may indeed already be in the second decade of the China century. Both Luttwak and Shambaugh, however, strongly challenge such assumptions.

Luttwak stresses China's strategies and search for a grand strategy, with comparisons to Australia, Vietnam, South Korea, Mongolia, Indonesia, the Philippines, Norway, and the United States. He makes the following assumptions: (1) China's economy will continue to grow very rapidly, twice as high as the biggest sustainable growth rate for the US economy, with the caveat that the Chinese economy could slow down or increasing environmental impediments, such as China's serious pollution, which could significantly reduce overall growth; other problems can develop from increasing social tensions because of income and wealth inequality; the frequent riots against local government authorities provoked by land expropriations; ethnic unrest such as is occurring in the greater Tibet region and the Western Xingjiang area; threats to the morale and cohesion of the Communist Party of China, arising from the ideological bankruptcy of a nominally Communist regime dedicated to the advancement of capitalism; the increasing disaffection of the more and more educated elite who aspire toward more democracy and freedom from censorship of media, including books, television, and the internet.

(2) China's rulers and their security officials are far from being confident in the stability of their rule.

(3) China's leaders will continue to increase overall military and police spending in step with China's economic growth.

Luttwak offers the following conclusions: because of its magnitude, the Chinese economy, regionally and internationally and military investment, must naturally cause adversarial relationships, and alignments of forces against China, as governments of nearby states fear for their independence from China. He notes that: "These reactions, which express the very logic of strategy, ensure in themselves that China cannot concurrently increase its military strength and also its diplomatic, or more broadly, its political influence…. Individually, each component of the Chinese state that operates internationally is purposeful enough in pursuing its own institutional objectives, but the overall effect is frequently contradictory and damaging to China's overall interests by evoking hostile reactions" (pp. 258–259), (pp. 238–270).

David Shambaugh in his book, *China Goes Global: The Partial Power* (2013) proposes that any potential major world power should be judged by four criteria: diplomacy, military, economy, and domestic and exportation of culture (soft power). He agrees that China has become a major player in the era of globalization, but quotes vice Foreign Minister Cui Tiankai in 2012: "China's position is far behind the United States. We are not a peer of the United States. We have been elevated [in the eyes of others] against our will. We have no intention to compete for global leadership" (p. 307). Shambaugh asks "What does it mean for the world and how should the world respond?...To what extent should China integrate into the world order, on what terms, and what is the likely impact on China's own domestic order?" (p. 307). He argues, as do Kluver and Powers in their book *Civic Discourse, Civil Society, and Chinese Communities* (1999) that "it was not until the 1978 'reform and opening' policies of Deng Xiaoping that China seriously began the process of integrating itself, really for the first time into the international system" (p. 309).

Shambaugh discusses China's relations with Asia and notes that "not surprisingly, of all regions in the world, Asia receives priority attention in China's diplomacy. Geographic proximity dictates this.... With the exception of the brief Bandung interregnum in 1955–56 following the Afro-Asian conference in Bandung, Indonesia, China was at odds with most of its neighbors." Shambaugh stresses that only in the 1990s did ties begin to improve as a result of five factors:

> "The first was Asia's reaction to the June 4, 1989 'massacre' in Beijing. Unlike much of the international community, many Asian counties did not respond to the Chinese military's killing of civilians in Tiananmen Square and Beijing with condemnation, sanctions, or ostracization ....The second turning point was the 1997–98 Asian financial crisis. The government ...acted responsibly and in a stabilizing way by not devaluing its currency and by offering aid packages and low-interest loans to several South-East Asian states.... The third catalyst to a new regional policy was more of a gradual process than a single event.... By 1999–2000, Beijing's greater receptivity [to regional organizations and cooperation] had given way to full-blown participation in a range of regional multinational organizations (parallelling China's deeper integration into a

number of international organizations). Thus in a relatively short period China moved from passivity and suspicion to proactive engagement in regional regimes and institutions.... A fourth impetus came during a tour of Asia in 1997 by a group of Chinese diplomats and military officials who called for abrogation of all international alliances...Beijing's call fell on deaf ears both regionally and internationally.... The fifth catalyst to China's proactive Asia policy was, ironically, the mistaken US bombing of the Chinese embassy in Belgrade during the 1999 war in the former Yugoslavia....Chinese international affairs experts concluded that for a peaceful environment conducive to domestic development to emerge [as had been proposed by Deng Xiaoping],China needed to be less passive and more proactive in shaping its regional milieu" (pp. 95–99).

Because of these five factors, Shambaugh stresses that they "stimulated a thorough review and reorientation of regional policy toward neighbors" and stimulated four new incentives; "(1) stepped-up participation in regional organizations, (2) establishment of 'strategic partnerships' and deepening of bilateral relations, (3) expansion of regional economic ties, and (4) reduction of distrust and anxiety in the security sphere" (p. 99). Unfortunately for China, these positive relations with most of its Asian neighbors deteriorated significantly in 2009–2010, as "China got into diplomatic scrapes with virtually *every* one of its neighbors, with the net result that the previously positive perception of China in the region plummeted. This has become known as the period of China's 'assertiveness'" (p. 99). He believes that " Going forward, China's ties with its neighbors will be a mixture of continuing interdependence, frictions, and suspicions (on the part of Asian nations toward China). No Asian nation (save perhaps North Korea and Pakistan) fully trusts China. Yet they all have to live next door and interact with it" (p. 100). Concluding this section of his book, Shambaugh says that "Two things are not going to change: geography and history. All of these [p. 14] nations live adjacent to China (and vice versa), and memories of China's historical 'tribute' relationships still run deep for all parties. These factors will continue to simultaneously bind and divide China and its Asian neighbors" (pp. 104–105).

Shambaugh considers the four criteria for becoming a global power as follows: "Although Chinese diplomacy is active, I conclude that it is *not influential* in many parts of the world or on major international issues. China is not shaping events and actively contributing to solving problems....I conclude that China 'punches way below its weight' in international diplomacy....China is certainly more than a partial power in the economic realm — in terms of its global trade profile and energy and raw material imports — but the global impact of outbound investment and multinational corporations has been fairly minimal to date.... We also found various aspects of China's global cultural footprint to be expanding in tourism, education, art sales and exchanges, literature and film, fashion and design, and sports. But in all of these categories (save, perhaps tourism and art purchasing) the global impact has been relatively minimal.... Despite a rapidly modernizing military, we saw that China still has no conventional global power-projection capacities....Among all of these dimensions, I therefore conclude that China is *a partial power*" (pp. 309–310). Shambaugh challenges Martin Jacques' claim that China "will soon rule the world" as an unrealistic assumption. Luttwak agrees, and specifically names Jacques as unrealistic in his assessments of China's global importance.

Concluding his book, Shambaugh states: "One thing is certain: China's going global will undoubtedly be the most significant development in international relations in the years ahead. Since China's opening to the world in 1978, the world has changed China — and now China is beginning to change the world" (p. 317).

11. Social Media and Cybernetics in Asia: Implications for Regional Security

(Keynote Address, National University of Defense Technology Cultural Security Conference, Changsha, China, November 21, 2014)

Abstract:

In this presentation, introducing social media, especially in Asia, I shall define such terms as information/cyber security; national security systems; cyber mission; international cyber issues; cyber risk/threat; and cyber terrorism/war. Examples relating to Asia are provided according to the 2014 National Security Cyber Maturity in the Asia-Pacific Region report.
Key words: Asia, information/cyber security, cyber mission, cyber risk/threat, cyber terrorism/war, national cyber maturity

I. Introduction

Currently, I am coediting a trilogy of books on social media: Social Media in Asia, covering fourteen countries in the Asia/Pacific Rim (2014, 668 pages) coedited by Cui Litang of Tan Kha Kee College of Xiamen University and me; Social Media in the Middle East, covering most of the countries either from the traditional or a newer Middle East map, being coedited by me, Adil Nurmakov of KIMEP in Kazakhstan and Ehsan Shahghasemi of the University of Tehran, which is in progress and will be published in early 2016; and Social Media in Africa, to be coedited by me and Debhasis (Deb) Aikat of the University of North Carolina at Chapel Hill, and targeted for publication in early 2018, all for Dignity Press.

II. Cybernetics

Cybernetics comes to us from ancient Greece meaning "steersman, governor, pilot, or rudder." Cyberspace was coined early by Norbert Wiener as an electronic communication experience. In 1948, Shannon and Weaver applied the term to the physical/virtual space existing between two telephone conversations. According to Cui Litang,"BBS may have been a precursor of social media, prior to the web, though social media is typically described as the web of the web, the next web, or defined as a group of internet-based applications that build on the ideological and technological foundations of Web 2.... Sir Tim Berners-Lee, creator of the World Wide Web, called it "a collaborative medium, a place where we could all read and write." Punk cyber novelist William Gibson argued that cyberspace "has become a conventional means to describe anything associated with the Internet and the diverse Internet culture" (Cui & Prosser, 2014).

In our coedited book, *Social Media in Asia* (2014), Cui Litang and I suggest that social media can be considered both through cultural dialogue between members of different cultures, which promotes a macro sense of positive universalism or globalization or through cultural criticism, which promotes micro comparisons between different cultures or cultural organizations and institutions. We also note that social media, within the concept of cyberspace, can be considered functionally through its components such as surveillance; value-oriented interpretation; linkage between individuals who are not necessarily connected in direct physical demographics but who are interested in shared topics; a transmitter of values; and as an entertainment transmitter.

Cui notes that among the world's internet distribution, 45% of more than 700 million netizens utilize seven of the world's internet languages: English, Chinese, Arabic, Japanese, Korean, Russian, and Indonesian. Asia thus represents a very significant producer and recipient of social media within the context of cyberspace. China's current internet penetration of more than 618 million netizans, in a process with nationalization of Chinese characteristics, half of whom use social media sites such as Qzone, Renren, QQ, SinaWeibo, and Kazkin, provide the world's largest social media cluster and market with 2012 online transactions worth more than 3.2 billion dollars.

On November 11, 2014, "Singles Day" Reuters indicated that "E-commerce giant Alibaba Group Holding Ltd (BABA.N) reported more than $9 billion in online sales," illustrating the buying power of the Chinese consumer and the importance of the event in the retail calendar. Real-time figures on a giant screen at Alibaba's Hangzhou campus surged past 2013's record to 57.1 billion yuan ($9.3 billion) just after midnight after Chinese and overseas shoppers snapped up heavily discounted goods online. The shopping day, similar to Cyber Monday and Black Friday in the United States, comes less than eight weeks after Alibaba's record $25 billion public share listing in New York."

David Shambaugh, in his book *China Goes Global,* indicates that China definitely possesses global reach in its cyber capabilities. With the US, we can note that these two countries both have the largest world-wide global capacities for the use of cybernetics.

South Korea is home to the second largest blogging community, whose Cyworld has attracted more than 18 million users, followed by Japan's Mixi with 15 million users, and Vietnam's Zing also with 15 million users.

In our book, *Social Media in Asia,* William J. Brown and Benson P. Fraser note that "'There is no doubt that 'social media in its various forms have created an unprecedented global public space that vastly increases and amplifies the number of accessible voices and connections in all parts of the world.' They assert that social media and online communication have grown rapidly in India, Indonesia, and the Philippines, stressing that "the potential of online communication to expand political, social, and economic involvement of more and more people could and substantively enhance the quality of life among the people of Asia."

Also in our book, David M. Lucas proposes that "with a rapid growth rate in communication technology and with a tendency toward early adoption of technology, India's population seems poised to become the single most logged on people in the world.... The culture of India stands at the precipice of a great cultural revolution   to be ignited by the influence of social media.... The digital revolution provides new avenues for the Indians to explore and manipulate into personal avenues for communication.... India is the world's fastest growing industry in the world in terms of the number of wireless connections after China."

It is important to understand that not only are vast numbers of individuals throughout the world, as an integral aspect of globalization intensely involved with computer mediated communication, positively and negatively, but even more importantly, that social media are significantly impacted by multinational corporations, nongovernmental organizations, and especially nonstate actors and governments which produce, use, and disseminate social media within the context of cyberspace.

III. Definitions of Cybernetics Terms

I shall define such terms as information/cyber security; cyber mission; cyber security threat; international cyber issues; cyber risks and threats, and cyber terrorism. Finally, I identify some regional cyber issues in Asia as identified by the Australian *2014 National Security Cyber Maturity in the Asia-Pacific Region Report*.
Information/Cyber Security, National Security Systems; Cyber Risk, International Issues, and Cyber Terrorism
The term information security means protecting information and information systems from unauthorized access, use, disclosure, disruption, modification, or destruction in order to provide integrity, which means guarding against improper information modification or destruction, and includes ensuring nonrepudiation and authenticity; confidentiality, which means preserving authorized restrictions on access and disclosure, including means for protecting personal privacy and proprietary information; and availability, which means ensuring timely and reliable access to and use of information (United States Cybersecurity Act of 2012).

National security systems mean any information systems (including any telecommunications system) used or operated by a governmental agency or by a contractor of an agency, or other organizations on behalf of an agency — the function, operation, or use of which — involves intelligence activities; cryptologic activities related to national security; command and control of military forces; equipment that is an integral part of a weapon or weapons system; or is critical to the direct fulfillment of military or intelligence missions; or that is protected at all times by procedures established for information that have been specifically authorized to be kept classified in the interest of national defense or foreign policy.

Malicious cyber command and control includes the actual or potential harm caused by an incident, including information exfiltrated as a result of subverting a technical control when it is necessary in order to identify or describe a cybersecurity threat; any other attribute of a cybersecurity threat. (United States Cybersecurity Act of 2012).

Cybersecurity mission means activities that encompass the full range of threat reduction, vulnerability reduction, deterrence, international engagement, incident response, resiliency, and recovery policies and activities, including computer network operations, information assurance, law enforcement, diplomacy, military, and intelligence missions as such activities relate to the security and stability of cyberspace.

Cyber risk means any risk to information infrastructure, including physical or personnel risks and security vulnerabilities, that, if exploited or not mitigated, could pose a significant risk of disruption to the operation of information infrastructure essential to the reliable operation of covered critical infrastructure.

The term cybersecurity threat means information — that may be indicative of or describe — malicious reconnaissance, including anomalous patterns of communications that reasonably appear to be transmitted for the purpose of gathering technical information related to a cybersecurity threat; a method of defeating a technical control; a technical vulnerability; a method of defeating an operational control;a method of causing a user with legitimate access to an information system or information that is stored on, processed by, or transiting an information system to unwittingly enable the defeat of a technical control or an operational control. (United States Cybersecurity Act of 2012).

Cyberterrorism is defined by the Technolytics Institute as "The premeditated use of disruptive activities, or the threat thereof, against computers and/or networks, with the intention to cause harm or further social, ideological, religious, political or similar objectives. Or to intimidate any person in furtherance of such objectives." (Wikipedia)

The following identifies different types of individuals or groups who create cyber risks or threats.

Bot-network operators take over multiple systems in order to coordinate attacks and to distribute phishing schemes, spam, and malware attacks. (Wikipedia)

Criminal groups seek to attack systems for monetary gain. Specifically, organized crime groups are using spam, phishing, and spyware/malware to commit identity theft and online fraud. International corporate spies and organized crime organizations also pose a threat to the United States through their ability to conduct industrial espionage and large-scale monetary theft and to hire or develop hacker talent. Examples include recent cybercrimes in the United States for banking and commercial institutions such as Morgan Stanley, Target, and Home Depot. Personally, I have had three cybercrimes targeted against two of my internet accounts, twice allegedly from London and once from Madrid.

The disgruntled organization insider is a principal source of computer crime. Foreign intelligence services use cyber tools as part of their information-gathering and espionage activities. It is clear that many different nations' intelligence services are active in gathering such information as identified by Edward Snowden (born June 21, 1983) an American computer professional who leaked classified information from the National Security Agency (NSA), starting in June 2013 which included intelligence information from China and Hong Kong. He has recently released new classified documents. Wikileaks released US national Department of Defense and other classified US intelligence information as early as 2008, and as recently as October 2014.

Hackers break into networks for the thrill of the challenge or for bragging rights in the hacker community. The worldwide population of hackers poses a relatively high threat of an isolated or brief disruption causing serious damage.

Phishers Individuals, or small groups, who execute phishing schemes in an attempt to steal identities or information for monetary gain.

Spammers include Individuals or organizations who distribute unsolicited e-mail with hidden or false information in order to sell products, conduct phishing schemes, distribute spyware/malware, or attack organizations (i.e., denial of service). (Wikipedia) Some of these events began in Nigeria in the mid 1990's and now I receive several such spams soliciting funds monthly both from African and Asian countries.

Spyware/malware authors are individuals or organizations with malicious intent who carry out attacks against users by producing and distributing spyware and malware.

Cyber terrorists seek to destroy, incapacitate, or exploit critical infrastructures in order to threaten national security, cause mass casualties, weaken national economies, and damage public morale and confidence. This is an increasing problem for many countries, including in Europe, North America, and Asia.

(Source: Government Accountability Office (GAO), Department of Homeland Security's (DHS's) Role in Critical Infrastructure Protection (CIP) Cybersecurity, GAO-05–434 (Washington, D.C.: May, 2005.) indicates that:

Information technology is central to the effectiveness, efficiency, and reliability of the industry and commercial services, armed forces and national security systems.

Cyber criminals, terrorists, and agents of foreign powers have taken advantage of the connectivity of governments to inflict substantial damage to the economic and national security interests.

The cybersecurity threat is sophisticated, relentless, and massive, exposing all consumers in the United States to the risk of substantial harm.

Businesses are bearing enormous losses as a result of criminal cyberattacks, depriving them of hard-earned profits that could be reinvested in further job-producing innovations.

Hackers continuously probe the networks of governmental agencies, the armed forces, and their commercial industrial bases cause substantial damage and compromised sensitive and classified information.

Severe cybersecurity threats will continue, and will likely grow, as national economies grow more connected, criminals become increasingly sophisticated in efforts to steal from consumers, industries, and businesses and terrorists and foreign nations continue to use cyberspace as a means of attack against national and economic security of governments.

IV. International Cooperation to Protect Cyber Security Is Essential

Cooperating governments, consistent with the protection of intelligence sources and methods and other sensitive matters can inform each other of the expected disruption of which could result in national or regional catastrophic damage between governments of the countries in which the information infrastructure is located of any cyber risks to such information infrastructure; and coordinate with these government of the country in which such information infrastructure is located to mitigate or remediate cyber risks.

International agreements for cooperation of protecting cyber security and overcoming or mitigating the risks of cyber risks, threats, or terrorism are now regularly being made by an increasing number of countries and regional organizations.

As the Internet becomes more pervasive in all areas of human endeavor, individuals or groups can use the anonymity afforded by cyberspace to threaten citizens, specific groups (i.e. with membership based on ethnicity or belief), communities and entire countries, without the inherent threat of capture, injury, or death to the attacker that being physically present would bring. Many groups such as Anonymous, use tools such as Denial-of-service attack to attack and censor groups who oppose them, creating many concerns for freedom and respect for differences of thought.

Many believe that cyberterrorism is an extreme threat to national economies, and fear an attack could potentially lead to another worldwide Great Depression. Several leaders agree that cyberterrorism has the highest percentage of threat over other possible attacks internationally. Although natural disasters are considered a top threat and have proven to be devastating to people and land, there is ultimately little that can be done to prevent such events from happening. Thus, the expectation is to focus more on preventative measures that will make Internet attacks impossible for execution.

As the Internet continues to expand, and computer systems continue to be assigned increased responsibility while becoming more complex and interdependent, sabotage or terrorism via the Internet may become a more serious threat and is possibly one of the top 10 events to "end the human race."

Dependence on the internet is rapidly increasing on a worldwide scale, creating a platform for international cyber terror plots to be formulated and executed as a direct threat to national security. For terrorists, cyber-based attacks have distinct advantages over physical attacks. They can be conducted remotely, anonymously, and relatively cheaply, and they do not require significant investment in weapons, explosive and personnel. The effects can be widespread and profound. Incidents of cyberterrorism are likely to increase. They will be conducted through denial of service attacks, malware, and other methods that are difficult to envision today.

In an article about cyberattacks by Iran and North Korea, the *New York Times* observes, "The appeal of digital weapons is similar to that of nuclear capability: it is a way for an outgunned, outfinanced nation to even the playing field. These countries are pursuing cyberweapons the same way they are pursuing nuclear weapons," said James A. Lewis, a computer security expert at the Center for Strategic and International Studies in Washington. "It's primitive; it's not top of the line, but it's good enough and they are committed to getting it." (Wikipedia)

V. Recent International Cooperation and Issues: International Cyber Maturity in the Asia Pacific Region 2014 Report

The importance of cyberspace has been assessed recently through a report from the Australian *International Cyber Centre*. In terms of its assessment and understanding, as Cui and I proposed in *Social Media in Asia,* it can be studied through the spectrum of cultural comparative criticism on one hand among the Asian and Pacific region countries and through four functions described in the report: government, military, digital business and economics, and social engagement. Fourteen countries in the region, and the UK and US which both have highly sophisticated global cybernetics abilities are discussed for comparative purposes.

The Report notes: "In recent years, the Asia–Pacific region has undergone tremendous economic growth, political transformation and social change. The development of cyberspace and the information and communications technology (ICT) that powers it has proven to be an integral part of the region's socioeconomic growth. The online environment is also rapidly growing in importance as an avenue for political and social expression in Asian societies."

But the report states that while each country surveyed understands that cyber security is of great importance, technological development in the region varies. Countries with the most mature cyberspace abilities include Australia, which has announced the creation of the Australian Cyber Security Centre; India, Japan and Singapore have all updated or launched new national cybersecurity policies, plus the UK and USA.

Lack of resources or weak supporting legislation restrict efforts to strengthen cyber resilience in the Philippines, Malaysia, Indonesia, Cambodia and Thailand. In India, a lack of enforcement capacity hinders an otherwise fairly well-developed policy framework. For nations such as Myanmar, Papua New Guinea and Cambodia, lack of infrastructure severely impede their growth in cyber maturity.

China possesses strong cyber surveillance and technical capabilities but lacks solid cybercrime and cybersecurity policy, legislation and coordination and is also a problem in Thailand, Singapore, and South Korea (in the latter case as an issue between the two Koreas. (National Security in Cyber Maturity in the Asia-Pacific Region report).

However, increased awareness, often driven by international engagement, is leading to positive cyber outcomes. For example, Japan's increasing engagement with the US is helping to shape its cyber capabilities, and its efforts to help regional partners develop their own cyber capacities offer a strong model for regional engagement. Robust existing regional policing and cooperation between national computer emergency response teams (CERTs) lay the foundation for higher level cyber policy engagement, particularly at the multilateral level.

With the ASEAN Regional Forum expanding their efforts in 2014, the AsiaPacific has every potential to see improved dialogue across both technical and policy realms and increasing levels of cyber maturity across the board. Those governments that lack an adequate focus on their cyber policies include Cambodia, Myanmar, the Philippines, Thailand, Papua New Guinea, and Indonesia. A great deal of discussion continues in the region about confidence building measures, capacity building and transparency in the cyber domain, mainly through the ASEAN Political and Security Community. These discussions present an opportunity for nations to increase their cooperation and mutual assistance in cyberspace.

Nations leading the way in military aspects of cyber capabilities are the US, China, UK, Australia, Singapore and South Korea. The report cautions that the increased utilization of cyber capabilities by the North Korean regime over the past year has put the South Korean Government under pressure to respond to cyber incidents as they arise without an escalation between the two countries, creating another challenge for strategic planners.

Australia, Japan, Singapore and South Korea are some of the most digitally savvy economies for online business and economy growth. China and India are giants in the region and Indonesia is on the cusp, with clear potential. All have been marked as key emerging markets to varying degrees and have large populations to match their economic dynamism. With technological adoption driven by social media and mobile devices, Malaysia, the Philippines, and Thailand boast growing populations of young 'digital natives.' I have already noted the great success on line of Alibaba on November 11, 2014. Lack of infrastructure is the largest challenge to the development of a strong digital economy in Cambodia, Myanmar, North Korea and Papua New Guinea.

VI. Excerpts from the Report Provide the Following Paraphrased Information.

In terms of social media and significant public awareness, debate and media coverage of cybersecurity issues, the Australian individual internet usage rate is at 82.3%4. The country had 12.4 million internet subscribers at the end of June 2013, and 19.6 million Australians have mobile phones connected to the internet.

Only 4.9% of Cambodians are connected to the internet. There's some reporting of cybersecurity incidents in the Cambodian media, but little evidence of public debate on cyber policy and security issues.

China reflects the systematic approach to engagement in bilateral and multilateral international forums across the full spectrum of international cyber policy and security issues. In 2011, China joined Russia, Tajikistan and Uzbekistan in proposing to the UN an international code of conduct for information security, followed by a multistate proposal in 2012 to give the ITU greater control over the internet. The Chinese media are generally quick to report on cyber issues whenever China is accused of cyber-espionage and have been similarly active as the Snowden revelations continue. While urban areas are well served, poor infrastructure in the rural areas of China means that only about 42.3% of individuals use the internet. Mobile internet is becoming an increasingly important means of connectivity in the country.

India has only 13% of the population connected to the internet, but there has been a vastly growing media coverage of the topic since 2009. Regular efforts are being made to link into the international discussion of internet security and capabilities. As I noted, India is primed perhaps to have the most wired netizan system in the world. The increasing problem of cyber threats and terrorism is of great concern to successive Indian governments.

Indonesia is middle of the range of the Asian-Pacific countries in terms of its social media and concerns about cyber issues. Indonesian leaders are now publicly emphasizing cybersecurity issues, which may help to broaden the debate beyond its current focus on foreign surveillance. The individual internet usage rate in Indonesia is 15.4%. The Indonesian Government has stated that its goal is to roll out broadband services to 15 million households by 2015, which would constitute about 20% of households nationally.

Japan is a highly engaged and capable actor in cyberspace. The government has clearly demonstrated its intentions to be proactive on cyber issues, publishing a Cybersecurity Strategy in 2013 and having instituted a wide range of legislation. Japan has 79.1% internet penetration and strong fixed and wireless infrastructure. It was an early and enthusiastic adopter of mobile internet technology, leading to mobile broadband subscriptions equal to 113.1% of the population. Japan is highly engaged with the international community on cyber issues and has a published International Strategy on Cyber Security. Japan is heavily engaged regionally and internationally on cyber issues and continues to be a global leader in the digital economy. Japan has a fairly mature understanding and good awareness of private industry cyber risks, as is laid out in the 2013 Cybersecurity Strategy.

The internet is used by 65.8% of Malaysians, one of the highest rates in Southeast Asia. Malaysia is highly active in the region in bilateral and multilateral projects through ASEAN and ITU–IMPACT/ The Malaysian Government appears to be actively building a structure to manage cybersecurity risks in a coordinated manner through the establishment of CyberSecurity Malaysia. Malaysia put the cost of cybercrime at US$300 million for the first six months of 2013, a 100% increase on the previous year. Discussion of cybersecurity incidents is common in the Malaysian media, but there is little discussion of other cyber issues.

The Philippines participates in several multilateral cyber-oriented working groups and workshops led by organizations such as APEC, ASEAN and the UN, with a particular focus on the area of cybercrime. The Philippines' reflects an internet penetration of about 36.2%. Currently, only around 19.7% of the workforce is involved in knowledge-intensive jobs.

Singapore scores highly for its involvement in technical information exchange, anti-cybercrime collaboration. The new National Cyber Security Centre (NCSC) headed by the Singapore Infocomm Technology Security Authority is currently being established and is likely to enhance Singapore's capabilities in the early detection and prevention of cyber-attacks. Singapore has successfully implemented legislation, such as the Computer Misuse and Cybersecurity Act, to prevent and respond to cyber issues, including cybercrime and hacking. Singapore has high internet connectivity: about 74.2% of its population uses the internet.[38]

Mobile internet, with 123.3 mobile-broadband subscriptions per 100 inhabitants, is also very popular.

South Korea has highlighted strengthening international cyber cooperation in its 2011 Cyber Strategy and played host to the recent Seoul Conference on Cyberspace. South Korea has a strong organizational structure for cyber issues, centered primarily on the National Cyber Security Strategy Council and the National Cyber Security Center (NCSC). South Korea is a leading technological actor in cyberspace and has some of the world's most advanced digital infrastructure. As evidenced by clear governmental organization and a body of legislation on cyber issues, the South Korean Government is highly aware of and responsive to all cyber issue areas.

There is heavy coverage of cybersecurity issues in the South Korean media, mainly because of the pervasive threat from North Korea. The government has also taken a proactive approach to raising public awareness and preparedness, sponsoring numerous educational mass media and advertising campaigns focused on cybersecurity. The Mobile Security Forum, launched by the Korea Communications Commission in 2010, focused on smartphone and mobile internet use, and the Korea Information Security Agency aims to make South Korea the strongest, safest, most advanced country on the internet. South Korea has one of the most advanced cyber infrastructures in the world, and 84.1% of the population uses the internet. South Korea regularly ranks as having the world's fastest internet speeds.

North Korea's internet presence is one of the lowest in the world, representing only 1% of the 30 million residents connected. North Korea has often been cited as being an existential threat to its neighbors because of its capacity for cyberterrorism. [North Korea has been charged by the US government on December 20, 2014 has having hacked Sony Studio's internet for its development of the movie: "The Interview."]

Thailand's international engagement on cyber issues is largely focused on capacity building and less on wider cyber issues, such as internet governance. Thailand has established many international partnerships to improve domestic cyber capabilities, including with the International Council of Electronic Commerce Consultants and the SANS Institute. Thailand's organizational structure for cyber issues is reasonably developed, with several institutions in place and improving clarity about roles and responsibilities. Cyber policy is primarily owned by the Ministry of Information and Communications Technology. However, the government has recently raised the profile of cyber issues by launching the National Cyber Security Committee, chaired by the Prime Minister. Social media adoption in Thailand has been high, but wider knowledge of cybersecurity and cyber safety remains low. In Thailand, approximately 26.5% of individuals use the internet, and the spread of mobile technologies has greatly improved connectivity.

VII. Conclusion

It is apparent in Cui's and my book, Social Media in Asia, where major accomplishments in social media have benefitted many of the fourteen countries discussed by the authors, and as Cui points out, that social media establish dreams of the millenniums, provide a long way towards solidarity, and develop an international Asian/Pacific Rim social media manifestation. He calls it "a reflection and celebration of the millennium-long international solidarity or by the current Zietgeist of globalization, focusing on the social media, as the internet landscape continues to extend, sometimes, become mapped and chartered by national and cultural boundaries, sometimes by no boundaries at all, amid unanimous efforts by the governments, institutions, organizations, businesses and individuals in developing and reaping return of investment of social entrepreneurship, social capital, and eventually the public sphere as a powerful mover [of society]" (Cui, 2014).

At the same time social media's relationship in cyberspace means that all of the countries in the Asia-Pacific region most seriously need to cooperate internationally and regionally to overcome cyber risks, threats, and terrorism either by state or nonstate actors whose efforts can be as dangerous in the current period to the global society as extreme physical or nuclear threats and terrorism. The 2014 report of the *National Security Cyber Maturity in the Asia-Pacific Region* makes this abundantly clear.

[This address is to be expanded as my keynote address at the June, 2015 International Academy for Intercultural Research conference in Bergen, Norway, with more information especially related to China and its censorship and cyberterrorism, as the subject was too sensitive at the Cultural Security conference in the National University of Defense Technology in November, 2014, requiring me to self-censure myself.]

12. Bicultural Japanese-American Research Conference, Nihonmatsu, Japan: 1974

Richard Harris's article on John C. Condon, "A different Way of Knowing: With Respect to John C. (Jack) Condon," (2012: November) discusses his very productive professional period teaching at International Christian University, during which his contributions to founding the field of intercultural communication was very significant, and he notes: "A significant development in this respect was instigated by a letter he received from Michael H. Prosser late in 1970. Prosser was head of the Intercultural Communication Commission in the Speech Communication Association (now the {US} National Communication Association), and wrote to Condon suggesting that he organize an intercultural communication conference in Japan. With the help of Mitsuko Saito, with whom he was developing a close professional relationship, Condon arranged the first ICU international conference for July 1972, which Milton Bennett has called a landmark event in the creation of the field....Papers from the conference, along with original material, were collected in a book, Intercultural Encounters with Japan, edited by Condon and Saito and published by Simul Press in 1975" (pp. 802–803).

Harris points out the second conference in Japan in 1974, "a meeting not organized by ICU, but attended by Condon, Saito, and a number of ICU students. Conceived as more of a bicultural workshop than as a traditional conference, this 9-day event involved splitting the participants into groups of eight and encouraging relatively unstructured spontaneous discussions, usually in English, on points of intercultural interest…. This experience has been well described by Prosser, one of the participants, in his book, *The Cultural Dialogue,* (pp. 216–289), although his recollections of the conference are more positive than those of many of the other attendees, particularly on the Japanese side. For various reasons, some cultural, some technical, but others more connected to process or personality issus, the conference proved a tense, difficult, frustrating, even traumatic experience for many, including Condon, and his well-established conciliatory role was on this occasion particularly vital, soothing frayed tempers and saving face. As Prosser recalls, "Jack was a model of reason in that conference"' (pp. 802–803).

Janet M. Bennett's article, "The Public and Private Dean Barnlund" (2012: November), describes the conference as follows:" In 1974, several senior interculturalists, including Dean Barnlund and Clifford Clarke, invited a select group to a hot springs resort named Nihonmatsu, where Americans and Japanese were gathering in an experimental effort to explore group building across cultures. Cliff [Clarke] suggests that this powerful learning opportunity 'was the turning point of many of the participants' lives in greater self-awareness because of the intensity of the interactions' (personal correspondence, April 2, 2012)….The well-intentioned efforts at intercultural dialogue ultimately proved challenging, and the event remains a source of divergent perspectives to this day."

Jacqueline H. Wasilewski and Holly Siebert Kawakami's essay, "Edward C. Stewart: Cultural Dynamics Pioneer" (2012: November) offers this comment about Stewart's involvement in the conference: 'Stewart went to Japan for the first time when he participated in the nine-day long Japan-US Bicultural Intercultural Communication Workshop in Nihonmatsu in 1974. One quarter of Michael Prosser's (1978) book, *The Cultural Dialogue,* is about the Nihonmatsu Workshop (pp. 216–289). It was during this time that Stewart met the key people at International Christian University (ICU) in Tokyo who were also developing the field of intercultural communication, including Professors Mitsuko Saito and John C. Condon from the Department of Communication in the Language Division at ICU.'

In his introduction to our coedited "Special Issue: Early American Pioneers of Intercultural Communication" (2012: November), Steve J. Kulich identifies the Nihonmatsu conference as one of the founding events for the creation of the academic field of intercultural communication: "… with most prominent interculturalists from each country at that time attending [Japan and the United States], seventy-six total representing academic institutions, government agencies, counseling associations, second-language societies, international exchange organizations, and independent consultants."

My first actual experience in Asia occurred with my participation in the Japanese-American bicultural research conference in the summer of 1974 noted above. With six days of dialogue, six hours a day for each of the eight groups, including four Japanese and four Americans in our specific group which was later analyzed by Clifford H. Clarke and Kenneth Kanatani in an essay published in Japanese (1979), and later, when the entire conference was analyzed by Paul B. Pedersen (2005). I was one of the American leaders who helped organize the conference at a planning meeting in San Francisco in late 1973 or early 1974, including a dinner at the home of the American chair of the conference, Dean Barnlund. I was a roommate with Muneo Yoshikawa, a Japanese professor in Hawaii, who later wrote: "Some Japanese and American Cultural Characteristics" (pp. 220–230) for the one fourth of my book, *The Cultural Dialogue,* dedicated to a paraphrased bicultural dialogue between the eight participants in my group.

In the dialogue itself, I gave the other seven participants-pseudonyms and I included very little of my own contributions, as there were often sensitivities that needed to be respected, especially since there were some heated intracultural disagreement and communication breakdowns, primarily among the American participants, more than interculturally between the Japanese and Americans. In my chapter, 'Beginning the Dialogue," I note that: "Our early dialogue was interesting primarily because it quickly involved us in discussing various interesting Japanese and American communicative and cultural tendencies, and interests among the group itself" (p. 2410). In this first dialogue, we discussed the process of naming in each society, the role of sexism, a day long field trip and the Mayor's luncheon, which unfortunately had a very serious communication breakdown. On the following day, we processed the communication breakdowns that had surfaced in our group and at the Mayor's luncheon.

As our six days of dialogue ended, we again returned to the communication breakdowns in our group and at the luncheon. [Names are pseudonyms.]

> *Florence,* the older American, asked Mark: "You say that we haven't dealt with anything personal. Should we?"

> *Mark:* "I hoped for much more."

Mr. Osuzawa: "What do you want? Actual cultural confrontation?"

Mark: "There really was very little confrontation, which was good. I wanted more personal interaction."

Mr. Shirai: "I've been frustrated for two or three reasons. Why am I here? Where am I going? Being confined in the small room, sitting all day for several days in the same position, discussing and discussing, was all very frustrating. The whole workshop seemed to have only the vaguest purpose. Why did they spend so much money for us to sit in such a small group for so long with no real purpose?'

Mrs. Nishikawa: "We use words to work out something. Here communication is the goal itself — not a task orientation as I am used to. There must be a motivation for communication. Here, after the first couple of days, we had no goal beyond just communicating…."

Miss Takahashi: "It doesn't mean that we don't get anything out of the communication. Behavior is communicated."

Mrs. Nishikawa: "I've never been exposed to this type of workshop before. Usually there is a plan. Here there I deliberately nothing to do."

Florence: "We aren't meeting your expectations, Mark, and perhaps that of the researchers."

Rachel: "They want us to do something, but won't tell us what they want us to do."

Mark: "But, we made a statement here, which should be the goal of the workshop — a task-orientation instead of a process orientation…."

Florence: "We are sorry that we let you down as a group."

Mark: You haven't let yourselves down. That is important."

Following this rather pessimistic exchange, group members made the effort to find commonalities in the dialogue, and to ease the tension, I suggested that we sing the song that both sets of participants knew: "When you are happy and you know it, clap your hands." Then I note: "The group laughed about their efforts at bilingual harmony as the formal aspects of this part of the workshop ended" (pp. 240–275).

When this phase of the workshop/conference finished, the Japanese and American women discussed their feelings, with several Japanese explaining their discomfort with some American women attempting to push a feminist agenda on them. The women had held extra sessions outside of the six hours a day for the groups of eight, and they noted some positive accomplishments meeting interactively as women: they were more personal with each other, they were more honest and open with each other, they offered a safer physical and nonverbal environment for each other, and they were more supportive of each other. They proposed three topics: "How would this conference have been different if more women had been present and if time had been provided officially for the meetings of the spontaneous women's group? What were their personal relations with their own mothers and children? How did personal touching help to support or nonsupport each other?" (p. 277).

There were several separate evaluation groups, Japanese women, Japanese men, American women, and American men at the end of the conference. The fifteen American male participants (identified as a paraphrased dialogue, with pseudonyms): was the only group, naturally, in which I was involved. This is a condensed and partial summary of their remarks.

Lawrence: "Basically, our whole question is one of motivation and cognitive approaches to intercultural communication. One way to do it is to talk about ideas, data, and results. In our group, the Japanese-language group, there were impossibly different perceptions about how to incorporate these approaches…"

John: "Another dimension which has to be considered besides whether the conference should be largely academic or experiential is how the group is loaded with Japanese men. You have to give Japanese men time to discover their relationships before they are even able to move onto any sort of content dimension…."

Jim: "We had a very sharp division between those who wanted a problem-solving approach versus a feeling approach. The older participants, especially the men, were much more problem-solving oriented, whether Japanese or American, while the younger Japanese and Americans liked the intense emotional feeling approach."

Ralph: "By some luck, we used our mornings on the interpersonal levels and the afternoon on the more abstract levels…."

Bill: "This isn't the real world, with experiential in the morning and cognitive in the afternoon. It all blends together….The key issue is why people are here and what they expected to get out of it."

Mark: "Are we agreed on any specific ideas for our report?"

Douglas: "No. I suspect that the report should say that these were observations and recommendations which individuals offered, and tie those which fit well together into the same sets of observations and recommendations, and where there is conflict, tie the appropriate conflicting opinions together too. This seems to typify our own individuality best."

(This approach was generally accepted by the group;)

In my personal evaluation, I noted that there was too much expectation that caused major stress and overloads on the participants, staff, and technology. Many of the Japanese men felt that it was basically an American conference transplanted to Japan. At one point all eight videotape machine completely lost their sound capacity for a large part of the day. I indicated that "With the best intentions on the part of its planners and participants, certain communication breakdown was inevitable by the very nature of the differences in patterns of linguistic, nonverbal, attitudinal, and cognitive dimensions between the Japanese and Americans, and between the younger and older, or male and female participants. The workshop was neither an unqualified success nor a failure…. As a final widespread view of the participants, I would suspect that it was generally considered a success. At the same time, as the workshop ended there was still confusion among many participants as to its real goals, and some generalized frustration at the procedure that the actual workshop moved toward in its conclusions" (pp. 284–285).

However, it is important to note that my assessment of the workshop/ bicultural research conference was much more optimistic, as noted above, than the broader assessment of the participants. Originally, the major Japanese and American foundation funding had provided that there would be a book published on the conference, but there was so much tension, and the fear of losing face, that it was never published. Thus, except for my own attention to the conference in my book, *The Cultural Dialogue* (pp. 216–289), and the noted articles above, and while its impact on the founding of intercultural communication has had significant implications interculturally and internationally, most of the academic potential for sharing the research has not materialized. Clifford Clarke has retained the videos that were produced from the eight groups of eight Japanese and American participants, and perhaps at some time in the future, and with the passage of forty years since the conference new scholars can carefully analyze the collected results of the research, and provide new theories for the field of intercultural communication.

In my own case, this bicultural conference was the beginning of my own journey to the East, and was thus a very important development in my own development of intercultural communication competence and movement toward a more multicultural individual, and possibly world citizenship. Forty years have now passed, and the intercultural communication field of study and practice has expanded far beyond these early Japanese-American foundational efforts, including of course, its great development in Chinese educational institutions and associations.

13. India, 2003, 2005, 2011

From February 4 to 14, 2003 and again in 2005, I was invited to give lectures at Lucknow University and local institutes and as the house guest of Dr. Sangay Gupta, a professor of political science at the University. He and I visited Delhi; Varnassi, the birthplace of both Hinduism and Buddhism; and Agra in 2003. In 2005, I was accompanied by Beijing Language and Culture University postgraduate student in Chinese language David Li. He and I visited Delhi, Agra, Jaipur, and Mumbai. In

2011, I spent six days with several other shipmates in South India when the University of Virginia Semester at Sea ship was docked in Chennai.

Lucknow is among India's biggest cities, in the largest state of Utar Pradash (UP). Its official language is Hindi, and the second language for those educated or becoming educated is English. The majority of the population is Hindu with a minority of moderate Muslims. My longer visit there and short visits to Delhi, Junpur, and Varanasi–the holy city of the Buddhists and Hindus, suggest the confusion of cows, dogs, bikes, motorbikes, motorcycles, three wheeled auto or bike rickshaws, cars, and trucks all vying for space on the congested streets and roads.

In 2003, I was present in Lucknow for the Muslim feast of Eid: celebrating the Old Testament rescue of Isaac from the intended sacrifice by his father Abraham, and the miraculous appearance of a goat/sheep in the burning bush causing Isaac to be rescued. Muslim markets were filled the last two days before the festival (also a state holiday) with sales of many young goats bred especially to be slaughtered and eaten by families on this festival day. I was a guest with my Hindu friend Dr. Gupta at the home of his Muslim friend, where we had the opportunity to enjoy the goat that the family had selected for the festival. Women served the food and then retreated to the back of the house while the men and boys held lively conversations in the front rooms of the home.

In my lecture series from February 4–14, 2003 I gave eight lectures at Lucknow University and other local institutions. On February 7, I spoke on intercultural communication to about thirty very young MA students in mass communication, and I had a conversation with faculty on sustainable development at the Preperatory Institute for young rural men with a promising future in the civil service. On February 8, my lecture on the Universal Declaration of Human Rights, with comparisons of the rights for teenagers in the United States, Swaziland, and China, was given to 100–110 fifteen-seventeen year old boys at the Montfort School (sponsored by the St. Louis Montfort Catholic brothers). On the same day I spoke in the Public Administration Department of Lucknow University for faculty and about thirty MA students on the American presidency. On February 11, I spoke to thirty-five undergraduate students in the same department on intercultural communication. On February 12, I was the keynoter for a three hour symposium sponsored by the Sociology Department of the Jai Narain Degree Post Graduate College and the Circle for Child and Youth Research Cooperation on the

Universal Declaration of Human Rights with special emphasis on the rights of the child. My audience included forty very senior researchers.

On February 13, I spoke to 100+ eighteen and nineteen year old students at the Christian (Men's) College under the sponsorship of the Methodist Church on globalism and English as the global language, and I held a faculty conversation in the Department of Political Science at Lucknow University on the potential coming US/UK attack against Iraq. On February 14, my final lecture was to faculty and about 100 eighteen and nineteen year old students in the Law Department at Lucknow University on the Universal Declaration of Human Rights and international human rights law.

As Valentine day was a rather troublesome event in Lucknow, because of parental insistence of arranging their children's marriages through match making, traditionalists claimed that it as an example of the worst excesses of Western cultural invasion of Indian values–because it breeds romance in country with 95% of arranged marriages, where "love should not be the determining factor, but the wisdom of the parents in choosing correct choices for marriage." The Head of the Political Science Department canceled my scheduled lecture as "there could be troubles because of Valentine's Day and we don't want to put students in jeopardy." The newspapers, however, were filled with positive information about Valentine's day, as well as many short ads "I luv u." Several people with whom I discussed the issue, including students, estimated that still 95% of Indian marriages were arranged by the efforts of the parents for their children. Those who appreciated the ongoing Westernization of the culture argued that it was a day for love, not only in a romantic sense, but also for parents, family, and friends. Gupta's father started an aggressive quarrel with me as a Westerner for helping to bring such Western holidays as Valentine's Day to Asia and India. I was rather shocked, as except for that issue, which I didn't bring up myself, it was a very pleasant visit to their home.

Based on my experiences in India, the frequent Indian claim which I heard often from faculty and students that the Chinese were much more efficient than India seems justified. The extremes were very clear–with many middle and upper middle class Indian families, and the contrasting extreme poverty of most Indians. China then was still more than 50% rural and India remained 80% rural, but on the Eastern and southern coasts of China, a great deal of positive development had already occurerd, with many joint western ventures taking place. Around Lucknow, I saw no McDonalds (perhaps partly because of the Hindu relationship to the cow as sacred), but also no KFCs or Pizza Huts which were in clear abundance in many places in China where I traveled. Visual trends toward western development, thus, seemed to be much less in India than in China. A number of knowledgeable persons with whom I discussed the topic at their initiation, indicated that perhaps India had already surpassed China's population because so many poor Indians were uncounted in the census. Researchers claimed that with shifting populations, and many poor uneducated Indians having a child almost yearly for several years, India could already be larger than the 1.3 billion population of China.

Asked after my lecture to about seventy-five young men students in a three month course at the Rural Development Institute preparing them to take the civil service exam, why China was so much more advanced than India, Professor Gupta replied that India had a loose and often chaotic democracy with many parties, but a very tight and rigid bureaucratic regulation system which discouraged Western entrepreneurs to enter the market, while China had a tight one party system but a continually loosening control system for foreign companies entering the Chinese market. Statistics do show that systematically China has lifted more than one million peasants, rural and migrant workers, every month out of extreme poverty for the last decade or more. China has a very tight houkou or residence permit process, despite the large numbers of peasants who are flooding into the cities as migrant workers. This system controls population growth in the cities, but also actually creates problems as it often prevents migrant workers' children from entering local city schools. Fortunately, as this problem is being gradually solved as more country-wide benefits are reaching the poorest members, China is also making considerable progress in extending the benefits of primary and junior middle school education to more and more of the rural and migrant worker population. Education of course is a key to development everywhere. In India, while the caste system has officially ended, side by side, there are signs of great wealth, the increasing middle class as I saw at two lavish Hindu weddings there, and the most extreme forms of poverty.

Many young Chinese seem to hate the Japanese for the atrocities of the 1930's and 1940's, but many of the young Indians with whom I talked appeared to despise the Pakistanis, and wondered why the US had recently given Pakistan 2 billion dollars in aid, but hadn't done the same for India. I had no reasonable answers for the group and I realized more and more how little I knew about India. I discussed with Gupta the possibility of teaching a year at Lucknow University, but he indicated to my surprise that the University had essentially had no foreign teachers in the last decade, suggesting some academic isolation on the part of faculty and students there.

Later, in 2008, the terrorist attack in Mumbai was tracked to young Pakistani extremists. In Mumbai, it appears that 172 persons died, nearly 300 were injured, some seriously. CNN reports said that the terrorists had enough weapons, grenades, and ammunition to kill 5,000 people. The home minister of the area resigned. Apparently, there was intelligence chatter eight days before the attack that a large number of explosives were coming to shore on an Indian trawler, and then the inflatable rafts were coming into the shore. Indians protested on the streets near the hotels, angry that the Indian intelligence did not catch the problem earlier and because the Indian commandos took so long before trying to rescue the hostages and to confront the terrorists, but apparently some of the best Indian commandos had to fly from Delhi to Mumbai.

Following David Li's and my 2005 visit and my lectures then at Lucknow institutes of rural development, our host, Dr. Gupta, wrote the following about my essay "China continuing: Cross-cultural observations with India "in which I made more positive statements about Chinese statements than for India:

Your description/analysis about India is quite objective and worth reading. I agree to almost all what you say and also agree that China, more than any other country, today should become for us a role model of development. In spite of our humiliating defeat at the hands of China in 1962, I have always held China in great esteem because of the great vision of the Chinese leaders and statesmen. They have quite successfully pushed back the so-called disadvantage of their population behind their back. They have emerged as one of the greatest powers- military and economic- in today's world. They have minimized corruption and beggary, the two biggest evils of the developing countries. In some of the seminars on development, I have suggested that instead of our bureaucrats and politicians making yearly trips to the US or European countries, they should better go to China if they want to study about development and planning. Unfortunately, hypocrisy is so much embedded in the psyche of Indian leaders, that has most pathetically percolated in the masses, that nothing other than despair is visible in the near foreseeable future. But we can only hope that a silver lining comes up in the dark clouds soon.

Ford and Rockefeller Foundations made great efforts as early as the 1960's and following to help India voluntarily get its population situation stabilized. These efforts may have served to bring the average families down to 3–4 children instead of 6 or 7 in the past and reasonable success has been achieved in the 300 million middle class families and young singles who are now entering marriage and professional careers. However, in Mumbai, which has the reputation of having the most and worst slums in Asia, in 2005 David Li and I clearly and consistently saw this problem: the lack of effective population measures, extraordinary poverty, squalor, rubbish on the city streets, lack of proper sanitation, and loose roaming of cows, pigs, and other domestic animals, plus inadequate infrastructure which all have contributed to India's lack of development. We saw hundreds of shanties which may have measured not much more than two meters square with large families sharing the small space. Fires outside the shacks with a big wind could have easily caused a very large multi shack conflagration, destroying many kilometers of shacks in a row, and killing hundreds or probably thousands of extremely poor families in the process.

At the same time, early in the next decade, China may face a major population crisis as it now has only 100 girl babies being born annually to 119 boy babies. Recent statistics indicate that there are thirty million more males than females in China. There are rural loopholes for having a second child, and major cities are beginning to allow a second child under certain circumstances such as two single children marrying, the first child being a girl, wealth, and advanced education. In fact, Xi Jinping has now permitted a second child for couples who are both single children. Presently, however, as young adults enter the period of marriage, typically older for well-educated individuals and younger for less-educated ones, and an expected delay in having their child, the possibility for young men to find suitable wives will become increasingly difficult. It is an interesting contrast for them if they are now majors in universities related to the arts or foreign languages where they are outnumbered by about six or seven women to one man, but too young for marriage. Young Chinese women who have not married by about thirty are negatively perceived as "left over women." It is likely that China now has only about five years to begin seriously shifting even swiftly to a more relaxed one child policy supplemented by an increasing two children policy in an orderly fashion or the population crisis will be quite different than when the one child policy was implemented in 1978. Before that time, Mao Tsedong had urged couples to have large families to make China's development more rapid and powerful. In a sense, marriage could be considered more systematized in India as 75–95% of all marriages are still arranged by families and marriage brokers. It is a curious irony. India is striving to bring the population down by fewer births, and it is clear that the more educated middle class Indians are doing that. On the other hand, China is now having to begin allowing more couples to have two children to change the balance of far too many men and too few women at marriage age.

In terms of development, it seems obvious to me by my reading and observation with three trips to India that China is far more developed than India. When one comes into major cities like Beijing, Shanghai, Guangzhou, by plane, train, or car, there is the strong feeling of being in a highly developed society. I have not been in the much less urbanized areas in China's west. Going by taxi over twenty kilometers to the Mumbai airport, however, it took nearly two hours because of streets clogged with cars, motorcycles, three wheeled taxies, people, and animals. as a twenty kilometer distance, we should have gotten to the airport in a half hour. Complicating the situation, the vast rows of shanties and a Muslim festival parade coming in the opposite direction meant that thousands of very poor people were watching the parade and spilling into our road direction which already had four taxis cars, and motorcycles abreast in a road width that at best could handle two or three cars. For our taxi driver, it was a start-and-stop situation every few meters, and at each pause, there were a dozen different small hands or young mothers pushing their babies in the taxi windows begging for food or money.

Tourism is of course a major income goal for many developing countries, including the national tourist slogan "Incredible India," often accounting for 25% of the GNP of the countries, but both the lack of infrastructure and the overwhelming poverty of a country have a severe hampering effect on this sort of development and income production as is occurring in India. Rubbish and litter everywhere, roaming animals, the lack of sanitation, and the high amount of petty corruption that we faced, made it seem that India has a long road toward rural development, while China's rural development is much more steady and promising.

In the small group of shipmates for the 2011 Semester at Sea docking for six days in Chennai, one of the world's largest cities, we saw hopeful signs of sustainable development progress among 500 poor children being well educated in a privately owned school, and in a vastly expanding NGO Working Women's Forum, founded in 1978, and described as "a pioneer in social mobilization-strategy committed to transform over a million women in extreme poverty into powerful and confident leaders of many households, equal partners in community-neighborhoods." As identified in its literature as consisting of 11,030,726 women in 3,676 villages and 2,270 slums in three southern Indian states, whose credit initiatives reached five million poor women entrepreneurs, with 99% repayment rate, where 41% live on less than $1. Daily.

In July, 2011, Secretary of State Hilary Clinton, a long-time international advocate for women and children, visited the Forum and stated that the US Government continued to provide financial assistance in southern India to help women overcome violence against them and their children, and also to assist in the development agenda of creating smoke-free stoves for the women in their homes to help protect their respiratory health. The Forum had made a major grant proposal to the William J. Clinton Foundation, whose members were optimistic to receive because of Hilary Clinton's strong support.

In sum, it appears to me that while China is far ahead of India in most ways of developing more rapidly and poverty is gradually and systematically being overcome in China, but it appears to be growing exponentially in India, leaving more and more without education, health care, or normal social services. Religion, even in a secular state such as India, including Hinduism, Sikism, Jainism, and Islam, always has had a major function in development. In India's case, religious conflict is often detrimental to rapid development. Both countries have massive corruption, but China's tightly controlled media make it less visible than in India, the world's largest democracy. In my first two trips to India, 2003 and 2005, I had many good dialogues with faculty and students about poverty, their own comparisons with China's more rapid development.

On the Semester at Sea in 2011, we had two very good talks about the work of Oxfam India to alleviate poverty and promote sustainable development, and in Chennai, I was glad to see the progress of the excellent private family school for 500 poor, and very bright children, and to learn of the work of the NGO Working Women's Forum to help the women to help move out of abject poverty through its interactive programs and leadership.

14. Vietnam: 2004, 2011

My Beijing Language and Culture University senior student Nick Deng (19) and I completed a twelve day tour of Vietnam in February, 2004. Chinese leaders might call it our "Vietnam Inspection Tour." We began in Hanoi and proceeded south to Ho Chi Minh City (Saigon) on an open bus tour, returning to Beijing from there via Hanoi. Our travels took us to Hailong Bay (closest to China's Hai'nan Island and the scene of the US spy plane incident in 2000); Hue, the former imperial capital (with a deteriorating "forbidden city)"; Hoi An (near the central highlands and the setting for an old quarter during the French colonial era); Ho Chi Minh City; and the Mekong Delta in the far south (for a three day water tour of the delta and Mekong River). With visas for Cambodia from Hanoi, because of incorrect information we had too little time to enter Cambodia and return to Ho Chi Minh City to obtain a new Vietnamese visa since we only had a single entry visa.

Meeting many especially young Vietnamese among the population of about 80 million, we found them almost uniformly friendly and very kind, including to me as an American. Tourism was increasing steadily in the last few years, mostly with a large annual influx of Europeans. In fact, I saw many more western tourists in Vietnam than I was used to seeing in Chinese tourist locations. One reason was the very high value for very low costs. Europeans were making visits of several Southeastern countries as a part of their broader tours. Though there were Japanese, Korean, and Taiwanese tourists, Vietnam has a substantial Chinese diaspera population, we saw very few mainland Chinese tourists. This led various Vietnamese and European tourists to ask if Nick was my grandson. While Vietnam is considered among the poorest countries in Southeast Asia, but better than Laos, with the usual daily wage less than 15,675 dong ($1), most people in the cities were well dressed. All of the city streets and highways were clogged with motor bikes (usually considered a second step in development after bikes as a means of transportation). Many people also had mobile phones (certainly a major development step beyond transistor radios). We saw many operational Buddhist temples throughout Vietnam and Roman Catholic churches south of Hue. In the Hanoi international airport, we met several Vietnamese students returning to BLCU who had either seen me on campus, or had attended our Christmas concert in December, 2003.

"February 23, 2004 edition front cover showed John F. Kerry and George W. Bush: "The Battle Is Over Vietnam as much as Iraq." Thus it appeared to have been a very auspicious time for us to visit Vietnam. Robert S. McNamara's 1995 book, *In Retrospect: The Tragedy and Lessons of Vietnam* pointed out that during the 1962–1975 American undeclared war against Vietnam the United States mobilized 6.5 million young Americans, with a total force at one time of 543,400 men and women, 70% from the army, 60% from the air force, 60% from the marines, and 40% from the navy. He reported that 7,850,000 tons of bombs were dropped on Vietnam, plus 75,000,000 liters of defoliants, including dioxin, which were dropped on croplands, farmlands, forestlands, and villages in the southern part of the country. According to figures made public by the US government, 352 billion dollars were spent for the war. In North Vietnam, bombs and bullets destroyed or seriously damaged 2,923 school buildings, 1,850 hospitals, 484 churches, and 465 temples and pagodas; most roads, bridges, and rail lines in northern Vietnam were destroyed and had to be rebuilt after the war ended in 1975. Nearly 3 million Vietnamese died, and another 4 million were injured. More than 58,000 Americans died in the war. (McNamara, 1995).

During our travel, I read McNamara's book; Bao Ninh's independent foreign fiction award book, *The Sorrow of War* (1990); much of the 2003 *Lonely Planet: Vietnam;* and *The Many Faces of Vietnam: The Man Who Made a Nation* (2002). I also read Neil L. Jamieson's *Understanding Vietnam* (1999) and Frank Snepp's *Decent Interval: An Insider's Account of Saigon's Indecent End Told by the CIA's Chief Strategy Analyst in Vietnam* (1997). These books were widely available from street peddlers. Much earlier, I had also read parts of the *Pentagon Papers* from 1967–1969 which became a Supreme Court case: New York Times vs.US. In *The*

Sorrow of War, Ninh's final page notes that he and his fictional author "shared a common sorrow, the immense sorrow of war. It was a sublime sorrow, more sublime than happiness, and beyond suffering" (p. 217). *Lonely Planet: Vietnam* makes the very interesting point that in fact despite the victory of Vietnam militarily, the South won the war economically. We observed this as well.

In Hanoi, in addition to seeing Ho Chi Minh in his mausoleum (and in 1959, I had seen Stalin and Lenin in their mausoleum in Moscow), we visited the Ho Chi Minh Museum. His displayed writings suggest that Uncle Ho (as he is widely called in Vietnam) was more of a nationalist than a hardline Soviet/Chinese styled Communist, but in *The Many Faces of Vietnam,* it is quite clear that he was not only a nationalist, but an ardent and very early Marxist-Leninist. While the one yellow star on red background flag was dominant wherever we visited in Vietnam, there were also various red flags with the hammer and sickle flying (no longer present in Russia nor China) and sculptures and large poster drawings displaying the hammer and sickle. *Lonely Planet: Vietnam* notes, however, that for the most part Marxism-Leninism has disappeared in Vietnam as a guiding philosophy in favor of the market economy.

In a long private conversation with a hotel manager in the Mekong Delta, he indicated that while there were still a lot of official government statements relating to Communist principles, the market economy was now the dominant guideline for the rising lower, but still relatively poor middle class in Vietnam. As I saw in Russia in 1959 and 1989 and currently in China, the children wore the required red scarves of the Young Pioneers. Apparently also, as is the case of the Chinese Communist Party, the Vietnamese Communist Party controlled almost all aspects of life at least in principle but not in terms of the thriving market economy. The hotel manager said that all of the very nice looking homes throughout Vietnam belonged to VCP members, and that corruption at various levels remained one of the major problems that the Vietnamese Communist Party was trying to eliminate, often without success because many top leaders were also corrupt.

From Saigon, we visited the reconstructed Cu Chi tunnels which the Vietcong and Vietminh had built over a 200 kilometer network in the southern tropical forests which helped them wage a low level guerilla warfare against the Americans and South Vietnamese troops. Our guide had been a child during the final French-IndoChinese War in the early

1950's and later a soldier working with the South Vietnamese army and the American Air Force. After 1975, he spent two years in the Communist reeducation camp. Before the mid1960s, his goal had been to become a Catholic priest. He said that he was reconciled to life under the Communist government, or he would have been among the three million Vietnamese from the South who fled in the 1970s.

The war Remnants Museum in Saigon (called the War of American Aggression Museum before the restoration of diplomatic relations between Vietnam and the US in 1995) displayed many photos of American brutality and cruelty as documented by American publications such as *Life Magazine*. It may not have been an exaggeration to compare the somber reflections which the scenes in this museum appeared to cause tourists, mostly Europeans, while we were present with the equally shocked reactions toward the Nazi atrocities of those visiting the Holocaust Museum in Washington, D.C. which I visited in 1993.

My 1960's-1970's contact with the Vietnam war as a young faculty member was based primarily on media images and the protest demonstrations against the war which occurred both in America and throughout the world. At the State University of Buffalo where I taught from 1963–1969, there were many "teach-ins" on the war toward the end of the 1960s. In 1978, I taught as a visiting faculty member at Kent State University where the May 4, 1970 killing of the five students still remained a dominant and controversial theme particularly around the anniversary itself. While teaching in Beijing, I decided to visit one Asian country during each Lunar New Year university holiday, beginning by giving eight lectures at Lucknow University in Lucknow, India in 2003. For 2004, Vietnam seemed to me a most appropriate place to visit to get a better understanding of the Vietnam-US 1962–1975 conflict, and to see how the current Vietnam was developing, now with massive American investments and aid. It was an enlightening experience particularly with this theme resurfacing in the early 2004 US election period between the two Yale University graduates in the 1960s, Kerry who served briefly in Vietnam, and Bush who served during the war in the Texas National Guard.

In 2011, with a group of Semester at Sea shipmates, I returned once more to Vietnam. In a public forum on board the ship, we heard two American veterans tearfully recounting their tragic experiences in the War, but in our six day visit, while many students visited the tunnels and museums in Hanoi and Ho Chi Minh City, and undertook volunteer work in Vietnamese orphanages and Habitat for Humanity, I am embarrassed to say that I joined a group which spent much of the period lazily at a Vietnamese resort, tailored to western guests. By this time, we had already spent more than half of the voyage visiting five countries in Africa and India, and so perhaps a break in our hectic experiences before was warranted. Nonetheless, I was sorry that I was unengaged in social justice issues in my 2011 visit to Vietnam which had dominated our African and Indian experiences earlier on the voyage. So many of the Semester at Sea students, faculty, staff, families and lifelong participants were involved in social justice issues in Vietnam while I and about fifteen others were lounging at a Vietnamese resort, designed for European visitors of whom quite a few of them were present.

15. Cambodia: 2005, 2010

For the Spring Festival holiday and Chinese Lunar New Year, 2005, my senior Beijing Language and Culture University student Sean (Shawn) Chen and I planned to visit Indonesia (which Jacky Zhang and I did visit in 2010), with our air tickets booked, but we changed plans after the December 26, 2004 earthquake and tsunami. We considered traveling to India or the Philippines, but finally we decided to go to Cambodia. We visited the world heritage Angkor Wat, and traveled on a number of nearly impossible country roads, with our own driver and his assistant, kindly recommended by Professor Thomas M. Steinfatt of the University of Miami whose book *Working at the Bar: Sex Work and Health Communication in Thailand* (2002) had been published in my "Civic Discourse for the Third Millennium" series. He also organized having me give a lecture to seventy-five students at the Royal University in Phnom Penh.

Early Chinese records report the Cambodians "as black, ugly and naked" (*Lonely Planet 2002, Cambodia,* p. 11). At that time, the Cambodian government estimated that there were 50,000 ethnic Chinese in the country, but unofficial estimates were close to 500,000 out of the total population of twelve million. In 1970, after a coup against Norodom Sihanouk, he took up residence in Beijing as a government in exile, nominally in control of an indigenous Cambodian revolutionary movement to which gave itself the name Khmer Rouge. (Red Khmers). The Chinese government was eager to destroy the successor government of Lon nol. The 1969–1973 US bombing in Eastern Cambodia against the 40,000 Vietcong and North Vietnamese troops there probably killed more than 250,000 Cambodians.

On April 17th, 1975, two weeks before the fall of Saigon, Phnom Penh surrendered to the Khmer Rouge whose goal was to transform Cambodia into "a Maoist peasant dominated agrarian society from the 1958–1960 disastrous model of Mao Tsedong. The capital and other major cities were almost completely emptied of residents. Sihanouk had returned to Phnom Penh as titular head of state, but was imprisoned in the palace and kept alive only at the insistence of the Chinese government which was providing the Khmer Rouge extensive military aid in exchange for nearly Cambodia's rice produce during that period. Later, during some of the worst excesses of Khmer Rouge's brutality against all levels of Cambodian society, the Chinese helped him return to Beijing in 1978 during the Vietnamese invasion of Cambodia (*Lonely Planet, 2002,* p. 19).

This period of Khmer Rouge's brutality has been amply illustrated in the movie "The Killing Fields" (1984) and in such books as Ben Kiernan's 1994 book *The Pol Pot Regime: Race, Power and Genocide in Cambodia under Khmer Rouge, 1975–1979* (1996) *(1;* the book "*Children of Cambodia's Killing Fields*" edited by Kim de Paul, compiled by Dith Pran, and introduced by Ben Kiernan (1984); and Loung Ung's 2000 book, *First They Killed My Father: A Daughter of Cambodia Remembers* (2000). Kiernan discusses Chinese aid for the Khmer Rouge regime when more than two million Cambodians were tortured, forced to work as peasants for 12–15 hours a day and executed.

In April 1975, China agreed to provide 13,300 tons of weapons to the Khmer Rouge plus supplies such as tools, salt and rice. "Brother Number One," Pol Pot, met Mao in June, 1975 in Beijing and in September China agreed to provide the Khmer Rouge government $ 1 billion in interest-free economic and military aid, including an immediate $20 million gift, "the biggest aid ever given to any one country by China (Kiernan, pp. 125–131).When Zhou En-Lai died in January, 1976, the Cambodian foreign ministry stated,"We must beware of China…She wants to make us her satellite." Still, Cambodia continued to request military and non-military aid and equipment from China (pp. 135–139). A leading Khmer

Rouge government slogan in 1976 was "The organization excels Lenin and is outstripping Mao" (p. 148). During this period, besides killing many educated Cambodians, and especially those speaking French, or wearing glasses, many of the Chinese diaspora and the Cambodian Buddhist monks were also killed.

Sean and I visited many of the Phnom Penh's tourist attractions such as the national museum, the royal palace, and the Buddhist pagodas, as well as the spectacular temples at Angkor Wat near Siam Reap, and the northwest Thai border at Poipet ("The wild west frontier"). However, one of our most important visits was to the Genocide Museum: Tuol Sleng, Khmer Rouge's-21 prison, and earlier a secondary school in Phnom Penh, established in the former school in May 1976. Is meaning in Khmer was "a poisonous hill or mound to keep those who bear or supply guilt [against Angkor]." Here, 10,499 adults and 2,000 children were photographed, tortured, and later killed. The shackled prisoners had to request permission for any change of position or even to relieve themselves. All prisoners had to abide by the following ten regulations:

"You must answer accordingly to my questions. Do not turn them away. 2. Do not try to hide the facts by making pretexts of this and that. You are strictly prohibited to contest me. 3. Do not be a fool for you are a chap who dares to thwart the revolution. 4. You must immediately answer my questions without wasting time to reflect. 5. Do not tell me either about your immoralities or the revolution. 6. While getting lashes or electrification you must not cry at all. 7. Do nothing. Sit still and wait for my orders. If there is no order, keep quiet. When I ask you to do something, you must do it right away without protesting. 8. Do not make pretexts about Kampuchea Krom in order to hide your jaw of traitor. 9. If you do not follow all the above rules, you shall get many lashes of electric wire. 10. If you disobey any point of my regulations you shall get either ten lashes or five shocks of electric discharge" (Prison flyer).

Additionally, we visited the actual "killing fields of Choeung Ek," fifteen kilometers south of Phnom Penh, with the mass graves and the monument filled with skulls, mostly cracked open during the executions to save bullets. Like the images from Nazi death camps, the Antiwar Museum in Ho Chi Minh City and, the Holocaust Museum in Washington D.C., Tuol Sleng and the "killing fields" provided an overwhelming portrait of evil such as that described in Bao Ninh's 1998 book *The Sorrow of War* related to the 1962–1975 Vietnam conflict.

Besides meeting a number of Chinese tourists from mainland China and Taipei during our thirteen days in Cambodia and celebrating the Chinese Lunar New Year, an incident in Phnom Penh gave me my first experience with traditional Chinese medicine. On February 13, I fell in our guest house bathroom, breaking my left wrist, badly spraining my left ribs, and sustaining various minor bruises. Our guide and diver took us to Tong Seng Chinese Hospital where a traditional Chinese bone setter, newly arrived from Harbin, took x-rays and then massaged my broken bones back into place, using only rubbing alcohol as an anesthetic. Though I was not swearing, I repeated the vowels in the alphabet several times, and sang to ease my pain for the nurses and Sean. Over three days, with a combination of ivis and Chinese herbal soup daily, the doctor took additional x-rays and massaged the bones more tightly into their position with a cast made out of cardboard, cotton and tape. A dark joke that we made was that the bone setter was actually a member of the Krmer Rouge torturing me as one of his victims.

I was unable to continue traveling to Sihanoukville, and as we sat along the Mekong Delta, meeting many persistent Cambodian vendors, and three young Buddhist monks. We spent several hours daily talking to them, as they returned to meet us daily, discussing their Buddhist beliefs, their educational progress, especially in learning English and computer competence, and the possibility that when they completed their education supported by the monastery, they would leave the monastery and get married. We learned when they used their begging bowls without sandals and when they would give coins to poverty-stricken women, children, and old men during the periods where they wore their sandals. In this way, they contributed to the monastery both by begging, particularly from the Western tourists and wealthy Cambodians, but also distributing their received funds to those who were poorer than they were.

On the day before returning to Beijing, facilitated through the kind assistance of Thomas M. Steinfatt, I gave a previously committed power point lecture on intercultural, cross-cultural and multi-cultural communication to seventy-five freshmen and sophomore English, media and tourism majors at the Royal University of Phnom Penh with my left arm in the cast and sling. Because of frequent electricity outages, I had more time for questions and answers as the lecture proceeded. I compared Mao's Cultural Revolution and Pol Pot's brutal excesses during the 1975–1979 periods. Also, having my Chinese English major Sean with me, I asked him to give comments about being Chinese and an English major in a Chinese university. Though a number of the students took notes from the power point slides, and there were several good questions, it was not clear how much most of the students understood as I had very little personal dialogue with them. Despite my injuries, it was a good ending to our Cambodian visit. Sean certainly was a good caretaker for me after I broke my wrist. He spent two years as a translator for Chinese managers of a lumber export company in Guyana, and now, married, he works for an emigration service in Xiamen University in Xiamen, China.

During my two week travel to Thailand in 2010 with Jacky Zhang, we decided rather spontaneously to spend several days in Cambodia, crossing the border from Thailand in "the wild west" so that he could see the World Heritage site at Angkor Wat, which also included our first elephant ride. We became aware that Cambodian young people whom we met were poorer than those that we met in Thailand, but they seemed equally happy, seeing a more prosperous future for themselves and their families. Even though their grandparents had suffered greatly during the 1975–79 "end of history and beginning of a new history from day 1," the influx of Western investments, aid, and tourists was making their future looking much brighter.

We also had a desire to visit Laos during this brief period in Cambodia and Thailand, but there was not enough time to visit all three countries.

16. South Korea: 1980, 2004

In January 1980, under the sponsorship of the United States Information Agency and as guest of the US cultural attaches, I had the opportunity to give several lectures at South Korean universities in Seoul and in Pusan during a very bitter winter and also in Singapore with tropical weather, giving me two very different experiences, plus travel in Malaysia as a side trip from Singapore. Visiting the National Museum in Seoul, my South Korean USIA guide gave me several very strong South Korean anti-Chinese reminders on the many generations of China's occupation of South Korea, and of Chinese aggressive volunteer involvement in the

Korean War, where more than a half million Chinese soldiers died in the battles and from the harsh cold, whose involvement he claimed could never be entirely forgiven. Despite these past national aggressions, he praised the much improved relations and trade between the two countries, and stressed their joint antagonism against the Japanese for multiple transgressions against the two countries in the 1930s and 1940s. He also predicted, incorrectly, that before 2000, the two countries would be reunited, but impoverishing South Korea with the efforts to improve the collapsing North Korean society. Personally, this experience in South Korea, Singapore, Japan where I visited several of my previous Japanese MA students, and Malaysia moved me more towards becoming Asiacentric, as it developed more rapidly during the early 2000s.

From May 1 (International Labor Day) until May 10, 2004, my 21 year old BLCU senior student, Tony Weitong, and I visited Seoul, Pusan in the south, Gyeonjui in the east, Gwangjiu in the west, plus their corresponding coastlines, and Incheon in the northwest. We also spent some time related to learning about the earlier North/South war, including the assistance to South Korea of American and other United Nations forces against North Korea, and also the aggression of the Chinese volunteer army. We visited the 1953 established DMZ (demilitarized zone), and the monument and museum for the allied landing in Incheon in 1950 which led to the War's cessation (still never concluded with a peace treaty). At the DMZ which is patrolled by South Korean and American troops in the South, we saw the "freedom bridge" where the exchange of South and North Korean prisoners of war had occurred in 1953. Looking over the DMZ, we could see the long four kilometer horizontal strip separating the two countries, ("no man's land") which has become one of the most pure natural environmental and ecologically balanced areas in Asia. We also toured one of the five North Korean "infiltration tunnels" which had been found in the late 1980s by the South Korean military. The five tunnels together would have allowed 200,000 North Korean soldiers to enter South Korea undetected in an hour's time and able to advance to Seoul directly to Seoul, less than forty kilometers away. One potential tour which interested us was a visit to Pyeonggang Village where 200 South and North Koreans lived reasonably harmoniously at that time, but it was closed to South Koreans and Chinese, meaning that Tony could not go there.

The South Koreans were uniformly kind and helpful to Tony and me, some going blocks out of their way to assist us. We were surprised that English was much less familiar to many of the ordinary Koreans than Nick and I had found among ordinary Vietnamese. I was a natural magnet for children, then having eight grandchildren, plus newly arrived Luke Patrick who was born while Tony and I were in South Korea. Because we were also there on their children's day holiday, May 5. In a group of 12 or 13 year olds at a museum, one very humorous boy, would say: "my name — Michael Jordan [then] oooooooooohhhh, [then] my name — Michael Jackson [then] oooooooooohhh, [then] my name — George Bush [then] oooooooooohhh [then referring and pointing to my white beard] my name — Santa Claus [then] oooooooooohhh." Each time that he would do this, the children would all join in the chorus. All over South Korea, teen aged girls would go into fits of giggling when they met Tony [perhaps the first Chinese that they had met?] and me. Or were they giggling at meeting both of us or just me? With 37,000 American military still stationed then in South Korea, I was surprised that it seemed the first time they had met an American and making such an enthusiastic response to my presence.

In Pusan, there was a very large and graphic street exhibit of Falun Gong (Falun Dafa) persecutions in China, including Tinanamen Square beatings. Though I had talked about such events more generally in my classes at BLCU, it was profoundly disturbing to Tony to see this criticism of his own government's actions toward Falun Gong members. He was torn between his intense anger that the Korean authorities would allow such an Anti-Chinese government exhibit on a well-traveled walking street, and his incredulous amazement that the Chinese government might be persecuting its own citizens so brutally and that neither he nor his student friends had been aware of these persecutions. Often when I had mentioned such activities in classes at BLCU, I could see the polite but highly skeptical raised eyebrows by my own students doubting whether I really knew what I was talking about since neither the regular or social media covered such events. If there was a rare student verbal response, it was often framed in "well, they are an evil cult and would do great harm to China if the government didn't control them." When I gently mentioned this event in some classes the following week at BLCU, students who were now regularly watching CNN in their dormitory rooms rejoined: "But see what the American soldiers are doing to prisoners in the Iraq prisons!" It was sort of a "gotcha" moment for those brave enough to make such comments in class.

English language media seemed much more limited in South Korea than in Vietnam. On tv in our small and low budget South Korean hotels, we could see CNN and South Korea's Arirang TV, which I could also see in Beijing, but almost nothing else in English. Where the small Vietnamese hotels had several English language programs and China's CCTV International in English on tv, we weren't aware of much else in English in South Korea. We did find *International Herald Tribune, Korea Times,* and *Korea Herald* newspapers at the newsstands. The latter two papers had lots of factual and opinion articles both about the prisoner situation in Iraq, as well as about Chinese Premier Wen Jiabao's "cooling down the economy" decision, which the two Korean English language newspapers argued was highly detrimental to Korean and other Asian country interests as it would seriously reduce their exports to China.

My grandson Luke was born in the US during our 2004 visit to South Korea. On our last night before returning to China from Incheon, we located a low price hotel some distance from the airport, but found to our rather innocent surprise that it was a "red light" hotel. I warned Tony not to answer the door of our room as it could be a man expecting to meet a woman there.

Tony became a China Radio International reporter after graduation, with a five minute daily positive story about different African countries, and later he served for two and a half years as its reporter in Eastern Africa and located in Nairobi. He has now completed his master's degree in international communication in London and was an intern at a company in Montreal for some time in 2014. He remains one of my best Chinese friends and visited me when I was teaching in Ocean University of China in Qingdao in 2011 and Yangzhou University in 2013–14.

I have been in the Incheon Airport several times traveling to or from China and in 2011, I spent a very quiet night at one of the airport area hotels going to and from Qingdao, China.

17. The Semester at Sea: 2011

As I have noted above, for the autumn semester of 2011, I was the faculty advisor for sixty-one lifelong learners on the University of Virginia/Institute for Shipboard Learning around the world Semester at Sea study voyage. There were 451 undergraduate students on board, thirty-six faculty, thirty staff members, fifty-four dependents, including about twenty-five children (with their own classroom), sixty-one lifelong learners for the whole voyage, plus an extra twenty who joined us in Costa Rica, and 187 mostly Filipino crew members. Traveling twenty eight thousand nautical miles, we spent fifty-five days at sea, and fifty-six days on land. We were on land six days each in Morocco, Ghana, South Africa, India, Malaysia, Vietnam, China, and Japan, as well as shorter visits to Mauritius, Hawaii, Costa Rica and Honduras and passing through the Panama Canal from the Pacific Ocean to the Atlantic Ocean. Beginning in 1974 and continuing while teaching in China, I had already been to South Africa eight times in 1990–91, plus the five Asian countries which we visited on the Semester at Sea voyage, but the 2011 visits added to my knowledge base.

Recently in a conversation with an American university graduate student, wearing a Semester at Sea shirt, we discussed whether an experience with many short country visits such as the Semester at Sea or a longer period in an overseas location a more in depth semester abroad period in a single country is a more valuable global learning experience. She strongly favored the latter experience, while I argued in favor of both opportunities as beginning to open students' minds toward becoming more intercultural, multicultural, and global citizens. One of my sons spent a Denmark International Semester in Copenhagen, giving me some thoughts on both a multicultural experience such as was provided to students on the Semester at Sea voyage. Naturally, the young woman and I both agreed that living, working, or studying either as a sojourner or a settler for a long time in another country is the most important possible situation for expanding our global vision. For me, the Semester at Sea experience enhanced my living and teaching in China and gave me the opportunity to discuss this experience with many Americans on the voyage. My professional writing in the Communication Research and Theory Network (www.crtnet.org) and my own blog (www.michaelprosser.com) as well as my articles and books about Asia and China have further extended my knowledge and contributions for Asia and China in focus. In my preface, I have noted my own publications related to Asia and especially China, which developed out of my life-world experiences in the broader region and in four cities in China.

The opportunity for those who have not traveled much internationally on a study voyage such as the Semester at Sea offers, or a semester abroad, becomes an option and creates future possibilities for global openness. In my case, it was an experience near the end of my professional career. The period from 2001–14, was a complement and a still broadening period for my already forty years of teaching, including summer teaching in Canada (1972 and 1975) and my Fulbright teaching in Swaziland (1990–91). An important advantage of a study voyage such as the Semester at Sea over a regular cruise (which I have done two — Australia and New Zealand with Jacky Zhang, and my cruise trip alone, Argentina, Uruguay, and Chile) is that it provides a more intense active learning environment rather than a passive one. In my case, I was not teaching undergraduate students on the Semester at Sea. It nonetheless reconnected me with many North American and other students and their current values and habits after teaching for a long time in China. Additionally, since our program in 2011 was oriented towards global studies, with a strong emphasis on social justice and empowerment, such a program leads many students to suggest that it was a life changing experience. There are statistics which demonstrate that it is often the first step toward a greater sense of global citizenship, future travel, study or living overseas, and volunteerism in their future lives.

PART FOUR
MY JOURNEY TO THE EAST: CHINA IN FOCUS

18. Contemporary Chinese Youth: Language and Culture

In *Olga Leontovich (Ed.). (2010). Chinese Linguoculture in the Modern Global World. Volgograd: Peremena Press.*

Abstract: Contemporary Chinese youth is a concept which can be applied to the People's Republic of China since its founding in 1949, the Great Proletariat Cultural Revolution and the 1989 Tiannamen Square tragedy, or in its even more contemporary setting, since the since the death of Chairman Mao Tsedong in September 1976, and the "opening up" of China beginning in 1978. This essay explores the more recent contemporary period as today's Chinese youth were born at about the time of the "opening up" or more recently and are frequently called "the post-80s generation." the author discusses the importance of the Chinese and English languages in the Chinese educational system, and the cultural characteristics of these Chinese youth. Conclusions and references are provided.

Keywords: Chinese youth and Chinese language; contemporary Chinese youth and English language; contemporary Chinese youth culture; post-80s generation.

Introduction: We can recall Chairman Mao Tsedong's famous quote calling Chinese students in Moscow in 1957 the future of China: "The world is yours as well as ours, but in the last analysis it is yours. You young people, full of vigor and vitality, are in the bloom of life, like the sun at eight or nine in the morning. Our hope is placed on you. The world belongs to you. China's future belongs to you" (1957).

    John H. Powers and Randy Kluver describe the emergence of a civil society in China: "contemporary China is heir to a civilization that traces its ancestry continuously for at least for at least 2,500 years. So, in one sense, China may have the longest sustained history of civic discourse of any nation in the world. In a different sense, however, contemporary China has been in the process of building a truly civil society only since the death of Mao in 1976.... The period between the end of the imperial system in 1911 and the founding of the People's Republic of China (PRC) in 1949 was characterized by fragmentation, civil war, and Japanese occupation, wherein little progress was made toward the evolution of civil society in the modern sense. From the founding of the People's Republic to the death of Mao, the development of "civil society with Chinese characteristics" floundered while the nation lurched from one top-driven political movement to another as Mao sought to implement his rigid ideological program. Only with Mao's death, in some views, did the seeds for a budding civil society find the conditions for sustained growth and development" (1999, p. 1).

In the study of intercultural communication, we have many theoretical, conceptual, and practical dimensions to understand. for example, it is possible to say that intercultural communication relates to communication taking place at the intersection between cultures; on one hand, (cultural dialogue) which stresses unity, universal harmony (a very Confucian concept, strongly endorsed by Chinese President Hu Jintao) and similarities among cultures, and on another hand, cross-cultural communication is a comparative and contrastive understanding of cultural phenomena between cultural groups or societies, often implying that one is better or worse than the other (cultural critique) and demonstrating differences and division between and among cultures (Stewart 1972; Prosser, 1978). A study of China's youth is increasingly a study of intercultural and cross-cultural communication particularly as they compare themselves more and more to American youth and as there are 350 million Chinese learning English.

Molefi Asante, Cecil Blake, and Eileen Newmark began their co-edited *Handbook of Intercultural Communication* (1980) by identifying these two major trends at the time in the study of intercultural communication, and noting that my books were an exemplar of the "cultural dialogue" approach while the social psychologist, early Peace Corp trainer and author of American Cultural Patterns, Edward C. Stewart (1972), represented well the "cultural criticism" approach (1980). There are various levels of difficulty in studying or even communicating interculturally: language or sociolinguistic elements; nonverbal cues, behaviors and customs; subjective versus objective culture (the intangible culture of the mind versus tangible objects or artifacts of culture); including at the subjective cultural level, attitudes, stereotypes, prejudices, beliefs, and the deepest, but most invisible aspect of one's mental culture, values (Prosser, 1978).Young Chinese must work through these levels just as international students, managers, teachers, and employees in international trade in China or those without a university education must do. Language would appear to be at a very high level of intercultural difficulty, but in China it is less difficult to overcome linguistic problems than it was even a decade ago, particularly for those who are college or university educated or are living in very cosmopolitan cities.

During the 1958–60 period, the grandparents of contemporary Chinese youth suffered greatly in the man-made famine that killed nearly 30 million people (see Becker, 2002). The Great Proletarian Cultural Revolution (1966–1976) is gradually being discussed among Chinese leaders and current young people, though many young Chinese prefer to adapt Deng Xiaoping's statement "To get rich is glorious," before they concern themselves very much with politics, which they leave to Communist party and government leaders (typically the same leaders). The Cultural Revolution very seriously affected their grandparents and parents often in a highly negative manner. More than 600,000 died in the Cultural Revolution at the hands frequently of extremist young "Red Guards" (see J. Chang, 1991; CNN: "The cold war series: 'The Chinese, 1949–1972,'"1998–99; Prosser for a review of three dozen books about China, 2007). "Cultural revolutions" occurred not only in China but in the west for example in France, Germany, The United States and even in Russia from approximately 1965–1975. (See CNN "The cold war series: 'The sixties: make love, not war.' and 'The sixties: the Russians,'"(1998–99).

The United Nations defines youth as between the ages of 15 and 34. James Farrer, for the purpose of his study of Chinese youth, in his case writing mainly about young single women, (qingnian) in Shanghai during the 1990s, identifies youth as from the ages of 18 to 34 (2002). In the midst of this unprecedented social and cultural change, and wondering publicly about the world-wide youth revolt, while speculating on the future of youth, the anthropologist Margaret Mead wrote: "As I see it, children today face a future that is so deeply unknown that it cannot be handled, as we are currently attempting to do, as a generational change with cofiguration [cultures without the presence of grandparents, or as demonstrated primarily through one's contemporaries — often young themselves], within a stable, elder-controlled and parentally modeled culture in which many postfigurative elements [typically in the presence of three generations, but often in an unchanging cultural pattern — a culture of the past] are incorporated.... for the figure of migration in space (geographical migration), I think we must substitute a new figure, migration in time.... even very recently, the elders could say: "You know, I have been young and you have never been old." But today's young people can reply: "You have never been young in the world I am young in, and you never can be." Today, suddenly, because all the peoples of the world are part of one electronically based, intercommunicating network, young people everywhere share a kind of experience that none of the elders ever have had or will have. Conversely, the older generation will never see repeated in the lives of young people their own unprecedented experience of sequentially emerging change. This break between generations is wholly new; it is planetary and universal (1970: pp. 48–50).

During the long period of the Mao cult (see Sun, 2006), he insisted on being called "the four greats: great leader, great helmsman, great commander in chief, and great teacher." Jung Chang has provided a particularly poignant first-hand account of her life as a youth and her mother and grandmother during the Cultural Revolution, when she moved from being an ordinary teenage student, to a Red Guard, and then losing and regaining her ability to achieve an education during that period: *Wild Swans: Three Daughters of China* (1991). Later she and her husband Jon Haliday, after ten years of research, published *Mao: The Untold Story* in which they claimed that Mao was responsible for 70 million deaths in peace time and was willing to lose half the population of China for his nuclear weapons ambitions (2005). Chang and Haliday seriously challenged all four of "the greats" which Mao attributed to himself. A few of my close young Chinese friends dismissed this book, without reading it, as "rubbish," despite the fact that it has more than 80 pages of reputable notes (see also Shuyun, 2006; August, 2007).

Following the death of Zhou Enlai in January, 1976 (see Gao, 2007) and after the September 9, 1976 death of Chairman Mao (the title a designation given him by Stalin in 1938), Deng Xiaoping (see Evans, 1993;

Deng Rong, 2002), was in and out of power again, but only briefly out of power after Mao's death. He called Eleventh National Party Congress, August 12–18, 1977, which was often identified as "a major turning point in modern Chinese political history." At the Third Plenum, the Party announced that the formal end of the Cultural Revolution had occurred and its later extremism was entirely the fault of the "Gang of Four." Madame Mao- Jiang Qing and her partners, Zhang Chunqiao, Wang Hongwen, and W. Jiang and Zhang's death sentences at their trial were committed to life imprisonment; Wang was given a life sentence, and Yao was given twenty-years in prison. Jiang died in prison. At the Plenum, the Party identified that "The fundamental task of the Party in the new historical period is to build China into a modern, powerful Socialist country by the end of the twentieth century." Two "corrections" were made, recognizing the "left" errors, and the two "Whatevers policy ("support whatever policy decisions that Chairman Mao made and follow whatever instructions Chairman Mao gave") The new policy was no longer to support class struggle, but to replace it with the "four modernizations," articulated first by Zhou Enlai in 1974 and promoted by Deng in 1978 with a dedicated 36% of China's GCP (agriculture, industry, technology, and defense) and "seeking truth from facts."

At the September, 1979 Fourth Plenum, Vice Chairman Ye Jianying stated that the "Cultural Revolution" was an appalling catastrophe" and "the most severe setback to [the] Socialist cause since [1949]." At the sixtieth anniversary of the founding of the Communist Party of China, not long after, Hu Yaobang announced that "although comrade Mao Zedong made grave mistakes in his later years, it is clear that if we consider his life work, his contributions to the Chinese revolution far outweighs his errors … his immense contributions are immortal" (www.countrystudies.us).

Currently, Chinese university students are hard pressed to remember the day or month that Mao died, but all of the modern currency bills have Mao's photo; it hangs above the entrance from Tiananmen Square entrance to the Forbidden City, his mausoleum lies at the opposite end of the Square; and at the October 1, 2009 Sixtieth Anniversary parade, four immense banners featured Mao, Deng, Jiang Zemin, and Hu Jintao (representing the fourth generation of leaders in the PRC). Some commentators argued that instead of celebrating the entire sixty years since the founding of the People's Republic, only the last thirty years should have been remembered. In fact, in 2008, there were widespread celebrations of the thirtieth anniversary of China's "opening up" policy under Deng Xiaoping. Additionally, every Chinese child, teenager, student admitted to a college or university, and every student admitted to a postgraduate program must pass tests on Marxism-Leninism, Mao Tsedong Thought, Deng Xiaoping Theory, and Zemin's "three Represents," promulgated in the Chinese Communist Party Constitution at the March 2002 Sixteenth Party Congress: advanced social productive forces (representing economic production); advanced culture (representing cultural development); and interests of the overwhelming majority of the people (representing political consensus). (*Baidu Encyclopedia,* 2010).

During this period (1979) under the leadership of Deng for China and President Jimmy Carter for the US, the two countries established diplomatic relations, seven years after president Richard Nixon's historic visit to China in February, 1972 (see Macmillan, 2007; for a time line for China from 1960–1999, see Heilig, 2008, May 15).

Also, during this period, the one-child policy was promulgated which over time has, according to government accounts, reduced the population by 400 million or by nongovernmental sources, 250–300 million (Yardley, 2008 March 11). It appears from my very informal questions in various classes that among my 2200 Chinese students, approximately 80% have been single children. The rising nationalism in China's youth has been described as in the Mao Zedong era, "Chinese people have stood up" (referring to the 1971 'ping pong diplomacy'), in the Deng Xiaoping period as "Rejuvenate China!" (referring to the women's volleyball successes), after 1990, as "The great revitalization of the Chinese nation" (referring to the success of China in the Asian games), hampered, however, by the unsuccessful Chinese bid in 1993 following the Tiananmen Square event of 1989 for the 2000 Olympics, which made the Chinese remember "the hundred years of humiliation — 1840–1949") (www.chinadigitaltimes.net, 2008, July 20, see also Zhang Liang, 2001–2002). Contemporary Chinese Youth and Chinese Language: The Nature of the Chinese Language
The Chinese language has 162 radicals, and thousands of ideographic characters, many of which are shared in Japanese and Korean (Davis, 1999). The Chinese child entering the second grade typically has already learned 750 characters, and by the end of the second grade has mastered in proper form nearly 1500 characters, plus a large amount of

memorized recitable ancient Chinese poetry. In math, he or she is usually more advanced at the end of the first grade than an American child at the end of the second grade. For a foreign adult learning both the Chinese written characters and the four oral tones, one year with fifteen hours a week, plus homework, might yield 2,000–3000 characters and a moderate speaking ability. As a native speaker, of course, the young Chinese university student probably has a command of 6,000 or more characters (Zhang & Prosser, 2010).

Chinese characters are one of the most ancient forms of writing in the world, bearing perhaps more than 4,000–5,000 years of Chinese culture and civilization. Chinese characters developed from early pictograms. Today, we can still see traces of these pictograms in the form and structure of some characters, allowing us to easily guess their meaning. In addition to their pictographic nature, the general ideographic nature of the Chinese writing system sets it apart from alphabetic writing systems. Chinese primary school children have a very rigorous learning process. Chinese students at each entry level, junior and senior middle school, colleges and universities, must demonstrate their proficiency in Chinese to be able to advance to the next level of instruction. The major form of Chinese learning is based on Mandarin Chinese, though there are fifty-five minority groups who may learn a native language first, and Chinese second. Written Chinese is not an alphabetic language, but a script of ideograms. Their formation follows three principles (see *Origin of Chinese Characters,* 2008; Zhang & Prosser, 2010).

Hieroglyphs or the Drawing of Pictographs

This was the earliest method by which Chinese characters were designed and from which the other methods were subsequently developed. For instance, the sun was written as 日，the moon as 月，water as 水, the cow as 牛. As is also well-known in Chinese linguistics, these picture-words experienced a gradual evolution over the centuries until the pictographs changed into "square characters," some simplified by losing certain strokes and others made more complicated but, as a whole, from irregular drawings they became stylized forms.

Associative Compounds

The principle of forming characters by drawing pictures is easy to understand, but pictographs cannot express abstract ideas. So the ancients invented the "Associative Compounds," i. e., characters formed by combining two or more elements, each with a meaning of its own, to express new ideas. Thus, the sun and the moon written together became the character 明 (*ming*), which means "bright"; the sun placed over a line representing the horizon formed the ideogram (*dan*) which means "sunrise" or "morning."

Pictophonetics

Though pictographs and associative compounds indicate the meanings of characters by their forms, yet neither of the two categories gives any hint as to pronunciation. The pictophonetic method was developed to create new characters by combining one element indicating meaning and the other sound. for instance,爸 (*ba*) the Chinese character for "papa" is formed by the element 巴 (*ba*) which represents the sound and the element 父 (fu) which represents the meaning (father). Likewise the character 芭 (*ba*) is formed by 巴 (the sound) and ++, indicating a plant. In this way, more and more characters were made until such pictophonetics constitute today about 90 percent of all Chinese characters (Chen, 1987; Yen, 2005; Zhang & Prosser, 2010).

As an ancient world language, the development of the Chinese characters of today has been a process perhaps 4,000- 5,000 years long. In their earliest form, characters were inscribed on oracle bones. Since the time of this oracle bone script, the evolution of characters has gone through periods of inscription on ancient bronze objects, large seal script, small seal script, clerical script, and finally, regular script (from 220 A.D to the present). Additionally, for thousands of years, Chinese people wrote with original complex Chinese characters ancient books, which rendered great service to the recording of history and the spreading of culture. However, these characters, with many strokes, are hard to recognize, remember, and write. Thus, people created some simplified Chinese characters during each historical period; this process continued to sort out and regulate them. From the development of Chinese characters over several millennia, the overall evolving trend of Chinese characters is simplification. Simplified Chinese characters are those with fewer strokes adapted from complex ones with many strokes (Chen, 1987; Yen, 2005; Zhang & Prosser, 2010).

After 1949, in order to make Chinese education universal, the Chinese government simplified Chinese characters in a unified and relatively large-scale way, when more than 2,000 original complex Chinese characters were successively replaced by simplified ones. (See Chen, 1987; Yen, 2005; *Chinese Characters* 2010; Zhang & Prosser, 2010). In Hong Kong and Taiwan, there has been a great effort to continue using the more traditional Chinese characters which are the soul of calligraphy, and calligraphy is the soul of traditional Chinese art. Almost all primary school children in the mainland, Hong Kong and Taiwan, Korea, and Japan learn the art of calligraphy, and practice it regularly as secondary and university students. Because of the simplification of the Chinese language since 1949, in 1979, the State Council and PRC government officially adopted Pinyin as the standard system of phonetic spelling of Chinese words. Because of this simplification, the government reported that 100 million illiterates in China have learned to read and write Chinese since 1990, partly through becoming literate and partly as the country's economy develops, leaving only 26–30 million yet to come out of extreme poverty, (Chinanews, 2007, July 29; www.chinaprofile.com ; and Zhang & Prosser, 2010).

Children, Youth, Teens and Adults in Chinese Education

The Ministry of Education reports that in 1999, there were 145 million pupils in Chinese primary schools and 91 million students in Chinese secondary schools and in 2002, there were 12 million college and university students. The United Nations Development Program indicated in 2003 that China had 116,390 kindergarten classes, with 613, 000 teachers and 20 million students; 425,846 million primary schools, with 5.7 million teachers, and 116, 8 million students, with a 51% increase from 1998 to 2007. Most of China's better primary schools now begin teaching elementary English in the third grade. General secondary education included 79,490 schools, with 4.5 million teachers, and 85.8 million students, plus 3, 065 special secondary schools, 199,000 teachers and 5 million students. In 2003, there were 1,552 institutions of higher education, with 725,000 teachers, and 11 million students. This number surpassed 2,236 institutions in 2007, with more than 18.9 million undergraduates, and 1.2 million postgraduate students. Most Chinese speak Mandarin in the mainland, though there are 55 ethnic minorities who may learn their native language first and Mandarin Chinese second. All admission tests at the various levels of education require a strong knowledge of Mandarin Chinese for most applicants (China Ministry of Education, 2009).

Expanding the Chinese Language Overseas

Presently, there are 86 [now more than 480 in 2014] Confucius centers around the world, whose goal is to teach the Chinese language and culture. Sam Dillon notes that the Chinese government is sending Chinese teachers to schools all over the world and paying part of the teachers' salaries. In the US, for example, many schools are now eliminating some languages from instruction, while adding Chinese. Sixteen hundred American public and private schools are now offering classes in Chinese, up from 300 a decade ago. Among the 27,500 US secondary schools offering at least one language, now offering Chinese, the number has raised 4% between 1997 and 2008. The number in 2008 taking advanced placement tests was likely to pass German as the third most tested language, while 88% of elementary schools and 97% of us secondary schools surveyed, taught Spanish as their number one language, and French remaining the second most popular language taught. China has sent 325volunteer "guest teachers" of Chinese to US schools and has subsidized their salaries by $13,500 for a year, with a possible 3 year renewal. Thus, the Chinese language has been gradually making significant inroads into the American school system as a language with growing popularity (2010, January, 21). Contemporary Chinese youth and the English language

Chinese Children and Youth Learning English

Chinese children in the strongest schools in China often begin to learn English at about the third grade level. In the increasing number of foreign language primary and middle schools, they are often learning simple English as early as kindergarten. Many Chinese kindergarten children can recite the ABCs, count, and know the days of the week and sometimes also the months in English. If children did not begin learning English earlier, at least by the age of about twelve they will have begun the process of learning it. To be sure, while many of the 350,000,000 Chinese learning English (more than the total populations of the United States, Canada, Australia, and New Zealand), most as students at various levels may just be marginally competent, they only have to begin by learning a romanized alphabet of 24–26 characters, a little more than a dozen punctuation marks, and how to count reasonably in Arabic numbers. In this sense, learning basic English is less daunting than for a young foreigner to learn Chinese.

The first English that most Chinese children appear to learn, as well as Japanese children, and perhaps Korean children, is the response to "Hello. How are you?" "I am fine, thank you, and you?" No doubt, this is an aspect of learning one's initial English in the British Oxford University pattern. In 2001–02, as a volunteer on every other Saturday, I taught English to 200 primary and 200 junior middle school children each for an hour at a brand new foreign language school near Yangzhou, and three 20 minute sessions for about 90 kindergarten children. Later in Beijing, as a contracted teacher, I taught children and youth English classes in 2 different winter English camps during the spring holiday periods.

Typically, when students enter the university, they often shift to American English, perhaps because many of their foreign teachers, and the foreign teachers of their teachers, have been Americans. For example, at the Beijing Language and Culture University, there are usually nine to ten native speaking foreign teachers in the English department, most of whom are Americans, teaching a wide range of subjects to the Chinese English majors (oral English, intensive reading, extensive reading, listening, debate, writing, advanced writing, American literature, British literature, and until recently, the capstone course for seniors, western civilization). Additionally, among the 6,000 students at BLCU, 1,500 are foreign students (the largest number of international students in the world), many are Americans and thus constantly are modeling for the 4,500 Chinese students enrolled there. The international students have come to BLCU [Beijing Language and Culture University] and other universities, of course, to learn Chinese. One hundred thousand foreign teachers are hired annually in China, most of whom teach English. Gregory Mavides and Ken Hayes provide an excellent and lengthy "foreign teachers' guide to living and working in China," focusing especially on the opportunities and problems affecting English teachers at both the secondary and tertiary levels (2007).

    Every Chinese college and university has an English department or college, and usually the English major represents the largest institutional major even if the college or university is a science or technology college. At Shanghai International Studies University, for instance, there are now twelve classes of undergraduate students each with 30 students at the freshman and sophomore grade levels in the College of English. SISU's College of International Education has still more English majors who become teachers of English after graduation. Because it is a foreign language college, as is the case in many other specialized universities, women students outnumber the men students by a ratio of five to one. Often, in my experience, the women's English proficiency as beginning undergraduates was stronger than that of the men. In contrast, in scientific, engineering and technology colleges and universities, the men students are likely to surpass the women students by the same ratio, and conversely, their English tended to be at a lower level than that of the women. Over the period of teaching in 3 universities during my eight years in China, there were frequent English corners, speech, poetry, debate, drama and music contests in English. I hosted perhaps 150 Friday night open houses, which were primarily English corners, with an average attendance of 30 students at each open house. At BLCU, students from 7–8 nearby universities were often present. Those who were not English majors often had weaker English than the English majors. The Shanghai International Studies University's postgraduate College of English has more than 3,000 applicants annually, and accepts only about 225 as postgraduate majors, divided among eight different programs. The intercultural communication program, initiated in 2002 by Steve J. Kulich, by the end of June, 2009 had awarded 121 MA degrees, with all theses written in English (plus three in journalism and communication written in Chinese). It is the largest intercultural communication MA program in China, and in my opinion, probably in the world (see www.sii.shisu.edu.cn).

    All Chinese applicants for China's university admission or postgraduate programs must pass at least a written exam in English. The information for admission to the College of English at Shanghai International Studies University exemplifies the concept of making its English major students become "highly qualified international English talents with noble moral purpose, a sense of high social responsibility, polished professional knowledge, excellent foreign language skills and broad global visions" (www.shisu.collegeofEnglish.com). All undergraduate English majors in Chinese universities must take approximately two years of an additional foreign language, noting however, that very few students actually achieve "excellent foreign language skills" beyond English. In the college or university as undergraduates, sophomores must pass College English Band CET4, and many take college English Band CET6 or other English certificate programs to enhance their opportunities for employment in international trade. English majors must pass TEM4 and TEM 8 (Test for English Majors) before graduation. The Shanghai Maritime University boasts that 97% of its English majors pass TEM4, 66% higher than average of all of the national universities of science and technology (www.smu.com).

English Language Companies and English Language Tests

Besides pupils and students studying English who are enrolled in all levels of formal education, companies teaching English in China are among its most prosperous educational businesses. The New Oriental School (New Oriental Education and Technology Group), the largest private education company in China, founded by Michael Yu in 1993 is a primary example. Before the end of 2009, 7 million students were enrolled, including 1.5 million in 2009, with 270 learning centers, including 48 schools, 23 New Oriental bookstores, plus 5,000 third party book stores, and approximately 5200 teachers in 40 cities, and an online network of 5 million registered users. Nearly 100,000 copies of *New Oriental Magazine* are sold monthly (www.neworientalschool.com, 2010).

World-wide, 1.2 million take the IELTS (International English Language Test System) annually, which is accepted in 6000 secondary and tertiary institutions in most countries, but less often in the United States colleges and universities. In China there are 9 centers in the East, 15 in the North and Central areas, 8 in South China, and 5 in the South West. Cambridge English provides ESOL (English as a Second Language) certificates for learners and teachers at various educational levels, with 6 centers in China: 3 in Beijing, 2 in Shanghai, and 1 in Shijaz Huang. Various other English exams are available in different parts of China, for example, the Cambridge TOEFL (Test of English as a Foreign Language) which is the usual standard for American colleges and universities and is accepted by some Canadian universities. The Cambridge English language tests also include the SAT (Standard Admissions Test) for admission to colleges and universities in the US, GRE (Graduate Required Exam), GMAT (Graduate MBA programs), TOEIC (Test of English for International Communication), MCAT (Medical College Admission Test), which is computer based for Canada and the US, and Grammar (www.cambridgeEnglish.com).

English and Bilingual Teaching Reforms

China's former Minister of Education, Zhou Li, has identified three major proposals for the reform in the teaching of English, noting that "The Ministry of Education and the universities have always attached great importance to the teaching of English to enable Chinese students to communicate in the language and develop a global vision." (Zhou J., 2006, pp. 95–96). Thus, the Ministry has provided three major proposals:

First, the Ministry of Education has set new basic requirements for teaching English, with practicality and the students' comprehensive ability to use the language as the guideline. According to the new requirements, the teaching of English should shift its focus on reading to comprehension, and the traditional curriculum should be reformed to give universities autonomy and space for development.

The second proposal is to establish a campus-based English teaching network. The traditional reading mode of a blackboard, a piece of chalk and a textbook should be replaced by modern education technology to improve the students' self-learning ability.

The third proposal is to develop a new evaluation system to assess the teaching of English in colleges at different levels, from different angles, and during different processes.

The students' learning process as well as their final examination. The teachers' work should be evaluated with reference to the students' progress. The Band Four and Band Six college English tests should also be further reformed to help students improve their ability to use the language. (Zhou, J. 2006, p. 96).

As noted above, all college and university students in China must take and pass the CET-4 Band Test in English, usually in their second year of study. Many others take the CETt-6 Band Test to provide themselves this credential for later study or employment, especially for international trade companies, most of which require a written test and often an oral English test before candidates are chosen to work there. Among the CET 4 or 6 exams, typically on a formulaic framework (title, topic sentence or paragraph, a main paragraph with pros and cons on the topic, a final summary paragraph, expressions of one's own views or most likely solutions to a stated problem), L. S. Zhou, Michael Prosser, and Jun Lu created a text, introduced by Xhou in Chinese, with 100 cross-cultural Chinese and American English language essays by Prosser and Lu, plus essays by Chinese and American student writers, and cross-cultural analysis by Prosser (2003). The text, *Sino-American Compositions of Shared Topics,* suffered from inadequate proofreading by a native English speaker, but became reasonably popular, especially among senior middle school students preparing for the university admissions exams.

In addition to the reforms in moving English from a reading language to a comprehensively understood and spoken language, Zhou, J. identified education among China's colleges and universities which was intended to actively promote the use of English and some other foreign languages in the teaching of such fields as biotechnology, information technology, law, and finance and other specialty courses for undergraduates. In 2001, China began to send faculty of basic subjects to English native language countries to improve their English and subject-based training. By 2004, university and other presses had greatly expanded their English language

Social, Cultural, Political, and Economic Boundaries in Learning English

Xuxin Jia and Xuerui Jia stress that it is not enough simply to say that Chinese are learning English, but that the symbols which are a part of the social processes have meaning only in the context of cultural and social settings, thus requiring an understanding of the social, cultural, political and ethnic boundaries through the communicative processes that inform them: "The situation at present is that Anglo-American English has been considered as standard English…and as a lingua franca in the Chinese cultural context. …This variety of English used by the Chinese is generally called China English, which develops from both internationalization and indigenization of Anglo-American English. It has the native-speaker based world of English as its core system but integrates with Chinese symbolic systems, underpinned with Chinese cultural values." They argue that "English is used for every aspect of life in China. This is of great significance for both China and the international community, because China and the world need to enter one another's world in their pursuit of peace and further development. Without China-English, communication between China and the world is almost impossible today" (2007).

Nobleza Asuncion-Lande notes that while there are a variety of Englishes, including "new Englishes," "the ascendance of American English as the world's lingua franca means the dominance of American cultural values that clash with a country's native cultures." However, she replies that there is really no such thing as 'cultural purity' except in the minds of those who in search of the perfect culture.... As we move forward in the information age, the prospects for English as the dominant language of intercultural communication at least in the early part of the twenty-first century remains undiminished. It has become an international property that no one country can claim as its own" (1998).

Chinese Students Studying in the United States

Robin K. Cooper writes that in 2009 there were 671,616 international students studying in the US, spending $17 billion for tuition, travel, and living expenses, with 98,500 Chinese undergraduates studying in American colleges and universities (plus the postgraduates), a 21% increase over 2008 (*Facebox, Education in China, 2010,* January 15, see also Internet Reuters, 2008, December 12; UN Human Development Report, 2009). A comment about Chinese students enrolled in universities in California is often made that there no longer are just a few Chinatowns but that California's university system can now be called China-universities. Chinese students tend to do very well in the math portion of the graduate record exam, and are increasingly stronger in the GRE and TOEFL written English tests. Many universities in the US are now holding phone interviews for promising Chinese students to determine if their oral English is satisfactory. Both the IELTS English exam for universities in the British Commonwealth system, and TOEFL now also has oral components.

Contemporary Chinese Youth Culture: The Post-80s Generation:

The One Child Policy

In 1979, Deng Xiaoping initiated the "one child policy" as a temporary measure, but it is still somehow enduring in 2010 [and easing somehow in 2013 by allowing Chinese couples who are both single children to have a second child], allowing city dwellers one child, and in the countryside if the first child is a girl another child is possible after 5 years or ethnic minorities are allowed 2 children. Jasper Becker labels the policy as one of the most totalitarian efforts ever made by a government (2002). While the government claims that 400 million births have been prevented by the policy, often through enforced late month abortions, and nonetheless, the population continues to grow by 17 million a year. Matt Rosenberg says that "The result of such draconian family planning has resulted in the disparate ratio of 114 males for every 100 female babies" (2009, November 04). In fact, there are 38 million more males, from birth to the age of 20, than females. Some regions have as high as 160 males to 100 females. In the next decade, these imbalances will cause major problems for young men in their late 20s and early 30s who are eager to get married and they may have to turn to other Asian women. Already, many North Koreans are crossing the Youlou River in search of a better life, and they often become future wives of young Chinese men.

Additionally, China has the serious problem with single children of a married couple having two sets of parents, possibly one or more grandparents, as China is aging rapidly, and a child to care for. Zhang Weiqing, the Minister of the National Population and Family Planning Commission, in 2008 announced that there would not be any changes in the one child policy for the next decade as 200 million adults would enter child-bearing age by 2018, and therefore China could not prematurely end the policy (Yardley, (2008, March 11; see also Evans, 2001).

Nicole Kempton (2010, January 07) writes a very thoughtful essay on this issue, calling it an "unprecedented state intrusion concerning women's reproduction choices…It has resulted in a range of gross human rights violations. Women of child-bearing age are routinely subjected to monitoring of their menstrual cycle by family planning officials, and their employment is often contingent upon compliance with the policy.... Women who violate the policy are served with fines which may be several times their annual incomes, or worse, subjected to forced abortions and sterilization as punishment." She notes that it is easy to praise the policy for reducing the Chinese population growth so substantially, but while the policy favors the well-off who can afford the fines it punishes the poor: "Moreover, this policy punishes the children of the poor, because they are more likely to be kept hidden from the state, and thus will not have access to health care and the education they need to climb out of poverty....The one child policy is one of the most disempowering legal forces against women in the world today"(2010, January 7).Most of the university students whom I have taught appear to agree with the policy and because their parents usually each had several siblings, they do have a number of cousins, whom they often call "my brothers," or "my sisters." However, their own children will have very few cousins. Also, many of the approximately 80% of students whom I have very informally surveyed by a show of hands in classes have said that they do miss having an actual brother or sister, and often say that they personally would like to have two children instead of one. [A two Children Policy was established in 2013 for couples where one member was a single child. The government expected two million couples to register in the first phase for a second child, but only 700,000 couples did so.]

The Post-80s Generation, Students, Rebelliousness, and the Rise of Nationalism

James Farrer's *Opening Up* (2002) is a very good introduction to Chinese youth in the 1990s, many of whom did not pass the gao kao exam to enter the university and who lived a life, quite contrary to the university students whom I have taught in China. His academic study is of the young single youth, and especially the women, who were no longer in the educational system in the 1990's and were obsessed with romance magazines, exhibitionism, sexual promiscuity, and consumerism (2002).

On the other hand, among my Chinese students, graduates, and postgraduate students, a very large number of them appear to have experienced a "poverty of romance," often never having had a single date or actual romance. Many of my women students have greatly admired the nineteenth century novels of Jane Austin, for their idealized romance (see also Gittings, 2006, Sang Ye, 2006, August, 2007, Gifford, 2007).

Today, many private profit-based colleges have emerged, often as "self-study" institutions guided frequently by teachers whose own educational background may be quite limited, perhaps with only a BA degree or less and absent a library or computer center, but supported by parents wealthy enough to try by this somewhat desperate method to have their sons or daughters later admitted to reputable colleges and universities. teaching oral English to second year English majors one day a week in a for profit business college in Beijing in 2002–03, basically an often poorly trained guided self-study program, I saw this situation at first hand. Absenteeism was high among a very large class, because the class itself had no tests, as the students were only preparing to pass required local and national tests. Following through later with some of my more attentive and serious women students, I learned that a majority of my students in that class had failed at least half of these tests after three years of study at the college.

[Today, the vast number of the undergraduate university students are not post-1980s but post-1990s generation.]

"The Hardest Working People in China Are the Students"

For this saying in China that the hardest working people are the students, this is generally true, except in my view, university seniors at all three universities where I taught, as they were too busy looking for a position, or were preparing very hard for the January entrance exams for post graduate studies. In fact, they were still working very hard, but many of them had shifted their hard work away from classrooms. Students at all levels are taught to memorize constantly, in a considerably rigid educational system. junior middle school children must always study for the "make or break" test (zhong kao) to be admitted to senior middle school, as well as the senior middle school students who are preparing to take the two day "black June" exam (gao kao) for admission to university. All are under great pressure. Students who fail this exam end up with a very different life than those admitted to a university. Chinese parents are more and more competitive (hiasu) for their often only child ("the little emperor or empress"), forcing them into many extra classes out of school so that their son or daughter can be on the same level as or better than other students. They are often called "the most stressed students" outside of Japan and South Korea. Gao kao has been compared to "a thousand soldiers and ten thousand horses across a single log bridge" (Baoru, 2009, June 8; see also Jing, 2000; Mavides & Hayes, 2007). Education at all levels requires and tests an increasing understanding of the guiding political theories and practices of the CPC, and maintains the principle of the four modernizations.

The Rise of Nationalism and "Angry Youth"

We can see examples of this rising nationalism recently in youthful anger over different major events such as the NATO bombing of the Chinese embassy in Belgrade in 1997; the downing of the US spy plane on Hai'nan Island in 2002; the anti-Japanese protests in 2005 (see Dong, 2009, May 25); and the anti-CNN and anti-Carrefour (China's largest foreign-owned French supermarkets) protests, and protests relating to disruptions of the 2008 Olympic torch relays (see, www.chinadigitaltimes.net, 2008, July 20)

Peter Hays Gries discusses the great surge in youthful nationalism and anti-Americanism after the 1997 NATO bombing of the Chinese embassy in Belgrade and the downed us spy plane on China's southern Hai'nan Island in 2001 (2004). Julia Lovell suggests that this anti-western nationalism may stem from the growth in economic confidence on one hand, and on the other hand, the "angry youth" (fenqing) may be that young people need something to "get mad at — they'll grow out of it." Nonetheless, she argues that a more important reason is an "essentially state-engineered phenomenon, rooted in one of the communist party's most successful post-Mao political crusades, patriotic education (2009, April) after all, it had been Mao himself who encouraged the young Red Guards (hong wei bing) to crush the "four olds"(old ideas, old culture, old customs and old habits of the "backward classes") and to chant, as they read Mao's Little *Red Book,* "it is right to rebel!" (Meisner, 1986; CNN: "The cold war series:'China, 1949–1972'").

Stanley Rosen, writing in the *Journal of Asian Studies,* stresses that rather than seeing Chinese youth today (15–34 year olds, the post-80s and post-90s generation) as an homogenized group, they are clearly not unified in their beliefs, attitudes, values, or behaviors. He states that in the last several years up to mid2008, in much of China's government authorized mainstream media, China's young people were frequently under attack as the "me" generation who were "reliant and rebellious, cynical and pragmatic, self-centered and equality-obsessed" and at the same time, "China's first generation of couch potatoes, addicts of online games, patrons of fast food chains, and loyal audiences of Hollywood movies." However, he notes that the May 12, 2008 Sichuan (Yuanchan) earthquake, which claimed the lives of 69,000 people, including 10,000 students, changed the media's perception of China's youth. Then they began to celebrate their youthful virtues "'of great compassion, benevolence, and gallantness. Still it is hard to reconcile these compassionate youth with those who are angry. Some Chinese critics call them 'internet-savvy nationalists' and 'online Red Guards' infected by a 'populist virus'" he continues by saying that currently China's youth are influenced by contradictory and competing causes and events, especially in the rapidly modernizing coastal areas, affected so much by global and internationalizing trends. These young people are indeed materialistic, he claims, who want to lead "the good life" and make money as quickly as possible. Those who are angry, argue, express it far less in adherence to the Party and government's pressures and more in the impulse to defend China from enemies from abroad, but also in a love of the country and self-sacrifice for those most in need, as was exemplified by the great outpouring of volunteer efforts following the Sichuan earthquake (2009).

Jieying Xi, Sunxiao Sun and Jian Jjan Xiao, in their book, *Chinese Youth in Transition,* (2006) explain that Chinese youth's increased self-interest shows a marked change from the group oriented behavior of their parents and grandparents. New Chinese policies have given them more personal freedom and autonomy, including more opportunities for consumerism, which the government is promoting, and a strong nationalistic freedom (Krayewski, 2009, January 11; see also Wasserstrom & Perry, 1992, 1994; Gries, 2004; Kynge, 2006; for 26 examples of moderate Chinese youth characteristics

Young Chinese's Different Views toward China

Entering college and university students are required to undergo two weeks of military training, and at most institutions it is held on campus, or sometimes on army bases, as one governmental method to curtail youthful rebelliousness. Some of my students have said that it is a good way to develop friends as freshmen and to build team work. Others have complained that it was among their worst experiences in their lives besides taking the gao kao exams for admission to university.

Han Han: Author, Blogger, Youthful Satirist and Hero

A very interesting illustration of youthful, playful and satirical rebellion is seen in Han Han, born in 1982, quitting high school and at seventeen, publishing his first of fourteen novels, *Triple Gate*, which was an instant bestseller. He is also a race car driver and musician, therefore appealing to various segments of the youth culture. In China, quitting middle school for good students is considered a major type of youth rebellion. Uln, a young Chinese blogger calls Han Han "a sort of Robin Hood of the Sinosphere. Han Han writes about injustice. He complains and makes fun of things that are wrong, by people who have power (political or other) in the older generations.... fighting injustice with irony, that is very much the style of Han Han" (2009, May 5). His blog has had 300 million hits, the most in the world. Named the "2009 person of the year" by both the *Guangzhou Southern Weekend* and *Asia Weekly*. *Southern Weekend* comments: "In the public eyes for ten years, and still young, he is called by his supporters as 'young master Han.' This nickname is flattering and lighthearted... an idol.... behind the 300 million clicks on his blog posts was a fresh, humanist radiating the wave of freedom (2010, January 10). *Asia Weekly* writes: "Han Han: youthful citizen vs. power: his clear and powerful writing has generated an enormous influence on public opinion. As a member of the post-80s generation, he lives authentically and freely, and demonstrates the energy of China's youthful citizens and the hope of civil society in China" (see *Asia Weekly's* two part interview with him (2010, January 26).

Simon Elegant called him in the November 2, 2009 *Time Asia*, "China's literary bad boy." Elegant quotes him: "No matter how rude and immature they are, how unskillfully they write, the future literary world belongs to the post-80's generation. They must be more arrogant. A writer must be arrogant." In the *Time* article, Lydia Liu, professor of Chinese and Comparative Literature at Columbia University is quoted as saying that "He has exemplified through his calculated rebelliousness the unspoken compact of his generation has forged with the ruling

Communist Party 'leave us along to have fun and we won't challenge your right to rule the country.' He is known for being a sharp critic of the establishment, but he isn't really, but a willing participant in a process that channels the disaffected energy of youth into consumerism." Elegant, however, also quotes the novelist Zhang Yueran: "Neither fame nor wealth have changed his honesty or the sharpness of his criticism. To me he's like the little boy in 'the emperor's new clothes,' whose provocative attitude doesn't allow people to be self-satisfied (2009, November 2). Some of my more recent freshmen Chinese students liked to say: "you know we are the post-90s generation and Han Han also speaks for us." [Han Han's book of blog posts, *This Generation* (2012] is his first book translated into English.]

Elite Education

The role of Science and Engineering Project 211's 106 universities represent 6% of the more than 1700 Chinese universities, but train 80% of the country's doctorates, 66% of all postgraduate students, and 50% of all foreign students (Mavidas), with 26,546 full-time students; 2. China Concord Medical University with 20,000 full-time students; 3. Harbin Medical University with 10,000 full-time students; 4. Capital Medical University with 8373 full-time students; and Southern Medical University (Chineseuniversities@0086.com). Nine of the best universities in China have agreed to create an Ivy League type of consortium called c9, including China Science and Technology University, Fudan University, Harbin Institute of Technology, Nangjng University, Peking University, Shanghai Jiao Tong University, Tsinghua University, Xi'an Jiaotong University and Zhejiang University. Students at any one of the universities can take courses at any of the others, receiving full credits; and postgraduates can be involved with research projects in the same disciplines with credits for six month work at another of the universities. The universities will share coursework materials and online lectures; nurture young professors; establish a joint committee for evaluating dissertations; and enhance exchanges with the American Ivy league universities and some in Australia (www.englishnews@ chosun.com. 2009, October 15).

China's very heavy recent emphasis on science and engineering, as the foundation of the four modernizations, which extends to all levels of education, was developed by Zhou Enlai in 1974 and articulated by Deng Xiaoping in 1978 and more extensively in the 1980s.Each year 450,000 engineering students graduate from engineering programs, 50,000 with master's degrees, and 8,000 Ph.D. degrees.

Most of the recent leaders of China have engineering degrees, including Jiang Zimen (electrical engineering, Shanghai Jiao Tong University), Zhu Rongji (electrical engineering, Tsinghua University), Hu Jintao (hydraulic engineering, Tsinghua University) and Wen Jibao (geological structures, Beijing Institute of Technology).... Xi Jinping (chemical engineering, Tsinghua University) [has replaced] Hu Jintao in 2013, and Li Keqiang (law,LLB, and Ph.D. in economics, Peking University) [has succeeded] Wen Jibao's as premier in 2013. Here, we note that as recent current leaders typically have had engineering degrees, and have led massive engineering feats in China in the last two decades, including road and rail infrastructure and the three gorges project, their successors, considered as the fifth generation of leaders since the founding of the PRC, will continue to lead the country with engineering degrees, or in the case of Li Keqiang with both law and economics degrees as illustrative of rising educational measurements of leadership when China has moved beyond Germany as an exporter, and by the end of 2010 [has moved] beyond Japan as well. China now sells more autos than the US and a large proportion of American debt is now owned by China.

Media and Internet Censorship; Google's Threat to Leave China's Internet Space; Han Han

Clinton Allison Klayman, speaking on the Voice of America, January 21, 2010, states that China not only blocks the internet sites of major foreign news organizations, the VOA itself, activist groups, and even social network services like Facebook, You Tube, My Space, and Twitter, but now has indicated that it would monitor the 600 billion text messages (in 2008 and growing) for sexual, unhealthy, pornographic, or other illegal materials. The internet service in Xinjiang in Western China, where July 2009 riots occurred, killing 200 people, has been blocked for a half year and is just gradually restoring internet service there (2010, January 21).In China, there is common information among students about four things that may not be discussed, at least not publicly in contradiction to CPC and government expressed views called "the 3 ts and 1 f" (Tibet,

Taiwan, Tiananmen and Falun Gong). China's censorship is becoming increasingly stiff, with You Tube, Facebook, My Space, and Twitter all currently blocked.

Eighty-million Chinese, generally college-age, and well educated college graduates, use Google for many academic endeavors (2010, January 21). On January 12, 2010, Google announced that its infrastructure and those of several other western companies had been very seriously cyberattacked from China, and declared that it was considering pulling out of China as a source and information engine. Han Han's blog (2010, January 26) "I am just speculating," satirizes the government's continuing denials that it was involved in the attacks against Google by looking ahead to 2016, saying that the internet is down to a million users. All with daily uploads based on the *People's Daily*, and in the same year, the internet disappeared entirely in China: "2116: the *People's Daily* wrote: 'An industry was sacrificed in return for the stability of the nation, but it was worth it'" (www.chinadigitaltimes.net, 2010, January 26). Another of his humorous and satirical blogs, "From today, I am a vulgar person," takes aim at the January 2010 government decision to monitor text messages to prevent "unhealthy, pornographic, and illegal material," stating that if he does not know what is unhealthy, pornographic, or illegal, perhaps a woman and he could repeat the usual words relating to female and male genitals over and over, and find out if these words are really unhealthy, pornographic, or illegal (2010, January 13). The unnamed irreverent magazine that Han Han had intended to begin publishing in the autumn of 2009, and paying contributors twice the usual yuan per character that was common among Chinese literary magazines, has been blocked by the government.

When he announced his plans in May, 2009, he immediately received 10,000 submissions. In his blog, "Three things," he writes: "my first idea was this magazine made a freer and more wild literary magazine, but it is regrettable that the publication in the existing constraints, the idea is difficult to achieve" (2010, January 5; see also, Loveland, 2010, January 11).

www.scoopworld.com on January 21, 2010, citing www.worldpublicopinion.org, has reported in a Chinese poll in January 2008 that "Two thirds of the Chinese public (66%) said that they 'should have the right to read whatever is on the internet' and only 21% said that the government should have the right to prevent people from having access to some things on the internet [such as pornography] (2010, January 21). Sharon Janiere, writing in the *New York Times,* (2010, January 16) states that Google's January 12, 2010 announcement of cyberattacks coming from China against it might cause Google to pull its information services out of China. She [and many other sources] reports that Google would no longer self-censor sensitive items which the government does not wish to have available on the internet challenges the government's claim "that constraints on free speech are crucial to political stability and the prosperity that has accompanied it" she writes: "the average age of Chinese netizens is still very young." she quotes Hu Yong at Peking University, "This is a matter of the future and whether the government's internet policy wants to fight with the future."Janiere postulates, "If this process goes on, more and more people are going to realize that their freedom of information is being infringed upon, and this could bring changes down the line." She concludes: "To many of the young, well-educated Chinese who are Google's loyal users here [in Beijing] the company's threat to leave is no laughing matter. Interviews in Beijing's downtown and university district indicated that many viewed the possible loss of Google's maps, translation service, sketching software, access to scholarly papers and search function with real distress" (2010, January 16).

US Secretary of State Hillary Rodham Clinton, on January 21, 2010, gave a major address on internet freedom. She identified four key freedoms of the internet age: 1. freedom of expression; 2. freedom of worship; 3. promotion of social and economic development to countries where people lack access to knowledge, markets, capital and economic opportunity; and 4. the internet as a great equalizer. Finally, from these four freedoms, she argued that governments or individuals engaging in cyberattacks should face consequences and international condemnation. "The freedom to connect," she stated, "is freedom of assembly in cyberspace." She announced that in the spring of 2010, the US State Department and USAID would launch new media to connect people, particularly young people, to expand civic participation and increase the new media capabilities for the civil society (2010, January 21).

Conclusion: Understanding Chinese Contemporary Youth Culture

This essay has important implications not only for understanding the contemporary Chinese youth and their involvement in both the Chinese and English languages, but also provides several illustrations relating to Chinese youth culture: the one child policy; rising nationalism; secondary and tertiary education; rebellion, as exemplified by the popular Chinese satirical blogger, Han Han; and media and internet freedom and attacks against them. Many more such illustrations are possible. I have written thirty-five 200 page notebook journals since going to China in 2001–2009. In this essay, my own personal involvement in teaching for eight years in China, 2001–2009 is only partly identified, but teaching 2200 Chinese students has greatly enriched my own life, and made it a colorful and productive period, [now 2001–2014, and more than 2550 students] including becoming good or close friends with a number of outstanding young Chinese in the age group from 18 to about 30, who illustrate well their promising future. Although often stressed because of course overloads, most of my students have appeared to be happy youth. Except for some intense anti-Japanese views. (see, for example, I. Chang, 1997), generally they would not be considered extremely nationalistic or very rebellious by their Chinese teachers or by me. However, I acknowledge that as a foreign teacher, and even among my very close young Chinese friends — almost all university students or beyond as I taught more years in China, I was still a guest in China. Thus, what they might discuss with their friends or classmates outside of class and in their native Chinese language often would not be shared with me. Because of watching various international tv channels not accessible to them, or reading many books banned in China, some of my views may have been more objective than theirs, but were also considered biased from my perspective as an American by my Chinese students and friends. Most of them accept the government and party's admonishment not to challenge its positions (not openly at least) about the "3 ts and 1 f" (Tibet, Taiwan, and Tiananmen and Falun Gong). In fact, many of them fully accept the government and Party's positions on these topics. At the same time, many of my young Chinese friends have been very open in their discussions privately with me and have shown me great friendship and an enduring affection, many considering me like a grandfather figure in their lives.

[Most of the information on the origins of the Chinese language was researched by Zhang Shengyong.]

19. Chinese Education

The increasing influence of China as an international stakeholder and strategic partnerships with many energy-producing countries in Africa, the Middle East, Latin America, and Russia, is often treated as the "China threat," by numerous authors, and books such as Martin Jacques' *When China Rules the World* (2009), Dambisa Moyo's *Winner Take All: China's Race for Resources and What It Means for the World* (2012), Edward N. Luttwak's *The Rise of China vs. the Logic of Strategy* (2012), and David Shambaugh's *China Goes Global: The Partial Power* (2013) clearly articulate the growing influence that China has economically, politically, and culturally through its "soft power" which includes its very strong attention to education.

With the rising educated middle class in China and the largest number of college and university students in the world, China may well reach President Hu Jintao's earlier goal of an "all round moderately prosperous" China by 2020, or even more likely sooner. The Chinese Ministry of Education has designated nine Chinese universities as China's nine most elite universities: Peking University, Tsinghua University, Nanjing University, Zhajiangu, Fudan University, Shanghai Jiaotong University, Harbin Institute of Technology, Xi'an Jiaotong University, and China University of Technology, but there is still some distance for Chinese universities to match those of the broad quality of the US and UK universities, as witnessed by the fact that there are now more than 100,000 Chinese students studying in US universities including more and more Chinese undergraduates. About 40% of these "talents" will return to China soon after their American (or other foreign education, including both the UK and Germany) depending on their opportunities for employment overseas.

However, the best US and UK universities are now suffering major budget cuts, still as a result of the 2007–2009 world recession. This means in an interesting way, that the American and British universities are also depending on Chinese student tuition who pay higher fees to help sustain them in a period of economic austerity. This current exceptional economic problem and conservative demands in the US and UK to slash spending in many areas, including education, may accelerate the rapid rise of Chinese universities, many of which, as Tsinghua University claims that it is "dedicated to academic excellence, the well-being of Chinese society, and to global development."

Jessica Shepherd writes that: Professor Richard Levin, [former president of Yale University] speaking to the *Guardian* on a trip to the UK, said that Chinese institutions would rank in the world's top ten universities in twenty-five years' time, squeezing out some of the west's elite campuses. At the moment, British universities dominate the top ten rankings, with Cambridge coming second to Harvard, University College London fourth, and Oxford and Imperial College London joint fifth. The rest of the top fifteen are US universities. China's highest-ranking institution is Tsinghua, at 49. but the Chinese government now spends billions of yuan — at least 1.5% of its gross domestic product — on higher education with the aim of propelling its best institutions, such as the Universities of Tsinghua and Peking, into the top slots (Shepherd, 2010: February 2)

Besides teaching 2550+ students at four Chinese universities and one Beijing area business college, I have been a volunteer or contracted part-time teacher for ninety Chinese kindergarten children, more than 500 primary, junior and senior middle school students, and adult learners of English. Additionally, I have given lectures to more than 8800 secondary and university students during this period in Cambodia, China, India, and Russia. I have reviewed more than 140 MA theses in intercultural communication at Shanghai International Studies University. Thus, I have a strong attachment to the role and importance of education, especially at university levels in China.

When I was first coming to China in 2001, D. Ray Heisey reminded me of three critical terms to remember (1) patience (2) patience (3) patience. These were among the wisest words that I have learned about teaching in China. Still, we might add one more critical term: *eternal* patience. The dean at one university where I taught said to the College of Foreign Language international teachers: "Welcome to our foreign teachers. You should remember three main ideas: be on time for your classes, keep a strict attendance policy; teach as you do in your own country." The third point left a lot of potential ambiguity for foreign teachers coming from four different counties: Australia, Ireland, the UK and the US. In my final semester of Chinese university teaching in 2013–14, I received a highly restrictive foreign teacher's manual, but fortunately it was more of a formal statement than practically possible. Even with some of these stringent rules, it was impossible to have a roll call each class period for one nine week class of 120 sophomore and another for 150 sophomore majors in Arabic, French, Japanese, Korean, business English, English translation, and English education as it took seven to ten minutes to complete a roll call of students in a weekly hour and a half class. Also, I noted that some students in the back of the lecture hall slipped out during the class.

As I continued teaching in the universities, new and unexpected courses were added frequently with such administrative statements as "You won't mind also teaching a weekly Monday night oral English course for our university teachers interested in going abroad"; "We are assigning you to teach seniors 'The History of the English Language.' You are an American; of course you can teach it"; "It's no problem for you teaching extensive reading and intensive reading" (but without identifying what these courses were about); "You are teaching five sections of sophomore oral English" (and without much warning finding that the oral English courses were switching the second semester to freshmen): "Take it or leave"; "You won't begin teaching these optional courses until three weeks after the semester begins" (and then finding two students in a class intended for 30 students in one class, and three students in the other class, intended for 60 students). At another university, I proposed and prepared carefully to teach a course on American literature, only to find that my dean, whom I never met, said after my arrival that it wasn't of interest to the majors in that college. Instead, I taught a very easy and non-challenging course in English newspaper reading to freshmen and sophomores, but where I developed close relationships with the students who asked and received my permission to give me an in class birthday party.

Teaching three sections of advanced writing with 30 students in each class for three years seemed rather daunting (biweekly assignments; creating magazines, two research projects), but I later met another American faculty member at a different university who had four classes of 70 students each in advanced writing, or 280 students where writing assignments were expected biweekly, plus a semester research paper, and while finishing semester grades, being asked by his dean to proofread a 250 page book in flawed English within a two day period. Although this teacher had prior teaching to junior middle school students in music, it was not in the field of English. His wife, who had no university teaching experience, was assigned to teach post graduates in research, other classes in oral English, and a weekly evening English corner. They both fulfilled their duties very well, but at the end of the semester both were exhausted and did not return for another year.

The field of communication as we know is very diverse, but in my ten+ years of teaching English and communication, I found myself teaching the following courses: freshman oral English; sophomore oral English; newspaper reading in English; mass media; debate; extensive reading; intensive reading; advanced writing; the history of the English language; American literature; rhetoric and public discourse; intercultural communication; public speaking; global media and culture; model United Nations Security Council; and western civilization. As a caveat, I should note that several of these courses were of my own choosing. Fortunately, I had graduate degrees both in English and communication.

In our text book for Chinese students, *Communicating Interculturally* (2012) which now also has a North American edition, *Chinese Communicating Interculturally* (2014), Li Mengyu and I included several essays about the significance of integrity and high ethics, one entitled: "Honesty and integrity: the hallmark of an ethical university education and research." However, such search engines as Baidu, Google, Bing, Sina Weibo, Yahoo, and Wikipedia provide many instant papers subject to plagiarism. In the four universities where I taught, there was a significant amount of cheating in undergraduate research papers. In a western civilization class as a capstone course for seniors, one of my four optional final assignments allowed for an essay about the US Civil War, and sixteen of the 150 course essays began "There were a myriad number of reasons for the civil war." With variations, all of the papers had essentially the same content from several different Google/Baidu, Wikipedia sources. While passing these students with the lowest possible grade, I asked the dean what the college would do about these cheating students (probably only a handful of those plagiarizing in the course but others not getting caught on the other three options), and he replied that was not the college's business but my responsibility. His assistant dean also passed a student against my wishes who had never attended the class.

As a judge in a debate contest, I was surprised to learn that while it was announced that three of five Chinese and American faculty judges had awarded the victory to one side, a couple days later we learned that there had been a mistake (win or lose judgments, no numbers involved) and in fact the other side had actually won by a 3 to 2 vote. Incredible! More recently, I began to find several dozen senior students appearing in classes for the first time three weeks before the end of the semester, and expecting to get a grade for the courses with the plea that if they did not pass these courses, they could not graduate (and they would be humiliated in front of their families and friends). One senior Chinese faculty member wanted her advisees' BA theses "to be elegant" and she rewrote more than half of some of these theses to make them "elegant." On the other hand, I was promoting simplicity and directness in the student research papers and BA theses which caused some of my thesis writers to be criticized by some older Chinese faculty for writing so simply and childishly.

I became aware that entire paragraphs of mine in earlier gift books to some faculty members or their colleagues appeared in articles or books by Chinese faculty members without attribution to me or with only very marginal acknowledgement. One young very close friend submitted my own academic material as jointly coauthored by him and me and had it published in a reputable journal. I learned about this only when the falsified article was being quoted by several different authors in Cui Litang's and my coedited book, *Social Media in Asia* (2014). The journal editor agreed to withdraw the online version, without comment, but the printed version could not be easily withdrawn, without causing damage to the reputation of the young faculty member and the journal.

It is easy to speculate that when administrators and faculty members plagiarize or are unwilling to deal with massive cheating by students, then the students have less difficulty in justifying cheating or plagiarism. We must also remember that from Confucius forward, Chinese philosophy encouraged collective attribution rather than claims of individual authorship. More importantly, during the 1958–1962 Great Leap Forward and the 1966–1976 Great Proletarian Cultural Revolution, honesty could cause great harm, or even death, to those who were honest. Nonetheless, despite the massive educational cheating and plagiarism (not only a problem in China, but far more broadly), when I would ask various student classes their most fundamental values, honesty was almost always identified as one of their most important half dozen values. This requires a balanced approach on the part of American teachers and faculty members in China.

I taught second year English majors on Wednesdays in 2002–03 at the Beijing Business College, a private for profit institution, in Nangkou, northwest of Beijing, but within the Beijing administrative district. The school was then only three years old with three campuses and the campus where I taught was the site of an old closed very ugly State Owned Enterprise (SOE). Contractors were busy building classrooms, sporting facilities, and dormitories, but there was no library. There was a student population of 7,000, 4,000 of whom were freshmen. All of these students had to have classes in oral English. This placed a great strain on the College in finding adequate teachers for one or two days a week, many of whom were American university students enrolled in university Chinese language classes at area universities, without any credentials or teaching experience and often quitting in the middle of a semester or after one semester. The oral English classes for relatively uninterested freshmen typically had 75 students in each class. In early January, 2003, all of them had to take a major oral English test on a pass/fail basis, which many of them failed. I realized that my own grading was unimportant in contrast to passing the college exam. All of the students enrolled at this school had already failed the "black" or "dark" gao kao university admission exams, and their parents were paying a much higher tuition rate than was typical for the universities that I was aware of in China. Students could also have single or double dormitory rooms instead of the usual four to six person dormitory rooms if their parents were willing to pay for such accommodations. In my afternoon sophomore English majors' class, I had many students who left after the break, sometimes reducing the class by two thirds. Among some of the more serious students in my sophomore classes, we did develop some very nice and pleasant friendships.

In the People's Republic of China, from kindergarten, primary school, junior middle school, senior middle school and university, the goals and prescriptions of the Communist Party of China (CPC) and its enduring importance, are paramount. At increasing levels of complexity, Marxism-Leninism; Mao Tsedong thought; Deng Xiaoping theory, socialism with

Chinese characteristics; Jiang Zemin's Three Represents (advanced productive forces, advanced culture, and the broad masses of the people), Hu Jintao's pronouncements of cultural harmony, stability, and scientific development; and now Xi Jinping's "Chinese dream" are all required subjects to move forward in the students' educational progress. At the encouragement of teachers and faculty, students, especially postgraduate students, are joining the CPC's 88 million members, the largest political party in the world, many for the benefits in careers, housing, owning cars which CPC membership provides over non membership.

Most areas in China now not only accept the Universal Declaration of Human Rights Article 26 call for all children having six years of free primary education, but follow the Chinese law regulating nine years of compulsory education, including six years of primary education and three years of junior middle school education. There are more than 200 million elementary and middle school students, with 60% of graduating senior middle school students now enrolling in college or university education. To enter the senior middle school, students must take the zhong kao entrance exams, including Chinese, math, English, physics, chemistry, political science, and physical education. In June each year, students who have completed senior middle school take the gao kao university entrance exam, covering the same subjects and history. There are now more than 400 million Chinese students at all levels of education, the largest number for any country in the world. The literacy rate for Chinese fifteen to twenty-four old youth is now 99% according to UNESCO, including the ability to read and write 1500 characters in the rural areas and 2000 characters in the urban areas.

Beginning in 2000, the Programme for International Student Assessment (PISA) has accessed the mathematics, reading, and science literacy for 470,000 fifteen year old students in sixty-five nation and localities every three years. In 2012, skills in financial literacy were added. In 2009, the fifteen year old test group from Shanghai led the scores in mathematical, reading, and science literacy. In mathematics literacy, Shanghai youth were followed by Singapore, Taipei, Hong Kong, Japan, and South Korea. Seventeen countries and locations scored higher than in the US. In reading literacy, the assessment included the concepts of the ability to access and retrieve, integrate and interpret, reflect and educate. The fifteen year-old leaders in and immediately following Shanghai repeated the 2012 assessment achievement as well. Nine locations had higher scores than the US fifteen year old students. For the assessment of science literacy in 2009, the Shanghai students were again the leaders, followed by Hong Kong, Singapore, Japan, and Finland, with twelve locations having higher scores than the US students. With the addition in 2012 of an assessment in problem-solving, the Shanghai students led Singapore, South Korea, and Japan (PISA, 2009 and 2012 databases). President Obama called it a "sputnik moment" reminiscent of the 1957 Soviet sputnik launch which energized the US to catch up to the Soviet youth in math and science.

It is fairly well known that mainland Chinese students are expected to memorize material rather than be problem solvers. In Li Mengyu's and my intercultural communication textbook, *Communicating Interculturally* (2012), we made special efforts to encourage critical thinking/problem solving, particularly in the imaginary dialogues followed by the main material of the chapters. However, the process of memorization remains dominant at the primary and secondary school levels in the mainland of China with more creativity and critical thinking developing at the university level depending on the likely creativity of the teachers. The final year of senior middle school remains entirely devoted to a review of all that has been learned before. Many Chinese students have told me that preparing for the gao kao exam during that year is their "year from hell." When I have asked students at the four universities where I taught what had made them happiest in their lives, the typical response was passing the gao kao exam with a good score, and being accepted to a good university. This statement was followed by noting that their first day in their university was the next happiest event in their lives.

Higher education in China includes two and three year junior colleges, often called "short-cycle" colleges, four year colleges and universities which teach academic and vocational subjects with three year certificates and four year BA programs at the undergraduate level. Most of the two and three short-cycle colleges offer only a few majors, often emphasizing technology or business. The accredited colleges and universities offer as many as forty majors in regular academic curricular programs. An increasing number of universities offer the master's degree, and a smaller number offer the doctoral degree. Adult education includes radio/tv universities, cadre institutes, worker colleges, peasant colleges, correspondence colleges, distance learning colleges, and colleges within universities.

In a 2003 CCTV International program, it was reported that for the first time since the founding of the PRC in 1949, the government was providing 45,000 merit-based scholarships to poor students entering or at universities, 10,000 of which would provide 6,000rmb ($700) a year, and 35,000 of which would provide 4,000rmb ($500) a year. Now, however, as the Chinese middle class is growing rapidly, and because of the ever increasing number of university students, fewer students are receiving such scholarships. Since 1994, China has provided more than 1 billion rmb in subsidies to universities annually. Additionally, 4,000 enterprises for returning students ("talents") have been established at 80 enterprise locations. Of the 400,000 Chinese students studying overseas in recent years, 180,000 have been projected to return to work in China reasonably soon after their degrees are awarded overseas. A number of individuals with foreign post graduate degrees return to China and develop new enterprises. Others who do not immediately return to China nonetheless assist their families with a flow of cash from their overseas work. There are special annual celebrations for returning "talents" in many Chinese cities.

President Hu Jintao, on January 17, 2005 speaking at the national conference for improving ideological education for college students, stressed the need for "ideological and ethical education for college students to cultivate talents with noble minds, sound ethics, and abundant knowledge to meet the need of the country's modernizing drive." He argued that "education should make it possible for college students to keep pace with the time, share the fate of the motherland and work hard together with all the people" and that education must increase knowledge of sciences, and also raise ideological and political awareness and the cultivation of socialist builders and successors as fundamental goals for Chinese society. (China Education and Research Network, January 19, 2005)

The Twenty-First Century Newspaper (a student oriented weekly newspaper published by *China Daily*) of January 19, 2005, reported that about 1.3 million people had registered for the post graduate exam, scheduled throughout China for January 22 and 23, 2005. The People's Daily put the figure precisely at 1.172 million and said that the increase was 24% higher than in 2004 taking the exam, with 15% more students being accepted for the master's degree than in 2004. In 2003, there were 945,000 taking the exam. In Beijing sitting for the 2005 exam, there were 208,000 applicants, 21 % more than in 2004 and three times the 2000 figure. In Shanghai alone, there were 100,000 who registered for the exam. The Ministry of Education reported that post graduate recruitment at the master's level had increased by nearly 26% each year since 1999. Before 1998, official higher education reforms had occurred, 72,000 persons passed the post graduate exam. In 2005, 360,000 were expected to pass it and enter a postgraduate (master's) program in China, 34,000 more than in 2004. This number accelerates greatly each passing year.

January 18 and 19 are now the annual dates for the post graduate exams throughout China, the only time in many universities that students have been able to change their major. This practice is becoming more flexible. In most Chinese universities, the master's degree requires two to three years and there are now more than 270,000 master's students in China. Presently, China graduates 12,000 Ph.D.'s annually, and hopes to expand that number to 50,000 a year in a decade or two. As noted recently, there are several hundred thousand students taking the post graduate exams, and they must pass five exams: Chinese, English, politics covering Marxism-Leninism, Mao Tsedong thought, Deng Xiaoping theory, Jiang Zemin's Three Represents, and Hu Jintao's harmonious, stable and scientific development), plus two exams in their proposed subject area. Many students begin studying for these exams as university juniors. This and the need to receive internships or regular jobs after graduation mean that seniors appear to be the least hard working students. They are, in fact, working hard, but not in their senior classes, in my opinion as they are searching for professional positions and internships or preparing to take post graduate exams.

The two-day exam period for the master's programs includes a three hour test on English and a three hour exam on political theory. On the second day, students take such exams as math, finance, economics, information technology, or engineering, depending on their desired master's degree major. Science students take a three hour exam on mathematics, and a three hour exam on the core of their major. Language students take an exam on their second language, such as French or Japanese, and an exam on the core of their proposed major. Ministry of Education regulations called for subject exams related to political theory, foreign languages, and three professional courses. The papers for political theory, foreign languages, and basic courses are prepared by the Ministry of Education. In 2014 at Yangzhou University, I had a twenty-five year old student visitor, who took and failed the post graduate exam three times, due primarily to his inadequate level of English as he has been enrolled as an undergraduate student at a college with a rather poor quality of English teaching. He had self-taught himself French for the exam, and also failed that portion of the exam, while passing other sections. He remains determined to keep preparing to pass these two subjects in a future exam so that he can be admitted to an MA program.

The Ministry of Education identifies that "new candidates are admitted according to the principle of 'judging the candidates in an all-round way and selecting the best students who are good morally, intellectually, and physically.'" The Ministry notes that "candidates should be patriotic, moral, ready to serve the country's construction and well- grounded in basic theory. They should have solid and systematic knowledge and related techniques and methods of their respective fields, capable of carrying out independent research and work." *The People's Daily* reported that by 1980, there were only 21,000 university graduates, but by 2001, 43,000 doctoral degrees had been awarded, 430,000 master's degrees, and 4,600,000 bachelor's degrees.

The website www.edu.cn stated on November 25, 2004 that since the opening up policy in 1978, China had sent 320,000 students to more than 100 countries and had hosted more than 340,000 students from more than 160 countries. China had sent out 1800 teachers and experts, and had appointed 40,000 foreign experts and teachers for its educational system. More than 11,000 Chinese experts and teachers had made presentations at international symposia and conferences abroad and in China since 1978. On January 11, 2005, *The People's Daily* reported that China would begin sending 5,000 young and middle aged college teachers abroad annually to study for doctoral degrees or undertake academic research in top foreign universities, supported by the China scholarship council and 50 major universities. Today, these numbers have more than doubled and China has now surpassed the US as the leading destination for international students going abroad to study and occurring both in China itself from abroad.

Additionally, there are now annually more than 100,000+ foreign educators in China, 100,000+ foreign students studying in Chinese universities; 100,000+ Chinese students now studying abroad (mostly in the US and other English speaking countries). There are 450 Confucius centers worldwide, which teach Chinese language and culture. More than 550 million netizens in China have access to smart cell phones, and other wireless technologies. There is an ever increasing ability to get all sorts of foreign movies, television, and commentary on the internet, and English is the required second language for educated students and citizens, though with recent weakening of the importance of English in the gao kao university entrance exam by the Ministry of Education. This downgrading the value of this exam worries many Chinese teachers of English whom I met in 2013–2014.

The government/party has a double dilemma–the fact that the student body in China is the largest in the world, that more and more middle class parents want the best possible education for their children, and that citizens want access to the internet, cell phones, and emerging information technologies. At the same time, the perceived government/Party need to control the information available to students, citizens, and netizens is becoming more and more difficult. Leaders encourage students to allow the leading Party members to manage the political realm, while following the saying of Deng Xiaoping "to get rich is glorious." Thus, there is an ever expanding middle class, which challenges the rote memorization offered in primary and secondary education, and questions media authenticity. Many adults and students express their interest in the American education system where independent and critical thinking is promoted rather than the Chinese system of constant memorization. In the private school where two of my grandchildren attend, of about 180 students enrolled from the eighth to twelfth grades, more than forty are Chinese.

The government has propagandistically controlled the student and citizen views on the forbidden "three t's and one f" (Tiananmen, Taiwan, the 2008 Olympic torch relays, and Fallun Gong)," but allows short-term symbolic protests (the bombing of the Chinese embassy in Belgrade–1996; the downing of the American spy plane on Hai'nan Island–2001; the 2005 protests against the Japanese educational denials of the severity of the Nangjing massacre of 1937–38; the protests against France and Correfur over the torch relay disturbances in 2008;

and the recent protests against Japan over the South China Sea land disputes remain a difficult task to manage. Nonetheless, both the education of Chinese young people, and the expanding influence of the media, especially the internet, cell phone, and emerging information technologies, are high political priorities for the Chinese People's Republic now and in the foreseeable future. The problem for the government/party is both the desire to expand a broad education and media presence, especially social media in China, while with the perceived need to control both of them, increasing even more with Xi Jinping as the current leader.

At both Beijing Language and Culture University and Shanghai International Studies University, I offered a semester-long lecture series. One series developed the following pattern, typically for an audience of about 300 students, three times at BLCU and one time at SISU:

> Lecture 1: definitions and historical developments in the field of intercultural, international and global communication.
>
> Lecture 2: human rights, social justice, and war and peace.
>
> Lecture 3: poverty vs. sustainable human development.
>
> Lecture 4: Asian and Chinese vs. Western values and world view orientations.
>
> Lecture 5: Eastern and Western cultural views on identity.
>
> Lecture 6: Geert Hofstede's national cultural variables.
>
> Lecture 7: language, including Chinese and Asian languages.
>
> Lecture 8: nonverbal communication cross-culturally.
>
> Lecture 9: international relations and international law.
>
> Lecture 10: multinational organizations.

Lecture 11: international and global media.

Lecture 12: major conclusions relating to the linkages between the various lectures.

I also gave power point lecture series at BLCU and SISU on western civilization. These lectures were well received by the students, freshmen to post graduate students, many coming to hear American English. Naturally, the wide range of topics meant that I had to include a broad academic, practical, and autobiographical basis for many of the lectures. Eventually, these lectures contributed to the significant development and expansion of topics in my global media and culture course and also the ten chapters of *Communicating Interculturally* (2012) with eleven creative dialogues, ten chapters, case studies, and questions for discussion: 1. Culture, 2. Communication and intercultural communication, 3.Creating our own cultural stories, 4. Perceptions, beliefs, worldviews and values, 5. Cultural patterns and cross-cultural value orientations, 6. Verbal and nonverbal communication, 7. Contemporary youth, 8. Cultural media, 9. Intercultural communication in business, training, and education, and 10. Intercultural theories and research. There were also about thirty short guest essays, many of which were written by my own former Chinese students. In 2012–2014, 1,000 copies were sold for Chinese university classes in intercultural communication, mostly in English colleges and departments and some communication and journalism colleges and departments, plus 325 copies for my undergraduate classes at Yangzhou University in 2013–14.

David Shambaugh (2013, p. 243) notes that China now produces more engineers and scientists than all other countries and that it has moved ahead of the US in producing the most Ph.D.s annually. In the 2010 report of premier Wen Jibao, he stated that the goal was to make China "a global leader in several technological spheres in order 'to capture the economic, scientific, and technological high ground' singling out biomedicine, nanoscience, quantum control, energy conversation, information technology, aerospace, and oceanography." With its development of the most elite nine universities (China Nine), and other elite "211" universities, and the goal of becoming global leaders in graduate universities, the world university rankings for 2010–11, ranked the university of Hong Kong twenty-first, Peking University thirty-seventh, and Tsinghua University as fifty-eighth globally. *The Financial Times* ranked the Hong Kong University of Science and Technology's Business MBA program as number nine globally (Shambaugh, p. 243).

However, he notes that there are four reasons why China has not yet fostered a basic research environment:

The first is political. To do basic research (in all fields) necessarily means going beyond politically prescribed boundaries....Second, the culture of academic corruption in China is corrosive and widespread. Academic plagiarism, favoritism, and false credentialism are rampant, and intellectual property rights theft is endemic. Third, innovation requires open-ended intellectual exploration, not rote memorization of knowledge. Chinese educational pedagogy has yet to escape the latter and embrace the former. Fourth, it requires being thoroughly linked into global intellectual and professional networks. In so many areas of the sciences, humanities, and social sciences, Chinese scholars remain trapped in a domestic discourse in Chinese and do not engage in — or contribute much to — international scholarly discourse or publications in the global language of English (Shambaugh, p. 244).

Nonetheless, in my perspective, the Chinese educational system deserves much credit for its forward movement in pulling more than 100 million Chinese out of poverty and illiteracy; creating a substantial middle class, and many highly educated citizens, a reasonably large number of whom are becoming entrepreneurs and potentially national, regional, and global intellectuals and leaders.

Most of the Occupy protesters in Hong Kong in 2014 calling for direct elections of the chief executive, rather than being proposed by the Chinese government, were secondary and university students.

20. Chinese Media

In terms of security both within greater China's borders (The South China Sea, the East China Sea, the Yellow Sea, the Gobi Desert, and the Himalayan Mountains), regionally (especially as the present South China see disputes continue with Southeastern neighbors), and more broadly, the Party and Government not only control all educational institutions but also attempt to control all media, print, radio, television, internet and mobile phones. However, more and more independent media are attempting to provide a more clear reality, through such media as South Morning Post, Renren, Sina Weibo, QQ, Youkou, and the ability to climb over the "Great Firewall. The Government is becoming increasingly sophisticated in blocking access to information that might "hurt the Chinese feelings." Since Xi Jinping has become President, censorship has increased exponentially. Perhaps 100,000 internet censors and paid netizans regularly write posts and open up websites which will provide the approved messages that the Government and Party want available. David Wertime reports that Chinese websites deleted one billion posts in 2014, according to the state media sources (Wertime, 2015: January 17).

Peter Hays Gries' book, *China's New Nationalism: Pride, Politics, and Diplomacy* (2004), said that in 1998, the new China News Agency announced an official web site to promote China's public image abroad and at home, but banned cultural activities that might degrade the country's dignity. He noted that in such instances as the 1999. HE noted that in such instances as the 1999 Belgrade embassy bombing and the 2001 US spy plane collision, private internet chat rooms and websites proliferated, and so many Chinese email messages were sent to the US White House which shut their system down. The China Internet Information Center, an English language government website, organized an extensive Belgrade bombing site with a whole section for international responses. Gries argues that the Belgrade bombing protests were largely a bottom-up movement. They were not, as most western insisted, a topo down Party affair." (p. 133). Currently, a pop-up now appears on the main page of the Ministry of Foreign as Chinese-language web site soliciting the opinions of ordinary Chinese, a relatively new feature for the politically relatively closed However, presently, all web users are now required to use their real names, rather than pseudonymns.

In *The Man Who Changed China: The Life and Legacy of Ziang Zemin* (2004), Robert Lawrence Kuhn contends that Ziang was intensely involved in surfing the internet, that both of his sons were directly working in information technology as careers, and that his grandson was far more proficient in using the internet than he was. Even while *The New York Times* website was often blocked, Jiang regularly read it both in the print and online versions (Gries, pp. 462–464).

After the 2001/9/11 attacks on the World Trade Center and Pentagon, Jiang's immediate public support of President Bush's "War on Terror," generated extensive debate on the internet, much of which was much more critical of the American government's responsibility for causing the tragedy, and much less supportive of Jiang's pledge to Bush (Gries, p. 471).

The April 2005 Chinese netizens' anger erupted publically with public demonstrations and internet commendations over the Japanese lack of sufficient official apologies about their atrocities against the Chinese during the 1930s and 1940's. 1940s, the Japanese children's textbook covering up the atrocities, and Prime Minister Kuizumi's annual visits to the Yasukuni Shrine honoring the war dead, including fourteen war criminals. More recently, Prime Minister Abe's 2014 visit to the shrine, the first by a prime minister in six years, has caused another multiple media and internet storm in China.

Philip P. Pan's February 19, 2006 Washington Post article, "The Click That Broke a Government's Grip," Demonstrates that power in China was seriously challenged in the August 2005, *China Youth Daily* assistant editor's internal criticism of the chief editor, which instantaneously spread both by instant messages, the internet, and quickly emerging websites. As soon as the internet police blocked emails and Chinese websites with headings related to the leak, new ones developed. The episode illustrated the profound impact of the impact that the web posed to its hold on power (Pan, p. A01). His February 22, 2006 Washington Post article, "China's Media Assail Google" comments that the Chinese Government insited that Google should stop telling users of the new Hong Kong Google site each time a search is censured. (p. A09). Google withdrawal to Hong Kong was still open when I was teaching in Yangzhou University during the autumn 2013/14 semester but in 2014 during my November/December visit to Changsha, I was unable to open my Gmail account or Google, while Bing remained open.

In Chapter 8 of *Communicating Interculturally*, "Cultural Media", an imaginary dialogue has a student named Tiger offering the following comment:

> Michael, have you heard the mythical story about the ancient Chinese dove, Gu Gu? It used to live in mainland China, but in March2010, it decided to fly from the mainland to Hong

Kong, as the giant river crab decided that they could no longer live together. Because of the change in the climate, the ancient voracious bird species Pidu ate all of the food that Gu Gu used to eat, and became bigger and bigger and increased the population of the Pidu in the mainland, the river crab which always walks sideways had to work hard to keep moving harmoniously without his friend G uGu to help point out the way (Li & Prosser, 2014, pp. 243–245).

Most of my students at Yangzhou University understood the meaning of this allegory and found it humorous. In the same chapter, we have a section, "Chinese Computer-Mediated Communication," in which Cui Litang has an essay, "Case Study: Wrangling the Media Market Place," as he states: "All media in China are centralized in the sense that they are controlled in ideology by the state government under the banner of China's socialist market economy,…Manifestations of media centralization in practice is cross-media censorship,… when the Google China rift eventually ended up in Google leaving the China upon its unilateral cease of censorship on March 23rd despite its "5,000-year patience" with China…." (Cui, 2014, pp. 258–259).

The increasingly rapid development of new internet users, beyond the 618 million identified netizans in 2014, the explosion of mobile phone instant messages, plus proliferating websites related to computer games, downloading foreign music, movies, and television programs, and every emerging chat rooms on sensitive topics means that more and more firewalls will be breached and that neither the CPC nor the government will constantly be able to halt the expansion of press freedoms. However, while on my first day at Ocean University of China, in 2011 an undergraduate student helped me to "climb over the Great Firewall," but during my 2013–14 semester teaching at Yangzhou University, the software no longer worked, and I found no students who seemed to know how to "climb over" it.

Hillary Clinton, in her book, *Hard Choices* (2014) writes:

> Around the world, some countries began erecting barriers to prevent their people from using the Internet freely and fully. Censors expunged words, names, and phrases from search engine results. They cracked down on citizens who

engaged in nonviolent political speech, and not just during periods of unrest and mass protest. One of the most prominent examples was China, which, as of 2013, was home to nearly 600 million users but also some of the most repressive limits on Internet freedom. The "Great Firewall' blocked foreign websites and particular pages with content perceived as threatening to the Communist party. Some reports estimate that China employed as many as 100,000 censors to patrol the web. (Clinton, 2014, p. 548).

Writing about the January 2009 Google incident, Clinton notes that Google "had discovered Chinese authorities trying to break Into the Gmail accounts of dissidents. The company said It would respond by rerouting Chinese traffic to Hong Kong servers outside the 'Great Firewall" (p. 556). More recently, Yahoo has also left mainland China. During my November/December, 2014 period in Changsha, I was able to open my Yahoo account, but not Gmail. It appears that neither Google nor Gmail can be opened at the present time.

My direct major involvement with the Chinese media, besides teaching about such media in classes, and writing several rather bland articles for the Yangzhou daily newspaper, included twelve interviews on China Central Television International's very well known "Dialogue" programs with three repeated broadcasts daily (2001–04), most of which were hosted by Yang Rui, the chief anchor for most of its history. I was the author of eight monthly articles for *New Oriental English Magazine* (2003–2004); and I was the subject of a feature photo essay in *China Talents Semimonthly Magazine* (in Chinese, 2005: July).

As a part of my various lectures and lecture series at a number of Chinese universities and colleges, I was often interviewed by local television programs or newspapers. In June 2009, Xinhua News Agency interviewed me for a national television feed. Over my period in Yangzhou, from 2001 to 2009 in Shanghai, I could reasonably estimate that several million people in China and beyond, especially in Southeast Asia, saw or heard me on Chinese television or radio. In this way, I gained a much broader reputation even than my dozen keynote addresses at Chinese communication conferences each with about 300 academic participants, and the nearly 9,000 secondary and university student who attended my lectures.

CCTV. English.com states that:

> Dialogue is one of the most acclaimed and influential programs on CCTV International. This 30 minute current affairs news magazine is an authoritative talk show designed to inform and educate viewers worldwide and influence decision makers in governments, businesses and academia. Dialogue provides fair and comprehensive analysis of current affairs within the framework of cross- cultural and multi-disciplinary comparisons. Chinese and foreign guests openly express their opinions on issues making headlines in China and around the world. Through frank discussions, and sometimes heated debates, viewers are encouraged to reach their own conclusions. (CCTV, 2003).
>
> An estimated five to ten million viewers watched "Dialogue" during that period in China with another million viewers outside China. Today, the number has far exceeded that number with 90 million viewers around the world (CCV Dialogue, 2014).

I often found Yang Rui to have a very subtle anti-American prejudice, and since the programs were recorded for five minutes longer than the actual broadcast, this allowed the producers to edit out any sensitive material] by foreign guests.

Challenging CCTV's statement about its "fair and comprehensive analysis of current affairs within the framework of cross-cultural and multi-disciplinary comparisons" the Chinese media, whether by television, or by radio, or in the print media or internet, were generally forbidden from discussing religion. Of course, such potentially violent situations as occurred in Tibet in 2008 and later, protests in Xinjiang, attacks against Falun Gong (Falun Dafa), or Tiananmen Square in 1989, as well as many rural protests against provincial land seizures, corruption, or environmental pollution could often not be discussed freely by much of the Chinese media. Teaching ten years and giving speeches on various topics at many Chinese secondary and tertiary institutions, I was always aware that I had considerable freedom of expression in private conversations; reasonable freedom in the classroom, less freedom in public lectures or writing, and very limited freedom when I was interviewed on television and radio if I was discussing topics relating to China. If I wished to criticize American policies, then I could have unlimited freedom of expression. My 2014 keynote address on "Social Media and Cybernetics in Asia" required considerable self-censorship.

For the November 2014 Inaugural World Internet Conference in Wenzhou, according to Charles Riley, the government allowed the 1,000 participants to have access to Facebook, Twitter, and You Tube for the three days of the conference: "The concession underlines the dilemma facing non-Chinese tech firms as they try to reconcile the country's enormous potential with its heavy-handed approach to censorship and market access. Executives from tech firms including Facebook (FB, Tech30), Cisco (CSCO, Tech30) and Qualcomm (QCOM, Tech30), for example, are at the conference. But Facebook is banned inside China, Qualcomm was recently investigated as part of an antitrust probe, and Cisco has been caught in the fallout of the Snowden spy scandal" (Riley, 2014: November 21).

My first of twelve "Dialogue" interviews was in November, 2001 with Yang Rui while I was still a professor at Yangzhou University, as I was also being interviewed for a position at Beijing Language and Culture University for 2003–2004. This was the first time that a faculty member from Yangzhou University had been interviewed on Dialogue, and the program was added to the university's website until after I left there in the summer of 2003. Subsequently, I participated in eleven more Dialogue interviews, often paired with a Chinese expert. An early interview was with Fred Casmir, discussing intercultural communication. My last interview was on Lunar New Year's day in 2004 hosted by both Yang Rui and his colleague Tian Wei with the Chinese editor of a popular magazine about Beijing and me as the guests. For an unexplainable reason, I was never invited to be a guest on another Dialogue program from that time until I left Beijing in the summer of 2005.

David Shambaugh assesses the two "Dialogue" anchors as:

"The two hosts present contrasting faces to the world. Yang Rui is an aggressive (often impolite) male interviewer, while Tian Wei is the opposite: female, attractive, suave, polite, inquisitive, and intellectual. While Yang Rui often gives a negative and nationalistic image to foreign viewers, Tian Wei offers a softer and more inquisitive face of China to international audiences. Yang Rui fancies himself 'China's Mike Wallace' and has consciously studied the late American anchor's aggressive on-camera style. He badgers and is often offensive to on-camera guests. When I asked him why this is so, he curtly replied; 'Hard politics, hard talk' (Shambaugh, 2013).

In my case, however, despite some frequent subtle anti-Americanism on Yang Rui's part, he was always very friendly with me, typically calling his Chinese guests by their formal names and calling me Michael. He still does the same with Chinese and many foreign guests. We had several very cordial conversations before and after the programs. I loaned him several books about American politics, which were never returned and which I sometimes heard quoted in later programs.

As illustrative of my early attention in my China university teaching to the media as the 2003 Iraq War developed, on January 29 and 30, 2003, Yang Rui conducted a two part "Dialogue' with Peter Trubowitz, an American Fulbright professor and Tao Wenzhao, a frequent program interviewee, both who were teaching at Beijing Foreign Studies University. They agreed that in his State of the Union address, Bush continued to encourage Congress and the American people to support the anti-terrorism campaign and to prepare them for a likely war with Iraq. Tao proposed that a time table was developing for a likely US war with Iraq, noting that with Hans Blix' Iraq inspection report to the UN Security Council, the State of the Union address, a visit by Prime Minister Tony Blair, and Secretary of State Colin next highly expected but inaccurate report of evidence to the Security Council on February 5 that there was clear evidence that Saddam Hussein had stockpiles of "weapons of mass destruction." The two professors agreed that Bush and Blair might take unilateral military action against Iraq by the end of February, 2003.

With Yang Rui's encouragement, Trubowitz and Tao argued that with worldwide protests developing against an anticipated war, and 70% percent of Americans polled by the *Washington Post,* the weapons inspectors should have an additional month or so to complete their inspections. Trubowitz also remarked that calling Iraq and North Korea "the two most dangerous governments in the world" was an echo of Bush's 2002 "Axis of Evil' phrase and while very appealing in demonizing the two governments, it was very bad diplomacy.

One of my most interesting "Dialogue" interviews was toward the beginning of the Iraq war in March, 2003. When Professors Howard Sypher and Jay Wang of Purdue University and I were interviewed on March 24 for two "Dialogue" Programs, there was a fast turnaround with the programs having a lively discussion about the now ongoing war airing the next two days. On April 23 and 24, Professor Mei Renyi of the Beijing Foreign Studies University and I were featured interviewees on the program about Bush's goals in the Middle East following the apparent "shock and awe" victory in Iraq. During this same general period, there were almost daily articles in *China Daily* about the war, often very critical of President Bush and Prime Minister Tony Blair, being shown in frequent derogatory political cartoons. I followed the news and opinion articles closely during the spring of 2003, first about the Iraq and later about the SARS crisis.

In 2008, while I was teaching at Shanghai International Studies University, an agreement was made with International Shanghai Channel for a cooperative linkage. I was among those named as an expert for the Channel. Subsequently, I was featured on the program "Culture Matters" for a program "Intercultural Friendship" and I included my own MA students in three of the programs: Anthea Yang Sha (now a Ph.D. student at Purdue University, married, and with a child); Zizi Zhao Zhao (now living in Wellington, New Zealand, married and a mother); and Jacky Zhang (now a faculty member at Dezhou University in Shangdong Province, married and with an expected child). A fourth program featured me and an Irish podcaster. These four programs were rebroadcast in 2009, and thus we reached several million viewers. During the 2008 US presidential campaign, I was featured on two programs with a Chinese faculty member from Fudan University. On election day, it was planned that a Chinese professor from Shanghai International Studies University and I would jointly provide about four hours of commentary. However, on the Sunday before the election, station officials contacted me to cancel my involvement as it would have been a live program, rather than being prerecorded, which was against the media rules for including a foreigner.

Over the period that I was teaching at Shanghai International Studies University, I was a monthly guest in Shanghai, prerecorded on China Radio International's daily program "People in the Know" hosted by a Canadian journalist from Beijing. Before each program, we discussed the topic, with his admonition not to introduce any sensitive information.

Summing up my own involvement in the Chinese media, it is fair to say that many million people, in and out of China, particularly in South East Asia, saw me on China Central TV's twelve "Dialogue" programs from 2001–2004 and Shanghai International Channel's four 2008 "Culture Matters" programs on intercultural friendship, which were rebroadcast in 2009; several million persons heard me on China Radio International's programs, "People in the Know" on a monthly basis while I was teaching at Shanghai International Studies University; perhaps several hundred thousand saw the featured article about me in the July 2005 *China Talents Semimonthly Magazine* (in Chinese); and more than 60,000 each month read my articles for *New Oriental Magazine*. Several million probably saw me in my Xinhua 2009 interview in Beijing as it was a live feed for all television stations in China.

Perhaps 4,000–5,000 people heard me give my fifteen or more keynote addresses in China, India, Japan, Russia, and the United States on topics related especially to intercultural and international communication. I taught about 2,500 Chinese students, and perhaps 8,500 secondary and university students heard me give lectures; and two of these university lectures appeared on Youkou as well. Chinese search engines such as Baidu and Sina Weibo include a reasonable amount of material related to me, including Peter Zhang Long's Shanghai International Studies University 2008 master's thesis about me, plus Li Mengyu's and my coauthored textbook, *Communicating Interculturally* (2012) and the three books published by Steve J. Kulich, Weng Liping, and me for Shanghai Foreign Language Education Press (2007, 2012, 2014).

How different my professional and personal life would have been if I had not answered the suggestion of my Chinese communication colleagues in 2000 when they suggested that as I was retiring from the University of Virginia and Rochester Institute of Technology simultaneously in 2001, I should go to teach in China, and I responded "Why not?" Had I resumed my tenure at the University of Virginia, it is unlikely that I would have taught in China.

21. Meeting the Chinese for the First Time: 2001–02

In Yangzhou in 2001–2002, my first Chinese living experience, I was delighted to meet my more than 300 students at the university, some who became very good friends. On the streets, friendly young teenagers would say, "Hello, how are you? I am fine, thank you, and you?" I began to call Yangzhou the "Hello" city because so many young people greeted me in this way. Foreigners were not so unusual there as in other smaller cities that I visited in China during my first year. Still, this was often the first time that these teenagers had talked just a little to a foreigner. Just after the two week military training for the freshmen at the university, sitting together at the basketball courts, I met a freshman chemistry student, Maxwell May, who later became one of my best young friends in China. He visited me later in Beijing when he assisted me in a winter English camp, in Shanghai, and in my last teaching in Yangzhou as well as at the hospital in Yangzhou in 2013 because of food poisoning. When I went to teach in Beijing in 2002, he encouraged a friendship with a second year chemistry major at Beijing Mining and Technology University next to my campus, Wing Mars, who in the spring of 2003 set up my webpage registered in China. He transferred it in February 2011 to an international Word Press blog. When I taught at Shanghai International Studies University, Wing lived with me for several months, and I often visited his home near Changzhou. He and his wife, Nightingale, have a lovely little son, Eagle. Maxwell and his sweetheart since 2001, Athena, married in February 2011, and they are now the parents of a small daughter.

Besides teaching English to juniors, seniors, and postgraduate students at Yangzhou University, as well as lecturers interested in going abroad, I held about thirty Friday evening open house/English corners in my apartment that year. Later in Beijing, I had about ninety more open houses/English corners, with students coming from several different nearby universities. In my ten years of teaching in China, I always had three big annual parties: for Halloween, Christmas and my birthday in March.

During the October 2001 week long national day holiday, I traveled eight days to see the magnificent three gorges: twenty-four hours by train to Chengdu, with a night in a small international hotel where a dozen of us from various countries chatted together in English. Then I went by bus from Chengdu to Chongqing, spending three days on a tourist ship coming east through the gorges, and later with a night in Wuhan. Then I traveled on an overnight ferry from Wuhan to Nangjing, and then by bus back to Yangzhou. I felt rather brave making my first such a complicated Chinese tourist trip alone, but I was also lonely. However, as I wandered into the train's hard seat car, two very kind young rural men with no English invited me to sit with them. They fed me oranges, peanuts and my first moon cakes. In Chongqing, I sat high on the steps going up from the bus station where I attracted a shifting crowd of about fifty curious and friendly people. A sixteen year old girl interpreted for me as I had friendly contacts with the people and many of them came to shake hands with me. A three year-old boy delighted the crowd as he came back and forth several times from his father to sit on my lap, causing applause from the nearby adults.

Walking slower than the tourists going to our ship, I lost sight of our tour group and got on the wrong ship. A pleasant young woman employee, with no English, led me back a half kilometer to the correct ship. As I was transferred three or four times to a different cabin, perhaps because those in the cabin didn't want a foreigner with them, a boy about nine went back and forth with me holding my hand as I was moved from cabin to cabin. Finally, two men and a woman accepted me as the fourth person in their cabin. The boy and other children, speaking a little English, spent a lot of time with me perhaps, as a friendly foreign (laowai) grandpa with no Chinese. Their mothers often fed me snacks. I understood that children everywhere can be most kind and friendly, if their parents have taught them to be so.

I took a twenty-four-hour ferry trip east to Nangjing. Where I practiced simple English, laughed, sang with a group of teenagers, and as a sort of Santa Claus, I gave many English names to those who had brought me to their dormitory. When I mistakenly used the woman's toilet, a little boy about four laughed, pointed to the correct WC and thought my error was very funny. There were two or three adults with reasonable English who chatted briefly with me as we traveled. One medical doctor urged me to keep my knees warm, and I later learned from various Chinese to keep my belly, feet, and back warm. It took me some time to appreciate drinking hot liquids regularly.

In October, 2001, I made my first visit to Xi'an for the fourth China association for the Chinese Intercultural Communication conference at Xi'an International Studies University where I was a keynoter, the first time of more than a dozen times in China. I was invited to join the faculty there in 2002, but the vice president of Beijing Language and Culture University invited me then to give some lectures there and to learn whether I would like to teach at BLCU in 2002–03. Subsequently, I did so and also was an interviewee on CCTV English international channel for the 'Dialogue' program, which was placed on the Yangzhou University School of Foreign Language website until I left there in the summer of 2002, as I was the first faculty member to appear on "dialogue" from Yangzhou University. It was a matter of prestige for the university that I was an interviewee on "dialogue" until I moved to Beijing Language and Culture University in the summer of 2002. I understood later that my interview was taken down from the school's website soon after I departed. The dean of the college of foreign languages hosted the young faculty and me, with guests also among the Chinese professors, for a very nice dinner about every six weeks. As the implicit protocol indicated, as the one older foreign professor, I was at his right side, except for one time when his own former professor was a guest, when I moved to his left, understandably. Interestingly, for our last dinner that spring semester, he placed me on his left, and a twenty-four old teacher on his right, probably symbolic of his potential displeasure at my leaving.

For an hour or two daily for about two weeks in November, I sat for fifteen sophomore Yangzhou University art majors who did pencil drawing sketches of me, mostly head drawings. All of the students gave me their sketches, after taking photos of them for their port folios. I had the sketches on a bedroom wall there as well as at Beijing Language and Culture University. During the academic year, I joined a number of their class parties. I was also invited to give talks or participate in their social events by the English college, international trade, physics, and chemistry student groups.

In November, 2001, I began as a volunteer, reinforcing the English teaching by their teachers every other Saturday in a new private primary and junior middle foreign language school in Yizheng, thirty kilometers from Yangzhou and part of its administrative district. The great enthusiasm of the children, whom I taught an hour for 200 primary school children, and an hour for 200 junior middle school children, really made me feel like an old rock star. When I came every other week, with a couple of my students as interpreters, the children would call out "Michael, Michael!" as I came into their auditorium. We laughed together, sang English songs, and we had some Chinese-styled cross talk with my students and two small stuffed pandas, Amanda and Randy, plus a yellow dog clock. The children would then repeat what my two accompanying students and I had said for the pandas and clock: "Hello, Amanda, how are you?" "I am fine, Randy, but yellow dog frightens me." "Don't worry, Amanda, I will protect you." "Go away, yellow dog. Don't bother Amanda anymore!" "Thanks, Randy." The children were always glad to see me, my students, and Randy and Amanda again.

In January, I began teaching simple English to three different classes of thirty kindergarten children. For the two different students who accompanied me each time, they had an opportunity to learn a bit about teaching in English, had a very exquisite lunch, and got to ride in a new blue Buick each time with Mr. Jin, the owner of the school. He gave us a regular luxurious lunch at his restaurant and he gave me many gifts, including a porcelain laughing Buddha, two Tang dynasty jackets, and a tailored leather coat which he identified as the same amount of leather as for three Chinese men. He took me and my students for several overnight trips in the vicinity such as Wuxi, where there is a giant golden Buddha, and Changzhou. When I was about to leave Yangzhou University in the summer of 2002, he offered me a fulltime teaching position as the English expert at a considerably higher salary than I received that year at the university. While this volunteer teaching experience was certainly one of my best and most pleasurable ones in China, my professional teaching career was at the university level since I taught junior middle school student Latin in the 1960s, and I had already agreed to teach in 2002–03 at Beijing Language and Culture University.

In March, 2002, I began teaching English the other two Saturdays a month to five or six classes of junior middle school students in a public junior middle school in Taizhou, forty kilometers from Yangzhou. I received the same enthusiasm from children as I had gotten in the foreign language school. These teaching opportunities made me realize how wonderful, kind, and generous the Chinese children and their parents could be.

For the 2002 spring festival, my junior student, Devon Yang and I traveled by bus to Xuzhou in northwest Jiangsu Province. While it was his "hometown," he had never been there. Coming out of the station, he urged me not to talk to anyone as he might be a criminal. I was shocked and teary eyed when a policeman knocked down a woman beggar with her child who had approached me. At the Xuzhou war memorial museum, he tried to steer a small battery-operated jeep, crashed through a hedge, and hit a large tree, as he had never driven even a small vehicle before. Luckily, he was not injured. It frightened him and worried me. We traveled by bus to his very poor rural home about eighty kilometers south of Xuzhou, where his very kind peasant family, five or six years younger than I, their neighbors, and friends or acquaintances paid very special attention to me and fed us very well. I was both Devon's guest, and the first foreigner (laowai) any of those in the village had met before. Their interpreted comments included statements like: "I have seen these foreigners on televison, but I have never met any of them face to face." "Oh! He is so tall!" We met his former teachers who were very proud of his achievements, as he was the only one in his graduating class who had gone to a university. The villagers urged me to come back again, which I did for his wedding in 2005. Devon is now an English teacher in Suining county, Northwest Jiangsu Province, his real hometown area. He is married, owns an apartment and car, and has an eight year old son, whom he has named Michael for his English name. During my visit in 2002, there were many mule and donkey wagons, plus ancient tractors, on the country roads, which I no longer saw in my more recent visits. In the larger city where Devon and his family live, three stone-mountain sheep stand at the center circle of the moderately modern city as its symbol, even with an "international" hotel, although I never met a foreigner there.

Then we traveled to Dong Hai, the crystal capital of China, where we met Devon's classmates, Garrett Pon and Jesse Zhang. Both Garrett's family in dong hai and Jesse's family in Linyanungang served us very delicious meals at their homes, typically with more than a dozen food items and they welcomed me very graciously. The four of us had a wonderful time at the yellow sea, taking our shirts off, wading in the water, and collecting sea shells. It was Devon's first time at the sea. Garrett is now a businessman and is married. In November 2013, I met him and a dozen of his former classmates at Yangzhou University who had come for a tenth graduation anniversary reunion. Jesse, with an MA in translation, translates English and Chinese legal documents for a legal company in Shanghai. He was my apartment-mate for several years in Shanghai. He and his wife own a luxurious apartment. Their new daughter, Jessica Jane, was born in May, 2013.

Also during the 2002 spring festival, another of my students, Jack QIn and I traveled by train to Guangzhou, Changsha, and Shaoshan, the birthplace of Chairman Mao. Someone tried to "pick my back pocket" in Guangzhou, but I caught his hand before he had slipped any money out. Jack decided after that to walk slightly behind me to protect me from future "pick pockets" and said that he would fight anyone who tried to take money from my pockets. It was Jack's first time to see the south sea, and he was happy to watch a dolphin and walrus marine show, to visit his first hard rock café, and to see the first harry potter film. When we arrived in Changsha, Jack became quite homesick as he had never been so far away from his home in Nangtong and it was his first time out of Jiangsu province. We were impressed with Chairman Mao's simple reasonably well-off peasant home. I compared it mentally to the grand homes that founders of the US such as George Washington and Thomas Jefferson had in the late 1700's. He also had a sophomore girlfriend, Ruth, whom he declared, he was 99% sure would be his future wife. There were no train accommodations back to the Yangzhou area, and in order to be back in time for the spring semester classes, we flew to Nanjing and too a bus from there. This was Jack's first train ride and first plane trip, something that almost none of my students at Yangzhou University had ever done.

After graduation, however, he worked for two years in Botswana. Now he is an international businessman, going regularly to Germany, Japan, Singapore, and the US. He is married to Sherry, not Ruth, with a daughter, living in Nantong. His parents also live with them. His parents and I visited him and his wife at the home of his parents-in-law for the 2009 lunar New Year in Taizhou. Jack and I also visited my former student, Richard Chen, called by his Yangzhou University classmates "the white boy" because of his light complexion. Ru Gao is popularly identified as the longevity city as many residents who had become centenarians were celebrated in a longevity park. Richard and his wife have a small daughter. When I left Taizhou by bus to return to Shanghai, Jack warned me to be careful about my seatmate, as he might be "a separatist or splittist." probably the young man sitting next to me was neither, and in fact, he spoke no English.

In April, 2002, during the two day sports holiday for Yangzhou University, my students, Terry (called by his classmates, "the mouse" because of his facial features) and Richard Chen, accompanied me to yellow mountain (Mount Hangshan) in Anhui Province. We took the cable car two-thirds up the mountain, where I remained while they climbed up and around the top. I was surprised to see so many Chinese men tourists wearing suits and ties and the women wearing skirts, dresses, and high heels. We guessed that they were perhaps first time mountain climbers, or wished to have photos of themselves for their family and friends in their best clothes at the top of the mountain. I was surprised also to see that many of them littered the ground around us with cardboard containers, empty bottles, and other throw-away items. This was an interesting cultural difference for me, as in American parks and tourist areas many signs prohibit people from littering, as well as guards imposing fines for those who disobey the signs. This was still in the early stages of Chinese tourism. In traveling with my Chinese students, I always had two main rules: "don't waste food" and "don't litter."

Subsequently, I traveled in China with students Joe Fan, his brother Frank Fan, and my student Jet Sun to Dallian; Tony Weitang to Chengda, Harbin, and Qingdao; Sean (Shawn) Chen to Yangzhou and Shanghai; David Xu to Wuhan and Jing Ming, Hubei Province); Charles Cheng to Anching, Anhui Province; Jessie William Zhang to Lianyungang; Steven Ru to Huaibei, Anhui Province; Jack Qin to Taizhou and Nantong; Jacky Zhang to Jillin, Qingdao, Fujian, Xiamen, and Guangzhou, and Jethro Jiang to Jinan, Shangdong Province. I took Nick Deng to Vietnam (2003); Shawn Chen to Cambodia (2004); Tony Weitong to South Korea (2004); David Li to India (2005); David Xu to Russia, Germany, Denmark, Sweden, The Netherlands, Belgium, France, Monaco, and Italy (2006); Charles Cheng to the Philippines and Russia (2008); and Jacky Zhang on a cruise from Australia to New Zealand (2009), to Japan, Thailand and Cambodia in 2009, Singapore, Malaysia, Indonesia, and the US in 2010. He has visited me in the US in 2010 and 2014. In 2015, we will travel in Scandinavia together.

Only a few Chinese faculty at my four universities, while being friendly, became close friends or maintained a long term friendship. Exceptions are Cui Iltang with whom I coedited *Social Media in Asia* (2014), Li Mengyu, my host at Ocean University of China and with whom I coauthored *Communicating Interculturally* (2012) and its North American version, *Chinese Communicating Interculturally* (2014) as well as Linda Zhang Hongling, Cherry Ruobing Chi and Weng ILping in the Intercultural Institute at Shanghai International Studies University. My former postgraduate student at Yangzhou University and now an associate professor in applied linguistics there, Lu jJn, and his wife, also my former student, Kathleen Jjin, are both very special friends.

22. Some Thoughts on the Beijing Language and Culture University: 2002–05

Beijing Language and Culture University was founded initially as Beijing Language Institute, and for its 40th anniversary in 2002, it returned to the Chinese name "Beijing Language University," but retained "Beijing Language and Culture University" in its English version for its international student programs. I was present for that autumn 2002 celebration as I had also been at Yangzhou University for its celebration of founding in the spring of 2002. BLCU has the largest foreign student population in the world studying Chinese, with about 1600 foreign students annually but not all are present at the same time. They come to study Chinese or Chinese culture, Chinese linguistics, or international trade taught in English. Typically, about 140 countries are represented with the two largest groups being Korean and Japanese. The number includes several hundred students from Asia, Africa, and the former Soviet Republics who are here on scholarships, with even a few older North Korean scholarship students. After a year of intense Chinese at BLCU, many of these students proceed to another Chinese university for a master's program or a science major in their chosen fields. Many have just come for a short course, semester, or year abroad. All students coming from outside China, except scholarship students, pay their fees in American dollars or equivalents. Some anti-Japanese sentiment existed among the Chinese undergraduates, who considered the Japanese students to be lazy, spoiled and cliquish.

About 4,500 Chinese students were at BLCU, of whom 2500 of whom were degree students. Six hundred and sixty extra students were entering the university over the usual rate each year since 2002. The ratio of Chinese men to women was about 1 to 7. The three largest degree programs were English with the most majors, plus teaching Chinese as a foreign language, and Chinese language, literature and culture. More recently, majors in information technology and finance were added. Many of the texts in information technology and finance were written in English. In 2003, a new arts department was introduced to the humanity faculty. Within the School of Foreign Languages, there were also majors in Arabic, French, German, Japanese, Korean, and Spanish.

The Continuing Education College had various majors for nontraditional aged Chinese students and the Pre-departure program enrolled mature Chinese students who expected or hoped to study abroad to or work in English speaking countries. BLCU had its own major Training and Testing Center for GRE, TOEFL, IELTS, ETSCOPE and other certificate exams for studying overseas. Most broad decisions for BLCU were generated from the Ministry of Education.

There were about forty foreign faculty members at BLCU, mostly from English speaking countries, but also including nationals from France, Germany, Italy, Japan, and Spain. The English Department had eight foreign faculty, representing Canada, ireland, the uk, and the us but oral English courses additionally were taught in several other departments with Australia and New Zealand also represented as well as Chinese professors teaching English and the other languages.

The CPC (Communist Party of China) with a total of about 88 million members plays a major role in all public universities in China, with each campus having a general secretary, and each school, college, or department having a nonteaching Party officer. It is my understanding that all Chinese faculty at the rank of dean or above or university officials usually must be members of the party. Just as in the former Soviet Union, and presently in North Korea, Vietnam, and Laos children become Young Pioneers; this is also true in China. Then, when students are in senior middle school and university, they are automatically members of the Youth League whose function is rather ambiguous even to the league members. Hu Jintao was a former leader of the Youth League.

I believe that 10–15% of the seniors at BLCU were Party members or candidates under the supervision of the Party. Among the English department seniors, about an average of four students in each of the six classes of twenty-four were party members or candidates. Among the junior English majors, there might have been only an average of two party members in each of the 6 classes. I have been told that students who were active in the school, college, or department level student unions, or who had served as class monitors for a long period often had the best chances of becoming Party members. Students who wished to enter government ministries after graduation usually were expected to become party members, while those in international trade related majors were less likely to become members. Students said that at other universities where there were mostly Chinese students enrolled, the average number of party members or candidates was likely to be much higher than at BLCU. Party members can often expect better jobs, housing, incomes, and more benefits in the future. Some however, who wish "to dedicate themselves with their whole hearts and souls to the people," are eager to become members because "to be a party member would be glorious," or because "my grandfather and father are party members, and my family expects me also to be a member" or "my family is proud if I become a Party member." Many students avoided becoming party members.

At various levels of education, to advance to the next level, for example, junior middle school to senior middle school, senior middle school to university, and undergraduate university to post graduate study, students must pass rigorous exams related to Marxism-Leninism, Mao Tsedong thought, Deng Xaioping theory, and Jiang Zemin's may 2001 "three represents" theory (advanced productive forces, advanced culture, and broad masses of the people), which is now enshrined both in China's and the CPC constitutions. Though Marxism-Leninism is almost never taught any longer in Russia, it remains the basis in China of "socialism with Chinese characteristics (or face)." Most students learn what they must do to pass the doctrinally rigid exams, and then they say that they discard the information for their own lives, especially since China's real working philosophy today is based on socialist-capitalism or the emerging market economy.

I found that to be true also in my visit to Vietnam with my BLCU student Nick Deng. Chinese graduating seniors were required to fill out an essay form in which they identified their major contributions the last four years and in which they could "provide honest reactions for the party, plus self-criticisms." One senior suggested to me that this might cause students to write: "if you are a party member you can exaggerate what you have accomplished to make the party look good, but if you are not a party member, you should be honest about areas of your weaknesses."

Premier Wen Jiabao argued that the peasants, farmers, and migrant workers were the 'most hard working people in China," but that saying was applied more and more to China's students which was a long-standing party axiom. In rural and small city junior and senior middle schools, many students boarded at the schools and had classes six days a week with unending homework. Later the ministry of education eliminated Saturday classes for these students. Besides being expected to be thoroughly familiar with politics as described above. Students entering the university ideally should have a strong background in such Chinese major classics as Confucius' *Analects*, Cao Xueqin's *Dream of the Red Mansion,* Wu Cheng'en's *the Journey to the West,* Luo Guanzhong's *The Three Warring States,* Shi Nai'an's *108 Generals' Rebellion by the Water,* Li Bai's and Du fu's poems, and *the Arrt of War* by Sun zi. Among twentieth century works, they should ideally also be familiar with Lu Xun's "Diary of a Madman," Guo Moruo's poem "Goddess," Mao Dun's "The Sun Rise," Ba Jin's "Home, Autumn, Spring," and Lao She's "Tea House." The reality is not always the same as the ideal as a number of BLCU students told me that like the political topics, their understanding of the expected classical and contemporary works was at best superficial even if they were required by parents or teachers to memorize famous quotes from these works.

Students in senior middle schools whose emphasis is "art" tend to go into university programs related to the humanities, languages, and social sciences, while those who stress "science," especially the men, are more likely to go into science or engineering programs. Thus most students at BLCU, including finance and teaching Chinese as a foreign language, and generally except for information technology majors, came out of the senior middle school art track. Students at the time that I was at BLCU were often selected by universities for majors other than those which they chose, depending on the Ministry of Education's announced needs for graduates in that major. Seven million senior middle school students took the two-day university gao kao entrance exam in June during the early 2000s, for about four million university slots. It used to be given in July and was called the "Black July" exam, but now as it began to be given for the first time in June, 2003 it is now called the "Black June" exam. Students who do not pass this exam are unlikely to go to a public university in China

One's future education is determined by success in that exam. At BLCU, most entering Chinese students tended to have reasonable English. This was not always the same for students coming from communities where the level of English teaching was less strong than in the best junior and senior middle schools and as they entered some of the other eighty-nine universities in Beijing. There were then 670,000 university students in the Haidian district, where BLCU is located. Somehow, in the college English test 4 (cet-4) taken by millions of non-English majors throughout China one year the composition question was posted on the internet at 2:30 am that morning. It created a serious educational problem for China. As time has gone by, apparently hacking of the various exam files has gotten more prevalent.

In my advanced writing classes for juniors, an assignment was expected every two weeks, and in an effort to develop the students' creative efforts, I had students learning to sing songs such as "oh where have you been Billy boy, Billy boy?" "Day is done," and "Where have all the flowers gone?" With an essay required for developing the topic more fully. In 2002, I learned that my junior English majors had never been assigned to write poetry. I had them write poetry in the form of the Old Testament psalms, simplified Shakespearean sonnets, and twelve-line free verse poems. I also gave them assignments to write short stories, and plays. Groups of six prepared a magazine during the semester which for the women students tended to be overwhelmingly romantic magazines. The students had not previously had any creative assignments like these. Once, with an assignment to create a simple fourteen line sonnet, one of the women students plagiarized "the Rose" by Bette Midler, and I invited her to the front of the class to recite her "sonnet." Then I suggested that together we could sing it which we did, but not mentioning that she had cheated on the assignment. Later, she privately apologized that she had used an already existing song, rather than creating her own sonnet. For a book review of a book of fiction that they were supposed to read, one woman student turned in a review of "a Rose for Emily," a short story by William Faulkner, as her book review. A term paper was required at the end of each semester, 3,000 words the first semester and 5,000 words the second semester, where plagiarism tended to develop among about 25% of the students. Considerable plagiarism occurred among the senior students' 10,000 word BA theses, with topics like the Chinese food or tea culture often copied almost word for word from original sources available on Google.

Beijing Language and Culture University, dominated by Chinese women, was separated from Beijing Mining and Technology University, essentially mostly populated by men in various sciences, by a tall brick wall. My women students often expressed their wish that there would be a gate between the two campuses so that the men and women students could move easily back and forth. Once for a semester advanced writing course final exam, I gave a creative assignment to my two classes in which the two universities were going to be merged into one university, and my students' task as advisers to the BLCU president was to advise him on the process of the merger. The students, used to rather formulaic exams based on memorization of standard topics, found it to be very interesting and asked me to continue that type of semester final exams. For another semester final exam, I provided the topic of falling in love with one of the campus' foreign students and I had the students write about the intercultural complications of such romances, as they were seen by university authorities, their classmates, and their families. Some of the women students did, indeed, fall in love with foreign student men, adding some heart-break situations when the foreign men changed quite easily to another romance or went back to their home countries.

Teaching two year-long classes of debate, in the first semester, all of the students were involved in group discussions, American-style debates, and British parliamentary style debates. In the second semester, for the first time in my teaching in China in the second semester, I had my debate students simulate a model United Nations Security Council with the students representing actual countries in the Council, and debating about six topics actually before the real Council. As a few English major students at BLCU went into the diplomatic corps or international trade, I received emails later indicating that this semester simulation had helped to make them more internationally oriented. A few of our English majors were actually involved later in model united nations simulations, both in China and in Singapore.

During December, 2002, 2003, and 2004, I showed six episodes of CNN's "Cold War" series to my 150 seniors in western civilization (which covered 3500 years of cultural development), including the ones about the early Soviet-Western cooperation before 1945, the Chinese developments from 1949 through the Nxon visit in February 1972, the Vietnam war, the sixties- "make love, not war," tearing down the Berlin Wall, and the concluding episode exploring the end of the Cold War. The English Department dean generously permitted the use of these videos but asked that I make a disclaimer for several of the episodes that the information might be at variance with other facts as the students had learned them, and that they should consider various perspectives carefully (with an emphasis on their learning in their politics classes, often quite different than the portrayal by the CNN Cold War series).

Still, according to some of my close senior student friends, some of the information was highly shocking, particularly relating to China's development and the demise of communism in Eastern Europe. However, it didn't generate any in-class discussion and only a little response directly to me by students outside of class. One student wrote out a question for me to discuss in class, saying that as a part of the politics preparation (Marxism-Leninism, Mao Tsedong thought, Deng Xiaoping theory, Jiang Zemin three represents) for the post graduate exams which he had taken, he was required to memorize a statement that the capitalist countries had been led up to the present time by those whose major concerns had been the dominant monied class and without concern for the proletariat poor classes. He said that the series gave him a different sense on this topic, but that he would still be required to repeat the memorized information for the politics portion of the exam. In the CNN episode on tearing down the wall in 1989, there was perhaps a minute given to the tragic June 3–4 Tinanamen Square event, and several people commenting in the video from Eastern Europe said that during this period they were highly afraid that the Soviet Union would apply the "Chinese solution" to their situations in Hungary, Czechoslovakia, Poland, and East Germany.

This Western and East European perspective on these events, and the last episode about the final collapse of Marxism-Leninism in Eastern Europe, were perhaps the most disturbing aspects of the episodes which my Chinese students viewed. Generally, the episode about China was seen by many of the students as reasonably balanced as there were authoritative voices from China, the Soviet Union, and the US. Some views seriously contradicted their own understanding from their courses on politics of the development of China from 1949–1972. They began however to get a sense of the importance of critical thinking as a potential benefit of having a foreign teacher's perspective.

The last class paper in my senior Western Civilization capstone course for English majors allowed a focus on the US Civil War, or comparing the Cold War between either the US or Europe and China or the Soviet Union from 1945 to 1989, or more recent developments between such countries. Sixteen students turned in a paper, "There are a myriad number of reasons for the US Civil War," all in various renditions, plagiarized from Google. As the papers emphasizing the Cold War were more informed by the CNN videos, made available to all the class members, they tended to quote more from the videos themselves with attribution to the videos than from Google. It was a good lesson for me to make such assignments more cheat-proof, which the later cultural story assignments were generally able to do.

In an informal but on random survey of BLCU Chinese students which I took in March 2003 in one of my public lectures, asking them for their six most important personal values, seventy-two women, ages 19–34, had listed the following most important values, but not in rank order: family (60), friends (50), career and love (both 37), money (33), health (28) freedom (17), happiness (9), good environment (8), leisure (7), relations with others (6), and knowledge, kindness, trust, marriage, and honesty each (5), plus others. Among the sixteen Chinese males at BLCU in the survey, ages 18–23, they ranked family (13), friends (11), career (9), happiness and money each (6), an enriched or colorful life (4), love, freedom, and music each (3), patriotism and sports each (2), and various single answers, including sex. The stress on "filial piety" as espoused by the analects as among their six most important values by most of the surveyed students.

Informally called the "Little UN," BLCU's integration of foreign and Chinese students could have been much better, for example, by having optional male and female dormitories set aside for foreign and Chinese roommates to live together. Ten years before or more, Chinese and foreign students could live together, but intercultural differences in living habits caused them not to do well together and the idea was abandoned. More contact could be also possible by providing classes in English in which both foreign and Chinese students could enroll, and by providing more scheduled foreign and Chinese student interactions. Basically, students interacted together informally, in campus restaurants, for sports or cultural events, or as language partners, but they had to take the initiative themselves, with no contribution by the university authorities.

Many Chinese students were too shy to make contacts with foreign students. Some foreign students, especially the Koreans and Japanese, clustered together rather than making friends with the Chinese students. The foreign student teaching building seemed very uninviting to the Chinese students and for the three years that I was present the foreign student bulletin board was absolutely clean, where notices about lectures or other cultural activities were routinely removed within ten minutes after being posted. Fortunately, because of the large number of foreign students, many of them took classes in the main classroom building, and thus had some opportunities by being in the same building with Chinese students at least for informal contact; though not in the same classes. Few foreign students spent time at the library where much informal contact would be possible, as their main subject was learning Chinese. Only a few foreign students used the campus indoor sports facilities and swimming pool, preferring to go to facilities outside the campus.

In my autumn public twelve week lecture series on intercultural communication, a large number of mature adult students attended, in a way which would be unusual in the typical undergraduate class situation, and asked serious questions or provided challenges. The younger students were thereby empowered to do the same. Because of one young American teacher sometimes being present, his highly critical questions and comments about China generated a lively Chinese-American debate, which made the lectures still more interesting than just with my monologues during the still popular lecture portions. In the 2004 US elections, two other American faculty members and I had a widely attended panel discussion on the election. One of the faculty members planned to vote for George W. Bush, and I planned to vote for John Kerry, which provided a very realistic debate

In my first year at BLCU, I had a Christmas concert with about twenty-five foreign faculty and Chinese students performing skits about the Jesus narrative story and religious music with no problems. However, in the second year's concert, because of religious skits and songs, some Japanese majors complained to the dean who then gave me criticism indirectly though other Chinese faculty members. They found themselves in some difficulties and they relayed the dean's displeasure to me. For my third and final concert in 2004, I gave that concert alone rather than involving Chinese students who might suffer punishment. I was forbidden from teaching my audience any religious songs or giving any readings from the New Testament, making it a much more secular event than in the first two years. Nevertheless, I continued to hold an annual Christmas party in my own apartment, with singing and silent gift exchanges, which caused no problems.

The year after I left BLCU to join the faculty at Shanghai International Studies University, it appears that a foreign faculty couple who were engaged in Christian missionary endeavors at their apartment were apparently dismissed, for that reason, and went to a different university to continue their teaching. Recently, on Facebook, one of the couple, now back permanently in the US, discussed their missionary activity while teaching in China. Brigham Young University has a contract with the Chinese Ministry of Education to send seventy retired Mormon couples to teach English in various universities annually, but their contracts specify that they are not allowed to give any oral or written information to their classes relating to religion.

On many Sundays, four students and four of us foreign faculty went in two taxis to Catholic Mass at the Immaculate Conception Cathedral. Twice a year, about fifty new Catholics were baptized, including one of my students, Michelle Cui, with an Irish Catholic woman and me as her godparents. Presently, she is married and a trader in Chicago. She is expecting the couple's first child. At the baptism Masses, there were always two men taking video pictures of each baptismal candidate. We could never learn if these men were doing so as parish staff (unlikely) or were government videographers (more likely). All sermons in Chinese churches must be vetted in advance of delivery.

Before and after the Mass there were always a dozen to fifteen beggars. As a group, we decided to bring a dozen oranges to give to them, as we thought that when they received money, they had to turn it over to their leader, but they could eat the oranges. Some embassies in Beijing had Sunday Masses, but Chinese without a foreign passport were not allowed to enter, for the foreign embassy staff and Chinese government's fear of them seeking asylum.

There were never more than about a half dozen foreign students among the approximately 150 in the audience each time for my lectures. Only very rarely did a Chinese student bring a foreign student to my ninety Friday evening open houses (English corners), but I had two or three African students who sometimes came. Some Chinese students privately expressed to me their general fear of African students. The Chinese students who attempted to create better contacts with foreign students by going through official channels were almost always denied the opportunity by the university's highest authorities. In fact, according to student comments to me, the university actually discouraged Chinese students from mixing too freely with foreign students, and on the first day when Chinese students entered BLCU as freshmen, the authorities told them to be very careful about their relationships with foreign students and the foreign teachers (perhaps for fear of contamination from foreign ideas). This practice still continues, based on comments from my former BLCU students who have visited me later.

Two twin tower dormitories, one for foreign students and one for the Chinese men students were joined together by a common lobby whose Chinese entrance was usually blocked and it was only open during class times, thus lessening opportunities for meeting there. There were optional outings organized by the university for the foreign students, but Chinese students could not participate. Foreign students could visit the foreign teachers' apartments without registering at the reception gate of the foreign faculty compound, but all Chinese, including even faculty, had to register to enter the foreign expert compound. Typically, out-of-beijing Chinese could not stay overnight with foreign faculty, but foreigners could do so. I had an implicit agreement that my former students could visit me overnight, until 2005, when the director of the international office got much more strict. My British neighbor regularly had her African boyfriend with her overnight, but a Canadian woman in our building was not allowed to have her thirty-year old Chinese boyfriend with her overnight.

Many Chinese students felt that they were very actively discriminated against in favor of the foreign students. Paying in dollars, foreign students had two students to a room and hot showers while the undergraduate Chinese students had four students to a room and had to pay two yuan ($.24) to take hot showers outside of the dormitory buildings. Many of the foreign students ate regularly in the more expensive campus restaurants, especially the Muslim Xingjang restaurant, while the Chinese students were more likely to eat in the student canteens. I often treated a dozen students in the restaurants, as group awards for having the best debates or writing assignments. One advantage that Chinese students had because of the foreign students was a television in each room with nearly forty channels available. Very few universities in Beijing had that accessibility and none of my students in other universities where I taught had television sets in their dormitory rooms. The large television screens in the BLCU canteens or in other universities showed no foreign programming.

The class load for Chinese students at BLCU was quite heavy. For example, freshmen English majors typically took such once a week hour and a half courses (equivalent to two credits in American universities) as oral English, British and American cultures, intensive reading, extensive reading, grammar, listening comprehension, ethics, Chinese linguistics, Chinese writing, fundamentals of law, politics — Mao Tsedong thought, physical education, computer education, and optional courses such as music theory and appreciation and movie theory and appreciation. Where most Chinese universities have a two week military training course the first two weeks of their freshmen year, the BLCU freshmen did not take this course until the following summer, which some of my students labeled as a form of torture, having for example to eat all of their meals standing up, and being bossed and harassed by active soldiers who were their age.

Sophomore English majors took English writing, audiovisual English, intensive reading, extensive reading, listening comprehension, English grammar, history of Chinese literature, philosophy, political economics: Marxist philosophy for the first semester and capitalism for the second semester, physical education, plus optional classes such as history of the English language, lexicology, stylistics, business English, scientific English, Chinese culture, and Chinese writing. They were also required to take the tem-4 (test for English majors-4) in the spring.

Junior English majors took debate, English advanced writing, intensive reading, politics — Deng Xaioping theory, politics and economy of the world order, English-Chinese translation, French or Japanese first year language, British literature four hours in the autumn semester, American literature four hours in the spring semester, and newspaper and magazine reading, plus such optional courses as foreign trade in English, and foreign affairs in English. One semester, I traded one of my assigned courses for an American literature class, usually taught by a British faculty member. I made it very creative for the students, having students develop short plays from some of the prose literature. I had previously taught American literature for postgraduate students at Yangzhou University.

Senior English majors took a second year of French or Japanese language, western civilization as a capstone first semester course, translation-Chinese to English, interpretation, linguistics, literary translation. They had to write a 10,000 word senior thesis, plus taking other possible options such as multimedia and website design. The second semester had only ten weeks for seniors as they had to take Tem-8, teaching for English majors-8) in March. They were expected to devote two weeks to social practice away from the campus, though many faked doing so and spent their time at home while providing a false report to the university

There were many public optional classes open to all BLCU students, such as music, film, art, history of tea, international business, international finance, marketing, international economic law, current world issues, mountain climbing and Confucian writings. Many of the students took extra courses at other nearby universities, especially in international finance and trade for certificates of completion in order to compete for positions in international firms.

Foreign experts, foreign students, and Chinese students began to get CNN in addition to the continuing twelve or thirteen channels of China Central TV (channel 9 in English), RAI (Italy), TV 5 (France), TWA (Spain), DW (Germany), Arirang (South Korea), NHK Jjapan), NOW (England), V (pop music from Hong Kong), STAR (sports from Hong Kong), Phoenix-a rival Chinese station network to CCTV (Shanghai or Hong Kong channels), a Taiwan station, several Beijing and other provincial stations. Because of its role as an international language university, BLCU students had far more international news and programs available than other universities at which I taught.

Our campus newsstand also had available *Twenty First Century, China Daily* (provided free six days weekly to all of the foreign faculty), *the Asian Wall Street Journal, International Herald Tribune, Newsweek, Economic Review,* and some other English newspapers and magazines from outside of China. These were all signs of progress for more media openness at BLCU, with the understanding that the same print media were not available in the newsstands outside the campus, but only at four or five star hotels. Used copies of *Newsweek* and *time* were often available.

Local students were watching "Friends," "Sex in the City," "West Wing," NYPD Blue," and "Prison Break,' and were beginning to get "Er," and "Chicago Hope" on their computers. A half dozen students and I weekly watched all ten seasons of "Friends." Students would watch and rewatch episodes to improve their own English and to get more of a feeling of youthful conversation among the six main cast members. In the imaginary dialogue in chapter six, "Cultural Media," in Li Mengyu's and my *Communicating Interculturally* (2012), I had one of the imaginary students, Mike, comment: "I watched all 10 years of 'Friends' and I have learned a lot of English. Since I own the whole set, I can watch a program and then watch it again to catch some of the phrases of Chandler, Joey, or Ross, and then practice them. 'How ya doin Rachel?' 'What's up, Ross?' my favorite character is Phoebe and her evil twin Ursula. She plays both parts, you know." The imaginary twin in the dialogue, Summer, then replied: "my twin sister, Spring and I like that part too, but especially when Phoebe had triplets. Since we are identical twins, perhaps we will have identical twins too." Such statements in the dialogue are modeled after specific students. Curiously, when I taught at Yangzhou University again in 2013–14, very few of my students had any familiarity with "Friends" or some of the other American television programs that were so popular at BLCU and still later at Shanghai International Studies University.

My daughter, Michelle, spent three weeks with me in July, 2005 while I was grading papers and preparing to move to Shanghai International Studies University. Several of my students became her tourist guides in Beijing. She and I, and two of my student friends, Cindy Zhao and Chicken Li, went with us to Xi'an for several days, where my daughter gave a very popular talk to about 400 senior middle school students who returned to school for it, even though they were on summer vacation. Professionally, Chicken Li's father was a driver for a company, and he spent considerable time to show us the Terra Cotta warriors and the Ming dynasty tombs. Cindy later was a singing member of "Up with People" and traveled with the group in several foreign countries. Chicken Li, has returned to his full Chinese name, Ji Li, is married, and living in Toronto, where they have a child.

After I left BLCU that summer, I went back to Beijing four more times for conferences, but the geographical locations prevented me from going back to visit BLCU. Nevertheless, I retain many fond memories of that experience. Several of my former students there have kept in touch with me and five of my students while I was teaching there, Nick Deng, Tony Weitong, Ideal Li, Shawn Chen, and Bob Zhang Bo came to see me when I later taught at Shanghai International Studies University, Ocean University of China, or Yangzhou University in 2013–14.

23. Two Chinese Weddings: 2005

Without any claim to understand typical Chinese weddings, some interesting intercultural comparisons can be made for my first two Chinese weddings which I attended. One was for an auditor in my postgraduate classes at Yangzhou University, Sim Amadeus Ting Tang's and my Yangzhou University junior English major student Fay's wedding in Yangzhou in June, 2005. The second was Devon Yang's small town and village wedding in Northwest Jiangsu Province in November 2005. I had known both men for four years and I am still a close friend with each of them. Both visited me in Beijing and Shanghai. I assisted Devon two summers in Suining County teaching senior middle school students English to prepare them for the gao kao university entrance exam.

Sim's family was reasonably well off with both parents in their late 50's. The father was a local party (CPC) leader, but he died of cancer several months after the wedding. The family had a two story apartment and an auto. An only child, sim had a master's degree in biochemistry with a good position in Yangzhou and his wife, fay, had a ba degree in English, and later also a master's degree in English. She taught in a technical college in Yangzhou. Sim had traveled abroad twice, once to Thailand and more recently professionally to Europe. He played the violin, was a Mozart enthusiast, and was an outstanding photographer. One of his highest values was friendship with both Chinese and American professionals. His income was 4,000 rmb monthly and his wife's was 1500 rmb. The couple's new apartment was very high scale, with contemporary furniture and art, including sim's enlarged photographs taken in Europe. Later, they had a son, first called Ben as his English name by his parents. Now at his insistence, he is called Gilberto, after a Brazilian soccer player. The family has moved to Australia where he is completing a Ph.D. science degree. It is likely that they will become Australian citizens.

Devon came from one of the two poorest villages that I have visited in China, eighty kilometers south of. His parents were peasants, both about sixty-six years old in 2005. Today, both parents receive about seventy rmb monthly as government social security. He has an older married sister with one child. His sister left school during her secondary education to get married, a familiar custom for many young women in her area. The major income producing work in this village activity was in recycling and bagging discarded plastic for sale to a recycling industry. The village brick homes were all one story, built by the local families themselves. Some of the families had a cow, pig or some goats and most had chickens. There were hay stacks near the uneven dirt roads, used both for feeding the cows and goats and as a means of cooking fuel. I estimate that the average monthly income for the village families was 300 to 400 rmb monthly. The village had a primary school, but no secondary school. Some students went outside the village for junior middle school, but few would go onto senior middle school.

When I visited his family and village in 2002, many villagers came again to the family home to meet me as their first actual foreigner they had ever seen outside of television. In 2005, Devon taught in a competitive senior middle school with 4,000 students, and his wife worked in Chinaunicom, both in the county seat of Suining County, 30 kilometers from his home village. The school had thirty Chinese teachers of English. His wife's only English was a few greeting phrases and expressions like "That's all right." Though one of the head English teachers at his school, Devon's English level appeared to be lower at the time of the wedding than it was when he was my Yangzhou University student. His third language in the university had been German, and he continued to self-study German, with hopes of studying in Germany for a post graduate degree in the future as some of his classmates were doing later. His headmaster, however, was not willing to release him for such study. As he had done in the university, he continued to listen daily to the BBc and Voice of America to improve his English. He was very diligent spending many hours daily teaching, monitoring students, or working to improve his own English and teaching skills. He continues this diligence presently.

Both couples had gotten their wedding licenses well before the celebrations and lived together, as is common in China, for several months before the actual wedding celebrations. Sim and Devon had known each other for a long time, mostly through me. They both accompanied me to Beijing in 2002 when I moved there from Yangzhou. Devon demonstrated a sharp tongue even when we traveled together earlier, and admitted to striking or kicking his students when they were misbehaving if they caused him to lose his temper. More recently, he has indicated that he no longer strikes or kicks his students.

I arrived in Yangzhou for Sim and Fay's wedding with my student friend, Shawn Chen, who also traveled with me to Cambodia in 2005. A day before the wedding, I revisited Sim's family home, and visited their new apartment on the day of the wedding. Fay's family and friends from Changzhou arrived on the morning of the celebration by bus, and appeared to be a rather ordinary group of Chinese, and far less sophisticated than Sim's family. As about thirty of her relatives and friends came into the new apartment, they carried very practical home gifts, probably duplicating what the couple already owned but at a less expensive level. Sim's parents hosted us all for lunch (typically called dinner in China) in a nearby restaurant.

For the evening wedding celebration supper, Fay wore a white wedding dress and then changed into a red one (the Chinese sign of happiness). There were about 300 present in a high class hotel, including three other American friends besides me, some European friends, several leading party members, including Yangzhou's former vice mayor, and coworkers of his father. One of Fay's older male relatives attended the feast in an undershirt, while most of the local participants were wearing suits or nice dresses. All of Fay's former Yangzhou University roommates participated in the event. I had attended Sim's grandmother's ninetieth birthday party in 2002, and I had met a number of his relatives then. I had invited Sim to travel with me on my first time to India, but he declined the opportunity.

At both weddings, cigarettes and rice/wheat wine were a major part of the socializing. After the dinner, the former Yangzhou vice mayor, party leaders, and coworkers gave short congratulatory speeches in Chinese. We were treated to a Peking opera type of male falsetto singer, a magician, an artist who created caricatures of the bridal couple, and a small orchestra playing Chinese and western music. Sim and Fay had one dance together on the stage. Wearing my red tang dynasty jacket, I sang three western songs which were well received, if not understood by the Chinese. One song was "I'm getting married in the morning" from "My Fair Lady." The young American woman teacher, Anna, from Yangzhou University with whom Sim, Fay and I had been good friends, told in English the stages of her getting to know the couple over a four plus year period, with simultaneous interpretation into Chinese. At the end of the celebration, sim's parents played a charming welcoming game with the couple to much applause. Fay's parents were much more shy and her father only said a few halting words of congratulations to the couple, but the mother did not speak. There were some probable class differences between the two families.

Devon made the nine hour bus trip to Shanghai to bring me back with him for his wedding celebrations and we returned to the county seat the next day by bus. That evening, her uncle hosted a supper for nine of us, including her father, her younger brother, and two male cousins. Her mother was not present, though we met her later that evening at her home. It seemed curious to me, but she may have been preparing for the wedding celebration at that time. The next day, I traveled with Devon to his village and family, where there were many people preparing the feast for the wedding celebration the following day. Wandering again in the village, many villagers came out of their homes to shake my hand. I watched a low stakes card game by some of the men in the village, while women nearby were loading heavy bags of plastic onto a truck for resale, and thus also cleaning all of the loose plastic out of the area for the celebration. That evening, Devon and his bride hosted a supper for about twenty-five of her Chinaunicom coworkers, including the twenty-nine year old local president, the manager, and her coworkers in their mid to late twenties. Devon was rather aggressive in forcing the male participants, except me, to drink many rice/wheat wine toasts. There was much good food and good country humor, but everyone left after about two hours. From past student celebration events, I had expected some kereoke singing, but there was none. Only Devon spoke any English, except for his bride's frequent happy "That's all right".

Early on the day of the main wedding celebration, Devon had rented two black cars (a favorite auto color in China for important events) and a truck for a local ragtag band of about seven men. We went to the bride's home through many local streets with the band walking in front of the cars as they played their simple instruments. When we got close to her home, two rounds of 5,000 firecrackers were set off. The bride, wearing a lovely pink gown, came down from the roof of her house (a custom that wasn't explained to me), and with another round of firecrackers preceding them, they walked to their decorated lead car. In the procession to and from the bride's home, several hundred onlookers clapped for the wedding party as we passed, either in the cars or on foot. Many townspeople wanted to shake my hand. For some reason which I didn't understand, Devon nearly got into a fist fight with some of the bride's neighbors, before family members hustled them away. At some point, two boy relatives had roosters in the car with us, before they were sent to ride in the truck with the band members. This custom was not made clear to me either. Since Devon was the only speaker of English and was in the first car, I missed a lot of the meaning of some of the customs which I was seeing. None of the bride's family attended the village celebration, which Devon said was the standard Chinese country and village marriage custom, but quite different than at sim and fay's wedding celebration. Still later, one of my MA student's, mother explained that the roosters were intended to call upon the couple to have a son. Also, there were sugar cane stalks, which symbolized the wish that they would have a son soon. I also saw this latter custom at a 2008 wedding in Suzhou.

    At the village, many residents came out to wave at the wedding party, which had now been joined by two vans of teachers from Devon's school. The band had gotten out of the truck and the men were playing their instruments as they led us to the family home, while another round of 5,000 firecrackers was set off. At Devon's home, we had a noon dinner, where well over 100 villagers participated, as well as the ten teachers from Devon's school, all of whom spoke fair to good English, his family and I ate at three tables in shifts at a neighbor's home which meant that there were some teachers with me then speaking English. Devon again insisted that the men teachers would accept frequent toasts with the rice/wheat wine. After the dinner, we went to the bridal chamber, as the couple was expected to spend their first night in Devon's parents' home. Some of the young single teachers were playing games with the bride, being knocked on top of her by other teachers, trying to steal kisses, and trying to get her to eat Chinese bread while one of them was eating at the other end of the bread. Two young men were especially aggressive. Devon was not in the room at the time, but we had about twenty-five children and adult onlookers.

    Older teachers asked me if I minded these games, as they said these were the usual customs for a village wedding. A married thirty-three year old teacher told me that he thought it was a custom with the bride which should be abandoned in China, and pointed to one of the very active young single teachers as "the naughty boy in our school." I told the young teachers that it appeared that the bride was no longer enjoying the games, and they stopped their activities, with apologies for offending me. The teasing actually did offend me, and in Sim's and Fay's wedding there was no such teasing of the bride, nor in other city weddings that I later attended.

At the end of the celebration, local villagers sat on a bench with a large bowl in front of them where they tossed in money for the bridal couple, including many fifty rmb notes, and the bridal couple bowed low before them after each donation. Following both the party with the bride's coworkers, the red envelopes with money gifts from the teachers, and this final custom, the couple quietly counted the money gifts received and Devon told me that the wedding had been much more expensive than all of the money which they received. I did not see any other gifts except some practical gifts that the bride had received earlier from her family. The custom at that time was for the red envelopes to include 500rmb in the cities, and five years later, it tended to be 800 to 1,000 rmb.

Both couples considered my intercultural presence important for their celebrations. I was glad to be a significant member of their weddings. Both shared some customs such as the heavy cigarette and rice/wheat wine consumption, but each was so different from the other, that I felt that I had been at two distinctive cultural events, even though within the same broader Chinese culture.

As I remained in China over the years, I attended a number of other weddings, one in a very wealthy wedding center where the one hour rental of a white grand piano alone had cost 800rmb. In still another wedding, I was publically introduced as the couple's professor friend from the United States, and when the couple visited our table, they remarked, "oh so you are our friend from America? Welcome to China." from these two weddings in 2005 onward, I was a participant in about four or five more weddings, where I always was acknowledged as the wedding couple's American professor friend, whether or not I knew them.

In the past, I attended Hindu weddings first in South Africa, and then two in India. In 2015, I attended a Muslim wedding celebration in Jakarta.

24. Michael, Are You a Chiamerican? A Photo Essay

1. Beijing Language and Culture University, Friday evening open house, 2002

2. American music concert at Beijing Language and Culture University, John Carey and Michael, 2002. Two performances in front of 300 students each

3. Michael ringing Buddhist bells, 2003

4. Audience for American music concert at Beijing Language and Culture University, 2002

5. Beijing Language and Culture University graduation 2004: Jay, Shawn, Sherry, and Michael

6. Shanghai International Studies University

MA student Halloween party 2005
7. Michael, Ronald McDonald, and webmaster Wing Mars, Changzhou 2005

8. Jimmy and Amy Weng and Michael, Shanghai International Studies University apartment, 2005

9. Shuman Lu, Shanghai International Studies University students and Michael, Xiamen University, 2005

10. Former Indiana University Ph.D. student Sherry Ferguson, Michael, and 2005 Shanghai University International Studies University student David Xu, Dresden, Germany, 2006

11. Michael and MA intercultural communication majors, Shanghai, 2006

12. Christmas concert at Shanghai International Studies University, 2006

13. Michael's international birthday at Shanghai International Studies University

14. Shanghai International Channel, Intercultural Friendship, Culture Matters; 4 programs, 2008; re-broadcast 2009

15. Rose, Sanders, Michelle, Sophia, Darya, Michael, and Jack with Lu Xun, Shanghai International Studies University Library, 2008

16. Christian Fellowship students and Michael, Huabei, Annui Province, 2009

17. Socratic dialogue about God, Christian students in Huabei, Annui Province, 2009

18. Shanghai International Studies University MA intercultural communication majors' graduation. Front row: Michael, Zhang Hongling, and Steve J. Kulich

19. Xinhua News Agency interview in Beijing for national TV feed, 2009

20. Michael's 75th birthday, Qingdao, 2011.
Front row: Tom, Wen, Michael, Susan, Jethro;
second row: Kevin, Li Mengyu, Victor, Yao, Robert, and Richard

21. Ocean University of China intercultural communication class, 2011

22. St. Michael's Cathedral, Qingdao, 2011

23. Michael and Victor at Qingdao wedding, 2011

24. Michael in Beijing with local children, 2011

A Journey to the East 249

25. Michael greets young pioneers in Beijing, 2011

26. Li Mengyu and Michael celebrate in Qingdao with friends the signing of the contract of *Communicating Interculturally* with Higher Education Press

27. *Chinese Communicating Interculturally*, the 2014 North American edition of *Communicating Interculturally*

28. Michael, Melissa Liles of AfS International, and Irid Agoes, my host in Bali, Indonesia

25. The Culture of Guanglinyilu Road: Shanghai International Studies University

Earlier in China, I lived inside the campuses at Yangzhou University and at Beijing Language and Culture University. Shanghai is the eighth largest city in the world but at Shanghai International Studies University, I lived in a foreign experts complex on a rather typical small Shanghai street, Guanglinyilu (Guangling Number 1 Road). I walked a kilometer to the postgraduate and main campus, or a half kilometer to the light rail and busses. It is an hour by shuttle bus to the Songjiang undergraduate and first year MA student campus in the suburbs, a university city with seven campuses and large student populations, plus its own large indoor swimming pool and ice skating rink. There are many restaurants and shops, filled with students from the different universities, except during the Lunar New Year period, when Songjiang becomes something of a ghost town. This has been a very rich cultural experience living quite close to the local population, and getting to know some of them, at least on a friendly "nihao" ("hello") only basis. After returning from Europe in 2006 with David Xu, many of the local people and merchants told me "Hao giu bu.jian" ("Long time no see."). Nineteen year old Yao in a wholesale clothing store and the women at the local roast duck shop smiled and waved at me as I passed by. In the 2008–09 academic year, nine or ten male students and I swam together in the autumn and spring on Tuesdays, and had a meal together at one of the Muslim restaurants in the business area.

Although I often walked up and down the 750–1,000 meter stretch of our street almost daily, I took two young Chinese friends, Jesse William Zhang and David Xu, on a walking tour so that I could more accurately understand the culture of this small but vibrant section of Shanghai. We figured that behind the street on both sides there were probably 50,000 inhabitants living in five and six story apartment buildings. The SISU foreign expert complex hosted more than 40 foreign professors teaching there and at its affiliated institutions such as the nearby SISU foreign language junior and senior middle school. I rarely saw the foreign experts except sometimes on the shuttle bus or at our SISU sponsored parties. The foreign expert complex restaurant attracted a rather small number of daily customers as SISU paid the staff whether or not there were customers. Inside the gate leading to the street, there was a rather relaxed guard station and in the parking lot, there were eight reproductions of art such as Da Vinci, Monet, Picasso and other classical European artists.

As a narrow street, we found a small hotel; sidewalk bike, shoe, and small appliance repair men or women; takeaways for noodles; steamed buns, lobsters, and rice; Shanghai outlets for tobacco and wine; electronic and mobile phone stores; household items, shoe, flower and plant shops; a spicy Sichuan restaurant; juice and hamburger shops and stalls; a roast goose shop; a roast duck shop; a small Korean restaurant; novelty shops; traditional medicine shops, twenty-four hour convenience stories, pastry shops, two supermarkets; two banks; hair salons; traditional feet washing and massage shops; a bath house; a large vegetable, fish, and meat shops with many independent stall owners; newspaper and magazine kiosks; public telephones; various clothing and tee shirt shops; and a popular upstairs internet cafe. There were many independent vegetable, peach, and small watermelon sellers along the street.

Sitting nearby the garbage collection site at the convenience store next to the foreign expert compound, there was a seventy-five year old woman, nearly toothless, every day who sold used magazines and books, with some regular time magazines for sale. She often took my hand and talked to me in Chinese. She told my two young Chinese friends that she looked younger than her age because she didn't have to use her mind, but, she said that I looked older than she because I was always thinking about different issues. Once when the police had taken away all of her books and magazines, she asked me to loan her 1,000rmb to buy new supplies. My student friend was astonished at her request and my agreement to loan her the money. She returned the money as promised, half each at two different times. Often she would encourage me nonverbally to eat garlic for good health. Once when I wanted to have a photo taken of us, she took off her apron and straightened her hair. "Why do you think that I sit here all day selling used magazines and books?" She asked me in Chinese to one of my students. She answered her own question through the interpretation of one of my young Chinese friends, "So I won't be so lonely in my little apartment." although we had little in common and could not speak the other's language, we were always very friendly. When I came back to give lectures in 2009 and 2010, I met her and we would say hello, always accompanied with mutual hugs, and urging me to eat my garlic. The last time that I was briefly at SISU for just an afternoon in 2013, she was no longer there, and I had no Chinese student to ask about her.

The primary school across the street for about 1000 children was labeled in Chinese and English "Model unit of the People's Government of Hongkou District," and had a slogan in Chinese and English, "Let the school be a paradise for the teachers and students to develop harmoniously." I would have volunteered to visit the school weekly and talk to students some in English, but it never materialized as my student visitors had no connection with the school. The health care clinic and hospital next to the school combined both western and Chinese traditional medicine. It's slogan in Chinese and English was: "Health is not only a sign of no disease or no weakness, but also a combination of healthy in spirit and happiness in the society." Next door was an affiliated dentist office. I went to the clinic daily for a week in 2008 to have my blood sugar tested. I was greeted by many patients in Chinese. There was a shop which I thought was for buddhist rituals, but it was for burial supplies, including fire cracker rounds for when a person died, which we would hear going off from time to time in the neighborhood. There was a small recreation and exercise area of about thirty by fifteen meters where many older grandparents would sit who were with their grandchild as he or she played on the exercise bars. I often sat there silently with the grandparents.

    Guanglingyilu was a very casual street with thousands of local residents, children, teens, and quite often older senior citizens walking along the street regularly. In the evenings, many men were in undershirts, or without shirts, and others wore a type of pajama that I had seen before on small streets in Japan. The area may have had a larger number of older citizens than behind other larger less traditional streets. Many people sat in nice weather in front of the shops and stores, conversing, playing cards, eating, smoking, or caring for small children. There appeared to be a very large number of elderly citizens whose lives might be located primarily here in this area. Many younger grandparents cared for their grandchildren, taking them to and from the primary school while the parents were at work. One grandfather who passed regularly on his bike spoke to his grandson on the back of the bike only in English and the boy responded only in English. Some children and teenagers regularly said hello to me, and others appeared frightened to meet such a large foreigner on the street. Several clerks in the supermarkets, or vegetable, fish, roasted chicken and duck stalls, and meat shops said hello to me as "nihao, Michael" when they would see me. The front of the bank of Shanghai regularly had two dozen middle aged and older women dancing or practicing Taji during nice weather in the evenings. A nearby dvd/cd shop was temporarily closed "for internal adjustment," as the police had recently closed several such shops because of raiding pirated materials being sold there. A noisy upstairs disco next to the foreign expert complex had driven some faculty to move to the SISU hotel near the light rail station. Around the corner of Guanglingyilu leading to the light rail station, there were several Muslim restaurants.

    The back gate for the Shanghai Finance and Economics University founded in 1917 poured out many Chinese, Japanese, Korean, African, and European students onto Guanglingyilu. The university was especially popular for night and Saturday CPA and MBA classes. It had its own training center in finance and adult education on the street, and served as a short cut to SISU. Its basketball courts were very popular with local youth and students. I often sat and watched the teenage boys shooting baskets with pickup games, but young women were a rare sight at the dozen basketball hoops. Although I had seen many full court teams of two men and three women playing basketball games at BLCU, I never saw such games at this university basketball courts. One young Russian told me that the boys didn't really know how to play basketball since there were no full court games, saying that Russian teenagers almost always played full court basketball games together.

The variety of small and large stores on Guanglingyilu had its own cultural interest for me, but the most important cultural experience was my regular daily contact with so many local residents and merchants who greeted me or smiled at me, and sometimes interacted with me, mostly in Chinese without my understanding, but sometimes also in English, or through the interpretation of one of my young friends, it was perhaps the most interesting cross generational and international street that I have ever lived on.

Shanghai International Studies University, 2005–09

Fortuitously, I met SISU Professor Steve J. Kulich at a language and intercultural communication conference at the Harbin Institute of Technology in January 2004. I was a guest lecturer at Kulich's invitation for a week at SISU and other Shanghai universities, in the spring of 2004. In May, 2005, I agreed to move from BLCU to SISU in the summer of 2005.

I joined Kulich in his MA program in intercultural communication as a distinguished professor in the College of English. The intercultural communication program was one of eight divisions of the College. Shortly after my arrival, in September, 2005, Kulich and I attended the Asia Education Foundation Conference in Beijing where we became acquainted with various Asian educational leaders, including several ministers of education, and former President Ramos of the Philippines. An educational official from Bangledesh indicated that he would ask his minister of education who was present at the conference to invite me for a week of lectures at Bangledeshi universities, a courtesy invitation which had no follow-up. Staying at a resort outside of Beijing, we had a full police escort to the Great Hall of the People on Tiananmen Square where we had a sumptuous banquet, a speech by a member of the politburo, and a Chinese children's dancing and singing program.

For the first semester of 2005, I taught four sections of thirty junior English majors in my model United Nations Security Council simulation, where two students represented each national delegation in the

Council, as I had done for nearly forty times. I served as the secretary general and advisor to all of the delegations. book, *the art of public speaking,* later published in China. Additionally, I began a four year autumn joint teaching program with Kulich for the MA students on the history of intercultural communication. It was a very productive learning period for me, especially with his emphasis on psychology, for which I had little or no academic background. He vastly expanded my knowledge of Geert Hofstede's (then) 5 national cultural dimensions, Kulich's extensive study of values crossculturally, and Shalom Schwartz' universal value indices. During my first academic year, I offered fifteen open lectures each semester: the first semester on western civilization, and the second semester on intercultural communication.

In September 2006, Kulich led an intercultural communication seminar as a part of the second biennial world forum on China studies, jointly organized by the Shanghai municipal government and the Shanghai Academy of Social Sciences, whose theme was "China and the world: harmony and peace." Our own subtheme was "China communicating interculturally and internationally." Perhaps this subtheme title subtly influenced our naming Li Mengyu's and my textbook. This initial gathering of cross-cultural China scholars organized research papers along two main themes: "a. the outer communication and interpersonal behaviors of the Chinese, b. the inner social psychology and communicative orientation of the Chinese."

Following this seminar, the official inauguration of SISU's Intercultural Institute occurred with Kulich as the director, and our colleague, Linda Zhang Hongling, as one of the two institute's deputy directors. I was appointed as the Institute's chair of its International Advisory Board and senior co-editor of the intercultural research series. Subsequently, Kulich and I coedited *Intercultural Perspectives on Chinese Communication* published by the Shanghai Foreign Language Education Press (2007), his, my and Weng Liping's coedited *Value Frameworks at the Theoretical Crossroads of Culture* (2012), and Kulich's, Weng's, and my coedited book *Value Dimensions and Their Contextual Dynamics across Cultures* (2014).

In the autumn of 2006, I taught five classes of sophomores oral English, including one class of Ughor Muslim students from Xinjiang in western China. We held Halloween and Christmas parties in all five of the classes. In the second semester, I taught five classes of oral English based on intercultural communication for freshmen English majors, where we used Linnel Davis's book, *Doing Culture: Cross Culture in Action* (1999). A new faculty member, Cooper Wakefield joined us to teach communication theory and international cinema. David henry transferred to our MA program from Overseas Training Center, assisted the program initially in the weekend MA program, and later more fully in the regular MA program. Later, Myron Lustig was a spring faculty member for two years. That year, I began teaching an annual autumn semester course on global media and culture to our postgraduate majors and a spring semester model un sc simulation to postgraduate English and international relations majors as well as the annual joint history of intercultural communication with Kulich. I advised my first set of first year MA thesis students, and read other MA theses. I have now read, as the final reader, more than 140 of the program's MA theses, plus the first three Ph.D. dissertations. I served as the external examiner for a large number of the weekend theses.

At the beginning of 2007, Kulich and I both became board members for the *Journal of Middle Eastern and Islamic Studies (in Asia)* and I served as the English proofreader of the Journal's forty-five articles from that time until the end of 2011. I wrote several articles for the Journal during this period. Kulich, I and a number of MA students attended the second triennial multicultural discourse conference at Zhezhiang University in Hangzhou. There, I met Evelin Lindner, Ph.D., M.D, the founder of the Human Dignity and Humiliation Network, which has led to a continuing professional relationship, particularly in terms of my publishing books with Dignity Press

In 2008, the Foreign Expert Board of Shanghai decided that no foreign teachers over sixty-five could teach in any Shanghai sponsored educational institutions. We were given a one year grace period. I left Shanghai in July 2009, but I returned and gave week long lecture series there and at several other universities. In 2010, we participated in a colloquium on the future of intercultural communication teaching and research in China and Germany led by Kulich.

My former MA student Charles Cheng and I visited the Philippines and Russia in the early and late spring of 2008. During the spring of 2008, Shanghai International Television featured me and three of my MA students on a series, "Culture Matters for a program entitled, "Intercultural friendship" which was expected to begin airing on May 12, but it was the same day as the Sichuan earthquake, causing the series to be postponed. Its presentations made my students and me well recognized as tv stars in the Shanghai area, with local Chinese stopping us in stores and in the main campus area and also in Songjiang. The full series was rebroadcast in 2009. This meant that for the programs' airings in the two years, several million people saw us on television. Frequently at this time, I was also an interviewee on the China Radio International program "People in the Know."

My daughter Michelle and her three children, Darya (then 11), Sanders (then 10), and Sophia (then 6) visited me in the summer of 2008. She had the opportunity to speak to 300 junior and senior middle school English teachers, as well as to the local Chinese Food and Drug Administration, and our MA students. We visited friends of mine in Suzhou, Changzhou, Yangzhou, in Jiangsu Province, and Maanshan in Anhui Province. In the autumn of 2008, I spent a week in a Shanghai hospital with pneumonia.

Steven Ru's and my holy week travel in 2009 to Huabei, Anhui Province was for the purpose of my giving two lectures to Christian fellowship student groups where we ran into some mild difficulties with the local police. During my lecture on Jesus' week when he was crucified, police came into the room, none of whom spoke any English. We suspected that neighbors had called the police to report a foreigner in the area. I had forgotten my passport, which caused some more small problems. While I was treated courteously, after Steven returned to Shanghai, local plain clothes police contacted him and harassed him about bringing a foreigner to a religious event in Huabei. I worried that some of the fellowship students would have problems later with the local police, but nothing developed. Steven had requested the Gideon Society to send me 200 New Testaments for him to distribute to these fellowship students, but he canceled the request after the incident and the warnings which he received in Shanghai not to bring a foreigner again to the fellowship students in Huabei.

When he wrote his exam papers to enter the doctoral program in international relations at Shanghai International Studies University, he failed the English exam, and was denied entrance into the program, even though he had been an outstanding MA student and had what I thought was very good English. Is it possible that his failure in the English exam had anything to do with our problem in Huabei? While I was living in Shanghai for four years, however, I took more than fifty Chinese students to one of Shanghai's four international Catholic churches for Sunday Mass, and even though some of them were members of the Communist arty of chins, none of them ever experienced any problems.

26. Shangdong Province, Qingdao and Jinan: 2011

Qingdao, China's Most Livable City, 2009, the City of Red Roofs,

Passing the Yellow Sea and going by shuttle bus to the relatively new main Ocean University of China's Laoshan campus and returning to the Yuoshan campus (built in the 1920s by the Germans) where I lived from February to July 2011, has been one of my most pleasant environmental memories. With the shuttle bus traveling by the sea on my right, and modern Qingdao on the left, and coming gradually to where both Laoshan Mountain and the Yellow Sea intersect, there were many bronze statues of women in different poses. Turning onto the seaside street, filled with traffic, there was a many meter tall statue of two hands holding, (perhaps the world?) resting on two legs, knees, and feet. Passing on the left, I found the Sea View Hotel and Restaurant, where I was superbly hosted several times with multiple ocean fish, lobsters, crabs, clams, shrimp, lamb, beef, pork, chicken, duck, cooked to order, many exotic vegetables, salads, and fruit dishes, fruit, fruit pizzas, noodles, rice, delicious pastry selections, and many flavors of fruit drinks, plus Qingdao beer, Great Wall red wine, and a special green tea buffet. The menu was so delicious and varied that even with returning to the buffet tables several times, it was impossible to taste all of the restaurant's delicacies.

Coming along the shuttle bus route, there were street vendors of fruits, vegetables, and meats, as well as the exceptionally rigorous Number 2 Senior Middle School, where the students lived from Sunday evening until Friday evening. My host and colleague, Professor Li Mengyu's seventeen year old son, Kevin, was a student there. He was eager each Sunday to return to the school because the academic atmosphere there was so attractive and where most of his young friends were studying.

The Ocean University of China's Laoshan campus, with the Laoshan Mountain encircling the campus was quite breathtaking! Like the Yuoshan campus, built by the Germans in the 1920s the classrooms, offices, dining rooms (canteens) and dormitories all have the German styled red roofs as are seen on many shorter and taller residence buildings in the city. While the Yuoshan campus has 90 year old mature lush vegetation and many annual flowering bushes and trees, most of the Laoshan campus trees and foliage are of recent origins, but also beautiful. The exceptionally well designed Laoshan campus links many buildings inside and out, helping teachers and students to move seamlessly through a large part of the campus, and in covered arcades, all still in a modern German design. The students have long walks from their dormitories. Each room is shared by six undergraduates who live their entire four years together, and generally thereby create life-long friendships. Almost all Chinese primary and secondary schools, colleges and universities, unlike educational institutions in the US, are surrounded by tall fences and gates with guards to protect the students from outside intruders and external harm.

Returning to the Yuoshan campus in the late afternoon, we passed many elaborate city buildings, taken over by the city government after the Germans, and then the Japanese left Qingdao. The former renaissance styled site of the German administration, built between 1904–06, is typical of the German occupation period. Since 1949, controlled by the Qingdao People's Republic of China, it was ranked in 1995 as the key cultural relic under the state level protection. Nearby, is the former site of the imperial court of Kiaochow built between 1912 and 1914. The former German police headquarters, also of German renaissance architecture style, was completed in 1905.

One of my favorite buildings constructed by the Germans in 1900 is St. Michael's Roman Catholic Cathedral with two tall spires and crosses on top, where I attended a Korean Mass on many Sundays. On weekends, in front of the Cathedral, dozens of couples were taking their wedding photos for their photo albums and wedding videos. One of the typical German medieval and renaissance downtown architectural city relics is the former site of the Bismarck Barracks. During the German occupation, built in 1899 it was the former site of the second German navy battalion headquarters. One of two early twentieth century prisons, the Kiaocho prison for Europeans, which began construction in 1900, was formerly the Kiaochow Imperial Court. It was once used as the first detention house of the Qingdao Public Security Bureau after 1949. Near the Yuoshan campus is the Christian church, restricted to European residents in the early twentieth century. It had a Romanesque and Jugendstil German style and today holds 1,000 worshipers. On Sunday mornings, the carillon's many bells offered me beautiful music at 7:30 and 930 am, and time is marked by the bells during the day. Intermingling with the bells are the harbor's frequent ship fog horns.

The former site of the German governor's residence, called also "The commander's building" is located on the south of Signal Hill, below the observatory on the top of the hill, and with a commanding view in and around the Yuoshan campus. It was under construction from 1905 to 1907. Chairman Mao Tsedong stayed there in the summer of 1957. In 1996, it was turned into a tourist "guest house" site, and has been under state level protection since. It is ranked as one of the fourth group of key cultural relics in China, and attracts thousands of tourists on a weekly basis. The Qingdao railway station, built by the Germans in 1900–01, features the public German architecture of its time.

Inside the Yuoshan campus, there is the former site of the Japanese Middle School, built in 1921 by Japanese architects and used for that purpose still lager during the Japanese occupation of Qingdao. With its proximity to the sea, this campus has many majors relating to fisheries, food sciences, marine biology, and oceanography. The university owns a ship for faculty, researchers,' student and teachers' studies of the ocean life in the region. The beautiful "May the Wind" pier (Zhangqiao pier), stretching far out into the Yellow Sea, is in front of the Qingdao government offices and is the symbol of Qingdao. The Chinese navy is very active around Qingdao, with many installations, including Chinese warships anchored near the shore. During the 2008 Beijing Olympics, Qingdao was the site for many of the sea sports. From spring to autumn, Qingdao's rocky and sand beaches, and very attractive ocean environment, naturally attract many thousands of local residents and tourists.

It is no wonder that Qingdao and its older and more modern German buildings and cultural relics was determined as China's most livable city in 2009. Living here was a delightful pleasure for me. I especially miss that weekly shuttle bus to and from the Laoshan campus with the spectacular view of the Yellow Sea, and then both Laoshan Mountain and the sea, coming together to form a wonderful linkage.

I had several hot pot dinners for faculty and student friends, including my seventy-fifth birthday dinner. After Professor Li and I traveled to Beijing to meet leaders of Higher Education Press to sign the agreement to publish *Communicating Interculturally,* we held a celebration dinner for about fifteen people, including five American teachers and several students.

In March 2010, Wang Chaolu wrote as a post script for his 2008 photo book, *Fifty Old Constructions in Qingdao:*

"Living in Qingdao, a beautiful garden city at the seaside, I love its mountains and waters, trees, and flowers, especially, the old constructions that add to the charm of the city.

Constructions serve as the major centers of the history and culture, as proved in a western saying that 'constructions are the history books of stones.' they demonstrate the esthetic standards of the old days and contain the profound culture despite the transformation of the history." (2008).

Unlike my earlier teaching to English and communication/journalism majors, many of my Ocean University of China students were majoring in various sciences, especially related to marine sciences. This provided a good contrast to the earlier students whose English tended to be stronger. I taught a freshmen/sophomore English newspapers class. These students especially bonded with me, and provided me a seventy-fifth birthday party. Additionally, I taught western civilization and intercultural communication to upper level students, and the model UN Security Council simulation. As there were not enough students for each of the fifteen delegations, various volunteer students participated in the class, without credit.

Jinan, the "Ciity of Springs" and Capital of Shangdong Province, China: Warm Hospitality for the Dragon Boat Festival: June 4–7, 2011.

On June 4, 2011 I went with Ocean University of China student Jethro Jjiang to his home town, Jinan, the "City of Springs," boasting 100 springs, where his father and mother greeted us at the train station as we had come from Qingdao. I was the first foreigner ever to visit his family, and the first foreigner that Jethro had ever traveled with. He called our friendship "a cross generational friendship." It was also my first time in

Jinan, except to pass through on the train. Jethro later studied for his master's degree in international business in the United Kingdom. In the information that Jethro had prepared for me, it noted that Jinan is a city with a heritage of more than 2000 years, "The cradle of longshan relics culture, the reputed prehistoric culture of China." Our first sightseeing was at the thousand Buddha Mountain (Qianfo Mountain), with many stone Buddhas carved into the mountain side, "since the times of the sui dynasty and its Xingguohan temple." There was a giant sleeping Buddha and the golden laughing Buddha overlooking the city. My first gift that I received in China in 2001 was a laughing Buddha and so I have a special fondness for them.

On June 5, we took an hour long boat trip in the river around Daming Lake (Daming Hu)-"The lake of great light" and into the lake itself, one of the biggest lakes in Jinan, and one of the three major sightseeing locations in Jinan (with the Thousand Buddha Mountain and Baotu Springs, containing 100 springs of which 72 are famous and maintain a year round temperature of 18% celseus). We traveled through two locks where the water level rose or lowered in order to pass into the next water way. Because of the Dagon Boat Festival, the river and lake areas, and around the springs were filled with many Chinese families and young people, enjoying the holiday. The luncheon that Jethro, his father and I had in the 49th floor of a revolving restaurant gave us a very good view of the entire city and surrounding area. Jethro's father, professionally a department chief in the local government, was an excellent photographer, and he took many photos of Jethro and me at all of the scenic sites. Jethro's mother, also a professional leader, had gone to the market, and spent four hours preparing an especially delicious Dragon Boat Festival meal for us at their apartment. The delightful hospitality the family gave me during the whole visit including the home of one's Chinese hosts made the experience all the more extraordinary.

We visited Baoto Spring Park, with "a history of 3,545 years, dating back to the Shang dynasty (16th-11th bc)" on the morning of June 6 where Jethro's father continued to take many very professional photos of us and the surroundings. Many young people wanted photos with me, a frequent happening during my years in China. I was the only foreigner on each day of our time in Jinan. Another delightful lunch was served by his mother in their apartment. I have visited about twenty-five homes in China since I first arrived in 2001 and always the families' hospitality was exceptional whether they were a poor or well off family. Jethro's family provided us a very happy time together. Jethro was very pleased to have me visit as his "cross generational friend." Certainly for me, it made my teaching experience at Ocean University of China and my travel a particularly happy experience as well. On June 7, after another Taiwanese rib steak meal at the same restaurant where we had eaten on our first day in Jinan, his parents brought us to the train station. Our trip back to Qingdao was quiet and restful on the very fast D train, which travels more than 200 kilometers an hour.

27. Yangzhou University Once More: 2013

With my previous experience teaching at Yangzou University in 2001–02, in the spring of 2013, I again suggested that I would like to teach there once more for the autumn 2013 semester, as sort of book ends for the period that I taught in Chinese universities. This request received a positive response from the then dean of international studies and the then director of the international office, Tommy Tang, whom I had known in 2001-02.

I recommended that I teach the following courses: intercultural communication, model United Nations Security Council simulation, global media and culture for undergraduates, and cross-cultural values for post graduates.

In fact, I taught intercultural communication for 55 senior majors in French and Japanese, using Li Mengyu's and my book; and for 15 first year post graduate women students in English education, using Steve J. Kulich's and my coedited book, *Intercultural Perspectives on Chinese Communication* (2007). These women students and I had a Christmas party at my apartment on Christmas day. They provided several interactive games which I had not seen before. In the second nine weeks, I also taught Western culture to 270 sophomore majors in Arabic, French, Japanese, Korean, business English, English translation, and English education, but also using LI Mengyu's and my book as the text. Using this book gave me the opportunity to see how well it worked for the Intended Chinese students. Previously, 1,000 other students in different universities had this as their text.NJJ

At the Lotus Flower campus where I lived, I heard that the University had given this campus to the Yangzhou municipality, in exchange for the new campus, where the College of International Studies/the Foreign Language College is now housed. Two American men English teachers taught oral English at four campuses. There was also a French teacher from Corsica, two Japanese male teachers with no English, and two Korean women teachers. It appeared that a Spanish language major was under serious consideration but there was an ongoing debate about whether yet another language would be productive. In 2001–02, there had been a German major, but it no longer existed during my teaching there in 2013–14. I stopped dozens of friendly 20–23 year old freshmen and sophomore majors at the Lotus Flower campus, in the nearby food sellers' lane, and at the adjacent agricultural college. Many had very weak English, to ask some simple questions: their name, home area, age, and subject which they were studying. Some were often unable to tell me the names of their majors in English, though others indicated that they were studying in technology, information science, nursing, international trade, interior decorating, English education, science, television news, and sports, and from the agricultural college, animal management, plant biology, and environmental studies. When I asked them the name of their institution at the Lotus Flower campus, they all said Yangzhou University rather than the name of the private college which had taken over the Lotus Flower campus. One rare philosophy major at the newest campus and I had a brief conversation about Socrates, Plato, Aristotle and Descartes (a surprise for me).

My former Yangzhou University postgraduate student and now a Ph.D. In linguistics and artificial intelligence, testing and collocation from Shanghai Jiaotong University, Lu Jun and his wife, Kathleen Jin and I had many very pleasant conversations. Lu Jun wisely recommended that instead of calling this book, *China in Focus,* I should call it *Journey to the East,* as a linguistic play off of the Chinese classic, *Journey to the West.* His wife offers private evening and weekend English lessons to six classes of children and teenagers, totally about sixty students with whom I had very nice conversations and lots of good questions. One thirteen year old boy asked two good questions and then just as the class was about to end, he asked: "Tell me all about America." Their English was very good for their ages, and in fact better than many of the freshmen students whom I met at the main university campus. They gave me several skits from

Two Japanese majors whom I met at the nearby food sellers' lane later joined me for dinner. Their spoken English was only fair, but one of the students told me that he was passionate about democracy in the US, Western Europe and Japan and he ardently wished that democracy would come eventually to China. He admitted that this would be unlikely soon at least at the national level. He hoped that after graduation he would have a chance to observe democracy more directly in Japan with a professional position there.

On Wednesdays for lunch, I voluntarily tutored a post graduate woman, Olivia, a nutrition MA student for her essays designed for TOEFL and GRE exams. One evening, she and a woman student friend cooked a delicious and nutritious dinner for me at my apartment. For New Year's Eve, I gave a dinner at a nearby restaurant for Lu Jun, Kathleen Jin, Olivia her friend, and five of my sophomore class monitors representing Arabic, French, Japanese, Korean, and business English. Adding to the Chinese cuisine, I included strawberries and oranges, which caused some quizzical commentary about American food habits in the wintertime.

In January 2014, I had many former students who visited me. I spent the Lunar New Year celebration in Shanghai, with David Xu, his parents, and ten year old nephew, little Daniel, just before returning to the us on February 5, thus ending my teaching experiences in China from 2001 to 2014. A former MA student, Jenny, her husband and child took me finally to the Pudong airport in Shanghai. I assumed that I would not be back in China soon, but in November/December, 2014, I spent two weeks in Changsha.

28. Cultural Health Detour, Food Poisoning: 2013

On September 27, 2013, at an upscale restaurant/ banquet hall, a dish with multiple eggs, which apparently was not handled well gave me food poisoning [Salmonella poisoning], and caused me to get a serious infection intestinally. Having the American habit of trying to solve health problems first by myself, and not understanding the seriousness of the situation immediately, it took me some time to make contacts for assistance. It was foolish on my part since it was not just a cold that I could overcome by myself, but with serious negative health implications.

The thirty year old, newly married doctor from Anhui Province, with reasonably good English at Yangzhou's best hospital, told me that there are standard procedures for curing food poisoning, but "like learning English, the process is slow." He said that even small clinics in China know how to treat the symptoms, but may not have the technology nor adequate communication to properly solve the developing problems quickly. Towards the latter part of my hospital stay, he said "There is an obstruction in the bowl." Asking him what that meant, I learned that he meant an obstruction in the bowel. I helped him correct that pronunciation, and he said that he needed to have more foreign patients so that he could improve his English.

When I entered the hospital, several days of my potential health crisis had passed already. I underwent four or five days of diarrhea, a loss of my voice for a full day, an accelerated blood sugar, two-three days of hiccups, and as a part of the recovery process I fasted two days without any food, and supposedly no water either. In that latter regard I was less faithful to the medical instructions than I should have been and I convinced my woman caretaker to have three bottles of water over the two days. Gradually, I was allowed to have rice porridge, vegetable soup with egg and tofu, then egg and tomato soup, and finally noodles, all vegetarian. Then overcoming constipation took until the last of my seven days in the hospital. The hospital appointed a special nutritionist for me, and some of my later food was prepared in a special canteen rather than the usual hospital canteen.

Yangzhou has two superior hospitals, and I was fortunate to be in the best and very progressive hospital in its medical procedures, technology, and care, meeting high international standards. Signage throughout the two buildings that I was in was both in Chinese and English. The hospital has seven buildings and a very professional, competent, and friendly staff. Younger doctors and nurses had reasonably good English; nurse aides, more likely had primarily hospital English, with expressions like, "good morning, how are you, I am your nurse assistant, speak English slowly, call if you need help, turn over, this way, wait a moment, I will be back, blood pressure check, blood sugar check, temperature check, be quiet, I am sorry, you give up? You give up? Etc."

While the American and German hospital systems, as the thirty year old doctor told me, who had spent a month in postdoctoral training in German hospitals, have basically oral medicine procedures, and the French hospitals use suppositories frequently, most often the Chinese medical practice is based on the belly as central to the entire health system. Chinese medicine mainly uses the injection and intravaneous fluid procedures, leaving my hands and arms bruised from the needles. Most of the days that I was there, I received two liters of antibacteria and antibiotic fluids.

The international office of Yangzhou University, was responsible for my care. "You are under the protection of Yangzhou University." the assistant to the Weiban [director of the international office at the university) was personally responsible for my care, and Lu Jun took me to the hospital by taxi. He was my main consultant, adviser, and interpreter as needed for my medical situation. I am very grateful to him and his wife Kathleen. After my hospital stay, they came every Tuesday evening to my apartment and he prepared dinner for the three of us..

From 6am to 6 pm, the hospital was fully alive and vibrant. The ward room for me and two other men patients in the digestive section of the hospital was a very clean, approximately ten to twelve meters long room and four to five meters wide, with its own toilet and shower, plus adequate storage areas. There were three chairs which converted into beds for the caretakers. The Chinese hospital practice, except for when I was in a western section of a Shanghai hospital in 2008 which had American style amenities and a thoroughly English speaking staff, was a "Bring your own caretaker, food, washbasins, towels, soap, tissue," policy. The bed itself cost only forty rmb nightly.

The first Chinese sixty year old patient in bed twenty-nine had his wife as his main caretaker, plus various rather noisy family members who were present at different times, and a good number of very old relatives visiting him. While the typhoon was moving outside from the South China sea up the coast of the East China sea with turbulent storms in Yangzhou, The man in bed twenty-nine at night seemed to have his own ongoing storm with coughing and hacking nightly. Apparently, his digestive problem was solved, but when he left, I had a feeling that he should be moving to the pneumonia section.

The second man in bed twenty-nine, aged sixty-two, was able to be fairly active. His caregiver was his son thirty-six, with red fingernails–too impolite of a question for me to ask why. On the day that they came I briefly met the twelve year old grandson who was able to speak some usual early English expressions. "Hello, how are you?" "I am fine, thank you, and you?" "What is your name?" "My name is — -." "How old are you?" "I am twelve years old." Pointing to the younger man, I asked, "Is this your baba?" "Yes, this is my baba." "Is this your grand baba?" "This is the baba of my baba." He did not understand the word "grand."

The older man's sixty year old wife had the appearance especially of a rural, ruddy, perhaps peasant background. Through interpretation, she said to me" You have nice teeth." She asked me, "Why are you in China, and why do you still work?" One of my two American colleagues at the University then visiting me, who spoke good mandarin Chinese, said that her Yangzhou country area dialect was so different that he could understand almost nothing that she said. The father and son were friendly and alerted the nurses or my caregiver when they saw that my injected fluids were running out or that I needed other assistance.

An older son with a deep ruddy peasant complexion was the caretaker for an old man in bed twenty-eight who was very ill when he arrived, but was talking again conversationally in Chinese when I left the hospital.

The thirty year old doctor told me that the difference between my bed, thirty, and beds twenty-nine and twenty-eight, was that while very few Chinese could even afford to be in this hospital at all, unless the patients in the other beds had reasonable health insurance, a one week stay in the hospital could cost several months of income or savings. They were not rich or they would have had private rooms, but they were richer than most Chinese. Additionally, any younger working caregivers would probably lose at least that week's income.

The director of the international office at the university brought me flowers. The assistant to the director also arranged for various students to come, walk in the halls with me, assist me, interpret for me, and keep me company. One of my earliest visitors with good English was Dr. Lu's freshman student Frank, and his roommate. Frank was nervous about helping a foreign teacher, but he appeared to like the experience and came to visit me daily, saying that it was a good way to spend the national holiday week, since it was too far for him to return home. Altogether, more than a half dozen previously unknown students came and visited me for several hours during the earlier part of my stay. There was of course a swirl of languages around me all during my stay–mostly Chinese, but at times with conversations going on simultaneously between English and also Chinese speakers — a gaggle of sounds and continuous code switching for those who were speaking English..

The Weiban office hired a middle aged woman caretaker for me, who took care of me twenty-four hours a day. She has two children thirty and twenty-eight. I met her twenty-eight year old son who came to visit her several times. According to the assistant from the university's Weiban office, she had been hired a freelance caretaker at the hospital for about twenty years when no family caretakers were available. She told him that she had never assisted a foreigner before so she was afraid to undertake my caregiving, but she adjusted well. Some things that she thought were funny which she told me, or to the other Chinese speakers in the room, were mostly at my expense and some of it seemed rather insensitive. Although I learned no Chinese during the process, she learned the word 'ok' as perhaps one of her first English words, since I often used it to indicate agreement or that the specific progress was complete to my satisfaction. As she was ready to wash me on my last evening, I had learned that the Foreign Language School dean and the supervisor of the foreign teachers would visit me at seven pm. There were no English speakers available, and she could not understand why I was refusing the washing. Calling the nurse's station, one nurse's aide came, and told me to speak slowly so that they could know why I did not want the washing. When my caretaker realized that guests were coming, she took the wash pan out until after they left. The dean said to me "You are the VIP in a common Chinese ward." it certainly was true that I did receive VIP treatment.

My hospital stay for one week cost 8,000rmb or about $1300, and 750 rmb for incidentals such as food, towels, soap, plastic pans, etc. (about $125). All of the tests, intravaneous fluids, and professional staff added significantly to the costs. During my hospital experience, I had blood tests, x rays, computer technology exams, body scans, etc. I gave her a generous cash gift. Later, Lu Jun told me that he had given Frank 300 extra rmb, but I had assumed that he was a volunteer.

In my last half hour in the hospital, I apparently did something in terms of the needle for the intravaneous fluid injection in my left hand that caused it to swell significantly, making me prone to shock. The nurse aide told me, "After twenty-four hours, you can use warm water to ease the swelling." She meant, "During the next twenty-four hours," but we both misunderstood the meaning. She wanted to shift the injection into my right hand, but I declined it as Dr. Lu was coming to get me shortly. "You give up? You give up?" she asked me. The woman doctor with good English released me, saying: "Take it easy. You are 90% cured, but no regular Chinese food for two weeks." Lu said, "In the future, if there are any problems, call me immediately." "The assistant from the international office had scolded me several times for not calling him when my first September 30th four AM intestinal pains began. Leaving the hospital, Lu and I waited for a taxi, while I felt that I might faint because of the shock to my left hand. I went to bed for several hours after I reached my apartment. It took several weeks for full recovery, but I returned to my teaching schedule as soon as possible.

The weeklong experience gave me new insights into Chinese medical practices in a very good hospital.,We can consider that this experience provides me some raw and rather isolated data about this above average Chinese intercultural medical practice. It was an expensive and somewhat troublesome experience, by ordinary Chinese standards. Learning that food poisoning is highly possible even in such an upscale restaurant/banquet hall as I had eaten the infected egg dish. Lu jun warned me not to eat food from the seller's food lane, but the two American teachers said that they had never had any problems eating from food bought at those stalls, and noting the irony that my food poisoning had actually come from an upper class restaurant/banquet hall.

29. Three Conferences in China, 2013/2014

Fourth Triennial Multicultural Discourse Conference, October 23–26, 2013, Zheziang University, Hangzhou, China

At the end of the Fourth Triennial Multicultural Discourse Conference, offered in large part in English, under the leadership of internationally recognized critical discourse analysis (cda) scholarship of professor Shi-Xu of Zheziang University, the largest university in China and perhaps the largest university in China, he offered his own discourse analysis of the conference.

1. The approximately 200 participants, many from outside of China, including Africa, Asia, Europe, Latin America, and the US, developed a number of different scholarly, cultural, and national forms and ways of understanding critical discourse analysis (cda). Among the remarkable topics under consideration was the prominence of regional and global development, economics, poverty, and national sovereignty. The African scholars present made a strong critical discourse analysis of China's discursive approaches to its aid for Africa, including the masked Chinese discourses that indicate the reciprocal need for energy from Africa. Chinese scholars at the conference were looking at the discourses taking place related to Africa, Asia, Latin America, Europe, and the US as a reasonably recent phenomenon since the first conference in 2004. Additionally, this conference now included a number of Chinese Ph.D. students studying overseas, who provided their own very interesting critical discourse presentations. Dambisa Moyo's book, *Winner Take All: China's Race for Resources and What It Means for the World* (2012), Howard French's *China's Second Continent: How a Million Migrants Are Building a New Empire in Africa* (2014) and Evan Osnos' book *Age of Ambition: Chasing Fortune, Truth, and Faith in the New China* (2014) are all especially critical of China along the same terms as the foreign scholars at the conference.

2. The effects and consequences of the conference included questions about the future directions of the increasing applications of critical discourse analysis in every continent. The plenary speeches, taking the entire first day of the conference, were specifically designed to offer a voice to a wide number of scholars from many different countries and cultures, with varying approaches to the subject of the conference. Using the Asian sense of shame, Professor Shi-Xu apologized for all failings that had occurred in planning and offering the conference by the organizers. One major suggestion by participants was that more discussion time should be available to interact with all of the speakers. This is not typical at most Chinese students that I have attended.

3. Professor Shi-Xu not only offered a half hour of final comments from members of the scholarly community present, an unusual event in my experience in more than fifteen conferences in China, but he invited the participants to submit articles for his edited journal on critical dis-

course analysis, as well as the series of books on the topic that are now published by Rutledge, and he invited participants to submit essays to his edited book which he planned to make on the topic. As he did in the 2007 conference which I also attended, he encouraged faculty from a different university to undertake planning and hosting the 2016 triennial conference. He had done this also in 2007, and I suspect that it was a courtesy offer, as these multicultural conferences were developed out of his own scholarship and background.

4. A symbolic weakness of the conference, and one which should be taken up in the 2016 conference, according to Shi-Xu, was the absence of topics such as discourses on the redistribution of wealth and resources from the developed countries to those still developing and emerging. Ending the conference, he offered the Chinese saying "all parties must end somewhere."

The plenary speakers included several African, Asian scholars from outside of China, Chinese, and Europeans, with a wide range of topics, and varying methodologies for conducting critical discourse analysis. The second and third day presentations were divided among such topics as cultural theory and methods; cultural concepts and historical discourses; women, gender and family; cultural/intercultural politics; power, politics, and governance; human rights and social prejudice; nationhood and foreign policy; multilingual and multidiscursive matters; academic discourses; urban and rural affairs; translation and rhetoric; development and the third world (which was strongly criticized as a topic by a participant from Nigeria); ethnicity/ minority/ migrants; and health and national disasters.

Personally, it is my judgment that the two multicultural discourse conferences that I attended under Shi-Xu's leadership, 2007 and 2013, were clearly among the best planned, hosted, and developed conferences that I have attended in China. He modeled a very strong attention to maintaining a serious academic well focused subject matter.. Conference participants were also a very friendly group.

The 10th CAFIC International Conference, November 21–24, 2013

With the theme, "Intercultural communication for a harmonious world: challenges and opportunities," the China Association for Intercultural Communication held its tenth biennial conference under the sponsorship of the University of Hai'nan Tourism College in Haikou, Hai'nan Island, China's southernmost tropical island, on November 21–24, under the leadership of dr. Sun Youzhong, the Association's incoming president, and dean of English and International Studies at Beijing Foreign Studies University. It was hosted by Feng Yuan of the Department of Applied Foreign Languages.

Professor Jia Yuxin, outgoing president, and professor of linguistics and intercultural communication at the Harbin Institute of Technology, provided an opening address in English about "intercultural personhood and bringing a harmonious global community into social reality" and an emotional concluding and personal address in Chinese. President Jia called upon the approximately 350 participants to "face the global challenges, think critically, reflect and act critically in the life of this global village, the concept which is becoming more and more real to us in the 21st century."

Keynoter. Sun Youzhong's address was entitled: ' A common framework for intercultural competence development in the discipline of English in Chinese universities: a preliminary proposal." In his address, he proposed, "on the basis of the latest scholarship in intercultural competence studies, a common [action-oriented] framework for icd" with nine sections; 1) defining ic; 2) the significance of ic for English majors [in Chinese universities]; 3) the relationship of ic and linguistic competence; 4) how to develop ic: curriculum design; 5) how to develop ic: teaching methods; 6) how to develop ic: extracurricular options; 7) ic assessment; 8) teachers' icd; and 9) recommendations for administrators.

Keynoter Carolyn Callaway Thomas, Ph.D., was the president of the world communication association, professor of communication and culture in the department of communication and culture at Indiana university, coauthor of *Intercultural communication: roots and routes* (1999) and the coeditor of *dr. Martin Luther King, Jr. And the Sermonic Power of Public Discourse* (1993). Her keynote address was entitled "Empathy: a global imperative" and she discussed several internationally known conflicts, while examining "challenges to humans' empathic impulses" and "how the practice of empathy influences human affairs" which she called "a significant tool for humanity" that "must be transformed into everyday linguistic and behavioral practice — a global imperative!."

Two senior scholars' forums were provided as plenary sessions, the first: "Intercultural communication studies: interdisciplinary research and application" had three presentations, but all in Chinese and without an interpreter, causing most of the foreign participants to be unable to understand them. The second senior scholars' forum, in English, and moderated by Steve Kulich, included presentations by Professor Ray T. Donahue (Nagoya Gakuan University, Japan); "Toward comprehensive discourse analysis; illuminating comparative culture, Professor Jane Jackson (the Chinese University of Hong Kong): "Intercultural sensitivity development through study abroad"; and Professors Alla Shevela and Victoria Timchenko (Far Eastern Federal University, Russia): "Gender and complementary discourse."

Forty-eight concurrent sessions were scheduled on the second day of the conference, most of which were mixed between presentations in Chinese and English. In past conferences, most of the simultaneous presentations have been given in English, while at this conference, about 60–65% of the presentations were given in Chinese, and without interpretation. It became a problem for foreign participants.

At the conference banquet, outgoing President Jia presented incoming President Sun the official seal as the Association's icon. There were many undergraduate and postgraduate student volunteers from the University for the conference. I was invited to sit between the two presidents, a nice symbolic honor.

I have attended the 2001–2013 conferences, and served as a keynoter at the 2001, 03, 05, 07, and 2011 conferences, plus giving a farewell address at the 2009 conference. I received a special recognition award at the 2009 conference, and Guo Ming Chen (University of Rhode Island), Steve J. Kulich (Shanghai International Studies University), Chen Ling (Hong Kong Baptist University), He Daokuan (emeritus, Shenzhen University) and I received special recognition awards in 2011.

The Cultural Security Conference at the National University of Defense Technology, November, 2014

Based, I assume, on past contacts, two other American professors, one Nepalese-American professor and I were invited as keynote speakers at this conference at the National University of Defense Technology in Changsha. The University is known informally as the West Point of China. Apparently for budget reasons, as Pesident Xi Jinpin has called for more financial thriftiness among state sponsored universities and especially military universities, the scheduled two day conference was squeezed into one day. My keynote address was entitled; "Social Media and Cybernetics in Asia: Regional Implications for Security." Professor Shi-Xu played an important role in this conference as well as at the Hangzhou conference. Later, I gave six lectures at the University and three at Central South University University, also in Changsha.

Part Five
Voices of the Youth

30. Winter and Summer Camps: 2003, 2013

Children's English Winter Camp, Beijing: 2003

At the Unicom (University of International Communication) in Beijing, I participated in teaching 171 children and junior middle school students for the New Century Youth English Club (camp) as one of four foreign teachers (the other three men, one from the US-about twenty-three years old, a nineteen year old from Columbia with a Scottish accent, and a twenty-four year old from the UK. The woman director speaking little English was assisted by a twenty-three year old woman Chinese teacher with good English, and 14 Chinese university students as "little deans." I was assisted by Bob Zhang Bo, a BLCU computer major student with whom I had already been a close friend.

I had the thirteen pupils with the best English, based on prior tests, five hours daily, ranging in age from thirteen to sixteen and including one seventeen year old student, George, who was a first year senior middle school student. Each student had a short oral English test before the end of the camp.

The families of these students each paid 1230 rmb (approximately $98) for their child for the ten days, including instruction, a trip to Beijing's Natural History Museum, lodging, meals, and awards. All thirteen of my children's families had a computer. Several students had their own mobile phones; all but two thirteen year olds had internet access. A number of well-dressed parents arrived for the final ceremony in their own cars and took many photos, a number with digital cameras.

Although the text book in oral English was designed for adults, and each of the seven classes only had to complete three units, the level of English for all but three of my students, and for many of the younger children, was reasonably good. In the class level immediately below

ours, there were children who were fourteen and fifteen, but with less strong English than in our class. Each class presented a play in English for the final ceremony, and our class presented "Beauty and the Beast" in about ten minutes with the parts memorized by the students. Also, each of the students participated in a public speaking contest over two evenings, with everyone involved first in an in-class competition, and five being chosen for each class in the camp-wide contests at the three levels of instruction. None of the speeches were actually speeches in the western context, but were short passages copied from children's English books. I have noted this situation at the university level both at Yangzhou University and at BLCU, where very little independent thinking was developed or expected in public speaking contests.
Students at the New Century Youth English Club winter oral English camp, January 22–31: 2003 made the following comments in my journal:

> *George, 17:* Hi, Michael. I have been here for five days. I'm so happy to live with you that we are having a good time. You are very humorous and kind. I think everyone can make friends with you, and so do i. You like playing games and telling interesting things, stories and singing English songs. I like them very much. I have never seen a teacher like you. My English teacher who is in my high school is very kind too. But she brings so many exams, so my listening and writing are so bad. You are better than her in my opinion. : People walk in and out of our life, but only friends leave foot prints on my heart. You are my friend. Thank you. George this was a memorized quote.
>
> *Grace, 16:* Hope you all the best. Please don't forget me. I will miss you. I'll remember all the joyful time that we spent together. Grace
>
> *Bill, 15:* I hope you are happy in China. I feel glad during these days with you. Don't forget me! Bill

Helen: 15: Dear Michael! : I'm Helen. I have been here for five days. During these days, I feel very happy, because I met you. I think you are very kind. We all like you. You are good at singing and you teach us many songs. We sing the songs everyday. We all like these songs. I hope you feel happy every day in China. Don't forget me. Your student and good friend, Helen! We are friends forever. Good luck for you. Helen

Sunny, 13: I have been here for five days. I think I am happy and I got joy there. Because I met you and you are my English teacher. Victoria and I like you very well. I think you are my best teacher and the most lovely teacher. I hope you are happy all the time! Best wishes for you, my good teacher. Sunny [She left a day early to travel with her parents to Hangzhou to visit grandparents for the festival.]

Victoria, 13: I really want to say something different, but I don't know what to say, just wish you good luck, be healthy and can you invite me to your own concert (for singing songs, famous singer: Michael)? God bless you! Victoria, 13 years old, in friendship, always. [She left a day early to go with her parents to Vietnam.]

Vera,13: I'm glad I can see you at there. In the five days, I am always very happy. You are a good singer and a good teacher, professor. I think you are very interesting, and I hope "your tomorrow is better than today!" *Vera*

Betty, 13: I'm Betty. I'm very glad to make friends with you. I always have a good time in your class. I really think you are a perfect singer. I hope you keep happy all the time and have a good luck! Betty

Mike, 14: Hi Michael. I hope you are happy. And friends are like the stars in the sky. You don't always see them but you know they always be there.so I can remember you. You are a good teacher. You are very interesting. Happy every day. Little Mike

Allen, 15: I'm very happy when I studied with you. I hope you are healthy forever. I will remember you all the time and remember when we had time together. Best wishes. Allen

Tony, 16: I hope you are happy every day! I'm glad to make friends with you. I'm very happy these days. I will remember you all the time. You can give me a letter when you are free.
[He came from Shangdong Province to visit his grandparents, but he had a serious anxiety attack just before the final ceremony, related to his small parts in "Beauty and the Beast," and he and his grandfather left before the ceremony.]

Simon, 14: Hello Michael. I'm glad to meet you and make friends. I hope you are happy every day. You are a very kind man. You are good singing. Of course you are a good English teacher. This is my card for you. Best wishes for you. Simon [He got ill on the night of the day that he wrote this message, and had to go home, missing the last half of the camp.]

Global Summer Youth Leadership Camp, Zhezhiang University: 2013

In the winter of 2013, an entrepreneurial twenty six year old leader in Beijing contacted me about being a part of a summer youth camp, in either Beijing or Hangzhou, initially intended for Chinese university students, particularly for students studying in the US and home for the summer. Several such companies have developed recently in China. He and his colleagues thought that it might be possible for such students to receive credit which could be translated into university credits at their American universities. As many Chinese do, his initial thoughts were directed towards the private Ivy League American universities such as

Harvard, Princeton, MIT and Yale, but as we discussed the possibility of developing a program, with at least half of its content as a study of intercultural communication, his company made efforts, unsuccessfully, to locate other public American universities where such credits might be transferred. Eventually, it was decided that the program for Chinese university students would be held at Zhezhiang University, China's largest universitiy, in Hangzhou.

After arriving at Shanghai's Pudong Airport on July 12, 2013, an MA student in intercultural communication from Shanghai met me at the plane which was three hours late arriving. We took the metro for an hour to the Shanghai train station, learning that the train tickets for Hangzhou for that day had been sold out. I took a charter bus going to Hangzhou, and arrived early in the morning of July 13, being met at midnight by Daniel, a staff member/ recent graduate of the Beijing Chemical University.

The summer youth camp, with only nine very bright senior middle school students enrolled, including three 2013 senior middle school graduates, and two students who had spent time in the US, but no university students, was already in session, with the first three days designed to teach them global leadership and world citizenship skills. The team leaders included a twenty-six year old German graduate from Oxford University, and a Hong Kong Chinese graduate, Feddy Luo, about the same age, who had graduated from Hong Kong Science and Technology University. Eight of the students' parents paid 2000rmb for the total ten day program and one had won a lottery which gave him free tuition. All of the students had the goal of studying in an American university, and had signed up for TOEFL and SAT exams. The information sheet suggested that they might wish to attend one of the following universities: Harvard, Caltech, Stanford, MIT, Princeton, University of Chicago, UC Berkeley, or Brown University in the US, or in the United Kingdom, Oxford, Cambridge, Imperial College, the London School of Economics, or University College of London, or in Canada the University of British Columbia. This is a typical mindset among many Chinese families, wanting their son or daughter, only to consider mostly private prestigious universities abroad.

At the start of the initial summer enrichment program, the Hong Kong- based inter cultural education limited team's three day intensive introduction and highly experiential program identified goals to develop critical thinking, global citizenship, and world leadership. Culture was variously defined and three main principles were identified: not mixing with one's emotions, morality, or with who makes a statement. Three main questions were offered: hidden assumptions, the actual meaning of a statement or question, and how it is applicable. The students were reminded throughout that the usual memorization technique of Chinese education had to be expanded always to ask why, and to be able to provide comprehensive reasons for why an assumption might or might not be reasonable. Students were taught to distinguish what rights and responsibilities would develop through critical thinking, with intended goals to assess whether the program had led them to think more about global citizenship, with more empathy for developing countries' considerations and for their own potential future as social innovators. I wished that Li Mengyu and I had included some of these materials in *Communicating Interculturally*.

Many practical illustrations were given about social innovations and the students' future in such efforts, which they discussed in two smaller groups and collectively. A major element of the program was connected to the development of fair trade practices such as current trade problems in third world countries, fair trade labeling and goods, the pros and cons of fair trade, and a fair trade flow chart, with specific examples for China, and practical applications which the students could make for their own future involvement in such initiatives.

The four earlier dimensions of Geert Hofstede were introduced as models for how such innovations might be developed, supplemented by discussions on culture, cultural differences, and underlying values in different societies. Both of the team leaders demonstrated how their own lives had moved them to make critical thinking and world citizenship a major aspect of their training and life agenda. The final exercise emotionally helped the students to imagine their future, year by year, through ten years from the present, and then back to an earlier three years when they had first started senior middle school. It was apparent that the students were deeply moved by this three day training workshop, and the students considered it to be very successful in developing their own interest as future world citizens and critical thinkers.

Fulbright philosophy Professor at Beijing Foreign Language University, Jonathan Scotiz, offered several sessions on the philosophy of the mind. He asked the students to think about the "mind-body problem" and he discussed the concept of "strong artificial intelligence," by saying that in this concept the mind is to the brain as the program is to computer hardware. In this approach, the brain is not biological, but simply another type of hardware computer that could sustain the programs which make up human intelligence. This group of computer experts/philosophers believes that we already have machines that can literally think, as intelligence is just a matter of physical symbol manipulation.

Scotiz emphasized, in contrast, that while the computer can recognize certain symbols, it has no semantic meanings as a part of its functions, but that the human mind has more than simply a syntax, as there is also interpretative content. He used this example in terms of questions and answers, with a set of questions that he asked the smart computer. To trick the computer's answer base, he asked provocative questions: "Do you have any interests? What do you think about the weather? Are you able to think like a human? Do you have any emotions or feelings?" The computer's response was that "she" had no interests, no interest in whether the weather was hot or cold, and that she didn't concern herself about thinking like a human. Thus, while computers could answer straight-forward questions, much as a gps system could provide directions from one location to another and recalculate when the car had passed an exit, or a computer could implement programs, Scotiz engaged the students in drawing the conclusion that it is clear that so far the human mind can interpret meanings attached to the symbols which deviate from the computer's programming, but the computer can only work with the symbols which are installed in its software. Thus, in the philosophical "China room" example, where random Chinese characters are entered into the computer, if the computer has no Chinese symbols, for example, it cannot reproduce the Chinese language system, nor if it has no English symbols such as letters, it cannot reproduce the interpretative nature of English meanings, no matter how many Chinese characters or English letters are entered into the "China room."

A recent woman Harvard Ph.D. Martha Ferede, offered the nine students a series of evening interactive programs on global citizenship initiatives and ideas for applying to elite American and other foreign universities with advice for creating a successful resume and personal statement. Later, she represented the company at a 2014 summer camp fair in Ningbo, which she later said was already a year too late for this type of summer enrichment program, as these students were already making decisions concerning such foreign universities to attend. Currently, many private college preparatory secondary schools in the US already have one fourth of their student population as Chinese students, and typically, they also proceed to four year colleges and universities in the US.

Using the chapter dialogues, short essays, and case studies in Li Mengyu's and my text for Chinese students, which all of the students had copies of as a part of the program, I provided critical thinking applications for the students' questions and answers about why one set of constructs was featured in the books over other possible ideas and how these particular ideas could lead to more critical thinking and global citizenship through a developing sense of social justice, gender equality, and positive human rights. We had reader's theatre with several of the book's dialogues.

Hjalmer Jorge Joffre-Elechorn, coming from Afghanistan, an internationally known leader of "theatre of the oppressed" and "forum theatre" for emerging communities, led the students in developing their own planned and executed short play which involved a young Chinese village woman who had received a full scholarship for admission to peking university, but who was confronted by a negative patriarchical Chinese parent, a bar tender who didn't want a young woman from a village to work for him, and finally, a young man tempting her to sleep with him, which caused her to become pregnant. In the spontaneously developing and audience interactive play, almost all of the men in the play oppressed her, with the kind intervention of an enlightened uncle and a teacher from Peking University leading to her own eventual taking control of her own life and enrolling there.

The nature of the "forum" type of play allowed the four experts and two staff members as the audience to intervene and thus to change the dimensions of the play itself. An eighteen year old young woman, who had spent two months in the summer of 2012 at the Yale University drama program, played the lead character. The final play offered a very important contribution to the students' development of critical thinking and a view of themselves as future global citizens especially with the positive interventions by audience members.

Overall, this ten day global leadership program was highly successful for the students. It is very likely that all of these students will enter and do well in elite world class universities. Their ages ranged from a fourteen year old boy to one nineteen year old, six males and three females coming from Hangzhou, Ningbo, and Wenzhou. Most of the students hoped to study in a leading California university.

Although the ten day program was excellent, the company's business model was unrealistic, with six experts over the ten day program and two staff members (the intercultural team coming for three days from Hong Kong; Jonathan Scotiz coming from Beijing, Martha Ferede coming from France, Joffre-Elechorn coming from Afghanistan, and I coming from the US) for eight paying students. Considerable promotional efforts were made at summer camp fairs in Hangzhou. Probably as the company's first such experience of this type, and since it was also sending its first group of students for three week homestays to Iowa in August, 2013, this entrepeneureal effort should have taught the members of the company valuable lessons for the summer of 2014. There is a saying highly favored in Wenzhou, known as the entrepreneurial capital of China: "Try once, fail; try twice, fail better; try three times, succeed." In my case, I was cheated 3,600 rmb by the company.

Summer English Camp, Suining County, Jiangsu Province, China: July 6–30, 2013

I have been to Suining County with a population of about 135 thousand people, probably six or seven times. I came first in 2002 at the nearby village where my former Yangzhou University English major student, Devon Yang grew up, and again for his village wedding; giving lectures in two county senior middle schools, and assisting him in 2011 for his annual summer English (and math) camp for senior middle school students. Considering the county development over these years, my first visits in 2002 to 2005 included seeing many mule and donkey wagons in the downtown area, many bikes, and very few electric motor bikes or cars.

Later, the city center in Suining County has seen the construction of many new buildings, many high fashion shops, an international hotel (although I have never met a foreigner there), improved major streets, parks, large supermarkets, exquisite restaurants, traffic lights, and three large sculptured mountain goats as the symbol for the county. The county has become more and more interested in a green environment and pollution- free atmosphere. While there are many bikes, three wheeled taxis (energy efficient, but easily crushed in an accident), and three wheeled trucks and wagons, the santanya vw is a frequent taxi in many Chinese cities. Electric motor bikes are an important means of transportation, and there are many cars on the roads (predominantly Volkswagons).

In contrast to the wide well developed major roads and streets, the cluttered and poorly maintained side streets appear not to have changed much since my earlier visits. My former student's parents in law still live within a small "bot" (somewhat like the earlier Chinese houtongs), with a poorly maintained communal Asian toilet. In contrast, his fifth floor apartment, where he offers the annual morning summer month-long English) camp for thirty seventeen-nineteen year old students, is well appointed with air conditioning. In his parents-in-law home where he teaches the younger thirty rising second year senior middle school students, aged sixteen-seventeen there is no air conditioning and the heat is quite stifling.

In contrast to the Zhezhiang University global leadership camp in Hangzhou, his summer English camp was highly traditional. He stressed considerable rote learning, the standard approach of many Chinese schools, which he said is necessary to prepare the students for the gao kao exam (where only 60% of the youth in Suining County could expect to pass and thus be admitted to a Chinese university). With the first summer camp in mind, I suggested that he might use more creative methods of teaching, His reply was that there was no time for creativity as the time for the students to prepare for the gao kao university entrance exam was too urgent. However, he has later informed me that he is trying to make his regular school English classes more creative, and with more critical thinking exercises along with the mandated teaching.

While several of my former MA students in Shanghai, which has one of the best educational systems in China, and even more broadly, have told me that they teach English with 90% in English language usage and only 10% in Chinese, Devon appears to teach English with 70–80% Chinese language usage and only 20–30% English language usage. He played a brief audio with American English at the beginning of each class, but since I was in a different room, it was not clear what the students did with this information afterwards. I did not hear them repeating the conversations.

In 2011 when I assisted him in his summer English camp, he left me in the hotel room more often than he had me speaking casual English on the fringe of the classes. This time, expecting to assist him for nine to ten sessions, we had agreed that I would have an hour of informal oral English every day each for the rising third year senior middle school students in the morning, and for the rising second year senior middle school students in the afternoon. However, he had me present for my hour of teaching only five times for the morning sessions and two times for the afternoon sessions, again having me staying in the hotel room for several other sessions with the argument that it was too hot for me to be teaching at my age. None of the sixty students had ever talked to a foreigner before me, seeing them only on tv or movies. They were curious and enthusiastic about my interaction with them.
  My impression of most of these students is that they would have a long way to go before they could have adequate oral English to compete in Chinese university freshmen classes. However, their teacher is to be commended as he was doing his best to assist them to pass the English gao kao exam. Besides the month-long classes, he tutored four- teen year old students, and we had several friendly contacts. They also had never met a foreigner before. These children, whose relatively well-off parents did not speak any English, were very keen to learn good English.
  Although this program was expected to last for about 30 days, with a math teacher, a holiday every six days, my volunteer participation for ten days, and costing the parents 500 rmb for the entire program, it suddenly ended, as there had been rumors that the County Education Department officials were going to start paying visits to such unauthorized summer camps and severely fining their organizers. It is a Chinese paradox in rural areas, wanting their students to learn English well in order to pass the gao kao exam on one hand, but not wanting to allow summer programs for the students to enrich their English (and math) competence.
  Considering the two summer camps, the differences were striking, between an elite group of nine students in the Zhezhiang University experience with six experts and two staff members and the very traditional rote learning of these sixty students in Suining County led bravely but traditionally by my former student, Devon. He is among my best Chinese friends, and I am proud of his efforts to improve English and

math skills for area students. The first group of elite nine students in the Zhezhiang summer enrichment program were likely to all enter leading world class universities in the US, UK, or Canada, while in the Suining County summer English and math camp the dream of the students and their parents was that they could pass the gao kao exam in the future, and thus be admitted to some Chinese university. All of the students in the two programs dream of going to the USA, but the first group was much more likely than the second group to achieve their goal.

31. Russian and Chinese Sophomore Cultural Stories: 2013

With thanks to Professor Olga Leontovich, and her eleven Russian students, I am grateful to receive these sophomore cultural stories. For comparison, among 240 sophomore cultural stories at Yangzhou University in the 2013–14 autumn semester, eleven Chinese cultural stories are also presented here, allowing comparisons between same level students in Russia and China..

1. Elena Belousova

My name is Lena and I come from Yolzhskiy, a town located near Volgograd. My town is very young, it was founded in 1951. However, the place where Yolzhskiy is situated was settled in the 14th century and was part of the golden horde. Later in the 17th century the village Bezrodniy with a population of about 20 000 people was situated there. But in 1942 — 43, during the battle of Stalingrad, it was almost completely wiped off the face of the earth: the only buildings that survived from the village Bezrodniy were an old school and an old mill.

I study at Volgograd State Socio-Pedagogical University, so now I am living in Volgograd. But during the weekend I am at home with my family, which includes my mother, father and myself. I also have cousins, aunts, uncles and (unfortunately) only one grandmother. Most of them live in Yollzhskiy, and some — in Saint-Petersburg.

Even though I am very busy with my studies, I sometimes get together with my friends, though not as often as I would like to.

I am in love with my best friend. A lot of interesting stories in my life are connected with him. His name is Vladimir, or Yova for short. I have known him since we were at school. So here is one of the most exiting stories. It was summer and we decided to go to the Black Sea resort. We decided spontaneously; we just opened a site and bought 2 tickets online. Approximately 3 days later there was a train. As we had e-tickets, the conductor demanded actual tickets which we did not have. So the conductor said: "You have 20 minutes to exchange your e-tickets for the regular ones." I was really worried and felt nervous. Fortunately, it was all right. It was not the worst moment and we did not know what was in store.

After spending several great days and visiting wonderful places we unexpectedly fell ill. We had to stay in bed with high temperature all day long and, feeling awful, to exchange our e-tickets on the way back. And then came the day when we had to leave. We arrived at the station just an hour before our departure. But there was a long queue to the ticket office. We waited for more than 30 minutes, but the queue moved slower and slower. It was 10 minutes before the train arrived and we stood and waited… if my friend had not pushed through the queue, we would have missed the train. That moment was the most intense I had ever felt! But I do not regret anything. And when we remember these moments, we cannot help laughing.

My story proves that I am fond of travelling. It is always fun and it makes my life diverse and full of adventures. I am also interested in foreign languages. I study English and German and I'd like to visit Great Britain and Germany in the future. My hobby is yoga, and I find it very useful.

In conclusion, i'd like to say that I try to avoid everyday routine, to develop mentally and physically. I hope I will be able to visit a lot of beautiful places.

2. Elvira Alieva

My name is Elvira; i'm 21 years of age. I live in a city that some locals call "a big village." I was born here, though I have never felt like I belong here, whether because this city is famous only owning to the people who fought for it, or because I am tired of its steppe climate and corresponding "landscapes." This city is of interest to those who are really into the history of Russia. Anyway, there's absolutely nothing to do and nowhere to go. Still, there are a few nice and more or less beautiful "nooks" I visit when I go out or want to stay alone and think up about something. I call my favorite one "the ledge," because there is a fence enclosing a hotel with a ledge I like to sit on. "The ledge" is located just in front of the local amusement park, which looks and smells lovely in autumn, my favorite season. In general, I am to a certain extent proud of the city I live in. However I cannot call myself a two-in-one — a lucky person and a happy citizen because of living here. Well, "it's not much, but it's home," they say.

As long as we talk about communication, I can safely say that I have never been good at it since I was a child, though I have always shown a lot of promise! My mom told me that I learned to speak before I learned to walk. Moreover, I never spoke the "baby language," I started to speak very clearly and distinctly from the very beginning. In fact, my experience of communication started off well — for example, in a new place I could get acquainted with everybody around in about 10 minutes. Quite a good result, isn't it? Nevertheless, it changed when I went to school. I never had friends while studying there, and not because I did not like people or I had some difficulties communicating with them, but I could not find anybody whom I found interesting enough. My classmates were not bad, they just were not right for me. I suppose, they thought the same about me and… my big black boots and spiky bracelets and chains on my wrists, as well as my black clothes. Perhaps so. Heh. My only friend at that time was my god-sister: we've been together since babyhood, doing a lot of funny things like recording our silly childish songs, playing self-made games, drawing, watching cartoons and so on. We even went to a musical school together and we always looked so alike that our neighbors used to mix us up. I was very upset when we eventually fell out and became strangers.

Later I made a new friend in college. When I first saw her, I thought: "what a wacky Emokid!," but over time she amazed me with her openness and cheerfulness, for I had a tendency to wear my heart on my sleeve, so I was very impressed by her behavior. Still, our friendship ended after a couple of years when her light-heartedness not only towards herself, but also to others started to irritate me, and as long as I am very forthright and do not watch the language sometimes I said everything I thought about her childish and careless attitude to everything in this world. Score: Elvira with the truth — 1, friends — 0.

I'd like to mention that I have never been afraid of loneliness and always felt entirely comfortable being all alone. I have never had the need for other people's company, furthermore, my hobbies and preferences do not require a partner: I prefer the north to the treeless and dirty Volgograd, soulful music to "singing pants," scary movies to snotty girlish melodramas and writing to talking with people.

There have been a few more unsuccessful friendships, not only between me and Russians, but also Americans and the British. In fact, Americans turned out to be the people with whom I can communicate best of all: I like their plain-speaking, absence of arrogance (unlike the British) and their hypocritical, but still charming American smiles. And yet, those people are too reserved to be friends with, at least for me.

Anyhow, when I entered the university I was sure that I would not make friends there. But I was wrong. The guys who were organizing a Halloween party at the Uni offered me the role of Wednesday (the character from "the Addams' family") in their play, and I agreed. Then I met my first best friend ever, he was playing Wednesday's brother Pugsley. To be honest, I had never been so close with anybody in my life, we shared so much in common and used to have such a great time together and helped each other in every way! However, we ended up arguing and yelling at each other nearly every week, so at last our wonderful friendship was ruined. That was my biggest loss, and I am not ashamed to admit that I had contributed to that breach. But the truth is that we were getting on each other's nerves so badly that it could not go on any longer.

The reasonable question then arises: if you're such an outcast and a sociopath, how come are you going to become a translator, Elvira?!

Well, there are a few reasons for it: first of all, I'm not a sociopath, I like people and I like to help them. Probably I just have not met the right ones on my way. And second learning languages is what I am most interested in and what I can do better than anything else. When I think about the future I see myself in a lovely town Camden, me, in my own little house, where I am sitting in an armchair among a lot of cats, sipping already my tenth mug of tea I cannot live without and writing or translating a book. Marginal life. Perfect. No people in my dreams, are there? Heh. Well, maybe I will make a loyal friend again, you never know. The only things I am sure of are that I want my dream to come true, that I agree to fight for it… and that if a marginal person wants to live in a private house abroad he/she needs to earn enough money for it.

Professors at the university are teaching me not to pay attention to insults and to always stay strong in stressful situations, so I am going on that "journey" in the big world of people with their difficult personalities, views, wishes and relations with the hope of finding my vocation, my place, my people and myself.

3. Anton Klimenko

Every person in the world is unique and has got his/her own interests, mind and beliefs. The causes of these differences can be national character, people that surround a person etc. As for me, as a result of these causes I have got my own outlooks on the whole life and every single day as well. But what were the reasons that made me the person I am? First of all, it is my family. It goes without saying that the biggest influence on every person comes from his/her family. Our parents teach us how to look at the world, what is good and what is not. And I am not an exception. The character and mind I have are not the same to my parents,' but I can say that my mother taught me to be a kind and compassionate person. Since my childhood, she has been telling me that animals are our friends, they are alive like people, they have they own feelings, mind and nobody can torment or kill them. And today I think the same way. Thanks to my mother, I like animals and I don't kill them like some other stupid adults do. She also taught me to help people, not to be an egoist. She explained to me that, for example, everyone can become homeless and poor one day. Of course, some people who ask for money on the streets can be just alcoholics, but still there are a lot of poor people who really need our help. Just imagine, maybe your ruble will save his or her life. That is why I always try to help such people.

My father taught me to be strong and brave. He always tells me "don't be afraid of anything or anybody, just keep doing things your own way.

I cannot insult women; it's just something men should not do. The second influence are my friends. I am very happy to have them. In the very first school-years I met the people who changed my life. We had our own rules, we were a really close-knit team. And these are not just words. We went all together (about 15 boys) to the gym for two or three years, it's something that not every class in a school of our country can boast of. We weren't addicted to night-clubs or pernicious habits like other guys — our interests were totally different. The third influence came from the environment and the russian national character. For example, I love winter so much; it's my favorite time of the year, and I am fond of skiing, which would not be possible in many other places of the world. I adore long walks in winter — the landscapes are so amazingly beautiful. I also like Russian food. In general, Russian culture has influenced my worldview.

To sum it up, I think that we can't find two identical persons in the whole world. It is because we are influenced not only by external factors, but also because our inner world molds us who we are.

4. Kate Kuznetsova

My name is Kate, I am twenty-one. I was born on April 26, 1992 in Volzhsky, Russia. I am the only child in my family. My mother is an economist and works at a mechanical rubber factory as head of her department. My father is an engineer and works at a tyre factory. My grandfather took part in World War II. After the war he married my granny in the Stavropol territory. 7 years later they moved to Volzshky. My mother's brother is a good friend of mine. He is young and works with my father. I have got a dachshund, her name is Nicole. I like to play with her, she is very funny. When I am away, my mom feeds her and looks after her.

I have many friends. Some of them are from my school; others are from my previous institute. My best friend's name is Dima. I have known him since the moment I was born. I have also made connections with people from the UK, US, Italy, Spain, France, Germany, Pakistan and Iraq. I do not really like the French — there is something about them that I find unpleasant — I think they are too arrogant. Most of all I like people from the UK, US, Italy and Spain. The British seem very intelligent and prudent to me, but also cheerless at times. Americans are friendly, patriotic but somewhat selfish. Spanish and Italian cultures are very close and their people are mostly emotional and responsive.

I met a Spaniard last year. He works in Russia, because, due to economic circumstances, it is quite difficult to find a job in Spain right now. I was afraid that cultural differences and the language barrier will cause a misunderstanding between us at first. But with time we have learned more about each other's cultures and traditions and have fallen in love with each other.

Speaking of my interests, there are many things that I like and a few that I dislike.

First of all, I like painting. I already have a diploma of a designer and artist. And with the help of my previous teachers and people who work in the field of art I hope to become a professional and famous artist in future. I have many works of my own — landscapes, portraits, still lives, compositions — and people admit that I am gifted. I have already taken part in several exhibitions.

I also like to learn languages. In addition to English and German, I have started to learn Spanish and Italian, but I am only a beginner. I wish to visit many countries in the future. I want to learn more about the cultures and traditions of different countries.

I enjoy reading and try to read books in the original, if I can. Now I am reading Sir Walter Scott's "Ivanhoe." Unfortunately, I do not have much time for reading books now.

I have a car and a driving license. I enjoy driving and always go to the university by car. I live in Volzhskiy, so it takes me approximately one hour to get there. I hate traffic jams (they are killing my mood), so I try to relax listening to music.

I hate getting up early in the morning, it is always a big problem for me. If I did not have to wake up so early, I would be the happiest person in the world!

Speaking of films, I prefer comedies and psychological movies, I do not really like dramas. I do not go to the cinema very often and prefer watching films on tv, dvd or via the internet.

I enjoy psychology. I am a people's person and really like to analyze people, trying to figure out how they think and why they do what they do. I have read a lot of books by Sigmund Freud and I like giving people proper advice. I guess psychology is a really good thing because it helps you understand people and give them a hand in difficult situations.

I made up my mind to get a second university degree and become a translator, because, in my opinion, it is rather boring to have only one speciality. It is much more interesting to work two jobs. I have always loved to learn languages and it is a great piece of luck I have an aptitude for studying them.

I'm interested in philosophy, especially Immanuel Kant's, Rene Descartes' and Friedrich Nietzsche's works.

To sum it all up, I can describe myself as a creative, positive, purposeful and self-confident person. In three years I hope to add the words "successful" and "educated" as well, of course, with the help of my teachers. I have had enough time to realize that I really want to become a translator and I have never regretted my choice.

I don't believe in God in the accepted meaning. But I know there is … something … beyond the reach of our understanding that affects this world powerfully. And I know there is a reason why we live in this world. No one will ever know… but I have learned that our choices always matter — to someone, somewhere. Each of our actions has a reaction. And sooner or later the consequences come back to us. I just want to leave something good behind…

5. Irina Merentsova

I am 19. When I look at myself in the mirror I see a brunette girl with long straight hair, green eyes and a slender figure. I think that I am even-tempered, rather reserved and calm. But sometimes I can lose my temper and become angry or sad. But I prefer to laugh and joke. I think I've got a sense of humour — I understand humour and appreciate it.

I was born on the 11th of August in Volgograd, Russia, where I am now living now with my parents. My early years, which I remember badly, were typical of a child living in town. I was sent to a kindergarten at the age of two, as both my parents were working, and I went to school at the age of seven. Here I should say that it was my lucky chance to study for 11 years at the best school of our district. There I got a proper training in such subjects as English, Russian, literature and history. I usually did a lot of home preparation for those classes and I liked everything about them. My teachers were very well-educated people with a broad outlook and deep knowledge of the subjects. But despite all my efforts, I was not good at maths.

School for me was not only learning — I am sociable, so I have got a lot of friends among my schoolmates. Sometimes we organized parties and other social activities.

In people I appreciate honesty, kindness, sense of humour and intelligence. I don't like when people are aggressive and rude.

I asked myself a lot of times what I wanted to be when I finished school. And three years ago I decided what profession I would most like to have in the future. I realized that my strongest desire was to continue learning foreign languages. I entered Volgograd State Socio-Pedagogical University, and I am now a sophomore. My future profession is an interpreter and translator.

Now I am going to write about my family, which is a very important part of my life. Understanding between family members and consideration for others are very important in the relationship. We are three in my family. My mother is thirty-eight. She is a kind and clever woman who is always ready to give me oral support and good advice. My father is forty-three. He is a very responsible person and the bread-winner in our family. We have a lot of common interests, such as going on trips and hikes together, visiting museums, theaters, and exhibitions. We discuss all the family plans together, exchange opinions and share the same joys and sorrows. I try to show my love and attention to my parents in everyday life because it can hurt if I am selfish, insincere or rude. I am proud that I don't have such a problem as misunderstanding with my family members.

And now a few words about my hobbies. One of them is singing. I have been singing for seven years, and sometimes I perform during different social holidays or festivals. I am also fond of reading books. They give me knowledge of people's lives and feelings and broaden my outlook. In my opinion, books and music are a source of emotional inspiration and romantic feelings.

And finally, the things I hope to achieve in my life are: a very successful career, making my parents happy and finding someone with whom I could share the good things in life.

6. Victoria Romakhova

My name is Victoria. I live in Volgograd and study at Volgograd State Pedagogical University, but I was born in Kamyshin. Despite the fact that my hometown is small, it has got a very interesting history. Kamyshin is the third largest town in Volgograd Oblast, located on the right bank of the Volga river, with a population of 119,174 people. Originally the town was built as a defense fortress in 1668. Later it was burned by Stepan Rasin. The town was revived after the arrival of peter the great.

For a long time Kamyshin was a merchant town. That is why nowadays there are a lot of old two-storied merchant houses in the old part of the town. During the great patriotic war (WWII) there were many hospitals there. Many refugees came to the town every day.

Residents of the town of Kamyshin have got a lot of traditions. One is the watermelon festival. It is believed that our watermelons are the tastiest in Russia and abroad. To sum it up, I am proud of my native town. Once every two weeks I go home by bus or electric train and visit my parents and friends. My family consists of four people. My mother is a teacher; my father used to be a military man, and now he is head of the heating networks. I have a fourteen-year-old little sister, a school student. I also have a lot of relatives in different parts of Russia, for example, in Moscow, Volgograd, Krasnodar and even the republic of Kalmykia (that is where my grandparents met). It a pity that I cannot visit these places every year, because I like to travel, see different sights and meet new people. I would like to travel abroad and I believe my dream will come true. I would like to visit a lot of countries, especially England because I have already been learning English for twelve years. I have also started to learn German.

I have got different hobbies. I finished music school, and I can play the guitar and sing. I sometimes sing songs at university events. When I have free time I usually read books. Most of all I like detective stories. Sometimes I read to music. Music helps me to relax and concentrate all the time. Cats also help me to relax, they are my passion. It is interesting that all my friends like music and cats. I have got many friends. Some of them live in my native town, that is why I see them very seldom. My best friend studies in Saint Petersburg, and I am going to visit her next summer, I am looking forward to the trip. In spite of the fact that I see my friends seldom, I am not alone — I have found good friends in Volgograd. They have taught me many useful things. Thanks to them I have become a more sociable and confident person.

7. Svetlana Malikova

My name is Svetlana, I am almost twenty. In Russian my name means "the light one." And the funny thing is that no one is completely sure when this name appeared. The common theory is that the name Svetlana was invented by the well-known Russian poet Vasily Andreyevich

Zhukovsky in the nineteenth century in his ballad called "Svetlana." But I want to believe that my name is rooted in Slavic culture when names could be given by some distinctive features like hair color or order of precedence in a family. In fact, every name in our culture means something, and you can hardly find a person who is not interested in or unaware of the meaning of his or her name.

As far as my family goes, nowadays in Russia there are few families with more than one or two children, so my family is one of the widespread families. My parents divorced when I was a year old; I have lost my granny and grandpa at the age of ten and that is a quite sad, but now everything is all right. I live with my mom, my stepfather, who is very kind and attentive to me, and my cat. I have a lot of relatives, but they are scattered all over our huge county: one of my aunts is in st. Petersburg, another one lives in Ural, and we try to stay in touch. And thanks to modern technologies and computer programs, we succeed in that. By the way, if you ask me to choose between a big and a small family, I would say that a big family with a large number of siblings and relatives is better, because it will never let you feel lonely. And in the future I want my family to be huge.

It is secret that though nowadays we are officially living in a classless society, classes do exist. They are now determined not by heredity, but by the amount of money people have. If you come to a school you will see that well-dressed children rarely play with their classmates who do not wear fancy clothes. Yes, they do communicate with each other, but not very closely. My family belongs to the middle class, as are most of other families in my country. I would not say that we had a strong class hierarchy at my school, but there was a boy who was very proud of his rich father. I do not think this is right, I believe parents must explain to their children from the very beginning that money does not define people's relationships.

As a student of the school of foreign languages, I want to go abroad not only to see the foreign works of art, famous museums, famous buildings, but also to learn how foreign societies live. I think it is exciting to turn into an English, French or Dutch girl for a couple of months. I am convinced this kind of experience helps people to understand each other much better. After all, it is one thing to read about another culture or communicate with the people of another culture — and a totally different thing to live for some time like a person of another culture.

8. Yevgenia Sumskaya

My name is Zhenya, I am nineteen and. I was born in Volgograd. This city is situated in the south-east of the European part of Russia, on the right bank of the Volga river, 1000 km south of Moscow. From 1589 to 1925 it was known as Tsaritsyn, and from 1925 to 1961 — as Stalingrad. It is a hero city because of the events of World War II.

One of its most famous places of interest, Mamaev Kurgan, is called the "main height of Russia." During the battle of Stalingrad of the most fierce fighting took place there. Today Mamaev Kurgan is a site of the memorial called "heroes of the battle of Stalingrad." The center of the composition is the sculpture of the motherland.

In Volgograd, there are very few historical monuments, unrelated to the WWII because the city was heavily bombed during the war.

I would like to say some words about my family which includes my father, mother, and grandmother. My father's name is Sergei, he is forty-four, but looks much younger. He is a businessman. My mother is forty-five, her name is Lydia. I admire her character — she is full of energy and a real optimist. My grandmother's name is Valya, She is seventy and long retired. I enjoy spending time with my family very much.

I want to be a journalist. I think it is an interesting and useful profession. Journalists meet many people, they try understand what is going on in the world, and explain it to other people.

9. Julia Tomasheva

My name is Julia, I am 18 and the most important things for me are my family and friends.

One of the most important people in my life is my mother, she has devoted all her life to me. Since my early age I have been spending a lot of time with my grandparents. Mother often sent me to visit them to the Ukraine. They love and have taught me to very many useful things. When I was a child it became a tradition with me to visit them every holiday and summer vacation. Every year I looked forward to it, I knew that I will get there as though to a different world, without problems, misfortunes, where I will always be helped and 1supported. My favourite holiday is New Year's Eve. It is bright and cheerful, and we always give each other beautiful gifts. My birthday falls on December 30, and

I almost always celebrate it in my grandparents' cozy and warm apartment, with a huge green fir-tree with father frost under it, a bright star on top, a lot of tasty food and a feeling that you are there where you want to be and a wish that this time never comes to an end.

My grandmother and grandfather are an example for anyone. They have gone through life hand in hand. They always support each other and almost never have arguments. It is a relationship of which everyone can dream. They know how to find compromises, to make concessions to each other and to be able to admit the guilt even if they are right.

Thanks to my family, I am very sociable. I have always had many friends, no matter where I was. I can be in a different city or on vacation — and I will always find myself company. People reach for me, and I for them. Friends are a very important part of my life. You have no right to be lonely if you have at least couple of friends who are like my second family. I know that when I come to them, they will always be able to understand me. If I cry they will cry together with me, and if I laugh they will do it together with me. We have many common interests, though we have very different personalities. I spend a lot of time with them and I am very grateful for everything that they do for me. With them I have learned to appreciate the good things in life, and to live in the present, we seldom speak about the future, but very often remember the moments in the past. I have a very interesting life.

10. Lilya Charova

My name is Lilya, I am nineteen, rather tall and slim. I have brown hair, blue eyes, a small nose and thin lips. I am stubborn at times. But I believe that being persistent is not always a bad thing. I always achieve my aim.

I enjoy reading. If I had more time I would read a lot of books. Nowadays it's almost impossible to imagine our life without books — they are a source of knowledge and a way to self-perfection. Books are my friends. Sometimes when I can't deal with some problems in my life and I think that books can help me. The time spend on a good book is never wasted.

I was born on February 5, 1994 in Volgograd, one of the largest industrial and cultural cities in Russia. I think I live in one of the most beautiful cities in the world. During World War II Volgograd (the former Stalingrad) was the site of a great battle that lasted 200 days and nights. On May

1, 1945, Stalingrad was awarded the status of a hero-city. We have a lot of memorials, of which Mamaev Hill is the largest and the most popular one. Another majestic memorial is the panorama of the Stalingrad battle, and I live just in front of it. Volgograd is situated on the bank of the Volga river, and I swim in it every summer. I am proud that I live in Volgograd.

I live together with my parents. I have a big family, and we are deeply attached to each other. Everyone in my family is my best friend. We like to spend time together. I live with my grandmother who is 80 years old, but she does not look her age. My grandmother is energetic and talkative. She went through World War II (we refer to it as the great patriotic war). I admire her courage and fortitude and try to help her with everyday chores.

My mother is the leader in our family. She is a doctor, which makes her very important. My mother is in a good mood most of the time and always supports me when I'm sad.

I also have many other relatives: uncles, aunts, and cousins. We are happy when we get together. We have a lot of traditions, one of which is celebrating the New Year's Eve together. I love my family!

I like being on my own, but at the same time I can't live without my friends, I like to laugh and joke with them. My best friend is Ann, I have known her for a long time, since we were in elementary school. We are looking at this world in the same way. Of course we have much in common: dancing, sports, books, films… we help each other a lot and try not to get into arguments. Ann is very creative and a great dancer. I hope we will be friends forever. "My friends are my estate," said Emily Dickinson, and I fully agree with this statement! They give me strength and self-confidence.

11. Nicole

First of all let me introduce myself. My name is Nicole. I was born on December 21, 1992 in Volgograd. Like many others, as a child I went to a kindergarten. It was a remarkable time of my life. At the age of 7 I went to school where in approximately the 8th grade I understood what I wanted to become in the future, and I started devoting more time to the study of foreign languages — French and English. After school I entered the university. So far I have not been disappointed in the choice of my future profession. I have many professional teachers, interesting disciplines, as well as very kind and clever classmates. Each of them has a unique character and their own points of view. I hope that after I graduate I will become a professional interpreter.

My family is very important for me. My family members — my mum and fiancee — always support me. During difficult times I can always rely on their help. My parents divorced 8 years ago, my father remarried and he gave birth to one more daughter. I am often in touch with my father and his new family. I love my younger sister very much and often spend my summer holidays in father's house where I feel at home. The atmosphere in the house is very positive, we have no innuendoes and claims to each other. It is a pity that my father lives so far.

I live with mother and my future husband who proposed to me last summer, and I said 'yes.' I love him very much and appreciate him. Next summer we will have a wedding. I am sure that it will be the best day in my life. I have already started beginning preparations for this event. I have never thought that it will be so difficult. I am very lucky that my fiancee helps me with everything. He is very caring, strong, and honest he works as a police detective. He has recently saved a little boy's life. The child had an attack of epilepsy at school. Before the ambulance arrived, my fiancee he provided the boy with all the necessary help. The newspaper "Komsomol'Skaya Pravda" held a competition "the national hero," and he won. I am very proud of him.

As for my mother, she is still very young — only 37. She works in a bank. She also goes to church and on pilgrim trips. I love her very much.

As for me, I am a good-humoured, very responsible, hard-working and emotional I like creativity and I appreciate this trait in others. I like creativity and appreciate this trait in others. I am fond of reading fiction and books on history. I try to read everywhere — in the subway, in a cafe, and at home. My favrite writers are Jane Austen, Charlotte Bronte, Alexandre Dumas, Jean-Jacques Rousseau and others. I adore watching fascinating films. When I am free I enjoy taking a walk with my friends, go to the cinema, museums, or theater. But my biggest passion is travelling. My dream is to see the whole world my own eyes. I am sure that my dream will come true!

The sophomore students which follow were enrolled in my intercultural communication course at Yangzhou University, Yangzhou, Jiangsu Province, China, in the autumn semester of 2013–14 representing Arabic, French, Japanese, Korean, business English, English education, and English translation majors.

1. Shi Mengyuan, Olivia, Business English Major

The importance of creating our own cultural stories

After the last class, for the first time I came to realize the importance of creating our own cultural stories. Culture is the one of the most important parts of a country. I feel proud as a Chinese, for China is a country with long history, aesthetic poems, delicate cuisine, beautiful language, etc. Everybody's cultural stories makes up a country's culture.

I am Shi Mengyuan, a sophomore at the Yangzhou University majoring in business English. I was born in Suzhou, Jiangsu Province, in the East of China. The city is on the lower reaches of the Yangtze River. Suzhou is often labeled as the "Venice of the East" because if you pay a visit to Suzhou, you'll see houses are all built on the sides of river. Suzhou is famous for its classical gardens which were added to the list of the UNESCO world heritage sites in 1997 and 2000.

My family is not very big. There are only five people– my grandfather, grandmother, dad, mum and I. At that time of my grandparents' age, a family had many children. My grandpa is the oldest child of the three. In that age when the living condition was poor, he had to shoulder the burden of his family at a very young age and was apprenticed to a builder. My grandmother is the youngest child of six. My father has a sister; my mother has a brother. At that time, it was common to see that a family had two children, mostly a boy and a girl. But coming to the 21st century, due to the one-child policy, many families gave birth to only one child. It is claimed that the policy has helped China achieve 400 million fewer births during the past thirty years or so. However, the children born under the one-child policy face the prospect of caring for an ever-increasing number of pensioners. I am the only child of my family, which means that I get the love from my family without anyone sharing it with me, but sometimes I feel lonely and think that what if I have a brother or sister.

During my early eighteen years, I lived in my small town and studied in a local school. I had a good command of the school's lessons and homework. After the college entrance examination, I was admitted into Yangzhou University. It was my first time to leave my parents and I knew that since then I had to learn to be independent and it's time for me to gradually become mature. College students must try to understand their developmental changes during this period and learn to store new knowledge or information. Also, they need to try to be independent in every way, not just emotionally but also academically. Another very important thing that we must do during this time is to internalize religious beliefs, values and morals, though, many people claim themselves as atheists.

I took a trip to Japan with my parents in the last summer holiday after my graduation from high school. It was a concise cultural experience– an adventure to discover the fashion of Tokyo, the pure, clean, and natural beauty of Mt. Fuji and the old style and grace of Kyoto. The workers of shops greeted us politely and served us with enthusiasm. Admittedly, japan is a country of fascination.

The exotic culture always has a fascination for me. This summer, I went abroad to Europe for a ten–day's trip. My tour route included Italy, Germany, Switzerland, France, Austria, and Vatican City.

The Vatican is the smallest sovereign state in the area, while it has the biggest church–basilica Di San Pietro. When I entered the church, immediately I got a feeling of bathing in the holy light. It is really worthy of the name of the world's most ambitious and most magnificent Catholic church. It has tight security to maintain order and safety. Women who wear dresses higher than their knees or off -the-shoulder clothes are forbidden to enter.

Venice is a city built on water. Do you know how to get around a city with no cars? The answer is by boat. There is a boat called gondola which is of local specialty. Take a gondola if you can afford it. It's expensive, but the sights along the canals are priceless. This city left the deep impression on me during my trip. I ate the traditional Italian dinner in a restaurant which faces the sea and had a pleasure of both food and natural scenery.

Speaking of Paris, there's no doubt that it's paradise for shopping. But centuries of cultural development makes Paris a variety of fashion, museums, architectural styles, and scenery. I appreciate the Seine's value in Paris. Nearly all novelists have once written about Paris. They must describe the beauty of the Seine river taking a ship travel on the Seine, there are coffee bars, the Eiffel Tower, and hundreds of classic or famous buildings on both sides of the river.

My cultural stories are continuing…but now let's end here, and I will write again in my later years of life.

2. Sha Wei, Chinese Name:沙威; English Name: Javert / Korean Name:사위; Korean Major

Walk on the road that God guides.

Hello! (안녕하세요!) Professor Ph.D., my Chinese name is Sha Wei. Besides, I have a famous English name made by a world famous writer, Victor Hugo. Among Victor Hugo's works,<Netherworld> is absolutely the great one. In this novel, a police sergeant is called Javert and if it is translated into Chinese the Chinese is my name. And if my name is translated into Korean, it means son-in-law. How magical it is! So, I'm proud of my name, not only is made by Hugo, but also by my kind parents under the guidance of God.

Ok, in the following, I will introduce you about my family. Which consists of 6 people including my grandparents, parents, older sister and I. My family is the home of Christ and all of us have faith in Christianity. In addition, we have a small church in my uncle's family. Perhaps because of this, our family is very kind and sincere. My grandmother and my mother like going to church with friends. And my grandfather and father like fishing.

Next, I will mainly show you about me along with my life. Time goes by, and now I am 21 years old. At this age, many things I have gotten but at the same time I also lost some. I have a dramatic character so that sometimes I'm active and sometimes I'm dissocial. However, I don't think it's a bad thing. In contrast, it is likely to help me experience a lot. The most important point in one's character is not worldly or sophisticated but of kindness and sincerity. Beside these, a sense of humor is a very important point and I like making jokes with my friends.

And so it is, I prefer foreign thoughts because foreigners are straightforward and easy. The thing I like I can say "I like" and when I hate I will directly say "I hate" without thinking a lot. Of course, I am a man of broad interests, such as drawing, sports, reading, writing, traveling and so on. Accordingly, I have many dreams whether they are realistic or not.In my opinion, having dreams is not a bad thing but a happy thing that can bring me from the busy world into a beautiful one. First, one of my dreams is to be a novelist. Not only do I want to publish my works, but also I hope to be its director and actor if it could be made into film. Possibly, this thing seems improbable but I believe that where there is a will there is a way. Second, I want to become a fashion designer because I am full of creativity and inspiration. Third, if I can't make the former dreams come true, the only thing I can do is to accept the reality and find a good job such as Korean translator in a foreign company in order to support myself and my family. In my life, there are so many interesting things having happened in which I have beautiful memories. For example, in my childhood, my favourite thing was catching fish or insects with little friends. In addition, according to custom we climbed a hill named "horse's head hill" in my hometown during the Chinese New Year is another thing I love. On that hill, the eating and drinking and playing are included.

My motto is that "Walk on the road that God guides, enjoy the most beautiful scenery." Thank you for reading. I wish you happy and healthy every day!

3. Flora, English Education Major

My cultural story: I hold that all our dreams can come true, if we have the courage to pursue them.

My name is Flora. I'm from Nantong, a coastal city full of various kinds of delicious seafood. Since it's near the big international city Shanghai, my hometown is developing rapidly both in economy and culture. I was born in a harmonious family. My family members are father, mother and I. They love each other and give me a happy family. My father is an engineer in an electricity supply company. He graduated from junior college about twenty years ago. In his daily time, he's busy with his work. So he spends less time with us. In contrast, my mother is a housewife. She spends more time taking good care of us carefully. Besides she has her own life to develop her own interest such as growing flowers, reading books, playing cards with her friends sometimes. What is worth mentioning is that she is good at cooking, which is really to my taste.

In school, besides concentrating on study, I also take part actively in various kinds of activities. I also entered the student union. What I learned in the student union is not only how to work together, but also how to communicate with others and deal with problems. It's a rewarding experience that I'll never forget.

Then I'll talk about my attitude to life. Just like the movie – Forrest Gump said "Life was like a box of chocolates. You never know what you are gonna get." It doesn't mean that life is full of unknowns and risks. But when I was in middle school, I always felt dejected and frustrated. Because I didn't know what the life would be in the future, I also doubted what I could do in the future. Fortunately, with time flying, I met a few people who treated me as real friends. For several years past, we are still best friends. They are the people who make me insist that life is full of beauty, hope and love. I become optimistic as I believe each person is kind in the soul. Now I am an undergraduate student. It's also a challenging and meaningful process.

Although I have been in Yangzhou for over one year, I'm still homesick often, maybe because I used to go to school near home from primary school to senior high school. So I'm going to work as an English teacher in my hometown after two years, which is relevant to my major and corresponds with my interest. Then I maybe get married and bear a baby. It's the stable and peaceful life that I pursue.

I think the most important thing in lifetime is health, which is the fundamental thing of everything. If we lose it, everything means nothing. The second thing that we should attach importance to is happiness, which can help us keep young. Only in this way, can we live better.

It's time that we should make our goals clear and try to achieve them. For us, although knowledge is important; promoting ourselves and learning to be a member of society are more necessary. I hold that all our dreams can come true, if we have the courage to pursue them. Flora

4. Wang Tianyu, Osama, Arabic Major

Languages and communicating are interconnected, including English and Arabic

My Chinese name is Wang Tianyu and my Arabic name is Osama. My birthplace is Huaian. It is a middle city in Jiangsu Province. As Chinese all know, Huaian is the hometown of Premier Zhou, a famous diplomat. My major is Arabic; it is another nation's language and most Chinese students think it is difficult to learn, but I am very confident to grasp this language.

I am very glad to be your student and I think that intercultural communication lessons are useful, especially for students who learn different languages. When I was young, I indulged in Arab culture such as the pharaoh, the pyramid, the sphinx, the mummy and so on. So when I graduated from high school, I thought if I mastered the Arabic, I could get comprehensive understanding of the Arab world. I chose Arabic as my major finally. My parents support all my decisions and I express my gratitude to them.

Michael, thank you very much to teach me how to communicate interculturally. Though I do not major in English, I think that languages and communicating are interconnected, including English and Arabic. Each nation has its own way of thinking. I think the best way of understanding the way of thinking of Arabs is to live with them and communicate with them, eat what they eat and enjoy what they enjoy. When I graduate from Yangzhou University, I plan to travel to the Arab world — the magic Islamic world, including Egypt, Syria, Saudi Arabia, Dubai, Iraq and so on. If conditions allow me to travel to Somalia, I will be completely excited. And my family will give me financial support. I think that will be fantastic. Michael, have you ever been to these places? If you have been to these places, can you give me some advice? At last, I wish you have a good health.

Yours sincerely, Osama

5. Jixing Hua, Alberta, Japanese Major 阿拉伯语 1201 班王田雨

Everybody has dreams.

Hello, everyone! My name is Ji Xing Hua. My English name is Alberta. I am 20 years old this year. I am from Nantong. My hometown is a beautiful city. If you come to my hometown, I will take you to many places. There are 4 people in my family. I have a sister. She is 3 years younger than me. Now she studies in the middle school and she is very hardworking. She likes painting; every week she goes to have painting class. She is crazy about it, and she wants to be an artist in the future. I am very proud to have such an excellent sister. My dad works in Shanghai. He is an engineer. Because his working place is not far away from home, each week he takes about 2 hours on bus and goes home. My mum is a housewife. She always does cleaning at home. My house looks so scrupulously clean. Mum looks after us so well. I am very grateful to her. I love my family very much.

    I am in the Yangzhou University and study Japanese. Though there are many classes every week and under the pressure of the study, I like my specialized subject very much. Not only do I spend time reading the books of my specialized subject, but also I often drop myself in the sea of other books. I like reading books very much. There are many students' organizations in the university. I think we shouldn't be crazy about it and join many organizations. If so, you will have no time to develop yourselves' interests and enhance your ability. In my opinion every minute counts. We have no excuse to waste time in the meaningless activities. We should spend time doing something to enhance ability. The university library is abundant in wide knowledge. It is a good habit to go to library to read books to broaden our horizons. Everyone has her own unique ideas and manifest different personalities. This is my own idea about how to live and develop in the university.

    Everybody has dreams, Now I want to say something about my dreams. I want to be a person who has devoted herself to do the exchange of culture and economy. The job is suitable to my specialized subject. However, I know very well that I could not succeed without painstaking efforts. So I will spare no effort to study in order to attain my goal. The access to success doesn't go smoothly. I have enough courage to be faced with the future's challenge. Perhaps other people will think my dream is not realistic. Yes! It is very difficult to do that but now do preparation to achieve my dream. Every day, I read a lot of books to get more knowledge. I like reading books about different countries' culture. No matter what difficulty I will meet with, I will never escape it. I believe that I can do it.

This is my introduction about my family, my university life and my own thought, my dream. Do you like my introduction and start to be interested in our life? I like everything around me! 季杏华 日语 Alberta

6. Zhou Di, French Major

My dream of my childhood: make a travel to Japan

My name is Zhou Di. I come from Changzhou. There are three members in my family, my dad, my mom and me. My mom is a saleswoman. She is very good at matching the clothes for others. My dad is a worker. He has been to japan for a year when I was young. All the people that have tasted his food agree that his cooking skills are getting better and better. I like painting, listening to music and seeing the films.

When I was a child, I wanted to be a painter, because painters are so free that they can travel around the world only taking the painting materials. I changed the idea when I became a high school student. My mother thought that painting could only be a hobby, not a career in the future. She wanted me to go to high school like other children. So I took her advice. During the first year of my high school life, I couldn't get a balance between maths and Chinese. When I was blamed because of my low marks in maths, my Chinese teacher was always proud of me, because I got the first place in Chinese of the whole grade.

After three years, I came to Yangzhou. At the same time, I met various kinds of people and made some good friends. The college life is so wonderful. However, it's annoying that we have a lot of free time to be planned by ourselves. My mom often calls me to complain that there is no fun without me at home.My dad prefers to sending messages to remind me to study hard. All in all, I think that they are worrying about me. And it's a good chance to depend on myself.

Luckily, we have nice teachers that teach us French. They are so kind and never blame students if we make mistakes. I wish that I can be a transformer. Then I want to realize my dream of my childhood: make a travel to Japan, because I am interested in this country and I have read many books and watched the programmes that were concerned about Japan.

That's all ~

7. Cherry, English Education Major

My story: we should not be afraid of failure. Failure is the mother of success.

My name is cherry and I am twenty-one years old. I think that you will be surprised at my age. I will tell you a story about why a sophomore student is over twenty years old. My home is in Jiangdu, which belongs to Yangzhou. So I am very familiar with Yangzhou, and I can be your tutor when you want to visit Yangzhou. When I was a child, I wanted to be a teacher as my mother was.

I have a very happy family. There are five parents in my family. They are my grandparents, parents and me. My father is a business man and my mother was a teacher. My mother went to Shanghai to help my father manage his business and look after my father after I graduated from high school.

In 2011, I attended the college entrance examination. However, I did not get a high marks in such an important examination. I felt depressed about the final result. I was thinking about my ideal and my future. Finally, I decided to go to high school again where I fell down. And I wanted to attend the examination in 2012. As we all know, for students in high school it is very hard in China. They have much homework, many lessons and little space time. As a repeat student, I had much more pressure than other students, because I did not allow myself to fail again. That time gave me the most deep memory during my growth. I spared no effort to study. And I almost lost contact with my old friends who had come to universities. They did not want to disturb me and affect my study.

But sometimes they called me to cheer me up and asked me not to give so much pressure to myself. With my hard working and their support, I was successful in the 2012's college entrance examination. I was admitted by Yangzhou University. When I was a freshman student, I majored in economics. When it came to my ideal, I felt very sad. So I decided to change my major. Because I was very interested in English and wanted to be a teacher, I transferred into English education. I will move to realize my ideal step by step.

Now, you must have known why a sophomore student is over twenty years old, because I have studied for four years in high school. That experience makes me more positive and mature. We should not be afraid of failure. Failure is the mother of success, if we try our best to pursue our dream and ideal. If I am a teacher in the future, I will try my best to teach my students well. I will not pay much attention to my salary.

8. Gao Gaoyu Anais, French Major

"Where there is a will, there is a way."

My name is Anais, a girl from an ordinary family in a small county, Datong, Shanxi Province. The county is famous for the coal mines and pared noodles. I have been spending nineteen years in my hometown. Now I am a student in Yangzhou University. I have a happy family; my parents regard me as their treasure so my Chinese name is Baoyu which symbolizes the treasure. I also have a sister and a brother. My sister is very kind who always has been popular at school. As to my brother, the boy seems like a little monkey because he is a real rascal. I love my family so much.

When I was a little girl, we lived with my grandparents; for me that time remains fresh in my memory. My grandfather is a doctor. When I was ill, he treated me at home. Maybe it can be said that he is only my doctor, because he retired when I was five. I remembered since I was the age of two, I lived with my grandparents until I was thirteen; that year my grandfather died of an illness. Although he passed away, in my mind, my grandfather is the most important person in my life, as he is not only my family, but also my first teacher.

Besides these memories, I also have a happy life at present. I am living in Yangzhou, a city that I like very much. When I was in senior high school, I dreamed that one day I could be living in a southern city like Yangzhou. Now my dream has become a reality. In the past year, I have experienced a different environment and a different culture deeply. In my ordinary life, I love literature and calligraphy. The calligrapher that I worship is Wang Xizhi.I also love reading; those romantic novels are my favorites, such as《Le Voleur Dombres.

If you say that the book《Le Voleur Dombres》is a book which is written by a French writer, you are right. Now French is my major in the university. After one year's studying, I could communicate with my foreign teacher in simple sentences. I believe that after four years studying, I can speak it better. My maxim of life is: "Where there is a will, there is a way."

As to my aim of the future, I want to be a teacher in the college of Confucius and spread the national culture of China all over the world as my foreign teacher Michael H. Prosser does for western culture. I want to take my parents to enjoy the Lavender in France and to have a travel in Manhattan.

9. Guo Yu Hong, Vicky, English Translation Major

About me: youth is not a time of life, but a state of mind.

My name is Guo Yu Hong and you can call me Vicky. There are 4 members in my family, including my grandmother, my father, my mother and I. My grandfather has gone several years ago since I was a student of grade 5. And we remind ourselves of him from time to time. My grandma is very laborious, just the same as the majority of the Chinese women. She on no account had the chance of receiving an education. However, there is no denying that she is a successful mother.

What I thought of success is not judging by the wealth or power. Her nerve and kindness won the reputation of our villagers. Thinking of my father, I just feel that I was a lucky dog. He didn't have the opportunity of getting further education, either. But the society is also a classroom in which my father has grown into a real man. In order to have a look at me, he could drive for a long time without complaining in the hot summer. The time when he quarreled with my mother, I was always astonished by her tolerance. Although he can't earn much money, he donated all his love to us. And my mother, actually, she is an alien to this province. It has been 21 years since she married my father. During this period of time, she only returned home a couple of times. We all know her complex emotions about her hometown. She had a bad temper; in fact, I know that she has a soft heart.

I was the only child of my family. The process of my school career is smooth as expected. I am that kind of person who easily gets satisfied of the current situation. At the age of 20, it is time for us to reflect our meaning of existence and our uncertain future. I hope that I will lead a life without regret and change myself before the world changes me. Youth is not a time of life, but a state of mind. I am young at the moment.

10. Celeste, Business English

Life is a journey: about life and values. I think that we should see the bright side of life.

My name is Celeste and I am a sophomore at the Yang Zhou University. My major is business English, in the midst of obtaining a degree in BEC. I was born is Lang Fang that is a small city of He Bei Province. Lang Fang has a special position; she is between the capital city Beijing and most important industrial city Tianjin. Because of the position, Lang Fang's economy developed very fast in recent years. It is also a good place to live. The city has good forests and many entertainment places. In the dawn or dusk, townspeople would go to square or park to do exercise. The city is very clean, neat street. I love my hometown.

My father is a businessman. He was born in the late 1970s. China was very poor. My grandparents did not have enough money to support my father's education. Because my parents have three children, this status made my father decide to work first to release the burden of family and then to look for opportunities to upgrade himself. He joined society when he was very young. So he has had rich experiences about living. My father is a very hard-working person. Nowadays, he is a very successful businessman. Learning from my father and his character has influenced me. His hard-working, persistence, studying steadily are worth learning. My mother is a full time housewife. She has to do much more housework than my father. Her work is taking care of the whole household and taking care of children and many insignificant things in family. She is very busy and tired. She finished her middle school but go no further. She has the basic knowledge of society, but has no interest for more things. She makes almost all the important decisions, because she has equal common sense with my father.

My grandparents have three children, two sons and one daughter. When they were young, they worked together in the local family business. They had a factory. Nowadays, their living level is improved, but their habits were formed in the hard old years. They now live quite a thrifty life and are strongly against any form of so called wastefulness and extravagance. They did not go to school when they were children. I have never seriously as well as thoroughly considered who I am and what constitutes my cultural background for the past twenty years.

About life and values, I think that we should see the bright side of life. Some things in life are bad; they can really make you mad. Do not grumble, give a whistle and this will help things turn out for the best. If life seems jolly rotten, there is something you have forgotten, and that is to laugh and smile and dance and sing. Enjoy the life. Happiness is the most important thing in my life. Do not look at material things so heavily. Healthy, happiness and substantial living are of more concern than substance.

During the next five years. I will graduate from Yang Zhou University. I want to study abroad further. The optimal country is United States. And then go back to my motherland, find a job, to be an office lady in Beijing.

11. Samson, Korean Major

I cultivate a heart of love.

In 1992, I was born in Shanghai, a city that developed rapidly in those years. My father and mother were ordinary workers leaving their hometown to chase their dreams at that time. I have three sisters, so my birth brought the whole family a great joy when the peoples' ideals were traditional. When I was 8 months old, I came back home with family because my sisters could not accept education without having local registered permanent residence.

After that, my parents worked exceedingly hard to support the whole family. Both my sister and I received a good education because of my parents' hard work. It was not easy for ordinary rural people to bring up four children. Not only did my father let us receive high quality school education but he gave us a good family education. My father was very strict with us, expecting us to learn the truth of being a real person and the spirits of struggle. I couldn't clearly remember how many times that I was criticized by my father when I was a kid. However I could understand him well, and I really learned a lot what I couldn't learn from the books. I became optimistic and self-confident, daring to face setbacks and challenges. I realized one thing which I treasure through my whole life. That is to never let anything stop me from chasing my dream, from working and falling in love.

Because of my parents' education I cultivate a heart of love. I love everything around me, my teachers, classmates, a tree and a flower. Shortly before I joined the communist party of China, I regarded it as a great honor for the party is a responsible organization having the ability to lead us towards a rich life, though it has some corruption to some degree.

My elder sister married two years ago, and now has a lovely daughter. She and my brother-in-law opened a small company in Shanghai with a stable income. Another sister works at pharmaceutical company in Nanjing, a state-owned enterprise providing considerable salary and welfare.

My parents are more than 50 years old this year, still trying hard to work in my hometown. I appreciate them for all these years of care and companionship and for everything. I hope my parents have a healthy body forever, and I hope my sisters have happy families, and for me, I hope I will be able to be myself, pursuing my dreams.

There are more Chinese cultural stories in my international blog, www.michaelprosser.com in the following posts: sophomores: 2020, 2021, 2023, 2024, 2026, 2027, 2028, 2033; seniors: 1953, 1954, 1961: postgraduates: 1951, 1969.

32. Beijing Language and Culture Students' Comments, Arguments, Debate, Essays, and Poetry

In my two spring semester junior English major open topic research papers, they included 3,000 words, with an: abstract, outline, key words, introduction, body, conclusion, five or more references, and notes and references. The students in these two classes prepared a 1500 word research paper for the first semester. As illustrations of the student research interests among the three junior men and twenty-one women, here are the titles of the papers for the twenty-four students.

1. Jay: A glimpse of Japanese and Chinese corporate culture

2. Dennis: Flame in violence: comparison of the representation of violence factor between occidental and oriental silver screen

3. Jim: Don Quixote de la Mancha and The True Story of Ah Q

4. Mavis: Chinese vs. American education system

5. Angel: Research on Chinese people's overseas study

6. Della: The beautiful authoresses in China

7. Mandy: Research on different concepts of love

8. Victoria: The outcry of two times: the comparison between the French Revolution and the [Chinese] Revolution of 1911

9. Aileen: One China in Europe: one France in Asia

10. Sharon: The comparison of education between China and Korea

11. Sarah: Chinese middle class and their American counterparts

12. Chelsea: Suicide!!!

13. Michelle: Shanghai and New York: International commercial cities

14. Shelley: Lookism — human nature or social prejudice

15. Catherine: Beliefs, influence and evaluation: a comparison between Chinese Confucianism and American Puritanism

16. Jessica: By some comparisons of animation and manga [animation artists but-never defined precisely] between Chinese and abroad to discuss the development of animation and Manga industry [This title is also a good example of Chinglish.]

17. Echo: Decoding their honest truth: an analysis of the similarities and differences between Zhou Enlai and Abraham Lincoln

18. Cynthia: What else can colors tell us [?]: a comparison of the connotations of colors between English and Chinese

19. Becky: The contrast between Chinese and American corporate culture

20. Julia: The balloon and the robot: comparison of cartoon cultures between Chinese and foreign countries

21. Vivien: The problems of taking a bus in Beijing

22. Hattie: Unload the mentally ponderous burden: a research paper on college students' psychology problems

23. Ada: Table manners: Chinese vs. Muslim

24. Lansing: What are we losing from the entertainment economics [?]

In my ten week (March 25-June 3, 2003) power point lecture series on intercultural communication at BLCU for my first of two lectures on values, I took a very informal and impressionistic survey of BLCU student views in the previous lecture and in the classes about their half dozen most important values. The results, noted here, are not based on rank ordering, but simply the most replies for a single value for students from different parts of China:

> A. Seventy-two Chinese women, ages nineteen-thirty-four: family 60; friends 50, career & love 37, money 33, health 28, freedom 17, happiness 9, good environment 8, leisure 7, relations with others 6, knowledge, kindness, trust, marriage, honesty 5 each, plus various others with less numbers.

> B. Sixteen Chinese men, ages eighteen-twenty-three: family 13, friends 11, career 9, happiness & money 6, colorful life 4, love, freedom & music each 3, patriotism & sports 2, plus various others with less numbers including 1 for sex.

The following comments were made by freshmen and sophomore university students in the age range of sixteen to twenty on November 22, 2002, most in connection with the Friday evening open houses:
Tom, 19, Freshman Japanese Major
[Tom suggested that we have students at the open houses write in my journal so that I would have the memories.]
   Because of a music party this night in BLCU, few people came to this open house. But we were still very happy. Sometimes we can talk better when there are few people. At almost 9:00, 3 foreign students came here. We all liked to talk to them and hope they will come as often as they can. Tom

Andi, 19, Freshman Japanese Major

I'm a freshman of this school, a freshman of this open house. But I hope I will be the old friend of it as soon as possible. Because I love it and you, Michael, like my grandfather. I hope your house will be open to us forever. Yours. Andi

Daisy, 19, Freshman Japanese Major

Michael, you are really a very nice person. You are so kind that I love you very much. Thank you for giving me such a nice night. Daisy

Carmen, 19, Freshman Computer Science Major

The party you hold is so great. I'll come next time. Carmen

Alice, 19, Freshman Computer Science Major

Thanks very much for your party. It is great. I love you. Alice

Jody, 19, Freshman Computer Science Major

Your open house is very good. Thank you very much. I will come next time.

Ideal, 18, Freshman Computer Science Major

Dear Michael, if one day you go back to America, what will I do on Friday evenings? Ideal

Sophia, 19, Sophomore English Major

Dear Michael, everyone here is nice. Every Friday night here is wonderful. I'll keep on coming to enjoy myself. I am wearing a new, nice sweater!! Sincerely yours, Sophia

Gymmy, 16, Freshman Computer Ccience Major

Michael,

I love you very much. I always look forward to Friday arriving. It's a really special time together with you on Friday evening. Kiss you. Gymmy,
November 25, 2002

Michael, 19, Sophomore English Major:

To Michael, I really appreciate your invitation and I am really glad to know you. I think you will be my foreign teacher when I am a junior student. I suppose we will spend more exciting and unforgettable times from tonight. Love you forever! Little Michael

Daisy, 19, Sophomore Computer Science Major

Dear Michael,
 It's the most special Thanksgiving day in my life, and I will never forget it. You are so kind, just like my grandfather. In your house, I thought I was at home. Such a feeling is really good, because I have been out of home for half a year. Carol, Elva, Steve, Bob and I came to your house, and we cooked a meal all by ourselves. Today's biggest prize should be sent to our Bob. He cooked wonderful fish and chicken which smelled very good for us. And the most popular food was the spring rolls made by Elva. Our Carol cooked eggs and I made hot pot. Carol did everything carefully and she seemed like a mother in the house. Our Steve did the heaviest work–washing the dishes for us. We had a wonderful meal. We were happy and the two boys ate a lot which made us felt even happier.
 I love you forever! Daisy

Steve 20, Sophomore Computer Science Major and President of the Computer Science Student Union

Today is Thanksgiving day, the one year anniversary of the friendship between dear Michael and me. One year ago, I met with you in BLCU. We enjoyed our Thanksgiving lunch together and built up our friendship. During the year which passed, we kept in touch with each other by email. And last month you were in front of me. Your big hug and beautiful smile impressed me so deeply that each day I missed you very much. Besides you told me lots of things to balance my life. You encouraged me to be positive towards life. I am lucky to know you Michael. Your house, books, pictures are always in my mind.

The dinner prepared today by Carol, Bob, Elva, and Daisy made this Thanksgiving day the most beautiful one I have ever had. We enjoyed ourselves so much that we were just like a family, three beautiful ladies and three handsome big potatoes. Time and words cannot describe the love between us. Happy Thanksgiving Day! Happy forever.

Big hug. Forever yours. Steve.
November 29, 2002 open house

Victor, 19, Sophomore in International Relations Major at International Relations University

I'm always looking forward to coming to the open house and chatting with Michael. You know why? Michael is such a fascinating person. I love every minute of it. Victor
December 2, 2002

Bob, 18, Sophomore Computer Science Major

Nothing special happened today. I went to Michael's house which is so familiar to me to have supper. Every Thursday and Sunday night. I together with this old gentleman have supper. But the problem is I don't have enough time day by day because my study becomes heavier and heavier. I have to overcome so many difficulties, learn how to design delicate programs, learn to communicate with other students. You know these are necessary for our future profit. The point is, I have to adapt to the society in the four years. So I have to do so. Every day is the same old, but this is life! Bob

December 8, 2002, my Beijing Business College sophomore English majors came from their campus in Nanko, south of Beijing for lunch

Holly, 20

It's 8 December, 2002 that I will never forget. I have ever visited lots of friends in my life. But I've never been to a house of a foreign man. A special, lovely, and happy house. Look! There are so many wonderful photos. And books, pictures, little things. I like most of them. But it's the international — UN flag and the USA flag that attract me best. I think it stands for something special.

Look, the other classmates are coming now. Oh! It's so cold outside. But it's better inside. Someone cooked very good food. They are busy with the dishes all the time. If they need, I'll give some help.

Michael is the closest teacher in our school. He makes us happy all the time, relaxed also. That would be perfect if I could see Michael every day. I hope Michael stays in China longer, longer, longer. Holly.

Gus, 20, A Freshman English Major Who Accompanied the Group, Not My Student.

It's a great day, isn't it? Today, I went to visit Michael.It's the first time that I came to a foreigner's home and spent a funny time. We spoke to each other in English, only in English, in a relaxable and happy atmosphere. It's a good way to improve our English and make us more understand the culture of USA and the style of life.

Michael is a very good man. Michael is gentle, kind, and amiable. He impressed me very much as all students said, "he is like our grandfather."

I'm so happy to be able to come here and appreciate Michael's warm reception.

Gus

Cammy, 19. Sophomore English Major

I'm writing the message next to Michael. I came to Michael's home first. I'm very happy. We speak English to each other, now I want to watch tv, All in all, I'm happy! Happy! Happy! Ha ha ha. Chinese girl Cammy

Frank, 21, Sophomore English Major

I came to Michael's home the first time, I am very excited. We speak English together; we play games. So happy, in the afternoon we have lunch together. I think Michael is a lovely man. I like him. I didn't want to leave, but I must leave. Bye. Chinese boy, Frank

Max, 20, Sophomore English Major

Today is my first day to come to Beijing this term because I don't like to go out. But I'm so happy today because I go to Michael's house–our teacher. He is very kind and we all like him. He makes me improve my English. I think I can make friends with him forever. Merry Christmas! Yours, Max

Olivia, 19, Sophomore English Major

It's a nice day, isn't it? We have a party in Michael's home. His house is very big and there are so many pictures on the wall. At noon, Anne and I cooked the meal. I think it's delicious, the plates are empty.

Today, I'm glad. I will come again to see you–our grandfather.
Chinese girl, Olivia
December 8, 2002. [the same day, several sophomore computer science majors from BLCU came to dinner.]

Billy, 19, Computer Science Major

How time flies! It's a long time since I met 'big papa.' I am sorry that I can't come so often because I have to hit the books or I can't pass the test. Anyway, I will try my best to come to papa's flat.

The last thing I want to say is — whenever we are in Michael's flat, we are having a good time. Billy

Cecilia, 19, Computer Science Major

It's the third time that I have come to Michael's flat. Whenever I'm here, I'm really enjoying myself. I want to come here every day if possible. But it's impossible I know. Because I have so many things to do every day, I always can't do whatever like. I really hate the computer science, but I have to study it; I really want to come to Michael's house, but I can't come here very often. I have no choice.

To enjoy myself, I will come here as much as possible. Cecilia
December 27, 2002

Cindy, 18, Freshman English Major

Dear Michael. Merry Christmas!
   I'm very grateful for your timely help! How can you be so knowlegable? Is it because you're on so many long trips? I'm longing to know sth [something] about the American way of life. You let me step the 1st step to this. Thank you! I love music. Do I have any chance to play piano and bring music to you? That'll be lovely. Wish you be happy and please let this happiness last not a year, but a life time!
   I'm crazy about English. I consider it as beautiful as music. I'm very glad to be one student of BLCU, and be with you–my Chinese Santa Claus!
   The other day, I was very sad because Roy changed his mind and didn't let me be the hostess of the Christmas party of our department. Since I worked very hard on it–I recited my speech (can we just say it is "speech"?)- deep into midnight. That's why I was very sad. But fortunately I have a grandfather-like-friend you. Thank you for offering me a job as your assistant [to Santa Claus] that night. I still think this idea is very creative, and it was the best way to solve a problem like this, I think, for I've been in this world nearly 20 years!
   Thank you!
   I wish you to live as happy as possible, live as long as possible, as young as possible, as good as possible, as wonderful as possible. Yours, Cindy.
   January 3, 2003

Charley, 17, Freshman English Major

I have a good time in Michael's open house. The open house gives me a kind of feeling just like my home and the host. Michael is more like my grandfather. Every time when I leave Michael's house, I sigh and say "How time flies!" Charley

Edison, 19, Freshman English Major

This is my first time to come to this house. It is really a lovely place. You can enjoy speaking English in this warm room, and enjoy meeting friends here and of course the important host– Michael.

Who is the most interesting person? Who is the warmest person? Everyone has his/her own answer. What is my answer? Of course– Michael. Though the wind blew hard when I entered this house, your hug made me feel really comfortable, staying by you, I really felt that I had come back to my childhood, just like staying with my grandpa.

I really enjoy coming here for fun, really glad to have you as my best friend and best teacher. Wish you to be happy every day!

Love you forever. Eddison

1. Chinese Student's Views in Argument and Poetry on China

In my two autumn junior English advanced writing classes, 2004, I assigned an open debate-like topic: "China should…"as a persuasive and argumentative essay. The following topics were the most frequent for the 58 students in the two classes, often topics already suggested in the oral communication workshop text for their year-long debate class: the college entrance exam, educational reform; psychological student health; environmental and industrial pollution; government corruption; abolishment of the death penalty; retention of traditional features, culture, and history; climate change; homosexual equality; abortion; agriculture, village life, and migrant workers.

Though I never assigned poems while teaching intercultural communication courses in the US, at BLCU, teaching English, I have included a twelve line free verse poem with each assignment.

At the sophomore, junior, and senior levels, when I first came, I realized that almost none of my students were aware of the importance of writing poetry regularly as English majors or as young people. With this assignment, each student had to write a poem about China. With justifiable pride, sometimes different from the "China should…" essays, here are some samples of this pride from Junior class 4.

> *Bridget:* "Red East": The east becomes red,/The sun rises,/ Chairman Mao appeared in the old China./It was he/ who rescued all people/from the extreme misery.// Chairman Mao was the golden sun./Where he went,/ where he became bright./It was he,/who brought the happiness/to people whose names were Chinese!

Ginger: "For China": Go to the west to see the great lands./Go to the north to see the beautiful islands./Go to the east to see the blue waters./Go to the south to see the beautiful islands.// This county has beautiful scenery,/This country has friendly people.//This country has profound culture,/It also has wonderful potential.// Being born in this country, we are lucky./Let us do something for her./Being born in this country, we are obligated to her.

Ivy: "China": China is a country with a long history./She has a history of five thousand years./She witnesses the rise and fall of many generations./She forgives her people's abuses./ China is a country with great culture,/from ancient times to the modern period,/From Confucianism to Marxism,/she is always a beacon of the world.// China is a country with beautiful scenery./She has pure snow in the north,/She has rain forests in the south./People see different scenery in different parts of China.

Marian: "A Promising Country": In the distant east/a once sleeping dragon named China/with the struggling by his posterity,/it soars up again as an unbeatable hero.// In the distant east,/a civilized country named China, with its bright and brilliant history, it attracts attention from the whole world.// In the distant east,/a promising country named China,/with its continuous development/it will have the brightest future.

Vivian: "My Motherland and I": No matter where I go/my heart will stay with you./No matter where I go/my soul will belong to you.// When you feel happy/ I'd like to listen silently, sharing your happiness./ when you feel sad/I'd like to be the tears in your eyes, sharing your sorrow.// Because you teach me to face the storms/ because you support me to grow up/because I fear nothing if you stand by me/because I can read your heart as you read mine.

Clare: "My Pride": when I was a little child,/mom told me to love you/but I knew not how./ In my adolescence, I grew more aware/of your significance.// Now wherever I go,/you are always/on my mind.// because I know/how to cherish you/as my ultimate pride.

Tammy: "Welcome to China": Welcome to China!/if I were your eyes,/i will not rest,/as long as I can see.// If I were your feet,/I will not rest/as long as I can walk.// If I were your hands,/I will not rest/as long as I can write.// Great wall, Yellow river//great China!

Sunny: "The Wind of Yangtze River": The wind of Yangtze river kisses my face; /it's cool taste in the air// I breathe./ The wind of Yangtze river caresses my skin;/its tender touch remains my dream.// The wind of Yangtze river blows my hair;/its odor overwhelms my soul everywhere./The wind of Yangtze river leads me to a distant voyage/unpredictable, but full of joy and wishes.// The wind of Yangtze river will never stop/ as my dream never sinks/i feel it now, and forever/ Yangtze river, my source of pleasure. [She writes that she lives in an apartment near the Yangtze River in Hubei Province.)

Summer: "My Motherland": You used to be feeble and weak,/ with the invasions and mistreatment,/you have suffered greatly,/in the dark old times now forever gone.// The wind of spring spreads all over the country,/ China has taken a totally different look./ It presents itself confidently in the new age/taking the whole world aback.// My heart beats with your pulse./I enjoy every progress you make./I've never known/I love you so much!

Susan: "China, My Mother": The brightest stars are your eyes,/ the beautiful scenes are your face,/the limpid streams are your blood/ the towering mountains are your body./You have centuries-old history,/that splendid culture comes from it,/You have brave people/who protect their motherland.// China–/my mother!/ China–/my only end-result!

Annie: "Great China:" Once, your vast, rich and beautiful land/ was trampled under those iron feet./Once, your kind, brave and diligent descendants/lowered their heads all the time./Once, you, such a large country/had no status in the world./In the past one hundred years/ you suffered a lot; you tolerated a lot./but now, all those have passed/by your constant struggles and efforts./You are full of energy again./You are still a giant standing in the east.

Sheila: "Yesterday, Today, and Tomorrow": Yesterday/poverty and backwardness are the character of China,/ invaded by big western powers,/looked down upon by all the world.// Today/open and upward are the symbols of China/developing with amazing speed/ making progress in all ways.// Tomorrow/democracy and strength are the hopes of China/trying to stand up through severe competition/being a powerful country in the world.

Robert: "The China Dragon:" There is a dragon in old Asia,/Its name is China./There are many people in old Asia./ They are the sons of China.// black hair, yellow skin./ They are the sons of the dragon/black hair, black eyes./ Forever, they are the sons of the dragon.// These sons love their mother./The dragon protects her sons together./No matter what happens/she wants her sons to be better.

2. Junior Debate Classes at the Beijing Language and Culture University in 2002–03

I had two year-long classes in debate for the junior English majors. We began the class with a series of group discussions on rather bland topics provided by our text book. Fortunately, I was an undergraduate university debater and so I remembered the American style of debate, with the affirmative and negative teams each having constructive and refutation speeches. In our case, in order to have two debates each class session. We had 6 minute constructive speeches and 3 minute refutation speeches for each debater.

In our second round, we added cross examination debate. The other two faculty members used a different format, with 3 debaters on each team, and a longer question and answer period.

Each student in my classes for both rounds of debate made a written proposal for a topic with arguments and evidence both pro and con. In the first round, the topic was framed as "China should…" and in the second round, it had to be an international topic, excluding "China should…" as the main theme. Out of the 24 proposals in each class, I selected a number, and the classes voted to narrow the topics to 6 for the round. We guaranteed that one male should be a part of each group of four, since there were only six men in each class, and students could choose the topic which they wished to participate in. When more than the required number wanted the same topic,

After the debates, our "election commissioner" distributed a ballot for those not in the debate on which the students would write either "affirmative" or "negative." I invited the 12 students in the class over three class periods who were declared the winners by the ballots to lunch at the campus "blue bar" as an award. In one case, 16 students had voted for one side and only 3 for the other side, but I expected exactly the opposite reaction in terms of the quality of the debate, and invited the team with only the 3 votes also to participate in the lunch. By these processes, we were using some "grassroots" democracy, which the students are regularly involved in when they select class monitors yearly after the first year, and in electing officers for the individual departmental or college student unions.

For the first round of debates, the following topics were chosen: class one: Group a: China should allow human cloning. Group b: China should encourage importing more Hollywood movies. Group c: China should support laid-off workers. Group d: China should prohibit the production and sale of chewing gum.

[I was surprised what an important issue this was, based on similar decisions by Singapore and the fact that Chinese workers had to spend many hours at considerable cost in cleaning Tinanamen Square after thousands of students and others had spent the night there for the flag raising on national day, October 1–sort of a national ritual especially for freshman students from many local universities.]

Group e. China should continue to have the household registration system. Group f. China should continue to charge postgraduates tuition for their education.

The class two topics were: Group a. China should entirely separate the sale of medicines from its hospitals. Group b. China should dramatically raise the pay of its civil servants. Group c. China should modernize all of its old and ancient cities. Group d. China should prohibit rural labor from working in the cities. Group e. China should seriously increase the level of university admissions in the country. Group f. China should eradicate copyright and patent piracy.

Second round topics for class one were: Group a. NATO should continue its enlargement in eastern and central Europe. Group b. The US and UK should drop their plan to wage war against Iraq. Group c. The UN should stop using economic sanctions to punish Iraq. Group d. The global economy should be greatly accelerated. Group e. International markets should prohibit the international sale of cigarettes and cigars. Group f. The United Nations should legalize the marriage of homosexuals.

Second round topics for class two were: Group a. The US should prohibit the commercialization of human eggs and sperm. Group b. Homosexuality should be legalized as an international human right. Group c. The Antartic should be further developed by international scientific teams. Group d. The United Nations should promote the human cloning technology. Group e. The United Nations should abolish the death penalty internationally. Group f. Asian countries should widely advocate sexual education for teenagers.

During the second semester in my classes only [Four other year-long classes were taught by two additional teachers.], we switched from American-style debate to a model UN Security Council with the 15 delegations debating such issues as resolutions relating to Iraq, the Middle East, and North Korea. After the opening speeches on each topic, there were many 1–2 minute speeches by the delegations on each topic. Some students said, "We don't have the background for this," but I countered, "We have a full semester to get the background and use it." "Ok." The first speeches after the students returned from the Lunar New Year/Spring Festival holiday were persuasive proposals on one of the three topics. Then delegations were chosen, with two delegates each as the five permanent SC members and other large delegations and one delegate for smaller countries.

3. Junior Class Advanced Writing Essays at Beijing Language and Culture University

The students had some sort of writing assignment every two weeks, which might have been writing a short play, short story, or set of poems, working in a group to create a magazine, plus a short term paper at the end of the first semester and a long one at the end of the second semester. All senior English majors had to write a thesis of 5,000 words. There was considerable plagiarism in the term papers and theses.

For an in class 45 minute assignment to prepare them for the upcoming exam with two essays, one on definition and one on process, during one class session, I allowed the class to select nine topics, and then to vote on the three most interesting topics for them to write about. The assignment emphasized definition, description, and illustration of the topic. They are basically as the students wrote them, with my present minor corrections. The three topics finally selected by the students were friendship, happiness, and beauty.

A) Friendship

Philip, 20

What is friendship?
It is kind of a relationship between you and your friends, you might say. Then, what is that relationship?

It is a close relationship that could not be seen or told, but be felt, not no matter how far you are your friends are apart. You could say you have a good relationship with some of your " acquaintances not friendship." friendship only belongs to you and your friends.

It is friendship that ties your heart and your friends' together and makes you miss each other. It is also a magic power that can make you do everything for each other. At this point, it is similar to love. However, love is only between two people, while friendship concerns more than that.

Of course, there is a difference between the two. If you are a man, your lover is usually a woman, while your best friends are usually men. And vice versa. If you have some real friends, the friendship can always last for all your life, while your marriage or the relationship between you and your lover may not. That is why, I think, nowadays, so many couples divorce.

A person may tell his or her friends what he or she is thinking about, but he or she will hide the true feelings to all the others, even family members, mostly his or her parents and spouse. So, the best ways to know a person, as you can see, is to know more about his or her friends.

Love is a necessity, while friendship is luxury. One can always find his or her lover, but a real friend is not that easy to find. Sometimes it will take a lifetime. You could not always compromise in your marriage, however, you could always find a peaceful way with your friends.

You can be the luckiest strike — one if your husband or wife is also your real friend. So, remember, friendship is always the most important.

Katherine, 19

Before we go deep into the topic of "friendship," let us answer these questions first: how many types of friends do we have, and which type of friends do we need or do we prefer?

In my opinion, "friends" can be divided into three types, among which, the first type can be called "acquaintance" friends. This type of friends is usually made in big parties, libraries and some other public places. We may have met them several times by accident or introduced to them by a third friend, and then may have struck up a conversation after greeting to each other. You might be a little bit dubious about this. Can "acquaintances" be called "friends?" think of the friendly smiles and nice words they share with us, think of the way they help us practice our communication skills; in a further sense, your answer should be ""yes."

The second type is characterized by "company," referring to those who spend most of the time together, like peas and carrots. The individuals in this group are often sociable and extroverts, therefore they need the intimate and bustling atmosphere all the time, in the form of having company around, instead of individuals.

While the third type is probably the most appreciated and highly praised one, for it is defined as "spiritual" type. In this group, two friends do not have to be together every day, do not have to agree on everything, and do not have to keep chatting all the time to show affinity or intimacy. But they do share something in common on fundamental things, as the goal of living and the passion for life. One of them may be outgoing, while the other is quiet, but it makes no difference to their communication and mutual understanding, on a spiritual basis. "a friend in need is a friend indeed." maybe this type is the most reliable one when we need help.

No matter which type do we prefer, we have to admit that each of them is essential with different functions, like the way we need different flavors and spices of life, "friends" being part of it.

Hans, 21

What is friendship? It is a kind of feeling that is deeply in one's heart; it is your only sunshine in a winter evening'. It is your resource of power. And it is the most lovely thing on this planet. Yes, friendship. As long as you have it, you will never feel hopeless.

Friendship is Chen's voice: "Come on! You can do it!" I was thin and weak when I was in junior school. Because of my poor condition, I could hardly pass the test of 1000 meters. Every classmate laughed at me. I was looked down upon by all people except for Chen, "You can do it," Chen's voice was strong, "Trust me and trust yourself."

Following his suggestion, every afternoon when classes were over, we would go outdoors and take exercises. Chen ran in front of me and tried to make my speed faster. One circle, two circles… I felt tired. I was out of breath. I was giving up — "Come on!" Chen turned around and cried at me, "Follow me! Hold on! No one can beat you. Quick!"

Finally, I had passed the exam. Though my progress was never a super one, I was so excited. "You know what? You are right! I have got it!" I cried out to Chen, who was clapping for me.

Friendship is Yan's pencil. After entering into senior high school, I was depressed for my mathematics. My teacher taught everything fast and my classmates learned everything faster. I was left behind and I could not catch up with them whatever I did. "Am I foolish enough?" I always asked myself.

Then Yan appeared. Nobody wanted to explain my trouble but Yan wanted to. He would like to use his pencil to draw a lot of pictures for my question: triangle, square…. And then I knew about maths.it was so easy.

"We're friends," Yan told me. I think that is one of the best definitions of friendship.

B) Happiness

Susan 21

I have been in this world for 21 years and in different times I have different definitions of happiness.

When I was a little child, 6 or 7 years old, when I began to remember things my happiness was playing with all my toys. I didn't have many of them, because my family was quite poor at that time and my parents would rather like to spend money on practical things. So when I got one or two toys on festivals, I got really really excited. Teddy bears were my favorite. My father gave one to me on my 7th birthday. Before that, I had pleaded with him at least 100 times for that. It was almost like a diamond to me. It was so precious to me that I cherished it in a metal box and only held it when I got my hands clean enough. Every time I opened the box, I felt I was the happiest child in the world. My friends didn't have this. Only I, who was more loved by my parents? I really thought so when I was that young, as I had the opportunity to play with such a lovely toy. How would my friends admire me. I saw their eyes sparkling when I showed them my teddy bear. Oh, how happy I was!

As I got older gradually, I began to go to school. My happiness changed into my high marks. All my teachers and classmates agreed that I was an excellent student, because I got very high marks in all exams. At that time, my happiest moment was when I showed my exam papers to my parents and got their praises in return. More often than not, my mother would give me some sweets and encourage me to go on working hard. She would wear big smiles on her face and when she got very happy, even her eyes were smiling. She seldom smiled in that period of time, for she almost had no time to do so. There were so many things for her to do, both in her family and in her factory. So, actually, my happiness at that time was to see my mother's smiles.

Fortunately, I got high marks in the college entrance exams and fulfilled my parents' dream as well as mine. Everything seems so bright in college and I am happy living and studying here.but there is one thing which makes me sad — I cannot see my parents very often. We're so far away from each other. So the happiest moment in my college life is when I talk to my parents on the telephone. We talk about almost everything. Sometimes, when I talk about exciting things, I will use both my legs and arms to show my feelings. Then, my mother would say: "are your arms waving?" and I would say," mamma, you bet." what a wonderful moment. I feel as if I were a child and on my mother's breast again.

I can say I am a happy girl, because I have good parents who love me with all their kindness. They're happy. So i'm happy. I'm happy. So are they. As long as they're happy, I have nothing to desire in my life.

Maybe in the future, I will share a boy's happiness, as well as his sorrow. You know, life is not so easy sometimes. I hope that no matter what we alone can face everything together, hand in hand, with our deep love in our] hearts.

This is my little happiness. Maybe it doesn't sound so exalted to somebody, but this is what I truly feel from the bottom of my heart. As long as you cherish the feeling of happiness in your heart, you can be happy even if you are a beggar. Happiness is not how much money you have in your pocket. It is what you feel in your heart. I wish everyone can live happily.

Felix, 20

Happiness is a very interesting word for all the human beings. Maybe it is one of the true basic meanings of our life. Maybe it is the goal that everyone in the world reaches for. Maybe it is the best present which god sent to us.

But, different from other things, happiness has various definitions from person to person, because everyone enjoys his own life and grows up in the different environment. We must keep our own meanings of happiness. For my father has the chance to enjoy the high level education is an amazing happiness. When he was twenty years old, he had to do the physical job in the factory. This was the tragedy of his generation, not only himself. He tried his best to get information and knowledge and read all kinds of books that he could find. After six year's hard study, he successfully entered the south-east university in Nanjing. He told me that it was one of the most exciting and happiest moments in his life.

For me, entering the university is still a kind of happy thing, but I was not so happy as my father was thirty years ago. Because the gate of the university is opening for most of us nowadays in China, anyone who studies hard and gets enough information can easily get into the university. Also I had to leave my parents, my happy life in my hometown, Nanjing, I was a little bit sad about that. When I entered BLCU, I found a new kind of happiness. I met some best friends here, as friendship helps me to avoid the isolation; I met some kind and knowlegable teachers here. As knowledge guides me to the cultural and civilized coasts. The new happiness I have found also includes, how to be a real man, how to be responsible. I am sure that I have learned a lot about this during this these two years.

Of course, happiness includes some basic elements. Just as we always say that happy families are all the same, but the unlucky families have different sadness. What are the basic elements? In my opinion, love must be an important one. In a family, we love each other and get together to face any difficulties and enjoy the happy life forever. This must be the happiest thing in the world.

There is a short message that my friend sent to me a few days before, "having a thankful heart, having a trustful friend, having a satisfying job, having a love who loves you forever, happiness will surround you forever."

Nick, 18

Life is a river, starting from those mountains which are covered by snow all the time and joining in the ultimate home for it–sea: then happiness is every drop of water in it.

River is full of water; life is full of happiness. Happiness is born when you are born, just like the way a river is produced by nature when snows begin to melt, developing little streams, then forming bigger ones. It is subtle! You can never tell where the exact place for water coming down from hills to form a river is. This new creature just jumps out and surprises you to a big smile. That is the way when we look back to our childhood. We do not remember when we began to feel happy but the whole meaning is sweet.

Then water cuts out some valleys and this river goes on and on. It winds all the way through "highs" and "lows," "wides" and "narrows." at any rate, it moves fast, as fast as how we would expect us to grow. And this time, as happiness is always with us, life becomes quite ambitious. Those water drops in the river–happiness–is "burning." great strength lies in these drops? Behold! Sometimes the river destroys villages and towns when we sometimes hurt many people. However, this full-blooded chapter is one of the most magnificent scenes under the sun, along with fast paced happiness.

As the river moves towards the sea, it slows down since more and more elements have joined it. In many cases, happiness, I mean, water in that river begins to be mixed up with them. The river starts to be a little dirty, especially when it is a big one. Even itsself cannot tell which is water and which is sand. Happiness? Sometimes ambiguous.

Fortunately, it figures and later when all the sand comes down to the bottom of the river, the river is clear again! Happiness shows up more clearly while it is more slow-paced. The river is coming to the end! But it is not the end of happiness, those small streams of happiness get together. Therefore a world of happiness comes out–the sea.

Remember, if your river is floating for that endless place; if your happiness is for everybody else's happiness which you could like to share with, your river will never end and your happiness will never fade.

In the first semester final exam, I was able to be creative in my writing assignments. However, in the second semester exam, students had one required essay and could choose an essay topic from an assigned list of four choices.

The one required essay was "How can students best prepare themselves to pass the Chinese college entrance exam? Please write your answer in the form of an explanatory essay (or exposition) plus the choice of one of these four descriptive topics: "Describe what a typical Chinese university student is like," "Describe how modern China has changed (or not changed) from its past"; "Describe the worst argument you have ever had with someone"; and "Describe the worst class you have ever taken." I was not involved in helping to design the test, but several of my students felt that they had answered such questions at various times in the past. Personally, I thought that such bland essay topics were basically devoid of much possibility for creative and critical thinking.

Several of the essays are illustrative of some of the students' cynical approach to this exam.

"How Can Students Best Prepare Themselves to Pass the Chinese College Entrance Exam?"

Selena, 21.

The Chinese college entrance exam is a fierce competition as the same as an army composed of thousands of men who intend to go across a river through a narrow bridge at the same time. Generally speaking, to best prepare themselves, students have to pass three stages. They "should pay any price, bear any burden, meet any hardship," to face the reality. They have no other choice.

The first stage is the first two years of their high schools. Their schools, teachers, authorities will help them to make a most "reasonable" teaching system. All the students should do is to follow the experienced teachers' instructions. Students will have the "privilege" to finish three years courses in two years. Students will not be distracted by "trivial courses" like music and art. Don't complain! It is the most happy period before your exam.

The second stage starts from the beginning of the third year of high school, and lasts to the next may. In these invaluable eight months, students should review all the knowledge they have learned in high school. They do exercises, of course not physical exercises, every day. They do exams every other day. They should be "rejoicing in hope, patient in tribulation" in this period. Don't go to bed before midnight; don't watch tv every day. Don't enjoy weekends before the final exam. Don't complain! There are some advantages in these deeds. You are tempered by pressure, hardship and sufferings. You will become a patient, strong-minded and self-disciplined creature. Last but not least, you can lose weight through these exercises.

The last period is from May to the day before the final exam. It is a short period. It is the end of the oddysey. Some lucky students are happy, for they have prepared very well for the exam. Some unfortunate ones are worrying about the exam all day long. Students will review the knowledge and all the exercises again before the exam. The point in this period is psychological preparation instead of knowledge.

Look at piles of exercise books you have used; hold the old and dirty text books you have studied. Whatever the result it is, students can't be not proud of all they have done. However, after the exam, all the sleepless nights and days, all the piles of paper, and all the beautiful ages will be thrown into the memory and gone with the wind.

Nick, 18

A brief introduction to pass the Chinese college entrance exam with "flying colors"

A flurry of interest has been consistently melting into the whole process of conducting students to pass the Chinese college entrance exam. There is a sea of books, tapes, videos, lectures, teachers, and training courses, waiting outside to be paid for. However, all of them, unfortunately have not paid enough attention to the "real mystery" inside that "magic exam," though they ae already well-paid for. Therefore, it is high time we should take a good look at this exam and think of some "creative" but really helpful ways to pass it with "flying colors." let us get started with some basic facts about what this exam requires labor. Of course, this is such an energy-consuming project. Not only you should be qualified, but also your parents, teachers, whoever are involved.

Less creativity. You might not want to bother your teachers with some "stupid" creative questions and answers. Otherwise, you are asking for troubles. "We want something standard!!! Ok?" your teacher will "gently" let you know about the fact.

More stupidities. [The class had recently read in intensive reading an article by Mark Twain on this topic relating to Europe.] Believe, not just totally believe in your textbooks and teachers. That is where your exam is going to come from. Stick to everything you own! "They are the most fantastic items I can get all over the world," you might want to say to yourself.

Time. There we go! And this means no hobbies, no after-class activities, no emotional relationships with your classmates, no vacations, and so forth because all these times will be completely devoted to a "holy" project.

Then, we can make a wonderful list of "do's and don'ts:

1. Get some marvelous medicine to strengthen your body. No exercise! We don't want to waste any drop of time.

2. Mask, rejection tools. Your parents or your baby-sitter if you have one might want to train themselves into professional doctors and nurses. No hospital stay! We have no time!

3. Shut your mouth all the time! No need to ask questions as well as discussion, consulting references, even going to the library. Oh my! Students with such stupid ideas should be punished to memorize some books. How could they come up with such ideas without consideration of time? 4. In terms of English, no oral English! No activities! Textbooks? Yes!!!

4. Memorize them and you will be fine. Who cares about communicating with foreigners what the hell does it have something to do with our "holy" exam?"

5. Do every other everyday-life-trifles as quickly as possible. Eat within 3 minutes while sleep less than 5 hours. You might want to have an alarm clock.

6. Since this introduction is getting to its end, let me remind you before I forget. You have to stick to these rules the moment you are in middle school. Otherwise, you are getting behind.

7. Bear this in mind: nobody cares about what you'd be like after the exam, while everybody cares about whether or not you will pass it. Go to the mattress! Fight to the death. Enjoy yourselves!"

"Describe What a Typical Chinese University Student Is Like."

Marty, 20

"Sleepy Sick Lambs"

This is how I describe the typical appearance of Chinese university students. For I don't know whatsoever reasons, Chinese students, especially those college students are sleepy all the time. I mean you see them on the road. They are walking in a mood which seems to me is sleepy. This probably is partly why they don't care much about their appearance. If you walk around in some campusesi think it is due to the poor English ability of students, Tsinhua university or others at this area, you could easily find it is really strange that people students from different places of this country, born in different years, of different nations] would dress almost the same way.

Compared with foreign students, Chinese students care much less about their appearance, which is a kind of national characteristic (I consider). In Chinese, this is called swi da lin (2nd, 4th, 2nd tongue)–means following suit.

This sometimes causes a lack of enthusiasm during classes also, which is another occasion you can find Chinese student s are likely to be sleepy. Then, talk about the "sick." this is not the students' fault, I have to strongly claim. This is due to the college entrance exam they have to take, and the educational system which exists in China now. As a result, most of the students who entered the universities, or can be called survived from the disaster–like exam worlds gives you an appearance of being sick. They seemed to lack physical exercises and seemed seldom to take outdoor activities.

At last, I want to talk about the "lambs. To most western teachers, their lovely Chinese students are really lamb-like in class. The education system required Chinese students to be so. In primary school when I attended it 15 years ago to be a good student and win a red flower every day, you should sit steadily in your chair and put your hands at the back of your waist.

And you should never talk during class time except to raise your hand and express what you want to say on the teacher's permission. If primary schools are like so, it won't be strange that a college student would act as a little lamb. But to me, what poor sleepy sick lambs.

Spiderman, engine and cloud.

You may be confused by the sentence I wrote. But as the words appeared in the sentence, students in Chinese universities are various. It's actually impossible to describe their appearance clearly in this article or even a book. Then, never think about the typical one. Just see some examples i'll show you and you'll see why. It"s much easier to describe students in BLCU as we only have three thousand Chinese students. But if we have ten times more, what the situation would be.

Take BUAA for example (which I'm familiar with, as my cousin studies there) a diligent student who woke up at seven in the morning and disappeared from the dorm all day long until 1 or 2 am. He would actually fail in several courses, which is the most common thing there. In that school, they have students who play all day but never study. I've even heard one of my cousin's classmates who failed his exam, just because when he woke up, he found it was late for the exam. So he continued to sleep. There are students who make phone calls 12 hours a day, 30 days a month also. Whenever you get up in the midnight for some washroom affair, you could find the guy sitting outside his dorm room–talking to somebody. There are students who study their subjects. Remember, I mean their personal chosen subject all day but never study their subjects they need to take exams in but they still could study in the university. It's strange because they never achieved anything but failed many subjects.

In this way, Chinese students would be at least, no less various than students of any other countries. Their appearance in the character field is as the shining star–you could see them, but how to count, or even give a typical description of appearance?

Chinese students, college students. Sleepy sick lambs. But how could you know if under the skin of this lamb, there actually is a wolf or even a whale?

"Describe How Modern China Has Changed (Or Not Changed) from the Past"

Jocelyn Li, 20

I was born in the year 1982, which was just the beginning of the reform of China. From then on, China has developed very fast and has had significant achievements. My father often tells me the life of his childhood, which was very poor and hard in the 1960's–far worse than it is today. But now I want to talk about my own experience. I also witnessed the great changes of China.

When I was three years old, my family was lucky enough to move into an apartment of a three-floor building. It might be very ugly and outdated today, but at that time it was the second "high" building in my hometown. Now, the number of beautiful and modern buildings in our city is countless. My family has moved into a much larger and more comfortable apartment as did many other families in our city 8 years before. Ours is just a small city of China, so you can imagine the changes in all of China.

During the 20 years, the economy of China is better and better, and Chinese people are richer and richer. My father's salary is 30 times higher than 20 years ago. We have bought a larger tv set, fridge, modern washing machine and micro-wave. More and more Chinese go out of the country to see the world. My father went to 9 countries in Europe and my family went to DPR Korea last year, which we cannot dream 10 years ago.

I remember when I was a little child, in winter, my favorite thing was canned fruit, which I can only get if I was ill or during festivals. Because we lived in the northeast of China, so there was hardly any fresh fruit in winter. But now we have everything. We can get things from every part of China and even abroad. We improved our planting so we have our own fruit and vegetables in winter. The improvement of the economy, technology and transportation has contributed a lot.

The changes of China are far more than I can describe. Every Chinese and the whole world witnesses the development of China. Being a Chinese, i'm very happy to see and fully enjoy these big changes. I have reason to believe that the future of my motherland will be better and better. It will be soon my turn to tell my children the life of my childhood which they can hardly imagine

"Describe The Worst Class You Have Ever Taken."

Most students who chose this topic identified a senior middle school physics class as the worst one they had ever taken

Yolanda, 20

A terrible class. The physics class in the first year of my senior high school is the worst class I have ever taken. Even now I can still remember the scene in the class. This had something to do with the teacher–an old man, tall and thin. I have forgotten his name, just remember his family name Wang.

Maybe because of Mr. Wang's old age, he had a very bad memory. He always could not remember what he had taught us or what he had not. He would teach the same chapter twice or three times. And what was worse was that he always did not admit his bad memory. When we reminded him that this had been taught, he looked at us with confused eyes and continued his repetition.

Physics was one of the most important and difficult classes in our study, so we all wanted to study it well. But Mr. Wang once and once again prevented us from doing so. Whenever he wanted to solve a problem for us, he had to spend a long time making himself understand the question. And most of the time, he made us more confused after his explanation. At the end, when we had problems, we would not ask him for help and this would be better.

Most of my classmates did not like him, not only because of his bad teaching, but also because of his bad temper. He always made mistakes, but whenever we pointed out his mistake, he got angry and always said it was our fault, but not his. When he asked us to answer questions, if we could not be able to answer them or we got the wrong answer, he would not encourage us but criticized us and even laughed at us. In this class, girls were always very nervous and boys were always very angry. The atmosphere of the class was terrible. No one wanted to listen to him, but everyone had to listen to his bad teaching. Another thing he made us dislike him was that he treated students unfairly. If he liked someone, he always smiled at him or her when he was teaching, and if he disliked someone, this student had bad luck. He or she would always be criticized by the bad-tempered old man, no matter whether he or she made mistakes. This caused many students' unsatisfactory grades. I remembered that once a boy quarreled with him in the class because of such a reason.

We learned nothing in the first semester, and many of my classmates did not pass the final exam. The teacher was changed in the second semester and we had to learn the theories or other things again. We heard that mr. Wang was retired and looked after by his grandson at home. We were lucky that we would not take such a terrible class in the future.

Xavier: Youth CCP Membership

[This is a statement by Xavier, a 22 year old senior student at Harbin University of Science and Technology, and a member of the CCP (China Communist Party) since 2004. It is his own view which he sent me after we had conversed about the topic on a train from Harbin to Beijing.]

I used to be a young pioneer in the primary school just as other children at that age. I entered the primary school when I was about seven and graduated at twelve. I think the most important thing as a young pioneer for all of the children are our red scarves. We had been told that the red color of the scarves represents the blood of the nation's heroes and they are also a part of the red Chinese five-star flag. As a young pioneer, the children are supposed to be kind hearted, helpful, and follow the model lei feng (19401962). When I was in the primary school, Lei Feng's diary was selected to be part of the text book.

But actually, a young child named Nai Ning, who was also a Young Pioneer at that time, left the deepest impression in my heart. He died in a forest fire as he was struggling to put out the fire with some other people. I kept thinking about what my behavior would be if the same thing happened to me during that time. Sometimes, the schools organized the children to clean the street, help the old people in the public places or something else. The most interesting thing is about the excellent Young Pioneers standing by the school gate early in the morning. The child who forgot to wear a scarf was not allowed to enter the school. Nearly every child becomes a Young Pioneer before grade five.

Students begin to learn politics as soon as they enter the junior middle school. First of all we learned about Mao Tsedong thought, which is based on Marxism-Leninism which had made quite a lot of development to fit the real situation of China. We've been told that the theory during the time in the Cultural Revolution is not a part of Mao Tsedong thought. Mao Tsedong thought it was all about the things that were true and correct. And then the Deng Xaioping theory with its most famous sentence which generally means that no matter if it's a white cat or a black cat, since it can catch a mouse, it's a good cat. That theory came out during the time from 1978 to 1985 with China's opening up. The government was allowed to use all of the economic methods that are good for the developing of the nation without considering whether its from capitalism or communism.

We had also learned that the reason why China is still so poor, though it has the most advanced Communist system in the world. Is because China didn't experience capitalism as the European countries did to accumulate wealth. So we have to go through a period of social development and that's the first stage of socialism. After that, we can see a flourishing of China's economy. When I was a little child, I still remember that we lived in a poor house and my father as a teacher then earned less than 30rmb a month. Everything is getting better now. In the early part of the middle school, only the outstanding students had the chance to be a Youth League member. But at the end of the senior middle school, almost all of the students were able to join the Youth League. Nobody refuses to be a member of the League because some of the students can't see any difference between being or not being a member of it. The members automatically quit the membership after a mature age.

I have decided to be a CCP member following the steps of my family members. My grandparents, father, and also uncles are all CCP members. My grandfather joined the Party before 1949 and my grandmother used to be the president of the local women's union. My father got a promotion opportunity after his graduation from the party school. I became a candidate during the second year in the university. We had to hand over essays about the new things we've been learning and the progress of our mind of politics regularly. Students working in the student union or as the monitor of the class have the chance to be a CCP member earlier than others. But after four years of campus life, about one third of the students in my program are able to join it. The

Party will first consider the outstanding students who are doing well in their job or their studies. My teacher used to tell me that it would be an advantage in finding a job if I am a CCP member. For the company, however, they seem never to take into that situation into account. A CCP member definitely has extra obligations but less people are concerned about that now.

I am very proud that I'm a CCP member now. For my part, I just keep telling myself that I should first of all be a successful person so that I can have more influence on the people around me and at the same time fulfill my responsibility better. It's not a good idea to keep telling somebody what to do and why to do it. We just have to be the model and do the right thing. When bad thing happen, I think all of the party members should stand out and be the strong assistance of the party with all their heart and soul because I think the party member's obligation is just all about helping other people.

33. The Sars Panic: 2003

Despite the spreading of the SARS epidemic (Severe Acute Resplratory Syndrome) in initially from Guangong to Shangxi Province, Beijing, Hong Kong, Taiwan, Bangkok, Singapore, and Toronto, China waited to report it to the World Health Organization until February 10, 2003. Then it announced that there had been 305 cases, including 105 health workers, and 5 deaths. Even though media reports indicated that the crisis had peaked in Guangdong Province in mid- February, later 806 infections and 34 deaths were reported. During the annual March, 2003 Peoples' Congress, the Chinese media were not allowed to report on the crisis in Beijing. Finally, on April 20, there was a public press report that the government had not been transparent enough about the crisis, and that both the mayor of Beijing and the minister of health had been replaced. On April 23, all private and public schools in Beijing were closed and on April 26, all entertainment facilities were closed, as well as any other public gatherings.

I Wrote the Post Below on my Blog in Late April, 2003.

SARS. There are now 588 confirmed cases of SARS in Beijing, with several hundred others who are possibly infected with the epidemic. The situation in southern China: Guandong Province where the first cases developed as early as last November 1, 2002, and Hong Kong, seems to be leveling off as there are now only about 10 cases reported daily. In contrast, in Beijing, the early reporting had 22 cases, then 37, then a fast jump to about 339, and then in the 400's, and now the 588 confirmed cases. There is considerable anxiety in Beijing and among the educational institutions. All of the primary and secondary schools have been closed until at least mid May (including the Labor Day shortened holiday), and there are rumors that many of the universities may begin closing for at least a couple of weeks starting next Monday.

At the Beijing Language and Culture University, we have no confirmed cases so far, but the campus is now closed to all outsiders, as is happening in other campuses nearby large classes have been canceled as have all public lectures, my open houses on Friday evenings, and other large gatherings. Many of the students are very anxious about the situation and would like to return home but some worry about the safety of the trains, especially since most can only afford the least expensive "hard seat" class, which could be expected to be very crowded.

My debate class today didn't want to continue our United Nations Security Council simulation, but wanted to talk about the SARS crisis. A number of them are wearing masks, which health officials say are not very useful unless the masks have 15–18 layers of protection. Most of the masks which the students wear only have 2–4 layers of protection. Also, the University authorities are providing the students a traditional herbal medicine which they are supposed to take twice daily. The foreign experts also have it available if they wish to use it. Health experts indicate, however, that some of the traditional medicines can actually lower the immune system rather than offering protection.

Where I am teaching on Wednesdays at the Beijing Business School in Nankou about an hour northwest from Beijing, there were not many students wearing the masks yesterday, but only 5 students attended the morning class and only 10 attended the afternoon class. Many of the students are leaving in the next day or two, and the campus gate for its students was to be closed today so that if they leave the campus, they cannot return. So far that campus has no confirmed cases

The Minister of Health and the mayor of Beijing have been dismissed by the CPC Standing Committee because of perhaps either the earlier underreporting, cover up of cases, or incompetence in regards to SARS. A high level person at CCTV International indicated to me that these two dismissals were actually most likely "scapegoating" for a much higher official now on the CPC Standing Committee who was the governor of Guandong province at the time that the SARS epidemic was first beginning in that Province, but who hasn't been publicly implicated in the ongoing crisis.

One of the Americans on our faculty said that this morning his class of 90 freshmen English majors was canceled at 8 am, just before he was planning to give them an exam. He predicts that in Beijing, the number of confirmed cases is likely to continue, and if the Guangdong/Hong Kong cycle seems to be about 5 months, then it may also be the same in Beijing. One major difference may be that since the 11 laboratories in almost that number of countries have actually isolated the virus, if an antidote is found quickly, the peak period of developing cases may be shorter than that in Guangdong/Hong Kong. However, he speculates that perhaps if the university closes early next week for the May 1 Labor day holiday and perhaps for another week, the closing might actually be in effect until about June. Presently, WHO has ranked SARS at the mid level: outbreak, less than an epidemic, and much less than advanced epidemic/ pandemic.

May 24, 2003
SARS Continuing

WHO has taken Hong Kong and Guangdong Province off of the advisory warning list for travelers, but not yet Beijing nor Taiwan. In the latter case, there still is a significant spread of the infectious disease. The total number of confirmed cases on May 22 in China's mainland is 5271, and in Beijing 2546 (May 23, 2003 *China Daily*). Twenty-three provinces have had between zero and 6 new confirmed cases on this date, with Beijing having 15 new confirmed cases. There have been a total of 300 reported deaths from SARS on the mainland since the reporting first began. Taiwan on May 22 had 65 new confirmed cases, and 487 new suspected cases.

Worldwide, there have been a total of 7,956 confirmed cases, including 666 deaths, according to WHO. The University of California at Berkely has withdrawn its partial ban on students coming from SARS infected countries, such as China and Singapore for summer ESL classes. The British Council has stressed that neither the Council nor any British university has put any restrictions on students coming to the UK for summer programs. WHO indicates that any travelers without any symptoms of SARS can freely enter other countries without quarantine. All public travelers in China by plane, train, or bus must sign a declaration about any symptoms which they might have, and anyone with a fever above 38% Celseus cannot board public transportation. Brief testing is done at each departure and arrival location in China

The 90 universities in Beijing, plus all other institutions of higher education in China remain isolated, with students still unable to go out of campus, except with special permission. Beijing Language and Culture University began shortened classes for the Chinese degree students on May 19. Most of the 1,500 foreign students and 1/3 or more of our forty foreign teachers have gone home. The campus is very lovely while quiet in its beautiful spring-time flowering, but students are being encouraged to participate actively in a variety of sports and outdoor activities.

All Beijing Grade 3 Senior Middle School returned to classes on May 22 in order to prepare for the national college entrance exams (gao kao) on June 7 and 8. This includes 158,000 students who have registered for the exams in the Haidian district where many of the universities in Beijing are located. Other students in rural Beijing (Administrative District) will return to school on May 26. Primary and secondary students in the more densely populated areas of Beijing will not return to school until July 14. Grade 3 junior middle school students, however, preparing to take the senior middle school entrance exams will return to school on June 9. Special hygiene measures are being taken for those taking entrance exams for college or senior middle school, and for all those returning to school in the near future.

In Beijing, because of SARS, the media, and students are using the metaphors for SARS as: "We are all warriors in the front line against this war SARS. When the party and the people call upon us, we must be responsible to fight this battle together," "As we have faced adversity over thousands of years, we Chinese people will triumph in this war against the evil SARS,"""Even before the Iraq war began, a new war was being waged on the Chinese: SARS, but we shall be victorious,." Praise to the frontline soldiers in the battle against SARS–the medical workers."

There are 670,000 university students in Beijing and 90 universities, the most in any city in the world. All Chinese university students here in Beijing and all over China are presently confined to their campuses until at least May 11.Thirty nine university students in Beijing have been confirmed as SARS cases.

Our most recent statistics indicate that there have been more than 3900 confirmed cases in China, and approximately 1660+ in Beijing. The May 3–4 *China Daily* 6 column headline reads: "SARS 'on plateau' in Beijing: official says outbreak will later decline." It is accompanied by a four column color picture of two special SARS ambulances with medical workers fully enclosed in protective clothing and gear. There are 500 students quarantined at North Jiaotong University and Central University of Finance and Economics. On May 1, a woman student at the Beijing Language and Culture University was suspected of possibly having SARS. Her entire dormitory floor is being quarantined for 10–12 days, including several of my juniors. On May 2, BLCU authorities announced that all classes would be suspended until May 16.

Of the 1,500 foreign students at BLCU, it is likely that more than 5/6 have left as those staying must now follow the same regulations of remaining in campus as the 3000 Chinese students. I wonder how many bikes of the foreign students have been abandoned?

Perhaps a few hundred of the Chinese students had gone home, but they can't reenter the campus until May 11, and then must be quarantined for 2 weeks. On May 2, BLCU Beijing residents were allowed to go home for two weeks. About 1/4 of the 40 foreign teachers have now gone home or are leaving this coming week. I have taken two extra advanced writing classes from an Asian-American teacher who has gone home.

I have talked regularly with my classes about SARS, but I decided to give the advanced writing classes a writing assignment to allow them to think through the situation more systematically and personally: 1. A ten line free verse poem either entitled "May day 2003" or "Beijing: May 2003." 2. A two page essay on "SARS." The assignment included both objective and impressionistic description with several paragraphs:

definition of SARS, international impact, national impact, Beijing impact, BLCU impact, and personal impact.

I am providing below several samples of the poems and personal impact paragraphs written by our junior English majors (all about 20 or 21 years old) to give a view of how they see the situation impressionalistically.

Cecelia

Blue sky and bright sun,/ beautiful city but sad men,SARS comes in no time./Everyone here grows tense./Doctors and nurses are divine./They make the patients healthy men./ If you ask who is the most lovely one,/ it is those who work at the e dangerous line,/ Let us all pay our sincere respect for them,/ and please let us take care of them all the time.

I was scared last month when I heard the situation turned out to be terrible. I even wept when calling to my mum. She is a kind and great woman who knows how to calm down others. I became understanding of the University's decision to lock the gate and relieved about the environment I live in after her warm and reasonable words. She gave me strength and confidence to be brave in the struggle for defeating the disease.

Tony

The sky is blue and clear/the grass is full grown/and the flowers are in blossom./ The more beautiful the scenery is/the more yearning for enjoying the outside world./ My body has been locked on campus/while my heart has flown/out of the hard wall, cold iron gate/to the flourishing nature,/the symbol of permanent freedom and eternal purity.

Most people tend to be quite nervous about SARS. On the contrary in spite of being quarantined on campus, because I never thought that the disease is so horrible as most people have imagined, the terrible scene reminds me of a word said by the former American President Franklyn Roosevelt in his inauguration speech that goes: "The only thing to fear is fear itself." Indeed, we don't have to be afraid. Just keep optimistic and relaxed every day. Don't focus too much attention on the negative and inactive impact the disease may lead to. That can only do harm to our health.

Jim

The sun is bathing,/The wind is swimming/in the most beautiful season in Beijing./ The campus is locked/the people are stocked/ in the most beautiful season in Beijing./ But we never give up/and we always expect/the rescue from god/the victory of the war against SARS

Anita

I walk slowly down the street on May day feeling lonely/the street is empty./ I continue walking, feeling frightened./ Why do people wear masks and keep their distance?/ I keep walking, looking at the bright sky/ and the beautiful flowers/ and the flying birds/ I smile/ I smell, I feel,/and enjoy May day

   The SARS war has started. It is a war without weapons but it causes fear. And to me, I am a little bit used to it. But I miss home and I want to stay with my parents. I can't concentrate in study among the surroundings where we are shut up and full of fear and anxiety.

Frank

Today I remember the "Diary of Anne Frank."/Sympathy was the only feeling I bore/ imprisoned at BLCU/which is better than the concentration camp./ I'm not afraid of being found by Germany/it is SARS!/ I am waiting/waiting for the end of SARS/or/waiting for the end of myself,/ After a darkest month/when SARS furiously attacks the capital- Beijing/ and takes away people's lives violently/Hopefully, May comes/It is a beautiful time when flowers and trees begin to grow.Iit is a new beginning; it is hope./ believe it./ we will overcome.

Jason

All the misfortunes and save all people's lives./ SARS may break people's bodies/but will never extinguish our hope./Time has feet./ Days flow away through the sink when I wash my hands./wears off in the bowl when I eat my meal/ passes away before my dreaming gaze as I reflect in silence./ I reach out my hands to hold them back but they flow past my withholding hands./ Tell me, why should our days leave us never to return?/ Tell me why should our may holiday leave us?/ If they had been stolen by someone/ who could it be?/ If they escaped themselves, where will they stay?/Because of SARS I cannot go out of campus./ And now I am studying hard to survive in this hell, with a strong will, good immune system, and a heart of tolerance./ Life is boring and dark. It is a torture.

Katherine

Can May day be called "a happy day?"/ Without reunion and travelling?/ can a holiday be called "a free day?/ Without a campus like prisoning?/ this is a May day for thinking/ thinking about the beginning/ thinking about the ending/This is a holiday of waiting./waiting for the mentally refreshing/waiting for a nation reviving.

    Apocalypse now--as a student of BLCU, I have witnessed the scenes of separation of previously close friends and white, thick foam on most mouths; I have gone through the paranoid fear of every small detail in daily life. Now it is time for me to reawaken my mind–boggling fear should be replaced by a peaceful and optimistic spirit.

Cynthia

Life on campus May 1, 2003/library, few people/ playground, few people/ dining hall, few people./ Do the students go out for holiday?/ Of course not, of course impossible./Foreign students go home' Chinese students cannot./ Then where are they now? Enjoying life in dormitory,/ May 1, 2003/ and enjoying the panic of SARS.

Angela

Once you have a dream-a pretty little castle/then came the rains out of the blue./ ever and always; always and ever/life appears to be so cruel for you./Now as you know, spring becomes autumn./ Youth is withering, falling from view/ever and always, always and ever./ Can anyone promise a dream for you?/ What is the dream? Pure white or dark shadow?/ Time is flying and life is changeable./ ever and always, always and ever./ No one can promise a dream for you/ the dream is elusive and trivial.

The virus has turned Beijing into "hell" at least in other people's eyes who are lucky enough to live in other places. BLCU is located in Beijing, so it can not escape. BLCU has already shut in on itself. As an unlucky member of it, I am also shut in and cannot go out. It becomes a prison. I'm now a prisoner! I never thought that one day this would happen to me. I would almost rather die than live in a prison! I have almost been driven crazy! Down with prisons! Down with the policy of imprisonment.

Richard

I want to go home to meet my mother/ but I can't./i desire to walk out of the campus and walk freely on the street/but I won't./ I really wish to cancel all classes/but I couldn't./ I plan to play basketball outside/but I wouldn't./ Maybe I should study in spite of playing "live NBA 2003,"/ but I don't.

This week, I will run out of money. However, I insist that all of this is temporary and everything will be over. At last, in terms of myself I will do anything I can to keep myself healthy. And I have decided to have a big celebration when this crisis passes.

Dean

If we add a stroke to "3" and make it an "8,"/the title could be Beijing-May 2008./At that time, all the Chinese will be hand in hand. expecting the coming Olympics with excitement./ However, in May 2003/Beijing is facing an unprecedented difficulty:/SARS is like an evil/intruding the bodies of innocent people./ but, we are not going to give in to it./Still we are hand in hand, believing the victory finally belongs to us/and last, a freshman sitting in my junior class as her class was canceled.

Cindy

Life on campus, May 1, 2003/the grass will be remaining green/the sky will be still blue/ and our faces will be as lovely as cream./Oh my, oh my!/ we are going to have a holiday leave./We cannot leave our campus/ since the gates are shut/but we can leave our hearts into the fine leaves of our campus young trees/so we can hear the Nightinggale sing.

Roy

Sitting in my dorm/waiting to die/MA, if I die, will you cry?/Pa, you never cry/so, why should I?/ I am only twenty/I've lived life a plenty/but, Ma and Pa, if I leave you/will you cry, too?

Part Six
Public Conversations

34. Bingjuan Xion, Applied Linguistics and Intercultural Communication

Professional Biography

Bingjuan Xiong is a doctoral student in the Department of Communication, University of Colorado at Boulder. She earned her bachelor's degree in English language and literature and a master's degree in applied linguistics from Zhejiang University, Hangzhou, China. Her current research interests are in discourse analysis, ethnography of communication, rhetoric and culture, intercultural communication, and Asian communication theory. She takes a discursive approach to the analysis of communication phenomena in the Chinese context, with a particular focus on mediated discourse from Chinese social media. She has worked on projects investigating cultural terms for talk in Chinese social interactions, Chinese discourse of trade disputes, and the sense-making practices in Chinese online discourse of defense. Currently, she works as a graduate part-time instructor in the University of Colorado, Boulder, teaching courses including intercultural communication, discourse, culture, and society, and perspectives on human communication.

> Question 1: Your BA in English language and literature and your MA in applied linguistics were both awarded in Chinese universities. Can you discuss the specific contributions that the study of applied linguistics makes to the broader study of English language and literature in Chinese universities?

There were fewer people doing linguistics when I was an undergraduate. Most of the undergraduates in the English major, if they had chance, would pursue their master's degree in English literature or translation as that was supposed to prepare them for a teaching position. When I was at Zhejiang University studying for my master's degree in applied linguistics, English literature, and translation were three different programs within the school of international studies. Usually faculty and students from these three areas did not communicate much with each other regarding academic topics.

In terms of the specific contributions, perhaps there are three things that deserve our attention. First, the study of linguistics definitely opens up more areas of study and research for people in the English department, such as second language acquisition, language assessment, business English, discourse analysis and intercultural communication. Secondly, there has been some influence from corpus linguistics in the study of English literature in Chinese universities. As a methodological tool, the techniques of corpus analysis have been applied to literature studies and language teaching. Thirdly, the study of linguistics has also motivated Chinese scholars' investigation of the language structure and usage of Chinese. Instead of doing research about English as a language, more and more Chinese scholars in the field of English language and literature turn their attention to the Chinese language, or comparative linguistic studies. Personally, I think this is a very important contribution for English language and literature in Chinese universities.

Question 2: Both as an undergraduate student at Henan Polytechnic University and as a postgraduate student at Zheziang University, you have received many prestigious awards. What were the motivations that led you to such diligent and industrious study which provided you these awards? What advice would you have for Chinese university students like yourself who can strive for awards such as you have received?

I was truly interested in the English language (and later English literature) during my undergraduate years. Most of the undergraduates in Henan Polytechnic University came from rural families and studying hard was the only chance for them to have a bright future. The learning atmosphere there was daunting as most of the students were working very hard. I too came from a poorer rural family and had all kinds of pressures to work hard and become a good student. Moreover, awards in Chinese universities came along with quite a considerable amount of money. It was also very practical for me to have that money and to make life easier for my family.

For college students from rural China, life could be very hard. Despite the material shortage, they might also experience different kinds of psychological instabilities. I like to talk to younger students like me, asking them: "please do not think less of yourself in whatever situations. Do not waste time, work hard and talk to people to enrich your life experiences. All the hardships you went through in the past are precious treasures to help you move forward."

Question 3: At Zheziang University, you had your first intercultural communication class, probably studying such topics as Edward T. Hall's high and low context, nonverbal communication, and monochronic versus polychronic time, and Geerte Hofstede's national cultural dimensions such as power distance, uncertainty avoidance, individualism/collectiveism, masculinity/femininity, and perhaps short and long term orientation. Can you describe whether such topics were informative for you in your later study of communication at the Ph.D. level at the University of Colorado? If you are teaching intercultural communication, how prominently do they serve as important contributor to this study?

I can't remember what was exactly taught in my first intercultural communication class, but the individual/collective dimensions of culture, high and low contexts were definitely the highlights in the textbook we used. I thought at that time, quite ignorantly, that intercultural communication was all about these topics that were not so interesting. After coming to the University of Colorado, Boulder, I came to see the limitations of focusing on abstract dichotomous concepts to categorize different cultures and the assumptions of culture homogeneity within a national boundary. The Communication Department in CU has developed a strong orientation to situated discursive practices in cultural contexts, this orientation has inspired me to look at how people from different cultural groups engage with each other on an individual and situational basis.

I have designed my intercultural communication course, mainly drawing upon studies of cultural communication within ethnography of communication, partly because that is the literature that I am most familiar with, and partly because of my strong belief in the importance of cultivating undergraduate students' awareness of and reflexivity on cultural differences. It is true that students can easily fall into those dichotomous categories (individualism vs. Collectivism) to label different cultures and further to assign meaning to communicative behaviors. These labels may give students some general ideas about cultural patterns, but I see it as problematic to apply them to situated cultural practices. What interests me most is the sense-making process in intercultural settings with a focus on what people are actually doing on the ground.

Question 4: You worked during your MA degree at Zheziang University with Professor Shi-Xu. He is widely known as a leader in the academic field of critical discourse analysis in China. What were the particular contributions which he made to your future professional career in communication, intercultural communication, critical discourse analysis, and applied linguistics?

I would not have decided to pursue an academic career in the US if I had not met Shi-Xu. I got interested in intercultural communication after writing my thesis on the differences of face and face wants between the Chinese and the Americans (as enacted in a movie "Gua Sha Treatment" in 2001). The idea that there are different (even sometimes competing) sense-making systems operating in an intercultural setting is just fascinating. Since then, I had been trying to figure out a "proper" way to approach intercultural communication, and I was immediately attracted by the scholarship that Shi-Xu has been doing in the field of critical discourse analysis when I came to Zhejiang University, in particular his advocacy for understanding and theorizing Chinese communication phenomena using Chinese cultural resources. Previous studies, especially in applied linguistics, were apt to apply western theoretical and methodological frameworks to understanding the language use of Chinese in social settings. For Shi-Xu, this is problematic in many ways, and he has criticized some of these western frameworks, such as the views there of critical discourse analysis (cda). His critiques inspired my curiosity to explore more about the larger field of language and communication. Therefore I came to the University of Colorado at Boulder, trying to understand the scholarship in this field and make my own contributions to Chinese language and communication through multiple dialogues with western scholars.

Question 5: In 1998, Ray T. Donahue and I *coauthored Diplomatic Discourse*, which includes both discourse analysis and rhetorical analysis as analytical methods to study communication messages and texts. I note that part of your background is the study of discourse. What major aspects of critical discourse analysis blend well with the study of culture and society and intercultural communication courses?

The area of discourse analysis is really broad and diverse, and every tradition in this area has its own distinctive approach to culture and society, and intercultural communication. Personally I have been influenced by Shi-Xu's cultural approach to discourse, Karen Tracy's action-implicative discourse analysis, and Donal Carbaugh's cultural discourse analysis. These approaches provide essential theoretical and methodological frameworks for understanding and examining the complexity of communication, culture, and society.

There are three things that I greatly benefited from these scholars' work on discourse studies. First, discourse analysis is an interesting and useful methodology for the study of communication. Its focus on discourse (although there are some traditions that examine not merely discourse but also the non-verbal mode of communication, such as multi-modal discourse analysis) provides a means to empirically investigate the complexities and situatedness of language use in social contexts, and this investigation further sheds light on our culturally patterned ways of speaking both in everyday life scenes and high-profiled socio-political contexts. Secondly, theories of discourse analysis have made their distinctive contribution to understanding communication in different cultural contexts. The very idea that any form of communication does not happen in a cultural vacuum necessitates the examination of discourse (and other forms of communication) sensitive to cultural contexts, knowledge and practices. Thirdly, some discourse scholars (like Karen Tracy) focus on the use of language in socio-cultural practices, especially around social problems or in some problematic contexts. This orientation to discursive practices adds a valuable "practical" dimension to communication studies, or in Aristotle's term, the "phronesis" of communication.

Question 6: In the International Communication Association, you have memberships in the Language and Social Interaction Division, Intercultural Communication Division, and Political Communication Division. In the National Communication Association, you also hold membership in the Chinese Communication Studies Group. What complementary aspects for you as a future Ph.D. In communication do your memberships in these divisions have for you?

I identify myself, primarily, as a scholar in language and social interaction, with particular focus on the study of Chinese contemporary political discourse. This is mostly the reason why I have become affiliated with these divisions. Additionally, because of my interest in communication and culture, I see it as a natural development to include intercultural communication within my academic territory. All these different affiliations brought me to these academic conjunctures which are quite exciting and challenging at the same time. I am interested in incorporating discourse analysis into the study of Chinese political communication, and the study of intercultural communication, I think these conjunctures within different areas of study will confront me with a wide scope of scholarship that I want to engage with.

Question 7: You have a publication, "The Practice of Reported Speech in Chinese News Reporting of China-USA Trade Disputes." What is your assessment of this news reporting? Does it seem fair or biased? Why? If there is bias, how can such reporting overcome such a problem?

This essay is a segment from my master's thesis in which I examined the discursive construction of Chinese news discourse regarding the China-US. Trade disputes. The China-US. trade war can also be seen as a "discursive war" between the two countries. If you read news about trade disputes between these two countries, it is not hard to see that news reports from both sides are biased in particular ways. In this essay, I looked at how reported speech is used, as a conversational device in the Chinese news reports to mediate this trade war. What I found interesting was that the Chinese news reports included a large number of indirect reported speech to present a one-sided story of the China-US. trade disputes; moreover, reported speeches are used to articulate a strong stance against the US and to portray a positive self-image for China.

Differing from the usage of reported speeches in the American news reports, the Chinese news reports on trade disputes were much more univocal. This led to a cultural explanation for the practice of reported speech in Chinese journalism, that is, reported speech was mainly used to fulfill the "ritual function of reporting" in China's mainstream media, such as People's Daily. The ritual function of reporting was mainly concerned with reporting news in alignment with the "official discourse" led by the Party, and not necessarily oriented to information disclosure and deliberation.

My suggestion for moving beyond this ritual reporting is to change Chinese journalistic practice through the ways that news reports are constructed. For instance, information-oriented ways of reporting ought to be given priority, especially when the covered topic is controversial or problematic.

Question 8: Ai Weiwei's traditional paper cutting was recently featured on cover in their lead story on Chinese perceptions of the world. Ai Weiwei is a leading artist in China, merging both traditional and avant garde art and sculpture, but he was forced to pay a large sum to the government in "taxes" and he was under detention for a period. What contributions can an artist like Ai Weiwei make to a better understanding of modern China? Why has he found himself both lauded as an artist and censored by the government?

To be frank, I knew almost nothing about Ai Weiwei before I came to the states. I got interested in him mainly because of the western media coverage (typically as a heroic figure). I can envision different responses to the question why Ai Weiwei is an important figure for understanding modern China, but for me personally, I think his actions draw our attention to the intersections of communication, public sphere, and new media in contemporary China. It is interesting to point out that new media have certainly made it possible for political activists (like Ai), reformists, critics, and ordinary citizens to critically engage with the government, however, this possibility has been restricted by various types of censorships imposed on those new social media. It is just fascinating to investigate the role that new media is playing (both as a chance and a constraint) in the Chinese society with regard to communication and social change.:

Question 9: You have made a conference presentation in the US, "The Chinese Online Discourse of Defense: A Case Study of Ai Weiwei." What were your major findings in this study? He is well known and much admired by many Chinese netizens. What were the major lines of defense for him in these online discourses? Were they reasonable lines of defense? Why? Or why not?

There have been discussions in the west about the "effectiveness" of China's political communication. Some of them argue that China needs to develop a "better narrative" to communicate with the world. In this conference paper, the broader project is to find out some patterned ways of speaking in Chinese political communication and to offer situated explanations to these patterns. Using *China Daily's* (the US Edition) reports on Ai Weiwei's detention in 2011 as a case study, I looked at the discursive construction of the Chinese defense discourse in terms of its salient strategies and frames. This study shows that there are particularities in choosing and practicing self-defense strategies in the Chinese context and the construction of a particular strategy (i.e. Transcendence) is situation-dependent: both negative and positive contexts are invoked in the Chinese defense discourse in order to transcend the focal action, and this transcendence ultimately set up the prerequisite for China daily to accuse the accusers in this case. Among all the frames identified in this study, western bias and conspiracy against China are frequently highlighted in the discourse. This discursive move to some extent works for the Chinese government in terms of shifting its responsibility in Ai's case and externalizing the accountability of its actions, but it also sends out "threatening" messages to China's western counterparts.

Most of the online comments on these news reports are critical about China's self-defense with regards to these strategies and frames. This suggests that the Chinese defense discourse is not well received by its global audiences, and the reasons for this failure mainly boils down to the lack of information. The contestation of information (i.e. What is the "correct" information to be disclosed in this case) and the public request for more information, are revealed as the most problematic issue in China's discourse of self-defense. In other words, the discursive move of information-disclosure needs to be given seriously if China wants to deliver an effective defense discourse to its international audiences.

Question 10: You are probably aware of the post 80s Chinese generation's enthusiasm for the now more than 30 year old blogger and race car driver Han Han, whose blogs in Chinese instantly create millions of comments by his fans. Earlier Ai Weiwei has been a major defender of Han Han and a collection of Han Han's blog posts have been published in English *This Generation*. Many post 80s Chinese call him "the voice of the post 80s generation." So far, his satire has not managed to cause him the same troubles as have negatively affected Ai Weiwei. How do you, as a communication Ph.d. student assess his immense popularity in China, and his success so far to avoid the same problems that Ai Weiwei has faced from the government?

It is very interesting to compare Han Han and Ai Weiwei in contemporary China, especially in the public sphere of new media. I did not follow Han Han as closely as his fans do, although I read most of his novels (or short stories) while I was in middle school. I think the reason for why he hasn't got into trouble with what he published on the internet, mainly resides in his portrayal of a young-literati identity. Not like Ai Weiwei, a self-claimed political activist, Han Han has secured his place in the Chinese popular culture, and his young-literati identity makes it a bit easier for the government to dismiss his critical stance and remarks appeared on the internet. Additionally, Han Han is mostly known inside China, while Ai Weiwei is very active on the international stage; therefore, from the point of view of the government, Ai potentially poses more threats than Han could, with regard to what they said about China and to whom.

Personally, I think Ai and Han demonstrate two different versions of critical engagement with the Chinese regime. For western audiences, perhaps Ai's approach is easier to resonate with and understand in terms of voicing open dissent and criticism as a political activist, but I see Han's approach of criticizing within the Chinese regime as having greater value than is normally perceived, especially his role of inspiring critical and independent thinking among the younger generations on the internet.

Thank you.

35. Man Cheong Tsoi: Hong Kong and Mainland China

Biography of Man Cheong Tsoi

Man Cheong Tsoi was born and grew up in Hong Kong. He received his tertiary education at the Hong Kong Shue Yan University and the Chinese University of Hong Kong. He was a trainer of customer service and career development before he gradually retired from his work from

2004. Participants in his courses came from all walks of life including celebrities, young leaders, entrepreneurs, and scholars.

Apart from his business, Tsoi is always actively engaged in social services and volunteer programs. As well as from monetary support to various charitable organizations and religious organizations in Hong Kong, Tsoi also participated in programs to build schools in poor areas in China, funding eye care programs in Vietnam, and supported programs for relief in South Africa. He was also a part-time clown for the past 15 years, hoping to bring joy and hope to the people around him.

After his retirement, Tsoi spent most of his time in travelling with his wife and furthered his research in medical ethics and China politics. He joined the Semester-at-Sea as a lifelong learner for its round the world voyage in the fall of 2011.

> Question 1: Having grown up in Hong Kong, you have experienced major changes in the society since the united kingdom returned Hong Kong to China in 1997 and Macau in 1998. Can you describe the general feeling of long-time Hong Kong citizens and your own feelings when Hong Kong returned to China at midnight in July, 1997?

Since the whole transition process had been continuous for years, the moment at the midnight of 1st of July was not too much excitement. As I had understood and even supported that HK should be returned to China ultimately since my childhood, I actually was quite 'well-prepared' for this to occur. However, I felt that the general public at that time was worried and even feeling helpless!

> Question 2: China guaranteed that for fifty years Hong Kong could retain its own cultural and political traditions. How much of this promise has been kept by the central Chinese government? What are the major changes that the central government in China has allowed for both Hong Kong and Macau? How many

of Hong Kong's cultural and political customs and values have been maintained in both former colonies?

I had been asked these kinds of questions over hundreds of times. In fact, it is not possible to answer them within a single conversation or by a few paragraphs of words. For an answer of question 2, I would like to start with the following questions:

   A. Could Deng Xiao Ping have another option when he talked to Margaret Thatcher on the sovereignty of Hong Kong?
   B. What does 'one country two systems' mean to the leaders of China? If HK politically does not follow the way which the central government prefers, then in the dictionary of the Chinese leaders, does HK and China still belong to a country?
   C. "All activities that could be performed before the transition would continue to be allowed after the transition"; is this the only criterion that the 'one country two systems' is feasible?

I am not pro-central government and certainly not pro-British. What I want to say is time flies and everything will change. As a civilian, I do not know what really is behind the curtain; thus it is not easy for me to differentiate what has been changed fundamentally. I will not focus too much on what has been preserved but rather how the HK people should fight for their welfare and autonomy in the days to come.

Question 3: Citizens of Hong Kong and Macau are now citizens of China. What are the general attitudes of those long-time residents of Hong Kong and Macau toward the central government in Beijing?

In response to this question, I have the following observations which may be only my assumptions:

A. In the past, what we learned from history and the schools, newspapers, publications and so on were all negative to the central government and communism. This seemed to have become a fundamental impression of the Hong Kong people towards the central government.

B. The weakness of the legal systems in the mainland and the rule-by-leaders above the rule-of-law in China has absolutely frightened the people of HK. About their personal safety and property rights.

C. The over-centralization of power by the central government is against the culture of the HK people who insist they always have the right to criticize the government for its wrong deeds. We know that HK people like to complain and leave no room for injustice in our society.

Would the HK people trust the central government under all these conditions? The recent implementation of national education in the schools of HK might prove my observation.

Question 4: How has your university education at the Hong Kong Shue Yan University and the Chinese University of Hong Kong impacted your future career and life? How do these two universities compare with other major universities both in Hong Kong and on the mainland?

HK Shue Yan University is a private university and receives only minimal financial support from the government. The years when I was in Shue Yan it was still a post secondary college. The principal and the headmistress had strong control over the whole college and this is still the same now though they are transiting their power to their next generation. I did learn a lot there and I remembered the days when we fought for a students' union, we received a lot of resistance from the headmistress in fear of that we would overthrow her! This 'incident' might have provided me with training and knowledge when I was involved in more social campaigns as I have grown up.

The Chinese University of Hong Kong is a very good university with a long history and gains strong financial support from the government as compared to Shue Yan. I joined the CUHK after my retirement and the greatest pleasure was I could become one of the students of the Faculty of Law. The Faculty of Law did help me to establish a concrete foundation and paved me the right path for future research.

I could not compare them with the universities in China as I have not studied there. I suppose HK Has a higher autonomy in academic researches than in the mainland.

HK is also an open society and you can collect information much more easily than in China. This is very important for academic studies.

Question 5: You have given extensive volunteer work in Hong Kong, mainland China, Vietnam, and South Africa. What differences do you see in your volunteer work in Hong Kong, mainland China and Vietnam? Has one of these volunteer activities helped to develop your own cultural and religious world view and your values more than the others? Which volunteer activity has had the most impact for recipients of your volunteer work and your financial contributions?

It is difficult to compare because different places have differences in culture. The project that I had the highest participation was one which helped to build schools in China. We started the program in 1992 and up to now we have built over thousands of schools and subsidizing many educational programs. This project was initiated by only a few citizens of HK without the back up of celebrities, big companies or entrepreneurs. Honestly speaking, the HK people lacked trust in the Chinese government in managing donations to the country. However the project received great support from the public. The most significant part of the program is that the members of this project do keep a tight surveillance of all their programs so as to make sure that the donations can really be given to those who need them. They even go to give money to the villagers directly and visit the sites regularly during the whole process of building the schools. The members of the project are all volunteers but willing to sacrifice their own time and efforts in providing schools and improving education for the poor children. What I have learned through my participation is "miracles can happen if you do something with your heart."

Question 6: You and I both participated in the University of Virginia/Semester at Sea around the world study voyage in the autumn of 2011. You were very active in taking classes, in being involved with the students, and also with the life long learners. What was the greatest impact that this study voyage had on you personally? Did it change your own values in any way?

It was really the greatest pleasure to join the SAS fall 2011 voyage! I got in touch with new people and new cultures and that I found I was still growing up at my age!

There is an old Chinese saying that 'Travelling a lot is far more worthy than reading a lot.' I think this is not true. I think 'travelling' and 'reading' are both important and symbiotic. We can get useful knowledge from books and in fact we use books as a tool for the world to exchange knowledge. On the other hand, if you only do readings but not travelling much, you cannot know what the actual world is and thus cannot broaden your horizon.

During the time when I was in the SAS for the 111 days, I especially felt that cross cultural programs were important to our world. What I had heard about Asia especially China and HK In the SAS, I would like to say I humbly disagreed with most of the information!

When people from different places are free to exchange their views and culture, we begin to understand each other more and be more considerate. Our world will thus become more peaceful!

Question 7: Since your retirement, you have actively engaged in medical ethics research and political contacts with mainland China. How have your volunteer efforts in Hong Kong, mainland China, Vietnam, and South Africa complemented your own interests in medical ethics and political involvement in Hong Kong or mainland China?

I do not have any political contact with the mainland and the Chinese government. The reason for me to have an interest in medical ethics is because my family members have been chronic patients for over 30 years. One of them passed away suddenly because of an acute stroke in 2005. Her passing away aroused my interest in medical ethics and patients' rights. As a close relative of chronic patients, a Christian and also a graduate of law school, I do think I can contribute a little idea to this area.

Question 8: Your beliefs, attitudes, and values are very much involved altruistically in helping less fortunate people in Hong Kong, mainland China, Vietnam, and South Africa. What led you from being a career-oriented business men to this altruistic spirit which you so strongly live by?

I humbly disagree again that I own a high altruistic spirit though I often woke up Prof. Prosser when we were in the SAS so that both of us would not be late for field trips!!
   I think the older generation in my family did shape my behavior. My god-mother believed that 'Do not think the evil things are very minor so you do it and do not think the kind deeds are tiny and so you do not have to do it.' My father was really a businessman but he taught me 'Let people take

advantage of you but not you to take others' advantages.' You can imagine what I had adopted when I was still very young. These words are stamped inside my heart.

Question 9: Your wife might like to join you on a future Semester at Sea study voyage. What opportunities do you anticipate for you and your wife from such a new voyage that would either be very similar or different than the 2011 study voyage? You met Archbishop Tutu on the 2011 voyage. If you could meet one other Nobel Peace laureate on a future such voyage, who would it be and why?

My wife and I have not talked about this yet but we are a couple who is fond of travelling. I had met several Nobel prize laureates before meeting Archbishop Tutu. I want to meet Mr. Nobel (maybe in heaven) because I have the interest to know his opinions about the recent peace prize laureates!

It may also be good to meet the students of the Tiananmen Square since what I had heard was that they were originally nominated as a group for the prize but were unsuccessful due to political reasons. We may meet and chat about the current issues of our motherland.

Question 10. Your spirit of bringing joy and hope to so many people by your part-time occupation as a clown for fifteen years was evident and admirable on the Semester at Sea 2011 voyage. What are the major benefits of being a clown for your recipients versus direct volunteerism in such cases as your volunteer work in Hong Kong, mainland China, Vietnam, and South Africa?

I think they are actually two things. Being a clown, you are enjoying a performing art with the people. In fact, you can have personal development by acting as a clown since it requires you to do something which others look upon as ridiculous! This is not what you can get from other volunteer work.

In addition, a clown playing with people of various nationalities can have a very creative and useful cross cultural function because the clown and the participants are communicating by a universal language!

36. Chew Fong Peng: the Chinese Disapora

Biography: Dr. Chew Fong Peng

Dr. Chew Fong Peng is a senior lecturer at the Faculty of Education, University of Malaya (UM). She is teaching Malay language education and early childhood education program at UM and Chinese language program at the University of Technology of Mara (UITM) and Sultan Idris University of Education (UISP), Malaysia. Professor Chew Fong Peng has presented approximately 98 working papers in national and international seminars and conferences in Malaysia and foreign countries including the United Kingdom, France, Switzerland, Greece, Japan, South Korea, China, Singapore, Thailand, the Philippines and Indonesia. She has published 5 books, 41 articles published in journals, 31 papers in conference proceedings, 21 chapters in books, 10 translated books including creative writings, 4 edited books and creative writings. She has completed 9 research projects of which 5 of them were led by chew. She won many medals in the academy and innovative expo. Um outstanding service award (2008), being listed in *Marquis Who's Who in the World 2011, 2000 and 2012*.

Chew is an article reviewer for international journals, namely *International Journal of English, British Journal of Medicine and Medical Research, British Journal of Education, Society and Behavioral Science (b, International Journal of Psychology and Counselling, Educational Research and Reviews, and African Journal of Pharmacy and Pharmacology*. She also supervises 20 masters' students (Malay language and Chinese language in education) in project and dissertation writing (14 completed), 8 undergraduates of TESL (Teaching English as Second Language) and early childhood education students in academic writing. Besides that, Chew recites Malay poems invited at the state and national level. Chew was invited as visiting professor at Peking university from October, 2011 to June, 2012 during her sabbatical leave. Chew won the "The World Outstanding Researcher" Award (2013).

> Question 1: I am conducting several public professional conversations with knowledge-rich Asian experts. Can you identify the number of people in Malaysia who consider themselves as of Chinese heritage? How has the Chinese heritage population adapted to Malaysian society, with its Malay and Indian populations?

There are many people in Malaysia who consider themselves as of Chinese heritage because we have a complete Chinese education system from primary, secondary to higher education. We have 1,142 national-type Chinese primary schools; 78 national-type Chinese secondary schools; 60 Chinese independent secondary schools, three Chinese higher education private colleges, one Chinese private university-college, and one Chinese private university. Almost 90% of the Chinese parents send their children to Chinese primary schools; 20% of these students will go to national-type Chinese secondary schools or Chinese independent secondary schools, and then they proceed their study in either local Chinese colleges or university or overseas. These entire education heritages maintain our complete Chinese culture from generation to generation due to our former educators/fighters who defended Chinese education, include Lim Leon Geok, Sim Mook Yi, Tan Cheng Lock, et al. Most of the Chinese-educated Chinese define ourselves as being of Chinese heritage while recognizing Malaysia as our nation. We love our country by contributing our effort, money, and blood.

Most are the descendants of Chinese who arrived between the early and the mid-twentieth centuries. Malaysian Chinese constitute one group of overseas Chinese and constitute the third largest Chinese community in the world, after those in Thailand and Indonesia. Within Malaysia, the Chinese represent the second largest ethnic group in Malaysia after the ethnic malay majority. As of 2010, approximately 6,960,000 Malaysian Chinese — the majority of the population (except those mixed ones) — self-identify as "Chinese".

As minority, nearly 25% of the population of Malaysia, Chinese here adapted to the Malays as majority 60% and Indian 7% in harmony and tolerance. We learn Malay language as national and official language, incorporate their culture by wearing Malay costume, namely batik especially on Thursdays, Malaysian Chinese eat all types of food, including Chinese, Indian, Malay and western cuisines. Malaysian culture accommodates Malays, Chinese, Indians, and indigenous culture as a whole; we have no much problem getting along with them, instead the Chinese here help to develop the country mainly in terms of financial, followed by political and social-cultural aspects. Chinese who born after 1970s are third generation in Malaysia that their grandparents migrated from China, so we are more Malaysia-oriented though most of us consider ourselves Chinese heritage.

Question 2: What is the role of the Chinese diaspora power in Malaysia, in terms of governmental, legislative, financial, and cultural aspects for the society? Is this power increasing or decreasing over time?

Malaysian Chinese are a socioeconomically well established middle-class ethnic group and make up a highly disproportionate percentage of Malaysia's professional and educated class, with a record of high educational achievement, a high representation in the Malaysian professional white-collar workforce, and one of the highest household incomes among minority demographic groups in Malaysia. Like in much of Southeast Asia, Malaysian Chinese are dominant in both the business and commerce sectors, controlling an estimated

70% of the Malaysian economy. They are also one of the biggest taxpayers, contributing almost 90% of the national income tax and 60% of Malaysia's national income.

Since early settlements during the 15th century, Chinese Malaysians are considered one of the wealthiest ethnic groups in Malaysia and have been more prosperous than other ethnic communities in Malaysia. In February 2001, Malaysian business released its list of the 20 richest Malaysians. Sixteen of the 20 and 9 of the top 10 were ethnic Chinese. A number of other wealthy Chinese outside the top 20 also control well-managed corporations. According to a 2011 *Forbes Magazine* list, eight out of the top ten richest Malaysians are ethnic Chinese. According to economic data compiled by the Malaysian daily in 2012, ethnic Chinese make up 80 percent of Malaysia's top 40 richest people.

Chinese Malaysians played a major role in the development of the tin, petroleum, and rubber industries and also continue to own 85 percent of Malaysian retail outlets. Chinese-owned mines produced nearly two-thirds of the tin in Malaysia. Many used their savings to open small businesses, where some grew into large enterprises. Typically, many of their enterprises have been family-controlled and family-run. In 1964, Sino-Malaysians accounted for 91.7% of the private corporate holdings in Malaysia and ownership of the Malaysian gravel pump and small-scale tin mines were completely placed in the hands of ethnic Chinese entrepreneurs. By 1970, glaring economic disparity between the Malays and Chinese was widespread as Malaysian Chinese entrepreneurs were estimated to control 26% of the assets in the corporate sector, 26.2% of the manufacturing and 92.2% of the non-corporate sector. Malaysian Chinese entrepreneurs operate as a more urban business community, dominating trade and commerce, primarily tin mining and agriculture. They are also dominant in both business and commerce sectors in Malaysia, where 70 percent of publicly listed companies were under Chinese ownership.

The Chinese in Malaysia are estimated to control 50% of the construction sector, 82% of wholesale trade, 58% of retail trade, 40% of the manufacturing sector, and 70% of the small-scale enterprises. In 2002, the Chinese Malaysian share of the overall Malaysian economy stood at 40% since the implementation of the Malaysian new economic policy and the Chinese share in the non-agricultural sector fell from 51.3% to 45.9% from 1970 to 1980. Despite efforts to reduce the share of Chinese entrepreneurial dominance, the overall Chinese share of the Malaysian economy increased to 60% in 2008. Chinese Malaysian businessmen are estimated to occupy 34.9% of Malaysia's llc companies, the highest percentage of ownership among the 3 major ethnic groups in Malaysia. In order to seek extra funding and seed money for potential business start-ups, many Malaysian Chinese entrepreneurs have turned to the Malaysian stock exchange for business expansion and potential ipos. Chinese Malaysians are estimated to control 62% percent of the stock market. In 1995, the seven biggest investors in the Kuala Lumpur stock exchange were all ethnic Chinese, with 90 percent of the smaller and younger companies on the second exchange of the KlSE are also Chinese controlled. Malaysian Chinese businesses are part of the larger bamboo network, a network of overseas Chinese businesses operating in the markets of Southeast Asia that share common family and cultural ties.

Home ownership and the utilization of property as an investment are also prevalent in the Malaysian Chinese community. Real estate investing is a common business and a source of wealth for Malaysian Chinese as it not only provides a steady source of monthly income from rental proceeds and a hedge against inflation, but also raises the standard of living for Malaysians who are not in the right economic position to purchase a home for themselves. In 2005, Malaysian Chinese owned 69.4% of the business complexes, 71.9% of all commercial and industrial real estate, as well as 69.3% of all the hotels in Malaysia, reflecting Chinese control over the various business and commercial establishments around the nation.

However, the underprivileged section of the Malaysian Chinese continue to be excluded from affirmative-action programs despite their genuine need for support in obtaining employment, government subsidized education, and housing. This perception of a zero-sum game amongst the races has unfortunately fueled protests by frustrated sections of the hitherto quiescent community — who consequentially faced a heavy-handed response from the authorities. Recently, the Malaysian government has at least pledged to change this by increasing assistance to needy Malaysians regardless of race, creed, or national origin.

Question 3: Malaysia is well known as "Asia truly Asia" in its tourist materials. What are the major contributions to this theme which are supported by religious and cultural traditions among the Chinese, Malay (largely Muslim), and Hindu populations?

The culture of Malaysia draws on the varied cultures of the different people. The first people to live in the area were indigenous tribes that still remain; they were followed by the Malays, who moved there from mainland Asia in ancient times. Chinese and Indian cultural influences made their mark when trade began with those countries, and increased with immigration to Malaysia. Other cultures that heavily influenced that of Malaysia include Persian, Arabic, and British. The many different ethnicities that currently exist in Malaysia have their own unique and distinctive cultural identities, with some crossover.

Arts and music have a long tradition, with Malay art dating back to the Malay sultanates. Traditional art was centered around fields such as carving, silversmithing, and weaving. Islamic taboos restricted artwork depicting humans until the mid-20th century. Performing arts and shadow puppet shows are popular, and often show Indian influences. Various influences can be seen in architecture, from individual cultures and from other countries. Large modern structures have been built, including the tallest twin buildings in the world, the Petronas Twin Towers. Malaysian music has a variety of origins, and is largely based around percussion instruments. Much earl literature was based on Indian epics, which remained unchanged even as Malays converted to Islam; this has expanded in recent decades. English literature remained restricted to the higher class until the arrival of the printing press. Locally created Chinese and Indian literature appeared in the 19th century.

Cuisine is often divided along ethnic lines, but some dishes exist which have mixed foods from different ethnicities. Each major religious group has its major holy days declared as official holidays. Official holidays differ by state; the most widespread one is Independence Day. Although festivals often stem from a specific ethnic background, they are celebrated by all people in Malaysia. Traditional sports are popular, while it has become a powerhouse in international sports such as badminton. Malaysia hosted the Commonwealth games in 1998, the first commonwealth games where the torch passed through more countries than England and the host.

The government has taken the step of defining Malaysian culture through the "1971 national culture policy," which defined what was considered official culture, basing it around Malay culture and integrating Islamic influences. This especially affected language; only Malay texts are considered official cultural texts. Government control over the media is strong, and most media outlets are related to the government in some way.

Question 4: In terms of the educational system in Malaysia, how does the highest level for Chinese ancestry students compare with the highest level of malay and Indian ancestry students?

Data (see next page) show that the total number of public university students' enrolment from the 41,267 students in 2011/2012 academic year fell to 38,549 students in 2012/2013 academic year, and the Chinese ethnic applicants were also reduced from 10,677 to 10,400; therefore, the Chinese enrollments decreased from 9,457 to 8,986 students.

Ethnics	2013/2014 session		2012/2013 session		2011/2012 session	
	enrollment	percentage	enrollment	percentage	enrollment	percentage
Malays	30,903	74,33%	27,455	71,22%	29,838	72,30
Chinese	7,913	19,03%	8,986	23,31%	9,457	22,92%
Indians	1,824	4,39%	1,384	3,06%	1,511	3,66%
Others	933	2,24%	724	1,88%	461	1,12%
total	41,573	100%	38,549	100%	41,267	100%

Table 1: Public universities' students intake from 2011/12 to 2013/2014 academic year
(source: *Sin Chew Daily*, July 12, 2013, p. 3)

The 2013/2014 academic year enrollments rose to 41,573 students and the Chinese applicants also rose to highest for three academic years (12,065 students), but the number of Chinese students enrolled did not increase, instead decreased to 7,913 students.

Therefore, in these three academic years of students' intake, the number of Chinese enrolment to the public universities increased from 22.9% in the 2011/2012 academic year to 23.3% in 2012/2013 academic year, but the latest 2013/2014 years fell to 19.03%.

In contrast, the Malay students enrolment is the highest in 2013/14 academic year with 30,903 students (74.33%) compare to 27,455 students (71.22%) in 2012/13 academic year and 29,838 students (72.3%) 2011/12 academic year; meanwhile Indians students and other ethnics enrolment decreased from year to year.

From the table 1, it clearly shows that Chinese, Indians, and other students' enrolment decreased from year to year and their total ratio was less than 25% from the total enrolment in public university students. So most of these ethnics tend to send their adolescent children to study at local private universities, private university colleges or private colleges, or study abroad for those who are rich. As a result, the majority of the post-graduates are Malays compared to other ethnic groups because the education fee is relatively expensive in private universities, private university colleges or private colleges, and even studying abroad is most expensive.

Question 5: You are teaching Malay language education and early childhood education program at UM and Chinese language program at the University of Technology of Mara (UITM) and Sultan Idris University of Education (UPSI) Malaysia. What are some of the major topics which you teach your students related to these subjects? Are there different teaching techniques that are appropriate when you teach Malay language education, early childhood education, and Chinese language programs?

In UM, I teach Malay language in education for the master's program mainly; the courses include planning and policy in language education, literature in language teaching, research in literacy development, and seminar in language education. I teach only one course for the early childhood education program for undergraduates, namely reading and early children literature. Meanwhile, I teach the Chinese language as foreign language for undergraduates (level I, level ii and level iii) at the University of Technology of Mara (UITM) and the Chinese language education program for undergraduates at Sultan Idris University of Education (UPSI), include the courses of sociolinguistic, Chinese education history in Malaysia, Chinese children's literature in Malaysia, phonetics and phonology of Chinese language, rhetoric of Chinese language, curriculum and Chinese language teaching in primary school. All of the above programs are under education categories except the Chinese language at the UITM; therefore the methods are totally different between them. For the education programs, since I am training pre-service teachers or in-service teachers, I emphasize more on the pedagogy, education policy, syllabus, and research methodology, hence fourth, I focus more on discussion, articles comments, seminar, and project writing especially at the master level; for the education undergraduate students, especially early childhood education program, I emphasize more on practical aspects, namely making big story books, presentation of their assignment and cultural on stage performance.

For Chinese language programs, since they are blended programs, I use mainly online interaction methods beside five lectures in one semester that carry out 2 hours per lecture. In the class, due to the time constraints, I have to use discussion and tutoring methods to cover the entire syllabus. For the UITM class, I emphasize more on students' pronunciation and conversation practice in pairs, meanwhile for the UPSI class, I apply questions and answers, experience sharing and group discussion methods because they are all in-service teachers.

Question 6: As the author of several books, many journal articles, and conference presentations, what is the impact of your personal Chinese heritage background and your professional interests related to Chinese language programs, and others, in your books, journal articles, and professional presentations?

My personal Chinese heritage background and professional interests are related very much to the Chinese language programs, and others. I am proficient in Chinese languages that made me become the part timer in teaching Chinese language programs at two other universities.

Occasionally, the Malay literary association tends to invite me to present papers either on Malay literature and ethnic relations, national integration in Malay literature, Chinese society and Malay language, etc. After presenting the papers, I send the articles to be published in journals. The national institute of book and translation also asks my help to do some creative writing translation jobs from Malay language to Chinese, or editing jobs. Since the market of the translation job is not only Chinese society in Malaysia, but include China, so there is a high demand of translators and editors in this field. As my mother tongue, I can write articles in Chinese languages well; I even stand a better chance to become the moderator to bridge the gap between two difference societies by doing the translation job.

In academic fields, at first I concentrated in doing research and writing articles in Malay language and literature in education; in recent years, I began diversifying my research to Chinese education as well; I found that the Chinese education issues in Malaysia are yet to be explored widely since there is nobody doing the study in quantitative methods compared to Malay education. In addition, the research on Chinese education attract more interest of the scholars abroad when I have presented papers in international conferences overseas. However I have never abandoned my expertise in Malay study that opened the chance for me to be invited as visiting professor at Peking University, an honor for overseas Chinese to teach there. One of the main reasons of the offer was because I can speak and write in Chinese well since China applies the monolingual education policy.

Question 7: We are both listed in the *Marquis Who's Who in the World*. Has your listing in this book been of general or specific importance for you, and the development of your own reputation as an international scholar of merit? With your many awards and honors, what do you consider your most significant professional accomplishments?

The listing in the marquis who's who in the world is an honor especially for Asians, I know that it is not easy to be included in the book, and not many Malaysians are being listed. For me, it is recognition of my status as an international scholar. All the awards and honors are an encouragement for me to be a better researcher and scholar.

My most significant professional accomplishments to the world scientific community were being appointed as a visiting professor at Peking University in 2012. Peking University ranked 57 in the world according to the 2012 statistics. They offered me the post when I spent my sabbatical leave from 1 October, 2011 to 30 June, 2012. I taught the Malay language to undergraduate students and Malaysia study for postgraduate students. They also recruited me as the panel member in selecting the postgraduate students' intake for Malay language program. At the same time, I did my research topic on "teaching and learning foreign languages at Beijing, China" that focused on English and Malay languages. The outcomes of the research were "English Language Acquisition among non-native Speakers" published in *Advances in Environment, Computational Chemistry & Bioscience: Proceeding of the 3rd*

International Conference on Arts and Culture (ICAC '12) and *"Language Attitude of University Students in China."* I am going to present at the 3rd International Conference on Languages, Literature and Linguistics (ICLLL 2013) in Sydney, Australia. On the other hand, in 2012.Beijing Foreign Studies University has also invited me to be a speaker to talk on the topic of "Malaysian Education System" and "Malay-Chinese Language Translation in Malaysia." All these invitations are an honor and recognition of my knowledge and expertise. I appreciate that I am highly recognized by the famous and established overseas universities.

Question 8: You have edited books and written articles concerning creative writing. What would you say are the most important aspects of creative writing? Would there be different creative writing aspects that might develop for Chinese ancestry individuals in comparison with Malay and Indian backgrounds?

Creative writing is the combination of reality and imagination of the author towards the reality. Therefore, the technique of delivering the philosophy of life from the perspective of the author becomes the most important aspect of creative writing beside the language, plot and setting of the story. In Malaysia, most of the Chinese authors write in the Chinese language and their literature is named as "Mahua literature." In Malaysia, only the Malay literature is recognized as national literature, while Mahua literature and Tamil literature (Indian literature) are named as "ethnic literature." Since each literature develops separately in their language, the development is found to be totally different among them. Mahua literature is closely related to China because its origins are from China literature, but the language used and the setting of the story in Mahua literature is local color; the same condition applies to the Tamil literature as well.

The Chinese authors who write Mahua literature focus more on their society, education, politic and social cultural issues in

Malaysia; on the other hand, they also tend to write their relationship with China due to the ancestry history. The theme that they cover includes Chinese ancestors migrant to Malaya to look for a better life; new economy policy and Chinese response; ethnic relations; the effect of the macro economy upon Chinese economy development; language, education and cultural issues; and Chinese beliefs; etc.

The same situation happens to the Indian authors who tend to write on their life, their culture and their problems comprise issues such as love and marriage; family problems; moral decay and social freedom; war; hypocrisy of politicians and their selfishness; economic life as laborers or small shopkeepers; poverty; rubber tape and oil palm estates problems; alcohol and prostitution; and education and so forth.

On the other hand, as the majority ethnic group, the Malay authors write on their own society too by focusing on their culture, the economy, politics in Malaysia with the setting of cities or rural areas. They write themes on love, rural problems and poverty; hypocrisy of life; moral decay and social freedom; prostitution; war and emergencies; contradictions of political ideology; the sailor world; country development; and Islamic values.

Question 9: You have participated in conferences in many countries, including China. When you are in western countries, versus China, how are you perceived? As a Malaysian? As an Asian professor? As a Chinese heritage individual?

I have participated in conferences in many countries. Wherever I go, I always perceive myself as Malaysian Chinese. I feel proud to tell the whole world that I am Malaysian because we have our uniqueness and identity: a multicultural society, our hospitality, Kuala Lumpur Twin Towers, beautiful beaches and Dr. Mahathir Mohammad, our charismatic former prime minister. Besides that, I perceive my identity as Chinese too; as a Chinese, I will always remember my origins and roots. I respect China as my ancestor's homeland. When I visit China, I feel the intimacy due to the similarity of our cultures, heritage and life. However, I know that my identity is Malaysian Chinese, not China Chinese.

Question 10. What influences in your own personal life, and in your family, have manifested themselves in your personal perspective as a Malaysian? As an Asian professor? As a Chinese heritage individual?

I like to convey my thoughts through writing. As a primary and secondary student, I scored well in language composition. This was due to my reading habit that I inherited from my father. As a secondary school teacher, he taught me to revise my studies every night. He also bought Chinese and Malay newspapers so that I might improve my language proficiency.

When I pursued the Malay study program at National University of Malaysia (UKM), the tradition of UKM is to train the students in academic writing properly and systematically. I am grateful that I could complete all my studies at UKM; from there, I learned a lot about the discipline of writing good articles, especially the guidance from an excellent lecturer from Faculty of Education Associate Professor Adnan Kamis. I started to write papers in conferences, articles in press and magazines under his mentorship and guidance when I started to teach in secondary school in 1998.

However I liked to upgrade myself and I did not remain in school; I did not have the opportunities to do research or get articles published in international journals since the school system only demanded that teachers focus on teaching. Therefore, I started to apply to become a lecturer at the public universities.

After failing 15 times in my application, in 2006, I was offered a lecturer post at the Faculty of Education, University of Malaya (UM). Since UM is the top university in Malaysia and the leader in research and innovation at the higher education level, I learned a lot of the research methods, scientific articles writing and data analysis there by attending courses, workshops and seminars. I started to learn to lead the small research projects sponsored by the university and major research projects sponsored by the Ministry of Science, Technology and Innovation. I am a research member of long-term research grant scheme entitled "AAA," led by Distinguished Prof. Dr. Shamsul Amri at UKM. The university offered me an environment that helped me to grow as a researcher and academician. And I was able to find job satisfaction; I enjoy teaching, doing research and writing

As a member at UM, I have to work hard to achieve the annual key performance indicator, and the criteria are becoming increasingly difficult to achieve. The competitive environment challenges me to work harder for better quality research and writing better articles in international journals. I am determined to publish at least three articles in journals per year, one or two in international journals and one in national journals besides writing books and chapters in books. I am still learning to write more scientific articles because the high quality journals are very demanding and competitive; the ground is wide open, and I am an infant who has a lot to learn in this era of globalization. UM is a good learning place for me to develop my knowledge and experiences in terms of research and innovation.

I am grateful that I have supportive family members who always give me moral support especially my father although he passed away in 2000. He is the one who always reminded me to further my studies and always work hard to gain the knowledge; he loved to study but had to quit due to financial and eye problems. So I am determined to fulfill his dream and made him feel proud that one of his

Children emerges as a bright star in the family. Secondly, Associate Professor Adnan Kamis was my main mentor who trained me in article writing and publishing at the beginning stage; that was the tough time especially for a Chinese who majored in Malay studies that is rarely found and it is hard to penetrate the hegemony of publishing in their press, magazines and journals. He always gave me courage and strength when my articles were being rejected. He would guide me to improve my writing and publications from time to time and urge me never to give up even though I was depressed. This later became the life philosophy that I have embraced till now. All the obstacles and difficulties made me become tougher and better able to chase my dream.

I also want to convey my gratitude to Prof. Tie who keeps on urging me to write in ISI journals regardless how many times there are rejections. He asks me to be focused in work and not be distracted by unimportant things. He gives me courage to go on my journey with a robust pace. With their support, I have become more confident now. They have manifested themselves in my personal life as a Malaysian Chinese among whom we are always hardworking to chase our dreams.

37. Laura Gostin (2007: 12–06) the Journey of an Intercultural/International Scholar: Dr. Michael Prosser

China Media Reports, pp. 104–117.

Abstract: This interview was conducted via email over a period of several weeks during the summer of 2007. Dr. Michael Prosser is a renowned intercultural communication scholar and one of the co-founders of the academic field of intercultural communication. During the interview, Dr. Prosser shared some of his personal experiences as an intercultural scholar and offered his valuable insights regarding the discipline of communication in general and the field of intercultural communication in particular.

Keywords: scholar interview, intercultural communication, founder, China.

Question 1: Would you please briefly introduce yourself and describe one of your typical workdays?

Growing up more or less monoculturally, something in my high school boarding school sparked my intercultural and international interest, now a guiding principle throughout my life. The western zodiac has me as an Aries, pioneer or warrior; my namesake, St. Michael, was a legendary heavenly warrior archangel. The Chinese zodiac has me as a rat, which jumped to the head of the 12 zodiac animals. I have been used to the role of leadership throughout my life. Following my university graduation, I traveled for two months in Europe, and in the following summer, I was among the first 15,000 Americans to visit Russia in 1959.

During my professional career, I have been among the founders of the field of intercultural communication; chair of the first three North American conferences to found the field; the founding chair for what is now the international and intercultural division of the [us] national communication association; a founding governing council member and later president of the international society for intercultural education, training, and research; the first teacher for communication majors as a Fulbright professor at the University of Swaziland; founder of six Rochester Intercultural Conferences (1995–2001); and for a period of time in the late 1990's I was called the "father of the South Sudan community" in Rochester, New York.

As the father of three children, with nine grandchildren, potentially I will leave a considerably large group of descendants behind me like those following the rat in the Chinese zodiac. Writing my doctoral dissertation on the United Nations speeches by us Ambassador Adlai Stevenson led both to my editing a 1969 collection of his international speeches over his lifetime and a 1970 two volume collection of addresses by heads of state and government at the United Nations.

My book *The Cultural Dialogue* (1978) was among the first texts on intercultural communication. Still later, my co-authored book *Diplomatic Discourse: international Conflict at the United Nations* (1997) illustrates how both rhetorical and discourse analysis can be used effectively to understand international messages in the UN. Recently, I have co-edited *Civic Discourse: Multiculturalism, Cultural Diversity, and Global Communication* (1998); *Civic Discourse: Intercultural, International, and Global Media* (1999); *Sino-American Compositions of Shared Topics* (2003); and *Intercultural Perspectives on Chinese Communication* (2007).

From 1998 to 2004, seventeen books were published in my series, Civic Discourse for the Third Millennium (Ablex/Praeger). Jointly retiring in 2001 from the University of Virginia and the Rochester Institute of Technology, I have since taught 1800 Chinese university students in three Chinese universities. Presently as distinguished professor at the Shanghai International Studies University, the SISU Intercultural Institute executive director, Steve Kulich and I co-edit an "intercultural research" series with our next two volumes on intercultural value studies in progress.

On every typical Monday for the last two years, I have taught five classes for undergraduates at the SISU undergraduate campus. This year in the autumn semester, I taught five classes of sophomore oral English for English majors and during the spring semester, five classes of freshmen oral English.

Question 2: What are the most challenging issues you are faced with in your teaching and research career?

My long-term teaching positions have included: junior high school Latin, 1960–63; communication in several American universities, 1963–2001; and English in three Chinese universities, 2001-present. I have now taught more than 10,000 students in my 47 years of teaching, including 1800 in China. In introducing new communication courses like classical/modern rhetorical theory at Suny-Buffalo and intercultural communication later, I found the development of the broad communication field always moving faster than I could keep up with it. I had to decide my main teaching and research focus: a classical- contemporary rhetorician; an expert on public address and discourse; or political or intercultural communication. Once, I introduced a seminar on communist rhetoric, quickly discovering that one undergraduate knew far more than I.

Later as a founder of the field of intercultural communication in North America, first, I had never taken courses in anthropology, sociology, or psychology. Although I required intercultural field studies in most of my intercultural communication courses in the American universities, I had no statistical background, nor the contemporary social science programs for empirical analysis. As the field matured in the 1980's until more recently, many teachers and researchers developed far more sophisticated theories and constructs than I was aware of. For example, though I knew generally about Geert Hofstede's multi societal surveys, it was more than a decade later when I introduced his findings into my own teaching.

In a similar way, before teaching at the Shanghai International Studies University, I had no knowledge of significant researchers such as Robert inglehart, Michael Bond or Shalom Schwartz and their seminal value studies. Fortunately, Steve Kulich and Zhang Rui gave me a broad understanding of these scholars' contributions. I can claim far more editorial competence than as an author. Among my books, edited or co-edited books leave only two authored ones, *The Cultural Dialogue* (1978) and my co-authored book with Ray Donahue, *Diplomatic Discourse: International Conflict at the United Nations* (1997). My edited and authored books are rather eclectic, with two on classical/medieval rhetoric; two on international public discourse, two dealing with communication at the united nations, and six involving my strongest interest, intercultural and international communication and media. However, these books all demonstrate my wide cultural and international interest, with the latest two books specifically on Chinese communication.

I am pleased with my intercultural co-editing collaboration with K.S. Sitaram. Preferring to work directly with book-length manuscripts, my scholarly journal articles represent a very short list. Because of my propensity for moving quickly toward a new project, unfortunately, several book ideas or books in progress have languished, sometimes leaving other contributing authors with their own committed but unpublished articles. Without any serious personal statistical or empirical background, I have not conducted any cutting edge research that the intercultural field demands.

While pleased at the number of my books that did get published, I regret those intended or committed but never published, especially for the authors whose chapters were not published. Steve Kulich, Zhang Hongling and I have more books in progress.

Question 3: Considering the impact of globalization, where do you see the discipline heading in the future?

"Globalism," like communication, is "the broad concept," while "globalization," like communications, is "the process," both positive and negative. We have not suddenly awakened to a globalizing society. The pre-Christian Greeks and Romans began the process for the west, where Aristotelian logic has formed a framework for modern deductive and inductive reasoning and Confucius, whose *Analects* is still a major life force in East Asian cultures such as China, Japan, and Korea, as well as Siddhartha, the founder of Buddhism, and Hindu sacred writings that developed eastern polytheocracies.

The Catholic Church, the oldest NGO (Non Governmental Organization) with the Orthodox and Protestant churches deeply influences 1/3 of the world's population. The sixth century creation of Islam is now the fastest growing religion with 1/6 of humanity. The probable visit of Marco Polo to Asia and China provided us with the first, though highly exaggerated, history of the world. Although the Chinese and Koreans perfected the printing press a thousand years before, the Renaissance and Reformation between 1400 to 1650 reopened the

West to the wisdom, art, and globalizing influence of ancient Greece and Rome.

At the same time, "the man of the second millennium," Johannes Gutenberg, opened up the West through the printing press, encouraging Europeans to become literate, to develop a middle class as well as great literature, art, and music and also scientific methodologies, and to conduct major geographical explorations. The eighteenth century gave us the American and French revolutions. The British, French, Portuguese, and Spanish colonization periods expanded globalization exponentially while placing Africans, Asians, and Latin Americans under their negative influence. The nineteenth century brought us early modern communication discoveries like the telegraph, trains, photography, telephone, light bulb, moving pictures, the bicycle, and the automobile. Marxism provided a counterbalance to the western development of capitalism. The twentieth century developed such positive major communication contributions as the radio, television, computer-mediated communication, and wireless technology. Negative impacts from World Wars I, and II, and in the latter case the horrors of the Holocaust led to the development of the modern field of communication.

The United Nations and later WTO further globalized the world. Genocides in Rwanda and Bosnia and other crimes against humanity negatively followed the "Cold War." in the midst of nuclear tensions between the US and the Soviet Union, China began opening up to the world, first in 1972, later with the 1978 and 1985 "opening up" by Deng Xiaoping in 1978 and 1985, followed economically by later Chinese leaders, Jiang Zemin and Hu Jintao.

Perhaps we are now in a post-cold war "Cold War" with new verbal skirmishes between Russia and the US, as President Putin reminds us that a new US missile system in Poland and the Czech Republic may reignite the "Cold War." other communication breakdowns as well include the devastating problems in the fifth year of the aftermath of the Iraq War, the resurgence of the Taliban in Afghanistan, other conflicts in the Middle East, plus nuclear technology and weaponry in

Iran and North Korea, the spread of hiv/aids and malaria, and terrorism, which continues to be a menacing global threat and the source of major communication breakdowns.

The serious study, critique and practice of positive versus negative communication scholars and media, organizational, intercultural and international communication have never been so important a global issue as it is today. Communication scholars and practitioners have the most critical responsibility to make the public in all sectors of society aware both of positive global communication and the negative communication breakdowns. It is a very special opportunity for us to recognize that while globalization is irreversible, our goal must always be to promote and analyze both positive communication and communication breakdowns.

We owe a very special debt to western communication innovators such as Johannes Gutenberg and Eastern leaders who continue to open up their countries to the world and the world to them.

Question 4: Many scholars believe that their role is solely to produce knowledge while others believe that scholars have an obligation to bring about social change. What do you consider to be the primary role of a researcher?

In my opinion, scholars have a vital double role, both to produce knowledge and to advocate social change, though not necessarily at the same time. Perhaps scholars who only produce knowledge but are removed from the real world as advocates are like cloistered monks or nuns. They have an important but limited function. We need thinkers and philosophers, but also "public thinkers" whose knowledge moves others toward one or another sort of positive action. The famous cloistered Trappist monk Thomas Merton's books moved millions of people world-wide toward a greater spirituality. He prayed several times daily with his fellow monks and taught the young monks theology, but he was clearly an advocate for spirituality.

Pope John Paul II had a doctorate in sacred theology, and wrote many books and papal encyclicals. He wrote and spoke eloquently for social change about religious and social issues, with addresses to more than 60 million people in his live audiences in nearly 90 countries. He was extremely powerful as one of the most significant world moral forces during the 25 years of his papacy. Some scholars credit him as one of the major influences both in a religious revival and in causing the collapse of Communism in central and Eastern Europe through his advocacy. When we advise graduate students for their theses, we encourage them to leave their call for social change out of their literature reviews, methodologies, and discussion of results.

However, we may also encourage them to call for social change in clearly delineated sections of the thesis such as recommendations in the conclusion. For example, a thesis, dissertation or book on educational reform first identifies the nature of the problem, offers various options to solve the problem, and typically advocates specific reforms that the writer believes should be introduced.

Sometimes at different times in our lives we produce knowledge at one point, and advocate social change at another stage. In this way, we have a significant double influence on society. We speak of the need for objectivity instead of personal subjectivity in our scholarship. The field of communication has many topics that specifically call for action, for example in public speaking, intercultural, organizational or mass communication. We provide our readers the information and then detail how to use the information to make them better speakers (or writers), better interculturalists, better organizational members or leaders, or better active users or producers of the mass media.

After all, we are interested in a particular topic first because of our personal subjective passion, and no matter how much we try or how objective the empirical research appears, our own biases and goals still remain a significant aspect of the research. In my view, this double perspective, as knowledge producers and as advocates of social change moves us out of the isolated "ivory tower" and makes us vital societal leaders through our advocacy for social change. Both should be complementary.

Question 5: You have been living in China since 2001 and have had extensive intercultural experience prior to your relocation. How, if at all, has this affected your personal and professional worldview?

In the late 1960's and the 1970's, I was an active founder establishing the intercultural communication field in North America. I led the first three North American foundational conferences to establish the field and participated actively in German-American communication conferences and the 1974 bicultural research conference in Japan. My own long and short-term teaching opportunities, including two in Canada, offered some of the first ic courses in the US and Canada. I actively developed professional divisions and organizations dedicated to intercultural and international communication (national communication association, international communication association, and the International Society for Intercultural Education, Training, and Research, for which I served as chair of the 1980 international congress and later as president from 1984–86).

In 1977, I was also a professor for mid-level executives and co-chaired scholar-diplomat seminars at the United States Information Agency working with L. Robert Kohls, one of the field's most outstanding interculturalists. Most of my edited and authored books have dealt with intercultural/international communication and media and the UN.

In the 1980's, I hosted international high school students each for several months from Sweden, Belgium, France, Brazil, Spain, South Africa, and Swaziland. Being an intercultural host father also thrust my own children into various positive or negative intercultural situations. I taught about 8800 university students such courses as intercultural communication, communication and social change, international media and the model United Nations Security Council.

I created ten high school Global Awareness Days at the University of Virginia from 1983 to 1990. During 1990–1991, as a Fulbright professor at the University of Swaziland, I initiated their first courses for the new communication major. Additionally, I got caught up in the military invasion of the campus on November 14, 1990, where two to four students were killed and 300–400 were injured. I actively assisted eleven students to seek safety outside the campus.

In 1994, I declined a Fulbright professorship in Bulgaria to assume a distinguished professorship in communication at the Rochester Institute of Technology. There I had funds for creative activities such as hosting 33 public lectures on intercultural and international issues, and presenting eleven of them. I hosted four high school model UN Security Councils for 800 Rochester-area students; and was the faculty advisor for RIT students at five model United Nations in Toronto and Montreal.

With K.S. Sitaram, I co-hosted six Rochester Intercultural Conferences, and co-authored or co-edited two books on intercultural and international communication. Overlapping the 1990s and early 2000s, I was series editor for 17 books in my series "Civic Discourse for the Third Millennium," two of which were on Chinese communication. Finally, I became "the host father" in the South Sudan community of Rochester, New York, including having young Sudanese adults living in my home over several years. I was a member of the growing welcoming committee for about half of the seventy-eight "lost Boys of sudan" who resettled in Rochester just before I went to China in 2001.

In a sense then, I blended my professional interests in developing the intercultural communication field and lived an intercultural life as well. Host father for various international high school students, host for many Swazi students in my University of Swaziland home and advocate for them because of the military campus invasion, finally I became a host leader for the South Sudan community in Rochester, New York. These personal intercultural activities have vastly enriched my life and have put into real practice the more theoretical constructs which I have taught and written about. It has been a pleasing intercultural life experience.

Question 6: You have been one of the founders of the academic field of intercultural communication as well as the founding chair of the International and Intercultural Communication Division of the National Communication Association. Do you believe the field has changed since its inception? If so, how?

As I have noted earlier, I was among the founders of the field of intercultural communication in North America, chairing the first three foundational North American conferences (1971, 73, 74). The 1974 summer NCA, ICA, and SIETAR International Chicago conference had 200 participants studying Edward C. Stewart's *Outline of Intercultural Communication.* NCA's proceedings were co-edited by Nemi Jain, Melvin Miller and me. At my speech on China at George Mason University in February, 2007, one senior faculty member reminded me that he was there, which began his life-long interest in teaching intercultural communication.

I was the third chair of the ICA Division of Intercultural and Development Communication founded by K.S. Sitaram and others in 1970. I was responsible for 13 intercultural and international communication programs at the 1977 ICA Berlin conference.

As a founding governing council member of SIETAR international, I was its president from 1984–86. In my essay, "One World, One Dream: Harmonizing Society through Intercultural Communication: A Prelude to China Intercultural Communication Studies" in Steve J. Kulich's and my co-edited book, *Intercultural Perspectives on Chinese Communication* (2007: Shanghai: Shanghai Foreign Language Education Press, pp. 22–91), I have included the following main sections: "The Significance of Values to the Study of Intercultural Communication"; "Early Intercultural Communication Development in the US: 1959–1979"; "Intercultural Communication: A Mature Field: 1980–2006"; "Practical Applications: Cross-cultural Training: 1950s to 2005"; "China's Contributions to 'One World, One Dream' — Harmonizing Society Interculturally"; and 12 pages of "References."

In my discussion on ic as a mature field since 1980, I highlight Geert Hofstede, Michael Harris Bond, William B. Gudykunst, Stella Ting-Toomey, Young Yum Kim, my "Civic Discourse for the Third Millennium" series, D. Ray Heisey's series on Chinese communication, selected books, and our ic program at Shanghai International Studies University, and others. In my section on practical applications in cross-cultural training, 1950s to 2005, I stress the US AID Communication Seminars and the Portland SIIC Summer Institute (now in its 31st year).

In the essay, I have not discussed ic developments in European, Latin American, Middle Eastern or African countries, or Asian countries besides China, intercultural business communication, interpretation and translation, comparative literature, social linguistics, cross-cultural psychology or intercultural mass media studies and my references miss reporting on several recent important books in ic, with much more historical work needing more careful consideration.

Thus, in my own review of the field, I have left out a lot of the important history, though some other essays in our book highlight sociolinguistics, for example by Steve Kulich and Yuxin Jia and Xuerui Jia, or cross-cultural psychology, for example by Michael Harris Bond, and the indigenous cross-cultural psychologist, Kwang-Kuo Hwang. Gudykunst's last edited book, *Theorizing about Intercultural Communication* (2005, Sage) provides a very strong identification of ic today as a mature field. Samovar and Porter's *Intercultural Communication: A Reader* (1972–2005, Wadsworth) has now been a significant student anthology for the last thirty-six years. Cultural competence and cultural identification are now major topics in ic studies.

The major point that can be made is that since 1980 as the field began to mature, ic has become a very important concept not only in North America, but in many other regions of the world. A remarkable contribution in China is seen in the ic development, especially since 1994. In the last year, I have attended conferences in Russia, Peru, Germany, and seven communication conferences in China, including the most recent June, 2007 intercultural communication conference in Harbin. All of them have had at least an intercultural communication component, with several having ic as the major feature.

The changes are very significant in theory, practice, and case studies since our nascent beginnings, and suggest that more and more theories, including an increasing number of indigenous ones, will push the field into greater maturity. In China, ic leaders are beginning to consider requesting that the ministry of education designate ic as a principal field in Chinese universities, with a national roundtable on creating ic as a discipline under planning stages at Shanghai International Studies University.

Question 7: In his presidential column from the June/July 2006 issue of Spectra, Dan O'Hair calls attention to NCA's failure to provide an "opportunity for interaction and collaboration with international colleagues," a concern which you yourself mirrored in your essay entitled "The Communication Field Reaching Out to International Scholars." What effect, if any, do you believe the opportunity to exchange ideas and scholarship with our international colleagues could have on the field in general and on the individual cultures in particular?

William Howell, President of NCA (then SCA) in 1971, earlier recommended that SCA should demonstrate its commitment to internationalization by holding its 1970 convention in Hong Kong, then still a crown colony of the UK. The small

SCA Committee for Cooperation with Foreign Universities, of which I was a member, enthusiastically supported this proposal, but the Legislative council reacted in shock with the idea that the organization was more than an American-based one, and that such a convention would be impossible for most American members to attend because of the transportation costs. At that time, our committee had already successfully co-sponsored the first German-American communication conference in Heidelberg, Germany, in 1968, and was going to co-sponsor the first Japan-US communication conference in Tokyo in 1969.

These, however, were only footnotes in the history of the organization. When the Legislative Council turned down the Hong Kong convention idea and selected New Orleans for the 1970 convention, Howell and our committee recommended that our keynote speaker should be Angie Brooks of Liberia, then the UN General Assembly President. Racial sensitivities on the part of our colleagues in the SCA leadership and local potential sponsors in New Orleans also found this idea to be unacceptable.

Nonetheless, under the leadership of K.S. Sitaram, the fifth division in ICA, Intercultural and Development Communication, was formed in 1970, and ICA may have held its first conference outside of the US with the 1973 Montreal site. SCA and the Canadian Communication Association held it first foundational meeting in 1971 for what later became our International and Intercultural Communication Division under my leadership at Indiana University.

In 1995, Sitaram and I co-chaired the first of six Rochester Intercultural Conferences, entitled "Intercultural Communication at Twenty-Five: The Present and the Future" to celebrate what we identified as the twenty-fifth anniversary of the founding of the intercultural field in 1970 under Sitaram's leadership for ICA and 1971 for SCA under my leadership.

Today, the Fulbright program, NCA, ICA, the American Communication Association, the World Communication Association, the Association for Education in Journalism and Mass Communication, the American Broadcast Association, the

International Association for Intercultural Communication Studies, the Chinese Communication Associations in North America, the Korean Communication Association, the Japan-America Communication Association, the African Association for Communication Education, SIETAR in various regions, the Asia–Pacific Business Communication Association, the Asian international Mass Communication Association, the International Academy for Intercultural Research, the China Association for Intercultural Communication Association, and many other communication organizations in Latin America, Asia, Europe, Africa, and the Middle East all are recognizing the critical importance of academic scholarly and practical exchanges in the field of communication.

I was pleased to serve as a co-keynoter with former NCA President, Dan O'Hair, at the May 31-June 2, 2007 Chendu, China, "Globalization and Western China Conference," where we exchanged useful views about the importance of the internationalization of the communication field. Later I was one of six co-keynoters at the June 22–24, 2007 Harbin, Seventh international China intercultural Communication Symposium, co-sponsored by the International Association for Intercultural Communication Studies, with more than 500 participants, including 30 from Russia, on the theme "Harmony, Diversity and Intercultural Communication."

Naturally, I have been convinced for most of my professional and cultural life that internationalization of the communication discipline and exchanges among communication scholars, practitioners, and students is every more critical. Middle Eastern scholars, for example, recommend that instead of a view toward Samuel Huntington's "clash of civilizations," we should instead be having a "dialogue of civilizations" as a way to better understanding between cultural groups throughout the world. As the internet used to be called the "information superhighway," for me personally, it now allows me frequent exchanges with faculty, professionals, and students in several countries. A few thousand people have viewed my website, www.michaelprosser.com and some remind me regularly to update my essays there.

Ongoing contacts through being interviewed earlier 12 times on China Central TV International and more recently regularly on China Radio International; at the ten international communication conferences which I have attended in the last years; and engaging with hundreds of students annually in my teaching or lectures in China all enrich my communicative world.

I hope that those who encounter me in these ways have their world enriched as well. Our goal should always be to move from communication breakdown to international communication competence, and from misunderstanding to understanding in the words of I.A. Richards many years ago in *Ideas Have Consequences*.

Question 8: Could you tell us some of the experiences you have had that are important to learning the ropes as a new student and scholar in the discipline?

With BA and MA English degrees (and communication and Latin minors), I first joined the University of Illinois Ph.D. program in English, but I switched to communication, making English my minor. Thankfully, significant reforms in MA and Ph.D. education have occurred since I was a student. In English for example, though I had already taken the History of English as an MA student, I was required to take it again. As English majors, we were required to take a semester of Beowulf in the original early English, but my intended major concentration was American literature. We also had to memorize hundreds of English authors, their works, and first lines, for an early departmental exam.

As a Ph.D. Student, I requested Latin as one of my two foreign languages, but was turned down because it was considered irrelevant to my study. Afterwards, I was a serious student of classical rhetoric, where both Greek and Latin were highly relevant. My year-long post graduate courses in French and German, only to translate 3 pages in 3 hours with a dictionary, meant that I learned these languages superficially, and with zero use as a scholar.

The first communication comprehensive exams dealt not with what we had learned as post graduates, but drama, phonetics, speech science, and debate, all learned as a college sophomore or junior. Fortunately, my Ph.D. advisor, Halbert E Gulley, had me audit communication theory for some background outside of rhetoric. He wisely challenged my early dissertation topics, but encouraged me to concentrate rhetorically on the addresses of Adlai Stevenson at the UN. He got me a $1000 grant to collect information there. This very valuable research led to 3 books, one, *Readings in Classical Rhetoric,* a second, a collection of Stevenson's speeches on international topics, and another, a two-volume collection of addresses by heads of state and government at the UN.

I did not have the reasonable time to study anthropology, despite the University of Illinois having outstanding cultural anthropologists such as Oscar Lewis who would have informed my later serious involvement in intercultural communication.

Hopefully, North American MA and Ph.D. programs now concentrate on what is really important for one's development as a scholar. Thus, an important recommendation is to remember that the ultimate educational goal develops in the thesis or dissertation, for which one needs to be passionate. All possible efforts should be directed toward that end, eliminating as much irrelevant material as possible. The right open-minded advisor is as critical as is the best choice of a thesis or dissertation. Post graduates should remember that very important future possible research topics may originate in their early research.

Additionally, post-graduate students should remember that they may forever be linked to their thesis or dissertation, so they should choose their topic wisely. As an MA student, Tom Bruneau got deeply involved in silence studies. He read everything possible on the subject, and today much of his reputation as a scholar is linked to that topic ("Silence, Silences, and Silencing"). Later, intrigued with the brain, he researched every possible aspect of brain study, and made it one of his recognized areas of expertise. In a similar way, one of my chief teaching and research topics today remains the United Nations, generated by my dissertation enthusiasm.

Question 9: Could you describe some of your most memorable experiences since your move to China?

Coming to China in 2001 began perhaps in the late summer of 1989 when I became a volunteer community host for a new physics Ph.D. student at the University of Virginia from Peking University. The dean of English in a Guangzhou university invited me to teach in Guangzhou in 1992–93. It was then impossible.

In November 2000, at the Seattle NCA convention, Kluver and Powers' 1999 book, *Civic Discourse, Civil Society, and Chinese Communities* in my Ablex "Civic Discourse for the Third Millennium" series won an outstanding book award. Chinese colleagues asked me about teaching in China after retiring from UVA and the Rochester Institute of Technology in 2001. My response was "why not?"

Shuming Lu organized my joining the Yangzhou University English Department in 2001. Wenshan Jia organized for me to be a keynoter in the 2001 Xi'an China Intercultural Communication Association forum. Beijing Language and Culture University's vice president invited me to come to teach there. Steve Kulich at Shanghai International Studies University encouraged me to join his intercultural communication program in 2005. I found myself teaching in English departments or colleges at these three universities. In Yangzhou, my teaching included mass media for juniors; intensive reading for seniors; intercultural communication, rhetoric and public discourse, and American literature for post graduates; and oral English for young instructors of various subjects whose English was limited.

At BLCU, where there are 1500 international students and 4,000 Chinese students, I taught primarily Western Civilization for all of the English major seniors, and debate and advanced writing for juniors. At SISU, I have taught freshman and sophomore oral English, my model UN Security Councill simulation for juniors and English and international relations postgraduates, public speaking, intercultural communication, and global media and culture. Numerically, I taught 1800 Chinese university students, plus many primary and secondary Saturday and winter English camp pupils.

I have given public lectures to more than 6,000 secondary and university students in China, India, and Russia. I was interviewed 12 times on China Central TV International's "Dialogue" program. I have visited many Chinese cities, plus Cambodia, El Salvador, Greece, India, Peru, South Korea, Russia, nine countries in Europe, and Viet Nam during my time in China. I have attended 15 Chinese communication conferences as keynoter for about eight. I have reviewed 32 books about China for the online *journal Review of Communication*.

I am known beyond China for my many CRTNET posts on China. I have co-edited two books related to China. I have read 24 MA theses in intercultural communication. Intellectually, and more importantly, I have vastly expanded my own knowledge base both in the field of English as it complements communication studies, and in intercultural communication, but particularly in values and Chinese communication studies, where some of our post graduates have had a much broader background.

Now, I have more or less caught up with the latest research trends in intercultural communication and am eager to continue to contribute to Chinese communication conferences and scholarly editing and writing, as exemplified by Steve Kulich's and my co-edited *Intercultural Perspectives on Chinese Communication* (2007), and the values studies books that he and I are co-editing for the Shanghai Foreign Language Education Press as a special mandate for SISU's new Intercultural Institute.

Question 10: As our interview comes to an end, we would like to thank you for your participation and ask that you make a final conclusion and share with us any final words of wisdom that you may have.

My two-month solo European travel at 22, again to Europe, including Russia, at 23 gave me a strong intercultural/international interest. Early attendance at conferences in Canada, Germany, Japan, Mexico, and the UK and teaching in Canada twice enhanced it. My Ph.D. advisor, Hal Gulley's openness, for my Ph.D. dissertation relating to addresses at the United Nations and collecting materials for six weeks there were very informative. Distant mentors like Fred Casmir, John Condon, Edward Hall, Ray Heisey, David Hoopes, Robert Oliver, Beulah Rohrlich, K.S. Sitaram, Edward Stewart, Lynn Tyler, and William Howell and having outstanding intellectually curious postgraduate students further developed my enthusiasm. Serving as chair of the first three North American foundational conferences to develop intercultural communication, publishing early books and my intercultural leadership in NCA, ICA, and SIETAR *International* all strengthened my intercultural/international background. In the 1980's as the field began to mature theoretically, I became very active experientially as an annual host father for several international high school students and organized annual Global Awareness Days for 2200, including 500 international high school students.

In this way, I began to live an intercultural life as well as being professionally dedicated to ic. I lived an intercultural life more fully as a Fulbright professor at the University of Swaziland in 1990–91.there, we faced significant cultural and intercultural conflict when the military invaded the campus on November 14, 1990, killing 2–4 students and injuring 300–400. On that single day, as we protected five women students and helped Canadian friends get 11 frightened students to safety outside the beleaguered campus, we and other expatriates thought we might surely die. Subsequently, we and our students lived through two months of university closure and later a national judicial inquiry. This extended event became for me one of my worst days and one of my best — seeing the yin and yang of evil and goodness.

In the 1990's at the Rochester Institute of Technology, I had the opportunity for significant intercultural creativity: as an advisor for university and high school model UNs in Rochester and Canada, hosting 33 lectures while delivering 11 on intercultural and international topics, publishing 3 books, serving as series editor for 17 books in the Ablex "Civic Discourse for the Third Millennium" series, and with K.S. Sitaram, hosting six Rochester Intercultural Conferences, in joint intercultural endeavors at the beginning and ending of our professional North American careers.

My 2001–07 Chinese teaching experience has brought me to a full circle for intercultural communication, both theoretically and experientially. Besides teaching China's youth, China's future, I have lived the most comprehensive intercultural life possible, including traveling and living with young Chinese. I have moved from being Eurocentric to Africacentric to asiacentric. I have traveled in and outside China extensively, opening up both my world and that of Chinese friends. As intercultural teachers and scholars, we have the opportunity to expand the field of intercultural communication exponentially in many cultural and national settings. Ideally of course, we are not just developing our now mature field theoretically, but practically through case studies and applications, and our own lived experiences. My favorite secular quote is that of Socrates: "I am neither a citizen of Athens, nor of Greece, but of the world." Our goal as interculturalists is becoming world citizens.

38. Intercultural Dialogue: an Interview with Professor Michael H. Prosser, Ph.D. by Li. Mengyu, Ph.D., Ocean University of China

Published by the Shangdong Foreign Language Teaching Journal, 2011, Vol. 32, 6

> Question 1: As we know you are one of the founders in intercultural communication in Northern America, and you are actively involved in the field; for instance, you started the early teaching of intercultural communication courses in the us, helped organize many international conferences on intercultural communication, and edited and wrote a large number of books related to the field, could you please introduce in more details about your major contributions to the field?

In 1967 when the Speech Communication Association Committee for Cooperation with Foreign Universities met, we began to discuss informally the need to create an academic field of intercultural or cross-cultural communication. We weren't quite sure of the precise name. In the mid to late 1960s, courses began to develop in various American universities. I taught my first intercultural/cross-cultural communication class at Indiana University in 1970, using Everett C. Rogers' book on innovation in Latin America. In fact, this made this course more of a class on communication and social change than just intercultural/international communication. In 1970, K. S. Sitaram and others initiated the Intercultural and Development Communication Division for the International Communication Association. In 1995, he and I co-chaired the first of six Rochester Intercultural Conferences

(1995–2001), celebrating the founding of the academic field of study, 25 years earlier.

In 1971, the speech communication association sponsored a consultation at Indiana University (Brown county state park) to begin to establish intercultural communication as a distinct subject of academic study. Speech Communication association President William Howell, Canadian Speech Communication Association President Grace Layman, Edward C. Stewart, Edmund Glenn, Fred Casmir, I and others plus about a dozen of my postgraduates, most notably, William J.Starosta (my first Ph.D. in intercultural communication). Barbara Monfils, Sherry Ferguson, and Iris Gonzalez met to discuss two key topics: the content of the future academic study field and the process of developing it.

In 1973, at the University of Virginia (Masanettan Conference), about 55 of us met to develop academic syllabi in intercultural communication and communication and social change. In practical terms, the US Navy sent a small delegation too. My book, was published that year. In 1974, 200 of us met in Chicago, under the sponsorship of the Speech Communication Association, International Communication Association, and the International Society for Intercultural Education, Training, and Research, using Edward Stewart's *Outline of Intercultural Communication* as a foundational document for building the field's content. A proceedings was published by the Speech Communication Association. Also, in 1974, a bicultural Japanese/American research conference was held in Nihonmatsu, Japan to discover the similarities and differences in the two cultures' communication patterns. I have described the dialogue which took place there in my book, (1978, 1985, and 1989) and translated into Japanese in 1982.

In 1974, Fred L. Casmir became the first editor of the International and Intercultural Communication Annual, published annually for twenty-five years under the sponsorship of the Speech Communication Association/National Communication Association, when it became a regular journal. In 1978, under the sponsorship of L. Robert Kohls at the United States Information Agency, I had the opportunity to teach a course in intercultural communication for midlevel executives, and served as a consultant to the vice director of the agency. Later, in 1979 and 1980, I was the coordinator for 23 half hour programs on intercultural communication for world-wide broadcast in English on the Voice of America.

These were the formative years of the development of intercultural communication as an academic field of study. As I described in my essay for Steve J. Kulich's and my coedited book Intercultural *Perspectives on Chinese Communication*, the 1980s and 1990s saw the maturation of this field of study, both in North America and abroad, including its rapid development in China. Professor Sitaram and I returned to work together by hosting the six Rochester Intercultural communication conferences (1995–2001) on specific themes, and by coediting two volumes on intercultural and international communication and media.

In 1998–2004, I served as the series editor for the publication of 17 books related to intercultural and international communication and media under the sponsorship of Ablex, Praeger, and Greenwood Publishing Group. From 2001 to 2009, I taught intercultural communication or global media at several Chinese universities, including most recently in 2011 at Ocean University of China. During the 2010/2011 period, you, Professor Li Mengyu, and I coauthored an intercultural communication text book, *Communicating Intercultur*ally, which is now in press with Higher Education Press. We hope that this book will become a model for understanding the importance of intercultural communication for Chinese students. In 2009 and 2011, I was pleased to receive a special contribution award for contributions to the development and study of intercultural communication in China by the China Association for Intercultural Communication.

Question 2: You like to quote Socrates' famous saying "I am a citizen, neither of Athens, nor of Greece, but of the world." What is the significance of the quotation to intercultural communication?

In 1986, the International Society for Intercultural Education, Training, and Research gave me an award entitled "Global Citizen" award, based on the statement of Socrates. This has encouraged me to make this my most favorite secular quotation in all of my teaching, whether in North America, Swaziland, or China. I firmly believe that it is an obligation for those of us who teach intercultural communication to assist our students both to become critical thinkers, and also to become more and more multicultural in their outlook, ending as true global citizens of the world. I have moved several steps in that direction, as explained in my keynote address at the Shanghai International Studies University June 2010 Symposium on intercultural Communication: "Being There: Steps Along the Way in the Development of Intercultural Communication as an Academic Study."

Question 3: You often call yourself "ChinAmerican," after many years of living in China, what do you think of your cultural identity now?

Actually, in 2009, some of our Shanghai International Studies University MA students started calling me "ChiAmerican" neither fully Chinese (as a foreign teacher), not entirely American (but retaining my American identity), and becoming broader in my outlook. Having spent nearly 10 years in China, I have assimilated some of the very positive aspects of Chinese culture, while also being fully American. There is a saying: "You can take Michael out of America, but you can't take America out of Michael." I like the term, ChiAmerican, and am pleased that some of my students began calling me by that name.

Question 4: You have taught in China for nearly ten years, and got to know Chinese culture and people quite well, what do you learn from Chinese culture and people?

Socrates not only made the famous quote above, but he said that his goal was to become truly wise, just, honest, and a good person, and if one were to accept the name of a philosopher, he would aspire to be such a person. In Plato's Socratic dialogues, he has Socrates give the impression that he seeks to know more, and in fact to be a "gadfly on the horse that is the establishment. Reading the dialogues, however, we become convinced that Socrates is indeed one of the wisest early thinkers and philosophers and seeks through dialogue (dialectic) to seek the truth by discussing ideas with wise others.

In China, my fondness for Western philosophy, and Descartes' famous quote, "I doubt, therefore I think; I think therefore I am" has blended with an increasing interest in the wisdom of Confucius and Mencius and their applications to modern Chinese life. Although, I have in fact learned almost no Chinese, I have been a serious student of contemporary China since its founding in 1949 and read as many books as possible to give me a clearer understanding of Chinese culture. Having taught 2,300 Chinese students, and giving lectures to another 8,500 Chinese secondary and university students, as well as giving volunteer classes for Chinese kindergarteners, primary school pupils, secondary students, and university students, I have developed a special interest in Chinese youth, as has been demonstrated in our joint book, *Communicating Interculturally* to be published soon by Higher Education Press.

Question 5: What do you think of the Western and Eastern civilizations' contributions to the world respectively? Particularly, what do you think of the far-reaching influences of the great thinkers such as Socrates and Confucius?

I have briefly discussed these points above. It appears to me that Western and Asian thinking, philosophy, and customs have often merged, although recognizing that there are still many major differences between the cultures. As Deng Xiaoping claimed, the Chinese have learned a lot from the West, and it is wise to take the best of each culture as complimentary, while acknowledging that there are major differences between the cultures. Now, there are 100,000 young Chinese studying in the United States alone on an annual basis, and perhaps 100,000 young Americans studying Chinese language and culture in China (including, for example, nearly 1,500 studying Chinese at the Beijing Language and Culture University, and also as exhibited by the many Confucius centers and Chinese language classes which have developed in Western countries. The fact that more Chinese are studying English than the entire populations of the US, Australia, Canada, New Zealand, and Belgium attests to that development in international and intercultural understanding.

Personally, without the ability to teach my courses in China in English, many foreign experts and I would never have had the opportunity to learn so much about contemporary China and Chinese youth. For this I am quite grateful.

Question 6: As we can see, there is a growing tendency of globalization in today's world, on the one hand, the American culture appears to be the most powerful, for instance, Hollywood movies, fast foods like Macdonald's and KFC seem to sweep over the world; on the other hand, with the rapid economic development, China seem to exert more and more influence on the world. What is your remark on the phenomena? How can globalization and localization be balanced for the world?

Martin Jacques, in his 2010 book, *When China Rules the World*, argues that although much modernization in China and more broadly in Asia is Western-oriented, which can be tested by such comparisons as clothing and cosmetics, food, language, power and policy, there are indeed many Western influences, depending on which Asian country we are considering. Nonetheless, he proposes that in the end, Asian, and Chinese society will determine its own modernization by what works in each of these societies. Although we think that Macdonald's and KFC have large market shares in several of these countries, in fact, Yum owns many more franchises than the Western restaurants — both with Western and Chinese franchises, in fact, at the end of the day, each Asian society adopts what is practical for it, and rejects what is not practical.

Question 7: Ever since intercultural communication has been introduced to China, it has developed quite rapidly; in your view, what are the strengths and weaknesses of intercultural communication teaching and research in China now compared with that of us?

With China just beginning to develop intercultural communication as a field of study in the mid 1980's as it was becoming mature in North America, it has indeed moved forward very rapidly, and is now entering its own mature stage. Progress is increasingly rapid today, both in technology and in idea development, but in the latter case, still within the context of traditional and modernizing societies. I like to think of two events in recent Chinese history, the 2008 Olympics, and the Shanghai World Expo, as major indicators of the possibility of positive intercultural interaction and exposure. Although the Han culture plus 55 minorities are in frequent interaction, more and more Westerners, Africans, Middle Easterners, Latin Americans, and other Asians need to come to China to work or study, and more and more Chinese should go abroad to work and study. Being a short-term tourist is a good start, but only when we spend a long time in another country, do we begin to understand our own culture better, and then see how it interacts with the new culture in which we are a part.

Question 8: Until now, you say you have traveled to 64 countries and numerous cities in the world. You seem to be a global citizen; what do you think of the international traveling experience helping to widen your horizon as well as your understanding of various people from different parts of the world?

Fourth-century Augustine of Hippo claimed that unless we have traveled, we have not yet opened the book of life. Personally, I traveled briefly in North America with my parents as a teenager; then when I graduated from university, I began to travel for a two month period in Europe. Then many more trips developed with my family and personally. Since I came to China in 2001, I have also traveled to Japan, India, Cambodia, Viet Nam, Thailand, the Philippines, Singapore, Malaysia, Indonesia, South Korea, Australia, New Zealand, Latin America, and Europe. I always encourage young Chinese to get a passport, as they never know when an opportunity might develop to go out of China, and have their world broadened. I have taken 7 young Chinese out of China, and almost all of them have a much broader world outlook because of this travel. Three of my young grandchildren have come to China, and one has gone to Spain, setting the stage for more broadening international travel in the future.

Question 9: You prefer to say "Thinking globally; acting locally," what does this suggest to be a global citizen?

This is an international slogan. Toward becoming world citizens, we need to know as much as possible, not only about our own society, but also other societies near and far from our borders. When an earthquake, or tsunami, or typhoon strikes one country or region, we all have an obligation to help in such situations to the extent possible. For Chinese, it may mean becoming friends with foreigners, or letting go of past national injuries or insults. If I had never gone to teach in China, I would have had contacts with American born Chinese, or Chinese overseas students, who are already Westernized, but I probably would never have learned to have deep friendships with Chinese colleagues and students.

Question 10: You have written one paper entitled *"One World, One Dream: Harmonizing Society through Intercultural Communication: A Prelude to China Intercultural Communication Studies";* then according to your opinion, how can we harmonize the world through intercultural communication when political, cultural and religious differences still prove to be hidden barriers to mutual understanding in today's world?

The late D. Ray Heisey gave me three pieces of advice when I was first going to China to teach in 2001: 1. Patience; 2. Patience; 3. Patience. The same holds true for Chinese going to work or study abroad. It is not so easy to promote intercultural and international harmony, but it is a requirement for a more cooperative and positive relationship to develop. The Confucian concept of "ren" (benevolence, kindness) helps to lead us all toward a deeper understanding, wisdom, and happiness as a means of moving toward "the good life" means that we all must seek this harmony together. Or, as the ancient Chinese saying goes, "If you want to travel 1,000 kilometers, you must begin with a single step."

As the anthropologist Margaret Mead said, it takes a community to begin to build a better world, or as Hilary Clinton proposed, "It takes a village to grow a child." While building a better and harmonious domestic, regional, and international society, we need to acknowledge and practice these words of United Nations Secretary General Ban-Ki Moon" the biggest crisis is a lack of global leadership. There are too few citizens with an entirely new vision for the world, a vision that is informed by a sense of global responsibility." So, truly, we need to think globally, and act positively on a local level.

Biography

Michael H. Prosser, a founder of the academic field of intercultural communication, received his BA (1958) and MA degree (1959) from Ball State University, and his Ph.D. from the University of Illinois (1964).

He has received prestigious awards from Ball State University (1978); the International Communication Association (1978); SIETAR International (1986 and 1990); and the China Association for Intercultural Communication (2009 and 2011). He is listed in the Marquis Who's Who in American Education; Who's Who in America; Who's Who in Asia; and Who's Who in the World. He is a Fellow in the International Academy for Intercultural Research. He was featured in China Semimonthly Talents Magazine (2005, in Chinese). He has a page in Wikipedia. He has been interviewed numerous times on China Central Television's "Dialogue" programs and China Radio International, and was featured several times on Shanghai International Channel. He has been a keynoter at more than fifteen conferences in China, India, Russia, and the US.

He taught Latin in Urbana Junior High School, Urbana, Illinois (1960–63); and Communication at the University of Buffalo (1963–69); Indiana University (1969–72); the University of Virginia (1972–94), Chairman of the Speech Communication Department (1972–77); and Emeritus Professor, (2001); Fulbright Professor, University of Swaziland (1990–91); the William A. Kern and Distinguished Visiting Professor, Rochester Institute of Technology (1994–2001); College of Foreign Languages, Yangzhou University (2001–02); Distinguished Professor, College of English, Beijing

Language and Culture University (2002–05); Distinguished Professor, College of English (2005–07) and Communication and Journalism College (2007–09), Shanghai International Studies University; Distinguished Professor, Communication and Journalism College, Ocean University of China (spring, 2011); Faculty Advisor to Lifelong Learners, University of Virginia/Institute for Shipboard Education, Semester at Sea around the world study voyage (autumn (2011); and Distinguished Professor, College of International Studies, Yangzhou University (autumn 2013–14).

He has been a visiting faculty member at Queens College of the City of New York (summers, 1966–67); California State University at Hayward (summer, 1971); Memorial University of Newfoundland (summer, 1972); St. Paul University and the University of Ottawa (summer, 1975); the United States Information Agency (autumn, 1977); as Distinguished Visiting Professor, Kent State University (winter and spring quarters, 1978); George Washington University (spring, 1994), and the State University College of New York at Brockport (1997–98).

He is the author/coauthor, editor/coeditor of several books dealing with classical and medieval rhetoric; international discourses by Adlai E. Stevenson and at the United Nations; diplomatic discourse; intercultural, international, and global communication and media; Chinese communication and culture; intercultural, international, and global values; social media in Asia; and social media in the Middle East. From 1998–2004, he was series editor for seventeen books for "Civic Discourse for the Third Millennium" (Ablex, Praeger, and Greenwood Publishers) and Senior Coeditor for the intercultural research series at Shanghai Foreign Language Education Press beginning in 2006. He was President of SIETAR International (1984–86). Prosser was president of the United Nations Association of Rochester, New York (1997–98); and is a Fellow of the International Academy of Intercultural Research; a member of the Board of the Journal of Middle Eastern and Islamic Studies (in Asia) (2007–present); and a member of the International Advisory Board of the Dignity and Humiliation Studies Network.

Michael Prosser is the father of three children: Michelle, Leo, and Louis, and the grandfather of nine: Christine Ann, Elizabeth Marie, Mary Catherine Rose, Darya Serenity Michelle, Sanders Stephen Gabriel, Sophia Lily Grace, Conner Michael, Jordan Faith, and Luke Patrick.

He has been the host father for high school students from Sweden, Belgium, France, Brazil, Spain, South Africa, and Swaziland, and young adult refugees from El Salvador, and South Sudan.

His special interests include youth, peace, social justice, human rights and peace. He has traveled to sixty-nine countries.

Michael and his nine grandchildren, 2014

Books by Michael Prosser

Benson, T. W. & Prosser, M. H. (Eds.) (1969, 1972, 1985, 1989). *Readings in classical rhetoric.*

Cui, L. T. & Prosser, M. H. (Eds.) (2014). *Social media in Asia.*

Donahue, R. T. & Prosser, M. H. (1997). *Diplomatic discourse: International conflict at the United Nations.*

Kulich, S. J. & Prosser, M. H. (Eds.) (2007). *Intercultural perspectives on Chinese communication: Intercultural research: V01.1.*

Kulich, S. J., Prosser, M. H., & Weng L. P. (Eds.) (2012). *Value frameworks at the theoretical crossroads of culture: Intercultural research: Vol. 4.*

Kulich, S. J., Weng, L. P., & Prosser, M. H. (Eds.) (2014).*Value dimensions and their contextual dynamics across cultures: Intercultural research: Vol. 5.*

Li, M. & Prosser, M. H. (2012). *Communicating interculturally.*

Li, M. & Prosser, M. H. (2014). *Chinese communicating interculturally.*

Miller, J. M., Prosser, M. H., & Benson, T. W. (Eds.) (1973). *Readings in medieval rhetoric.*

Prosser, M. H. (Ed.) (1969). *An Ethic for Survival: Adlai Stevenson speaks on international issues, 1936–1965.*

Prosser, M. H. (Ed.) (1970). *Sow the wind, reap the whirlwind: Heads of state address the United Nations.* two volumes, deluxe, boxed set, and numbered for the twenty-fifth anniversary of the United Nations,

Prosser, M. H. (Ed.) (1973). *Intercommunication among nations and peoples.*

Prosser, M. H. (1978, 1985, 1989). *The cultural dialogue: An introduction to intercultural communication.* (1982). R. Okabe, translated into Japanese; (2013). He, D., translated into Chinese.

Prosser, M. H., Nurmakov, A., & Shahghasemi, E. (Eds.). (Forthcoming). *Social media in the Middle East.*

Prosser, M. H., Sharifzadeh, M., & Zhang, S. Y. (Eds.) (2013). *Finding cross-cultural common ground.*

Prosser, M. H. & Sitaram, K. S. (Eds.) (1999). *Civic discourse: Intercultural, international, and global media.*

Sitaram, K. S. & Prosser, M. H. (1998). *Civic discourse: Multiculturalism, cultural diversity, and global communication.*

Zhou, S. L., Prosser, M. H. & Lu, J. *Sino-American Compositions of Shared Topics.*

References

Amnesty International (1991). Amnesty International Report, 1991. New York, NY. Amnesty International.

Anderson, T. (1995). The den of lions: A startling memoir of survival and triumph. Xxx

Asante, M. K., Newmark, E. & Blake, C. (Eds.) (1979). Handbook of intercultural communication. Beverely Hills, CA: Sage.

Asuncion-Lande, N. (2008). English as the dominant language for intercultural communication: Prospects for the next century. In K. S. Sitaram and M. H. Prosser, Eds. Civic Discourse: Multicullturalism, cultural diversity, and global communication. Stamford, CT: Ablex.

August, O. (2007). Inside the red mansion: On the train of China's most wanted man. Boston, MA: Houghton Mifflin.

Baidu Encylopedia (2010). Jiang Zemin. Baidu Encylopedia. Trans.SinoPop.Org.HTTP://Baihe.Baidu.Com/Views/545466.HTM.

Bao Ninh (1998). The sorrow of war: A novel. English version by F. Palmos, from original translation, P. T. Hao. London, UK: Vintage.

Barme, G. R. with Lang, M. (Eds.) (2006). China candid: The people on the People's Republic. Berkley, CA: University of California Press.

Beker, J. (2000). The Chinese. New York, NY: The Free Press: Simon and Schuster.

Bennett, J. M. (2012: November). The public and private Dean Barnlund. In M.H. Prosser & Kulich, J.R. (Eds.). Special Issue: Early American pioneers of intercultural communication. Intercultural Journal of Intercultural Relations. Vol. 36. Issue 6. 780–788.

Benson, T. W. & Prosser, M. H. (Eds.) (1969; 1972; 1985, 1989). Readings in classical rhetoric. Boston, MA; Allyn and Bacon; Bloomington, IN: Indiana University Press; Davis, CA: Hermagoras Press.

Bevor, A. (1998), Stalingrad: The fateful siege, 1942–1943.London, UK: Viking.

Brown, L. R. et al (2000). The state of the world 2000.NEW YORK, NY: NORTON

Brown, L. R. (1995). Who will feed China?: Wake up call for a small planet. New York, NY: Norton and Co.

Bruneau, T. (2007). Paper presented to the China Association for Intercultura 1Communication Conference. Harbin, China: Harbin Institute of Technology.

Calloway-Thomas, C., Cooper, P. J. & Blake, C. (1999). Intercultural communication: Roots and routes. Boston, MA: Allyn and Bacon.

Cao, X. & G. (eighteenth century). Dreams of the red chamber.

Chang, I. (1997). The Rape of Nanking: The forgotten Holecaust of World War II. New York, NY: Basic Books.

Chang, J. & Haliday, J. (2005). Mao: The Untold Story. New York, NY: Random House.

Chay, J. (Ed.). (2000). Culture and international relations. New York, NY: Praeger.

Chen, G. M. & Starosta, W. J. (1998). Foundations of intercultural communication. Boston: Allyn and Bacon.

Chen, H. (1987). Simplified Chinese Characters. Torrance, CA: Heian.

China Ministry of Education (2009). Educational statistics.

Chinanews (2007). 100 million illiterates learned to read and write in decade. (retrieved 2007, September16, 2007). Chang, K. C. (1977).Food in Chinese Culture: Antropological and historical perspectives. New Haven, CT: Yale University Press.

Clarke, C. & Kanatani, K. (1979). Turn-taking no shikume: Turn-taking in small group discussion — a cross-cultural study. Language, Education and Technology. pp. 12–24 (in Japanese).

Clarke, R. A. (2004). Against all enemies: Inside America's war on terror. New York, NY: Free Press.

Clinton, H. R. (2010, January 21). Address at the Newseum on internet freedom. Washington, D.C.; US State Department.

Clinton, H. R. (2014). Hard choices. New York, NY: Simon and Schuster.

Clinton, H. R. & Geithner, T. (2009, JULY 27). A new strategic and economic dialogue with China. Wall Street Journal.

CNN (1998–99). The cold war series: The Chinese. Video. Narrated by K. Branagh; Directed by C. Clifford. Atlanta, GA: CNN.

CNN (1998–99). The cold war series: The sixties: Make love, not war. Video. Narrated by K. Branagh; Directed by C. Clifford. Atlanta, GA: CNN.

CNN (1998–99). The cold war series: The sixties: The Russians. Video. Narrated by K. Branagh; Directed by C. Clifford. Atlanta, GA: CNN.

Condon, J. C. & Saito, M. (Eds.) (1974). Intercultural encounters with Japan: Communication-contact and conflict. Tokyo, Japan: Simul Press.

Condon, J. C. & Saito, M. (Eds.). (1976). Communicating across cultures for what? A symposium on humane responsibility in intercultural communication. Foreword by K. R. Boulding. Tokyo, Japan. Simul Press.

Condon, J. C. & Yousef, F. (1975). An introduction to intercultural communication. Indianapolis, IN: Bobbs Merrill.

[Confucius]. (1999). The analects (Trans into English: A. Waley; Trans. Into modern Chinese Y. Bojun) (1999). Changsha, China: Hunan People's Publishing Hoouse.

Cooper, R. K. (2010, January 15). The Business Review: Intl' students flock to US. Schools. Institute of International Relations.

Cui, L. T. & Prosser, M. H. (Eds.) (2014). Social media in Asia. Lake Oswego, OR: Dignity Press.

Dai, X. & Kulich, S. J. (Eds.) (2010). Identity and intercultural communication: Theoretical and contextual constructions: Intercultural research, Vol. 2.Shanghai, China: Shanghai Foreign Language Education Press.

Dai, X. & Kulich, S. J. (Eds.) (2011). Intercultural adaptation (1): Theoretical explorations and emperical studies : Intercultural research. Vol. 6. Shanghai, China: Shanghai Foreign Language Education Press.

Davis, L. (2001). Doing culture. Cross-Cultural Communication in Action. Beijing, China: Foreign Language Teaching and Research Press.

de Paul, K. (1997). Children of Cambodia's killing fields: Memoirs by survivors. Compiled by D. Pran, Introduced by B. Kiernam. New Haven, CT: American Library Association.

Deng, R. ((2002). Deng Xiaoping and the cultural revolution: A daughter recalls the critical years.Trans. S. Shapiro). Beijing, China: Foreign Language Press.

Dillon, S. (2010, January 21). Foreign languages fade in class except Chinese. New York Times.

Dominic,, J. R. (1999). The dynamics of mass communication: Sixth edition. New York, NY.

Donahue, R. T. (Ed.)(200A2). Exploring Japaneseness: On Japanese concepts of culture and consciousness. Westport, CT: Ablex.

Donahue, R. T. & Prosser, M. H. (1997).Diplomatic discourse: International conflict at the United Nations. Stamford, CT: Ablex.

Dong, D. (2009, May 25). Reproducing Anti-Japanese Nationalistic Sentiments: A case study of contemporary Chinese youth. Paper presented at the annual meeting of the International Communication Association, Dresden International Conference Centre, Dresden, Germany.

Elegant, S. (2009, November2). China's international bad boy. Time Asia.

Ellul, J. (1964). The technological Society. New York, NY: Random House.

English Peoples' Daily Online (2009: December 4).

Evans, K. (2000). The lost daughters of China: Abandoned girls: Their journey to America and the search for a missing past. New York, NY: Jeremy P.Tarcher/Putnam.

Evans, R. (1993). Deng Xiaoping and the making of modern China. New York, NY: Viking.

Farrer, J. (2002). Opening up: Youth, Sex, Culture and market reform in Shanghai. Chicago, IL: The University of Chicago Press.

Fergunson, S. D. & Shade, L. R. (Eds.) (2002). Civic discourse and cultural politics in Canada: A Cacophony of voices. Westport, CT: Ablex.

Fleichman, H. L., Hopstock, P. J.,Pelczar, M. P., & Shelley, B. C. (PISA Databases, 2009,2012). PISA results in focus: What 15 year olds know and what they can do with what they know.NCE52011–004, NCE52013 -004. Washington, D.C: U.S. Department of Education, National Center for Education Statistics. U.S. Government Printing Office.

Fontaine, G. (1989). Managing international assignments: The strategy for success. Englewood Clifts, NJ: Prentice Hall.

Frannier, S. (2010, January 16). China at odds With future in internet fight. New York Times. Retrieved by China Digital Times.

French, H. W. (2014). China's second continent: How a million migrants are building a new empire in Africa. New York, NY Alfred A. Knoph.

Freire, P. (1996). The pedagogy of the oppressed. London, Penguin.

Gao, W. (2007). Zhou Enlai: The last perfect Revolutionary: A Biography. Trans. Peter Rand and Lawrence Sullivan. New York, NY: Public Affairs.

Geertz, C. (1974). The interpretation of cultures. New York, NY: Basic Books.

Gher, L. A. & Amin, H. Y. (EDS.) (2000). Civic discourse and age communications in the Middle East. Stamford. CT: Ablex.

Gifford, R. (2008). China road: A journey into the future of a rising power. New York: Random House.

Gittings, J. (2006). The changing face of China: From Mao to market. Oxford, England: Oxford University Press

Global Times (2009: November 30).

Gostin, L. (2007: 12–06) The journey of an Intercultural/International Communication Scholar: Dr. Michael Prosser. China Media Reports, pp. 104–117.

Gries, P. H. (2004). China's new nationalism: Pride, power, and diplomacy. Berkley, CA: University of California Press.

Gudykunst, W. B. & Kim, Y. Y. (1998). Communicating with strangers: An approach to intercultural communication.: Third edition. New York. NY: McGraw Hill.

Gudykunst, W. B., Tinag-Toomey, S., & Nishida, T. (Eds.) (1996). Communication in personal relationships in personal relationships across cultures. Thousand Oaks, CA: Sage.

Guterriez, G. (XXX). The power of the poor in history. Maryknoll, NY: Maryknoll.

Hachten, W. A. (1996). The world news prisim: Changing media of international communication. Fourth edition. Ames, IO: Iowa State University Presss.

Hall, E. T. (1959). The silent language. Garden City, NY: Doubleday.

Hall, E. T. (1966). The hidden dimension. Garden City, NY: Doubleday.

Harris, R. (2012, November). A different way of knowing: With respect to John C. (Jack) Condon. In M. H. Prosser & Kulich, J. R. (Eds.). Special Issue: Early American pioneers of intercultural communication. Intercultural Journal of Intercultural Relations. Vol. 36. Issue 6. pp. 798–809.

Heilig, G. K. (2008, MAY 15). China profile: Facts figures and Analyses. [Includes 11 academic wesites about China].

Heisey, D. R. (Ed.). (2000). Chinese perspectives in rhetoric and communication. Westport, CT: Ablex.

Heisey, D. R. & Gong, W. (Eds.). Communication and Culture: China and the world entering the 21st century. Amsterdam, The Netherlands: Editions Rodopi.

Henry, J. (1963). Culture against man. Middlesex, UK: Penguin.

Hesketh, T., Lu, L., & Zhi, W. X.(2005, September 15). The effect of Chinas one child family policy after 25 years. The New England Journal of Medicine.

Hoopes, D. W. (Ed.) (1971, 1972, 1973, 1974, 1975). Readings in intercultural communication, Vols. 1–5. Washington, D.C.SIETAR.

Hu, J. (2005). Address. National Conference for Improving Ideological Education For College Students. China Education and Research Network.

Hu, J. (2005: January 19) (China Education and Research Network.

Huntington, S. P. (1996). The clash of civilization and the remaking of the world order. New York, NY: Simon and Schuster.

Jacques, M. (2009). When China rules the world: The end of the western world and the birth of a new global order. London, UK: Penguin.

Jain, N. C., Prosser, M. H. & Miller, M. H. (Eds.) (1974). Intercultural communication; Proceedings of the Speech Communication Association summer conference, x. Falls Church, VA: Speech Communication Association.

Jamison, L. N. (1999). Understanding Vietnam. Berkeley, CA: Philip E. Lienthal Book, University of California Press.

Jia, W., Lu, X.,& Heisey, D. R. (Eds.) (xxx). Chinese communication theory and research: Reflections, new frontiers, and new directions. Westport, CT: Ablex.

Jia, Y. (2014). Foreword. In L. Mengyu & M. H. Prosser. Chinese communicating interculturally. Lake Oswego, OR: Dignity Press.

Jia, Y. & Jia, X. (2007). The study of Chinese language behavior cross-culturally: A sociolinguistic approach to intercultural communication. In S. J. Kulich & M. H. Prosser, Eds. Intercullltural perspecctives on Chinese communication. Shanghai, CHINA: Shanghai Foreign Language Education Press.

Jing, J. (2000). Feeding China's little emperors: Food, Children, and social change. Palo Alto, CA: Stanford University Press.

Kempton, N. (2010, January 7). China's horrid one child policy continues. The Huffington Post. (2010, January 26).

Kiernan, B. (2002). The Pol Pot regime: Race, power, and genocide in Cambodia under Khrmer Rouge, 1975–1979. New Haven, CT: Yale University Press.

Kissinger, H. (2011, 2012). On China. New York, NY. Penguin Books.

Klayman, A. (2010, January 21). China maintains tight grip on communications. WWW.VOANEWS.COM

Kluver, R. (2009). Elite-based discourse in Chinese civic discourse in J.H. Powers & R. Kluver (Eds.) Civic Discourse, civil society and Chinese Communities. Stamford, CT: Ablex.

Kluver, R. & Powers, J. H. (Eds.) (1999). Civic discourse, civil society, and Chinese communities. Stamford, CT: Ablex.

Kohl, L. R. (2001). A survival kit for overseas living. Yarborough, ME: Intercultural Press.

Kraykowski, K. (2009, JANUARY 11). Contemporary factors shaping Chinese youth: Chinese adolescents are shaped by a variety of forces.. WWW.CHINA.SUITE101.COM /Article.CFM.Modern Chinese Youth.

Kroeber, A. (2010: APRIL 11). Five myths about China's economy. Washington Post.

Kulich, S. J. (2012: November). Reconstructing the histories and influences of 1970s intercultural leaders: Prelude to biographies. In M.H. Prosser & J.R. Kulich (Eds.). Special Issue: Early American pioneers of intercultural communication. Intercultural Journal of Intercultural Relations. Vol. 36. Issue 6. 744–759.

Kulich, S. J. & Dai, X. (Eds.). (2012). Identity and intercultural communication (ii). Conceptual and contextual applications; Intercultural research. Vol. 3. Shanghai, China: Shanghai Foreign Language Education Press.

Kulich, S. J. & Dai, X. (Eds.)(2013). Intercultural adaptation (II): Conceptual foundations and contextual applications, Vol. 7. Shanghai, China: Shanghai Foreign Language Education Press.

Kulich, S. J. & Prosser, M. H. (Eds.) (2007). Intercultural perspectives on Chinese communication. Shanghai, China: Shanghai Foreign Language Education Press.

Kulich, S. J., Prosser, M. H., & Weng, L. P. (Eds.) (2012). Value frameworks at the theoretical crossroads of Culture, Vol. 4. Shanghai, China: Shanghai Foreign Language Education Press.

Kulich, S. J., Weng, L. P., & Prosser, M. H. (Eds.) (2014). Value dimensions and their contextual dynamics across cultures. Vol. 5. Shanghai, China: Shanghai Foreign Language Education Press.

Kuhn, R. L. (2010) How Chinese leaders think: The inside story of China's reform and what this means for the future. New York. NY: Wiley.

Kuhn, R. L. (2005). The man who changed China: The life and legacy of Jiang Zemin. New York, NY: Random House.

Kynge, J. (2006). China shakes the world: A titan's rise and troubled future – and the challenge for America. New York, NY: Houghton Mifflin.

Li, M. & Prosser, M. H. (2012). Communicating interculturally. Beijing, China: Higher Education Press.

Li, M. & Prosser, M. H. (2014). Chinese communicating interculturally. Lake Oswego, OR: Dignity Press.

Lin, Y. T. (1938). Moment in Peking. Xxx

Lindner, E. (2010). Gender, humiliation, and global security: Dignifying relationships from love, sex, and parenthood to world affairs. Santa Barbara, CA: Praeger Security international.

Lonely Planet Cambodia (2002). Sydney, Australia: Lonely Planet, Inc.

Lonely Planet India (2003). Sydney, Australia: Lonely Planet, Inc.

Lonely Planet Vietnam (2003). Sydney, Australia: Lonely Planet, Inc.

Loung Ung (2000). First they killed my father: A daughter of Cambodia remembers. New York, NY: Harper Collins Publishers.

Loveland, G. (2010, January, 11) Han Han says magazine stalled: Cites government censorship. Asia Headlines Examiner.

Lowell, J. (2009, April). It's just history: Patriotic education in the PRC. www.Chinadigitaltimes.net.

Luo, G. (fourteenth century). Romance of the three kingdoms. Xxx

Luttwak, E. N. (2012). The rise of China vs. the logic of strategy. Cambridge, MA: The Belnap Press of Harvard University Press.

Macmillan, M. (2007). Nixon and Mao: The week that changed the world. New York, NY: Random House.

Mao, T. D. (1957). Quotations from Mao Tse Tung, Chapter 30: Talk with Chinese Students and trainees in Moscow, November 17, 1957.

Mavidas, G. & Hayes, K. (2007). Foreign teachers' guide to living and working in China. MHTEAM@MIDDLEKINGDOMLIFE.COM

McNamera, R. S. (1995). In retrospect: The tragedy and lessons of Vietnam. New York, NY: Vintage.

McPhail, T.L. (2010) Global communication: Theories, Stakeholders, and trends. Third edition. Malden, MA: Wiley-Blackwell.

Mead, M. (1970). Culture and commitment: Garden City. New York, NY: Doubleday.

Meisner, M. (1986). Mao's China and AFTER: A history of the People's Republic of China. New York, NY: Free Press.

Miller, J. M., Prosser, M. H., & Benson, T. W. (Eds.) (1973). Readings in medieval rhetoric. Bloomington, IN: Indiana University Press.

Mo, Y. (1992). The republic of wine. Trans. from Chinese. H. Goldbatt. New York: NY: Arcade Publishing.

Mo, Y. (1993, 1994). Red sorghum. A novel of China. Trans. from Chinese. H. Goldbatt. Penguin Books.

Mo, Y. (1996). Big breasts and wide hips: A Novel. Trans. from Chinese. H. Goldbatt. New York: NY: Arcade Publishing.

Mo, Y. (1998). The garlic ballads. Trans. from Chinese. H. Goldbatt. New York: NY: Arcade Publishing.

Mo, Y. (2001, 2913). Sandlewood death: A novel. Trans. from Chinese. H. Goldbatt. Norman, OK: University of Oklahoma Press.

Mo, Y. (2001, 2011). Shifu, you'll do anything for a laugh. Trans. from Chinese. H. Goldbatt. New York: NY: Arcade Publishing.

Mo, Y. (2006, 2008, 2012). Life and death are wearing me out. Trans. from Chinese. H. Goldbatt. New York: NY: Arcade Publishing.

Mo, Y. (2012). POW! Trans. from Chinese. H. Goldbatt. London, UK: Seagull Books.

Moyo, D. (2012). Winner take all: China's race for resources and what it means for the world. New York, NY: Basic Books.

Murdoch, G. (1945) Common denominator of cultures. In R. Linton (Ed.) Science of man in the world crises. New York, NY: Columbia University Press.

No author (2002). The man who made a nation: Ho Chi Minh: The many faces of Vietnam, Hanoi, Viet Nam.

Oliver, R. T. (1971) Communication and culture in ancient India and China. Syracuse, NY: Syracuse.

Oliver, R. T. (1962). Culture and communication: The problem of penetrating national and cultural boundaries. Springfield, IL: Charles C. Thomas.

Osnos, E. (2014). Age of ambition: Chasing fortune, truth & faith in the new China. New York, NY; Farrar, Straus and Giroux.

Pedersen, P. (2005). A lesson in humility. In J. A. Kottler, J. A. & Carlson, J. (Eds.). The client who changed me: Stories of therapist personal transformation, 153–160. New York, NY: Routledge.

Pentagon papers (1996). New York Times.

Powers, J. H. & Kluver, R. (1999) Civic discourse, civil society and Chinese communities. Stamford, CT: Ablex.

Prosser, M. E. (2008). Excuse me, your God is waiting. Charlottesville, VA: Hampton Roads Press.

Prosser, M. H. (1964). A rhetorical analysis of the speech-making of Adlai E. Stevenson on major issues in the United Nations during the fifteenth and sixteenth sessions of the General Assembly. Unpublished doctoral dissertation, Urbana, IL: University of Illinois.

Prosser, M. H. (1968). Selected sources on contemporary communication and politics: 1948–1968. Today's Speech. (Communication Quarterly).

Prosser, M. H. (1968). Selected sources on modern communication, human rights, and social protest. Today's Speech (Communication Quarterly).

Prosser, M. H. (Ed.) (1968–1970). Today's speech: The Journal of the Eastern Communication Association.

Prosser, M. H. (Ed.) (1969). An ethic for survival: Adlai E. Stevenson speaks on international affairs, 1936–1965. New York, NY: William Morrow.

Prosser, M. H. (1969). Selected sources on modern international communication. Today's Speech (Communication Quarterly).

Prosser, M. H. (1972). Cross-cultural communication: A review essay. Today's Speech (Communication Quarterly).

Prosser, M. H. (1972). Communication and development: A review essay. Today's Speech (Communication Quarterly).

Prosser, M. H. (Ed.) (1973). Intercommunication among nations and peoples. New York, NY: Harper and Row.

Prosser, M. H. (1978, 1985, 1989).The cultural dialogue: An introduction to intercultural communication. Boston, MA: Houghton Mifflin; Washington, D.C.: SIETAR International. (1982). Roichi Okabe, translated into Japanese; Tokyo, Japan: Tokai University Press. (2013). He Daokuan, translated into Chinese. Beijing, China: Peking University Press.

Prosser, M. H. (Ed.) (1978). USIA intercultural communication course: 1977 Proceedings. Washington, D.C.: International Communication Agency.

Prosser, M. H. (1999). Media Reactions to "Bloody Wednesday" in Swaziland. In M. H. Prosser & K. S. Sitaram (Eds.) Civic Discourse: Intercultural, International, and Global Media. Stamford, CT; Ablex.

Prosser, M. H. (2003–14) www. Michaelprosser.com

Prosser, M. H. (2007). China: Selected books in English. Review of Communication [on line].7. 2.

Prosser, M. H. (2007). One world, one dream: Harmonizing society through intercultural communication: A prelude to China intercultural communication studies. In S. J. Kulich & M. H. Prosser, Intercultural perspectives on Chinese communication. Vol. 1, Shanghai, China: Shanghai Foreign Language Education Press.

Prosser, M. H. (2008–09). The unrelenting war. www. Michaelprosser.com

Prosser, M. H. (2009). Classical rhetorical theory. In S. Littlejohn & K. A. Foss. Eds. Encyclopedia of communication theory, Vol. 1. Los Angeles, CA: Sage.

Prosser, M. H. (2010). Contemporary Chinese youth: Language and culture in O. Leontovich (Ed.). (2010). Chinese lingoculture in the modern global world. Volgograd, Russia: Peremena Press.

Prosser, M. H. (2009). Cross-cultural communication. In S. Littlejohn & K. A. Foss. Eds. Encyclopedia of communication theory, Vol. 1. Los Angeles, CA: Sage.

Prosser, M. H. (2009). Media diplomacy. In S. Littlejohn & K. A. Foss. Eds. Encyclopedia of communication theory, Vol. 2. Los Angeles, CA: Sage.

Prosser, M. H. (2010: December). Reading discourse on the Middle East for intercultural understanding. Journal of Middle Eastern and Islamic Studies (in Asia). Vol. 3. Number 3.

Prosser, M. H. (2010, December). Reading Discourse on the Middle East for Intercultural Understanding"The Journal of Middle Eastern and Islamic Studies (in Asia), Vol. 3. Number 3.XXX.

Prosser, M. H. (2012). Universal human rights as universal values: A historical perspective. In S. J. Kulich, M. H. Prosser, & L. P. Weng (Eds.) Value frameworks at the theoretical crossroads of culture. V01.4. Shanghai, China: Shanghai Foreign Language Education Press.

Prosser, M. H. (2013). Asian modernity and intercultural communication. In M. H. Prosser, M. Sharifzadeh, & S. Y. Zhang (2013). Finding cross-cultural common ground. Lake Oswego, OR: Dignity Press.

Prosser, M. H. (2013). Discourse on the Middle East for new intercultural understandings. In M. H. Prosser, M. Sharifzadeh, & S. Y. Zhang (2013). Finding cross-cultural common ground. Lake Oswego, OR: Dignity Press.

Prosser, M. H. (2013). Introductory essay: Ancient and contemporary views of attitudes and values. In M.H. Prosser, M. Sharifzadeh, & S.Y. Zhang (2013). Finding cross-cultural common ground. Lake Oswego, OR: Dignity Press.

Prosser, M. H. & Cui L. T. (2014). Introduction: A cross-cultural perspective on social media in Asia. In L. T. Cui &. M. H.

Prosser, (Eds.) Social media in Asia. Lake Oswego, OR: Dignity Press.

Prosser, M. H. & Kulich, J. R. (Eds.). Special Issue: Early American pioneers of intercultural communication. Intercultural Journal of Intercultural Relations. Vol. 36. Issue 6. 744–759.

Prosser, M. H., Nurmakov, A., & Shahghasemi, E. (Eds.). (forthcoming). Social media in the Middle East. Lake Oswego, OR: Dignity Press.

Prosser, M. H., Sharifzadeh, M..& Zhang, S. Y. (Eds.) (2013). Finding cross-cultural common ground. Lake Oswego, OR: Dignity Press.

Prosser, M. H. & Sitaram, K. S. (Eds.) (1999). Civic discourse: Intercultural, international, and global media. Stamford, CT: Ablex.

Qian, Z. [Ch'ien Ching-shu) (1947). Fortress Besieged. Xxx

Rogers, E. M. (1969). Modernization among peasants: The impact of communication. New York, NY: Free Press.

Saarimento-S. S. (2013, June 7). Is Xi's Chinese dream compatable with Latin America's?" The Diplomat Blogs.

Shambaugh, D. (2013). China goes global: The partial power. New York, NY: Oxford University Press.

Shambaugh, D. (2013). China goes global: The partial power. New York, NY: The Oxford University Press.

She, C. (1945, 1981). Camel Xamgzo; Richshaw Boy, 1945. Xxx, Reynal and Hitchcock; [Camel driver. Beijing, China: Foreign Languages Press.

Shepherd, J. (2010: February 2). "China's top universities will rival Oxbridge," says Yale University president. [Richard Levin]. Guardian.UK.COM.

Sitaram, K. S. (1995). Communication and culture: A world view. New York, NY: McGraw Hill.

Sitaram, K. S. & Cogdell, R. T. (1976). Foundations of intercultural communication. Columbus, OH: Merrril.

Sitaram, K. S. & Prosser, M. H. (1998). Civic discourse: Multiculturalism, cultural diversity, and global communication. Stamford, CT: Ablex.

Skinner, B. F. (1971) Beyond freedom and dignity. New York, NY: Knopf.

Slomanson, W. R. (2000). Fundamental perspectives on international law. Belmont, CA, West Thomson Learning.

Smith, A. (Ed.) (1966). Communication and culture: Readings in the codes of human interaction. New York, NY: Harper and Row.

Snipp, F. (1977). Decent interval: An insider's account of Saigon's indecent end told by the CIA's chief strategy analyst in Viet Nam. New York NY: Random House.

Snow, E. (1936). Red star over China.

Stewart, E. C. (1973). Outline of intercultural communication. Mimeograph released by the Business Council for International Understanding.Washington, D.C: American University.

The Gioi Publishers (2002). Ho Chi Minh: The man who made a nation: Eighth edition. Hanoi, Viet Nam: The Gioi Publishers.

US Census Bureau (2000).

Wall, S. (2008) Easier said than done: Writing an autoethnography. International Journal of Qualitative Methods, 7. 1.

Wasilewski, J. H. & Kawakami, H. S. (2012; November). Edward C. Stewart; Cultural dynamics pioneer. In M. H. Prosser & Kulich, J. R. (Eds.). Special Issue: Early American pioneers of intercultural communication. Intercultural Journal of Intercultural Relations. Vol. 36. 869–884.

Yogananda, P. (2001). Autobiography of a Yogi. Preface, W. Y. Evans-Wentz. Kolkata, India: Jaico Publishing House.

Zhang, S. Y. & Prosser, M. H. (2011). G2 Languages: Chinese and English, Intercultural Communication Studies.

Zhang, S. Y. & Prosser, M. H. (2013). A Comparative Review: Three Middle East Books. In In M. H. Prosser, M. Sharifzadeh, & Zhang, S. Y. Finding cross-cultural common ground. Lake Oswego, OR: Dignity Press.

Zhou, J. (2006). Higher education in China. Singapore. Thomson.

Zhou, S. L., Prosser, M. H., & Lu, J. (2002). Sino-American conversations on shared topics. Zheng Zhou, China: Henan People's Press.

Other Books from Michael Prosser at Dignity Press

Michael H. Prosser,
Mansoureh Shanifzadeh,
Shengyong Zhang

FINDING CROSS-CULTURAL COMMON GROUND

March 2013
511 pages, paperback
ISBN 978-1-937570-25-5
22.00$ / 17.00€ / 14.50£

Li Mengyu, Michael H. Prosser

CHINESE COMMUNICATING INTERCULTURALLY

May 2014
North American edition of *Communicating Interculturally*, Higher Education Press, Beijing

384 pages, paperback
ISBN 978-1-937570-28-6
19.80$ / 14.80€ / 12.00£

Cui Litang, Michael H. Prosser (Co-editors)
SOCIAL MEDIA IN ASIA

Feb. 2014
686 pages, paperback
ISBN 978-1-937570-36-1
26.00$ / 20.00€ / 18.00£

Forthcoming :

Michael H. Prosser, Ehsan Shahghasemi (Co-editors)
SOCIAL MEDIA IN THE MIDDLE EAST

Michael H. Prosser, N.N. (Co-editors)
SOCIAL MEDIA IN AFRICA

More about how to buy these books and about
other Dignity Press books at
www.dignitypress.org

Dignity Press
World Dignity University Press

www.ingramcontent.com/pod-product-compliance
Lightning Source LLC
Chambersburg PA
CBHW060055190426
43202CB00030B/1587